Unpredictable Plays

by

Mario Fratti

Volume compilation and preface copyright © 2007 by The New York Theatre Experience, Inc.

See p. 347 for individual play copyrights.

All rights reserved. Except for brief passages quoted in newspaper, magazine, radio, or television reviews, no part of this book may be reproduced in any form or by any means, electronic or mechanical, including photocopying or recording, or by any information storage and retrieval system, without permission in writing from the publisher.

CAUTION: These plays are fully protected, in whole, in part, or in any form, under the copyright laws of the United States of America and of all countries covered by the International Copyright Union (including the Dominion of Canada and the rest of the British Commonwealth), and of all countries covered by the Pan-American Copyright Convention and the Universal Copyright Convention, and of all countries with which the United States has reciprocal copyright relations, and are subject to royalty. All performance rights, including professional, amateur, stock, motion picture, radio, television, recitation, and public reading are strictly reserved.

All inquiries concerning production, publication, reprinting, or use of this work in any form should be addressed to Susan Schulman, 454 West 44th Street, New York, NY 10036; or schulman@aol.com.

Published by The New York Theatre Experience, Inc.
P.O. Box 1606, Murray Hill Station, New York, NY 10156
www.nyte.org
email: info@nyte.org

ISBN-10: 0-9794852-0-7
ISBN-13: 978-0-9794852-0-6
Library of Congress Control Number: 2007926039

Book and cover designed by Nita Congress

Dedication

To my wonderful children, Mirko, Barbara, and Valentina.

Acknowledgments

The publisher of *Unpredictable Plays* thanks Mario Fratti for entrusting these plays with us. We also must express enormous gratitude to Nita Congress, who designed and edited the book, and without whom it literally would not exist. Her dedication and excellence in working on this project cannot be overstated. We thank her for her remarkable contributions to this book and to all the work that NYTE does every day. Thanks too to M. Scott Douglass of Main Street Rag for his production assistance.

Contents

Preface, by Martin Denton iii
The Friday Bench 1
Suicide Club 17
Alessia 26
The Piggy Bank 35
The Fourth One 42
Dolls No More 51
Porno 59
Dina and Alba 68
The Bridge 77
Confessions 94
The Coffin 110
A.I.D.S. 123
Brothel (The Doorbell) 129
The Letter 142
Mothers and Daughters 147
Beata, the Pope's Daughter 163
The Wish 189
Erotic Adventures in Venice (Promises) 202
The Academy 225
Friends 238
Terrorist 264
Wars 280
    The Return 281
    The Seventy-Fifth 292
    Iraq (Blindness) 295
"Che" 303
Anniversary 312
Missionaries 328
Sincerity 334
About the Author 343
Copyrights 345

Preface
by Martin Denton

One of the great surprises and privileges of my life in the past decade has been that I have gotten to know Mario Fratti. Before I met him, I knew him chiefly as one of the creators of the musical *Nine*, and as the author of a number of other plays, going back to the 1960s.

Mario is also a critic, one of the most generous in our profession. And he's also a teacher of playwriting, sharing his nearly half-a-century of experience with young authors, helping them to become better and more skillful at their craft.

One of the secrets of great playwriting that Mario has shared with me is that the ending is supreme. Come up with a great ending, he says, and the rest will easily follow.

Surprise, of course, is one of the key elements of a socko finish, and Mario is the master of the surprise ending. In this volume, so aptly titled *Unpredictable Plays*, you will witness the master of the unexpected twist at work. There are twenty-eight plays on the pages that follow. And so, as you read this book, you can expect to be surprised twenty-eight times. At least.

Mario's plays explore all the subjects that make life interesting and varied. There are plays about love and sex and faithfulness and indiscretion and betrayal here; and there are plays that look incisively at war and disease and our obligations to one another as citizens of the world. All are characterized by Mario's trademark sly wit: they're serious and not serious at the same time, reflecting the world view of a man whose zest for living only seems to grow and deepen with the passing years. His delight in the quirks of humanity, for better and worse, is evident in every one of these plays. Count on that; but don't count on anything else, because as I said, Mario loves to surprise his audiences.

I am proud that he has entrusted these twenty-eight *Unpredictable Plays* to NYTE to publish. In July 2007, he will celebrate his eightieth birthday, and we're pleased to honor him in this milestone year with this new anthology. Here's to many more surprises from the master of unpredictability!

The Friday Bench

The Characters:

MONICA: a beautiful woman in her early twenties; serious and sad; she knows how to hide irony and contempt.

ALFRED: an elegant man in his late forties; distinguished and correct; the conservative type.

MARTA: a pleasant woman in her early twenties; modest and cordial.

Today. A cold autumn afternoon in the park. An isolated bench. Autumn leaves are scattered around upstage and downstage. To the right of MONICA—almost on the edge of the bench—is a long basket with a double handle. A baby is sleeping in it. MONICA is reading a magazine for mothers. ALFRED enters from stage left and approaches timidly. He cannot make up his mind whether to sit down or not. He does not want to be seen by anybody. MONICA ignores him. ALFRED sits down at the other end of the bench. He uses his umbrella to hide his nervousness.

ALFRED: *(After a silence.)* Good evening.

MONICA: *(Without lifting her eyes from the magazine.)* Good evening.

ALFRED: *(After a silence.)* It's rather chilly today.

MONICA: Rather.

ALFRED: The forecast is for rain—later.

MONICA: Later.

ALFRED: Or maybe snow.

MONICA: Maybe.

ALFRED: The first snow of the season.

MONICA: The first.

ALFRED: Sometimes it's just guesswork. They don't—

MONICA: They don't.

ALFRED: It was January, I remember—or maybe February—the weatherman assured us that it would snow. Bundled in overcoats and boots, we left— *(He refrains.)*

MONICA: We left.

ALFRED: Two friends and myself. Two of the best skiers I know. Old friends.

MONICA: *(Ironic.)* Old.

ALFRED: You probably guessed. It never snowed.

MONICA: I guessed.

ALFRED: It happens. But one must be prudent just the same. That's why I took my umbrella.

MONICA: Right!

ALFRED: I don't see yours.

MONICA: My what?

ALFRED: Umbrella.

MONICA: I don't listen to "weathermen."

1

ALFRED: Why not?

MONICA: I don't have a television.

ALFRED: So much the better…They often lie.

MONICA: Always.

ALFRED: Not intentionally. I'm sure of that.

MONICA: Are you really sure?

ALFRED: More or less. That's why it's practical to be well covered, at every change of season. *(He caresses the scarf that is well tucked up in his overcoat.)*

MONICA: I hate scarves. They suffocate me.

ALFRED: I understand. Sometimes, at home, they can be suffocating…

(MONICA smiles.)

ALFRED: You're smiling. Why?

MONICA: A scarf around your neck, at home? That's an amusing scene!

ALFRED: Only rarely. After a cold; or before.

MONICA: *(Ironic.)* Or before.

(A silence.)

ALFRED: What's new?

MONICA: *(Indicating the magazine.)* Nothing new.

ALFRED: *(Indicating with his head.)* How is the little angel?

MONICA: Like an angel.

ALFRED: Is he sleeping?

MONICA: He's sleeping.

ALFRED: Does he sleep very much?

MONICA: Very much.

ALFRED: Always at this hour?

MONICA: And at night, naturally.

(A brief pause.)

ALFRED: A real angel.

MONICA: *(Ironic.)* Like his father.

(A brief pause.)

ALFRED: *(Trying a witty joke.)* He doesn't snore, I hope.

MONICA: He doesn't. Neither does his father.

ALFRED: Silent nights, then.

MONICA: Silent.

ALFRED: That's better.

MONICA: Why?

ALFRED: The night was created for silence, peace, rest. "Stille Nacht." "White Night." Tranquil, silent, white.

MONICA: And yours?

ALFRED: What?

MONICA: Nights.

ALFRED: Yes—certain—certainly. Silent. Created for sleep. I sleep a great deal.

MONICA: Good for you.

ALFRED: Are you being ironic?

MONICA: *(Ironic.)* I wouldn't dare!

ALFRED: From the initial "Good Evening" to that "Good for you"—I sense a biting irony.

MONICA: Biting? I don't bite, no. I assure you, Sir.

ALFRED: Sir?

(MONICA stares at him defiantly, ignoring her magazine for the first time.)

ALFRED: *(Uneasy.)* The magazine…

MONICA: *(Offering it.)* Here.

ALFRED: I mean…it's better if you…continue to read.

MONICA: *(Stares again at the magazine, indicating it.)* It explains why some mothers can't breastfeed.

ALFRED: Why?

MONICA: Because they don't have milk.

ALFRED: Obviously.

MONICA: And the reason why they don't have milk.

ALFRED: Which is?

MONICA: Their hatred for those who made them mothers.

ALFRED: Exaggerations!

MONICA: Who's exaggerating?

ALFRED: Those doctors. I bet they're not even doctors.

MONICA: *(Handing him the magazine.)* Check it out yourself.

ALFRED: No, thank you. Go on, read.

MONICA: I read it three times.

ALFRED: Another page. There must be more…

MONICA: I've read it—cover to cover.

ALFRED: Here is my paper.

MONICA: No, thank you. I'd rather look at you.

ALFRED: *(Upset.)* Please don't, I beg you…People pass by…They might think that…

MONICA: Nobody passes at this hour.

ALFRED: One never knows. At times…

MONICA: If you're so afraid, you should go. Who's keeping you here?

ALFRED: You misunderstand me…Everyone knows me, in this town.

MONICA: They know me too. I was born here.

ALFRED: They like to gossip…

MONICA: *(Indicating the bench.)* Look at the distance between us! Who would dare to accuse you of…"courting" a mother? As a matter of fact, let's put the "angel" in the middle. *(She tries to lift the basket.)* It will be a "buffer state." *(Ironic.)* "The obstacle."

ALFRED: *(Alarmed.)* No, no! Better not!

MONICA: *(Giving up.)* All right. But don't you agree he is the "obstacle"?

ALFRED: *(Ignoring.)* Better leave it there. If it were closer—God knows what they'd think.

MONICA: *(Ironic.)* You're right. An infant between a man and a woman is like a condemned man between the priest and the executioner. He makes them partners in crime—accomplices.

ALFRED: …I had a cold yesterday… That's why I don't dare come closer.

MONICA: Last Friday too. It must be the day for colds. *(Ironic.)* So, on Saturdays and Sundays, you can rest at home. And enjoy the warmth of your family.

ALFRED: Not me…I have a lot of work to do. I'll be locked up in my study.

MONICA: *(Ironic.)* Poor thing! You have such a difficult life, really. I'm so sorry!

ALFRED: Don't exaggerate now!…I recognize that yours is…infinitely more difficult.

MONICA: Thank you.

ALFRED: Feeding, bathing, other things. Looking after a baby is indeed exhausting…

MONICA: *(Ironic.)* Indeed.

ALFRED: But they say—it's also a woman's shining hour. It's gratifying.

MONICA: Gratifying. For a father too "they say."

(A silence.)

ALFRED: A man's day begins at eight. He goes to his office and comes home late...when the children are sleeping. The mother, on the contrary, is always with them. That's why it's especially gratifying for her.

MONICA: *(Indicating the baby.)* He wakes up at seven.

ALFRED: Because he's hungry. Ten minutes to feed him...Then you can go back to sleep for two or three hours.

MONICA: He doesn't go back to sleep. And there are endless things to do in a house.

ALFRED: But it's up to you when and what you do. In an office, one is nailed down. Orders, more orders, always orders!

MONICA: Given or received?

ALFRED: Receiving orders is easy. The real difficulty is giving them.

MONICA: I understand. You're a real victim.

ALFRED: Let's not exaggerate. I was only saying that...a mother's life is hard but...only up to a certain point. You can postpone every action until you feel inclined to pick it up.

MONICA: The "angel" is wet! Should I leave him wet?

ALFRED: Oh no, not that! He could catch a cold!

MONICA: Then, when he's ready for his outing in the park, he has to be changed again. But this time he's full of sh—

ALFRED: *(Interrupting.)* I know what you mean. It's all so human!

MONICA: It takes us two hours before we're both ready for a little airing in the park.

ALFRED: Every day?

MONICA: Every day. The doctor recommended it.

ALFRED: Why? Is he sick?

MONICA: *(Slowly.)* No...

ALFRED: *(Worried.)* That's not a very convincing "no."

MONICA: The doctor wants to see him every Monday, but...

ALFRED: But?...

MONICA: I don't think he's really sick, no. He wants us to pay four visits a month instead of one. That's all!

ALFRED: Change doctors.

MONICA: Why? To save money?

ALFRED: Oh no! Only to be sure. A baby's health is precious.

MONICA: The week begins with that visit. We return home at two. A little nap for him only. Then the park. No time left to market, on Mondays.

ALFRED: But the other days...

MONICA: There's always something—you can't win! Cooking, washing, mending, shopping, keeping accounts. If I could only have some help...

ALFRED: *(Rapidly.)* Better not, better not.

MONICA: Why?

ALFRED: *(Vaguely.)* Servants today are all so demanding!

MONICA: I found one that would stay with me for...one hundred a week. Only one hundred.

ALFRED: No, better not. It's not worth the trouble.

MONICA: Why? Why isn't it "worth the trouble"?

ALFRED: I read that a baby should see his mother only—always. He must love her—and only her. It was demonstrated that all the youths of today who are...confused, deranged, or...slightly peculiar—had more than one servant, They saw too many faces. One uglier than the other. The result: confusion!

MONICA: The one I've found is young and attractive. And she's promised to stay permanently if I pay her what she asks.

ALFRED: It's not a question of money. It's for the good of the little one.

MONICA: And what about the good of the mother? You men are so selfish!

ALFRED: Calm down, please, calm down. *(Embarrassed, he looks around.)* They could see us and think that—

MONICA: Nobody is here at this hour! She could help me with the marketing—cleaning the house—change his diapers—ten times a day!

ALFRED: *(With pride.)* Does he really wet that much?

MONICA: He certainly does!

ALFRED: He'll have a fortunate life, I'm sure of it. How does that proverb go? *(He does not succeed in remembering it.)*

MONICA; What proverb?

ALFRED: ..."He who pours showers—will have all sorts of worldly powers!" *(Indicating the basket.)* He'll give and receive much in life. He's lucky.

MONICA: It doesn't seem so.

ALFRED: Why?

MONICA: To start with—he hasn't got a father.

ALFRED: What do you mean?

MONICA: He hasn't got a father who lives by his side, that can speak to him, that can protect him.

ALFRED: *(After a brief reflection.)* At times—it can be an advantage...

MONICA: How?

ALFRED: Men and women—husbands and wives—they frequently fight. A disgusting sight. Real poison for a child.

MONICA: Normal parents argue when the children are asleep.

ALFRED: The baby "hears" them just the same. Children sense everything. They can feel it. It is a traumatic experience for them.

MONICA: When they go to school, then! It's an ideal time!

ALFRED: Ideal for what!

MONICA: For everything.

ALFRED: For...?

MONICA: Arguing, fighting...everything!

ALFRED: What do you mean by "everything"?

MONICA: Making up.

ALFRED: Sex. That's another good reason.

MONICA: What reason?

ALFRED: Our little one is fortunate. If his father is not around to protect, he is not around to... *(Vague gesture.)* The mother is consequently clean, pure, adorable. A symbol to revere.

MONICA: Then all children who have parents "active in bed," are doomed to...confusion, inversion, and so on?

ALFRED: Not all of them. But many.

MONICA: In other words, for his sake—no maids, no father present, no sex?

ALFRED: A perfect environment!

MONICA: *(Incredulous.)* Three "passionate" Fridays—to conceive him—and it's all over for me—finished?

ALFRED: *(Proud, with ecstasy.)* "Three"..."passionate." He'll be lucky.

MONICA: And for me—twenty years without a man in bed?

ALFRED: Eighteen. At eighteen, he'll find a second mother and—

MONICA: What second mother?

ALFRED: The Army. While they make a real man out of him, you can return to being... *(He does not want to offend her.)*

MONICA: A woman again.

ALFRED: In a way.

MONICA: *(With increasing hostility.)* Eighteen years in white while you—"ardent lover"—

ALFRED: *(Flattered.)* Thank you for that "ardent"!

MONICA: —While you're having a good time! You're crazy! Absolutely crazy!

ALFRED: You're adorable when you're so insulting!

MONICA: And you—so formal and hypocritical! *(Sarcastic.)* "Good evening, Madam!"

ALFRED: I only said: "Good evening."

MONICA: So detached! Correct and proper. As if you had just met me.

ALFRED: I always find you hostile like this, all engrossed in reading.

MONICA: It's you who insisted that I read! Afraid, terrified that someone will find out that we know each other! Coward! Hypocrite!

ALFRED: It's all for the good of us all—

MONICA: It's all for your own good, it's always you, your own selfish self!

ALFRED: Please, Monica... *(Looks around.)* They can hear—

MONICA: *(Interrupting.)* Lucky for you there is no soul in sight! Very smart of you to pick this isolated bench, this hour! These damn days!

ALFRED: Just a moment ago you referred to the "passionate Fridays." You said it with genuine feeling. I'm grateful. "Three." "Passionate."

MONICA: *(Interrupting.)* The three Fridays that ruined my life!

ALFRED: Don't say that please! We've conceived an angel. Those afternoons of love gave us an heir—

MONICA: *(Interrupting.)* "Us"? You don't exist in his life! You show up on Fridays, just to reminisce, to humiliate! You're a hypocrite!

ALFRED: Don't call me a hypocrite, I beg you. I'm concerned—

MONICA: Concerned—you?

ALFRED: I've provided well, you must admit you have everything. I'm protecting your honor—

MONICA: *My* honor?

ALFRED: Yours—above all. If they spread the rumor that— *(A vague gesture.)*

MONICA: That?

ALFRED: —That you're not a widow, as you make them believe.

MONICA: I *am* a widow.

ALFRED: Not quite. I am here, very much alive...

MONICA: Alive—for whom?

ALFRED: For... *(He hesitates, uncertain.)* I'm here; you can see me.

MONICA: *(Sarcastic.)* I see you all right. One hour a week. But who are you with the rest of the time?

ALFRED: *(Vague.)* You know, I'm a prisoner. I'm always at the office.

MONICA: Always at the office? You—Jesuit!

ALFRED: Most of the time, you know—

MONICA: Yes, and seven nights a week, in bed with your fat wife!

ALFRED: The night was created for—

MONICA: Hypocrite! How is the old bitch?

ALFRED: Not too well.

MONICA: Pregnant?

ALFRED: Oh no! You know that's impossible. I never—

MONICA: Ready to drop dead?

ALFRED: Don't say such things, please…

MONICA: Is there or isn't there a chance that she'll die?

ALFRED: How can you? Please…It's not Christian.

MONICA: That first Friday you mentioned she would, you swore she would! You made a point of that.

ALFRED: *(Becoming uncomfortable.)* Only as an eventuality…perhaps.

MONICA: When?

ALFRED: I don't know. How can I know?

MONICA: The doctors, what did they tell you?

ALFRED: It's in the hands of our Good Lord now. If there is a breakthrough with that new medicine—

MONICA: *(Interrupting.)* With all the wars we're fighting—thank you, "Good Lord"!—they won't have time for new medicines. How much longer, without medicines?

ALFRED: *(Vague.)* …without…a few years.

MONICA: What does a "few years" mean? We all have a few years!

ALFRED: Less than ten, they say.

MONICA: And I should wait ten years?

ALFRED: To wait is not the right word.

MONICA: What do you mean?

ALFRED: I've told you many times…I'm ready to…

MONICA: Ready to…?

ALFRED: If you would only accept my plan.

MONICA: What plan?

ALFRED: A little apartment in the suburbs.

MONICA: No. I was born here. I want to live here.

ALFRED: I would come every weekend…

MONICA: To do what?

ALFRED: *(Vague.)* To…visit you.

MONICA: Who wants your "visit"?

ALFRED: Friday night, Saturday night—

MONICA: And Sunday morning! This way all three of us can go to mass together!

ALFRED: Three long days…

MONICA: Thanks! No.

ALFRED: *(Nervous, timidly.)* She…she sees me less, I assure you!

MONICA: Seven nights! SEVEN!

ALFRED: *(Timidly.)* Only four…

MONICA: Four? How come?

ALFRED: If I'm with you Friday, Saturday, and Sunday—

MONICA: I said no.

ALFRED: Three nights with the two of you, with *you*, Monica.

MONICA: To do what?

ALFRED: Whatever you want, Monica.

MONICA: *(Ironic.)* "The night was created for silence, for peace…"

ALFRED: Silence and peace, then.

MONICA: Thanks for the offer. No!

ALFRED: *(Vague.)* Or whatever you suggest—

MONICA: What do you mean?

ALFRED: …If it's silence and peace you want—you'll have it. If not…

MONICA: If not?

ALFRED: *(Vague.)* The absence of silence and peace. We could… *(Vague gesture.)*

MONICA: *(Studying him.)* Interesting… *(With irony.)* You're a man of character…Really admirable.

ALFRED: You gave me a son, Monica, and—

MONICA: You nearly passed out when I told you.

ALFRED: From surprise, from joy…

MONICA: And you fired me, out of joy!

ALFRED: I only wanted you to rest.

MONICA: You disappeared.

ALFRED: That stupid contract in South America. Those idiots said that our triggers are too sensitive! If you touch them they fire! Obviously! Imagine!

MONICA: I'm imagining.

ALFRED: But I came back, remember?

MONICA: When I threatened a scandal.

ALFRED: And I sent flowers.

MONICA: I thanked you a hundred times for those damn flowers. And I *told* you that I received them the day I left the hospital!

ALFRED: I was in Bolivia, where the telegraph is very slow. I ordered them five days before. Together with a check for your expenses. *All* the expenses.

MONICA: *(Sarcastic.)* Your generosity is very touching.

ALFRED: It was a pleasant duty.

MONICA: Easy, too easy!

ALFRED: What do you mean "too easy"? How else should I make money? Digging ditches?

MONICA: It could be healthy. It would help you grow up.

ALFRED: We'll dig in our garden.

MONICA: What garden?

ALFRED: …The little house in the suburbs…

MONICA: Now it's a little house.

ALFRED: It's better yes. A little house set back, with a garden.

MONICA: Naturally? The more "set back," the better. And a dog, tell me. Can we have a dog? Or are you afraid the dog too might emasculate the baby? *(Indicates the basket.)*

ALFRED: A dog? Oh yes, certainly! Good idea!

MONICA: *(Ironic.)* You're so agreeable!

ALFRED: A little house to ourselves—our very own. Think of—

MONICA: In whose name?

ALFRED: *(Indicating the basket.)* In his name. It's tax deductible if—

MONICA: No.

ALFRED: We must if—

MONICA: It's too late!

ALFRED: We'll have beautiful happy days, with him—

MONICA: Too late!

ALFRED: No, Monica. Think. Three long days and three long nights. Almost half a week.

MONICA: Half to me, half to her. You're a real gentleman—I always thought so.

ALFRED: You complained, before...

(MONICA stares at him.)

ALFRED: ...Eighteen years without... *(He hesitates.)*

MONICA: *(Tense.)* Without...?

ALFRED: ..."Without a man." You said that.

MONICA: Precisely. Without a *man*, I said. Not a creep who takes the plunge three times, gets you pregnant, and then disappears.

ALFRED: *(Puzzled.)* "Plunge"?

MONICA: And then disappears.

ALFRED: I'll make it up to you. Just think—three times a week. Fifty-two weeks a year. One hundred and fifty-six marvelous days of—

MONICA: You've even counted them.

ALFRED: I figured it out in my head, this very moment. You know, I have a good head for figures.

MONICA: How could I forget it?

ALFRED: ...One hundred and fifty-six nights...almost a lifetime.

MONICA: Almost.

ALFRED: And...if they don't come up with that new medicine—

MONICA: *(Interrupting.)* But what makes you so sure that I want you? Who wants a man like you?

ALFRED: *(Tense, vaguely hurt.)* What do you mean "like me"?

MONICA: A man without the courage of his convictions.

ALFRED: The courage will come, I assure you. If I have you near me. Please, I need you and the baby.

MONICA: It's too late, Al.

ALFRED: Call me Alfred—as only you can say it. *(Tries to imitate her.)* "Alfred"...Please!

MONICA: *(Exaggerating.)* "Alfred"...

ALFRED: Yes! Yes! It's at that precise moment that I...became excited... *(He slides toward her.)*

(MONICA stops him midway with a gesture.)

MONICA: Don't forget your cold—the people— *(Indicates the basket.)* the little one that suffers if we... *(Joins two fingers.)*

ALFRED: *(As he returns humbly to his place.)* He's too little for that.

MONICA: Naturally!

ALFRED: Together—we'll protect him, we'll love him, we'll educate him.

MONICA: *(Ironic.)* Without ever quarrelling, I hope, and without showing him that to kiss is human!

ALFRED: Whatever you say, Monica.

MONICA: *(Studying him, slowly.)* Whatever I say...And who will rule, in the little house with a garden?

ALFRED: *(Uncertain.)* The one who is right...The first months, you. You're right. Later...

MONICA: Later?

ALFRED: I will, if...I should be right.

MONICA: And if I say you're *not* right, that you're entirely wrong?

ALFRED: It would probably be true and...

MONICA: And would you..."obey"?

ALFRED: I would do what you want, Monica. Cross my heart.

MONICA: I don't want a man like you.

ALFRED: *(Ignoring.)* And...if you fall in love again—with me...everything is possible...

MONICA: Meaning?

ALFRED: He could have a little sister, maybe...

MONICA: I don't want another child from a man like you!

ALFRED: You're right! You're right! I've learned now.

MONICA: What have you learned?

ALFRED: There are ways...

MONICA: What ways?

ALFRED: To avoid having children. Eventually...many methods.

MONICA: Ah, yes! *(Ironic.)* When did they discover those methods? Yesterday?

ALFRED: Oh no! A long time ago. But I didn't... *(Vague gesture.)*

MONICA: *(Indicating the basket.)* Obviously!

ALFRED: True love is passionate and total!

MONICA: *(Ironic.)* Tell me about the half total!

ALFRED: When I found out... *(Indicates the basket.)*

MONICA: —The mistake. You passed out.

ALFRED: From emotion, I assure you. From sheer joy. And I told him... *(Hesitates.)*

MONICA: *(With curiosity.)* Who?

ALFRED: My best friend.

MONICA: I bet he's a doctor.

ALFRED: No. A lawyer. We were talking about a variety of subjects—

MONICA: Business, contracts, guns—and the conversation turned to—

ALFRED: —The happy news I had just received! *(Indicates the basket.)*

MONICA: No doubt he told you: "Stupid! Don't you know they sell lots of...?" *(She does not want to say the word.)*

ALFRED: What? What do *you* know about...those things?

MONICA: I don't know much. But more than you, you can be sure!

(MARTA, a beautiful woman in a modest coat, appears behind them.)

ALFRED: What do you mean?...At times I don't understand you...

(MARTA advances slowly. ALFRED becomes aware of her presence and is suddenly afraid. He stiffens immediately.)

ALFRED: Shhh! *(Indicates with the corner of his eye that someone is there.)*

(MONICA is motionless. MARTA comes near the basket. She stops and smiles at the baby. Suddenly she recognizes MONICA.)

MARTA: *(Exaggerating.)* Monica!

MONICA: *(Without enthusiasm.)* Marta.

MARTA: I didn't see you at first...Then I noticed the basket... *(Looks at the baby; then at ALFRED too.)* Sweeter than ever!

(ALFRED ignores her.)

MARTA: Beautiful! He's the most beautiful baby *in the world!* Have you seen him, Sir?

(ALFRED—petrified—ignores her.)

MARTA: You should. Congratulations, Monica! You must be proud. *(Looking down admiringly.)* All pink and blue. Such a beautiful baby!

MONICA: *(Giving her a dirty look.)* Thank you!

(A silence.)

MARTA: *(Changing tone.)* I was just walking...I know that you go to this park...I thought—perhaps I'll meet her...From way out there I saw this bench and...it seemed empty... *(Uncomfortable.)* Then I saw that it was taken...a man and a woman...I said to myself: impossible. That couldn't be Monica...she never speaks to strangers. Not Monica...

(MARTA stares at ALFRED, who is absolutely immobile.)

MARTA: When I saw that you were at the end of the bench—a good distance from him—

(A weak smile on ALFRED's face.)

MARTA: I thought...perhaps...I said to myself: Yes, that could be Monica...and little Frank.

(ALFRED is startled at the baby's name.)

MARTA: I was right. My heart told me...

(MARTA pulls up the baby's cover. She caresses him while MONICA and ALFRED exchange exasperated looks.)

MARTA: Is he warm enough?

MONICA: *(Giving her another icy glance.)* Very warm, thank you!

MARTA: With such weather...At times...

MONICA: There's no danger.

MARTA: The sudden change of season is always dangerous...

MONICA: I know.

MARTA: They're so delicate at that age...

MONICA: He's strong.

MARTA: I can see, I can see how healthy he is...

MONICA: Thank you.

MARTA: *(To ALFRED.)* You should see him, Sir!

(He does not move.)

MONICA: *(Icily.)* I'd rather not.

MARTA: *(Uncomfortable.)* As you wish, Monica, as you wish...

(A silence.)

MARTA: Are you going home soon?

MONICA: No. *(Picking up the magazine.)* I have to finish this article. *(She begins to read; she is obviously trying to get rid of her.)*

MARTA: Well, then...

MONICA: We'll get together soon. Bye!

MARTA: *(Realizing that MONICA does not want her around.)* Good...See you, Monica...Goodbye, Sir!...

(ALFRED ignores her. MARTA is embarrassed. She looks at the baby once more, smiles at him. She walks away and exits.)

ALFRED: *(When he is sure that MARTA is gone.)* Who was that? How does she know my son's name?

MONICA: Marta is a neighbor...

ALFRED: A neighbor? A neighbor where?

MONICA: We shop at the same market. She's crazy about Frank and always offers to help me. She is the one who wants to come and work for me, if I pay her—

ALFRED: *(Interrupting.)* How did she ever land here? Why?

MONICA: I don't know.

ALFRED: Did she *follow* you?

MONICA: I don't think so. This is a public park.

ALFRED: But no one ever comes to this spot! Do you think she suspects?

MONICA: Suspects what?

ALFRED: About the two of us. She asked me if "I saw the baby."

MONICA: It's normal. Solitary gentlemen sitting beside solitary ladies usually notice and compliment the baby.

ALFRED: But it was her first question! Why me? With this distance between us!

MONICA: *(Ironic.)* Maybe she saw your "passionate efforts"!

ALFRED: *(Worried.)* You're right. She did. She must have!

MONICA: *(Smiling.)* Don't be so suspicious, Al. You ought to get used to—

ALFRED: *(Nervous, alarmed.)* To what?

MONICA: To neighbors, to a maid.

ALFRED: No. We don't need neighbors, or maids.

MONICA: *You* don't but I do. I want this maid. I want her. It's a chance I cannot afford to lose. Did you see how she adores Frank?

ALFRED: Too much!

MONICA: You'll have to get used to this too!

ALFRED: To what? What do you mean?

MONICA: It's a fact that in many cases a maid can be more loving than parents.

ALFRED: It's not your case, I hope.

MONICA: No.

ALFRED: You allowed her to...touch him, to caress him. Why?

MONICA: Because I know she's very competent. She's too good to lose, Al, I need that girl.

ALFRED: Later, maybe.

MONICA: No maybe. I want *her*. She adores Frank. She's ideal for me. Only one hundred dollars a week. You can afford it.

ALFRED: We'll see...

MONICA: It's very little if you consider that she'll live with me. Except for her day off, I'll have someone in the house all the time. More than you can offer me.

ALFRED: *(Trying to change the subject.)* What were we talking about before? *(A gesture in MARTA's direction.)*

MONICA: A subject that isn't useful to...the future of children.

ALFRED: What is that?

MONICA: Your discovery of contraceptives. Congratulations! You're really growing up.

ALFRED: Don't be ironic, Monica. It doesn't become a mother.

MONICA: A mother! I wouldn't be one if you hadn't been so...naïve! We wouldn't have this problem!

ALFRED: What do *you* know about those things?

MONICA: It's everywhere for everyone to read—even if you're sixteen! And if you have the courage to ask a doctor, you'll get all your questions answered and demonstrated.

ALFRED: Did you ask a doctor?

MONICA: I was stupid. If I had seen a doctor, I wouldn't be in this mess.

ALFRED: What do you mean? Don't you love our baby?

MONICA: More than you. You haven't even bothered to look at him today!

ALFRED: Did you bring the pictures?

MONICA: Why pictures—when he's here!

ALFRED: You promised—

MONICA: I forgot them.

ALFRED: *(Producing a tiny camera.)* I thought...if Monica forgets...May I take a picture?

MONICA: No. You'll wake him up.

ALFRED: *(Pleading.)* Just one...

MONICA: No. How does Marta seem to you? Beautiful or ugly? One of those who gives complexes to babies? Do you think she's the type who..."emasculates"?

ALFRED: *(Getting up and going behind the bench, where he can see the baby.)* ...She didn't impress me one way or another...She's too aggressive, though...

MONICA: According to you, all women are aggressive—including your mother.—"A witch who chained you up"—was your description. Now, Marta is the witch. Maybe me too...

ALFRED: *(As he admires the baby.)* Oh no, Monica, oh no...You're so feminine...Look what you've given me...He is really handsome...He resembles me more and more—you're right...Every week a little more.

MONICA: Al, seriously now. I want that maid or else...

ALFRED: Or else?

MONICA: I'll go to Europe and take Frank with me.

ALFRED: *(Very surprised.)* Europe? Who's put that idea into your head?

MONICA: No one. I've been reading a lot, lately. The best schools are there.

ALFRED: Are you going back to school?

MONICA: Not me. Frank.

ALFRED: But how long would you stay in Europe?

MONICA: A few years.

ALFRED: *(Looking at the baby and taking a picture.)* And me?

MONICA: You can keep that picture—as a souvenir.

ALFRED: That's cruel, Monica. I'm his father...

MONICA: One is *not* a father; one becomes a father. For him, you don't exist.

ALFRED: But by now—

MONICA: By now?

ALFRED: *(Slowly.)* That could be true if...I had never seen him...

MONICA: *(Staring at him slowly.)* An interesting confession...Very revealing...You don't deserve to be a father. Pay us ten years in advance and we'll go to Europe.

ALFRED: Ten years? And I—for ten years... *(Takes another picture.)*

MONICA: Or else hire Marta—with an extra one hundred dollars in the...envelope. *(She indicates his pocket.)*

ALFRED: Yes, I brought it. I'll give it to you. *(He takes another picture.)*

MONICA: You saw her. She's young and full of energy.

ALFRED: A busybody...a gossip...And what kind of accent does she have? It would ruin our little heir. He would imitate—

MONICA: What kind of accent do you want? Oxford?

ALFRED: *(About to take another picture; suddenly notices someone in the distance.)* Who is that? There? *(He goes quickly to the extreme end of the bench; sits down hastily and remains motionless.)*

MONICA: *(Surprised.)* Where there? Where?

ALFRED: *(Through his teeth, still immobile.)* Behind those bushes, there!

MONICA: What bushes? I don't see anyone.

ALFRED: *(Through his teeth, still immobile.)* I saw it move! I saw it move!

MONICA: So what? Maybe it's two lovers...or two squirrels...

ALFRED: *(Through his teeth, still immobile.)* One person—alone! One! With two big eyes! I can see them! It's that repulsive friend of yours, I recognize her!

MONICA: I don't see her...

ALFRED: I do! She's there!

MONICA: And so what, if it is?

ALFRED: *(Muttering through his teeth.)* She's spying on me!

MONICA: What could she say? That you seduced me on a bench? At most, she just saw you take some pictures.

ALFRED: She's going to blackmail us—blackmail!

MONICA: *If* it's her, *if* she does ask me something, I'll tell her that her enthusiasm aroused your curiosity to look at the baby. And that you took three pictures for your newspaper.

ALFRED: What newspaper?

MONICA: Any newspaper, stupid! *(Looking toward the bushes.)* Do you still see her?

ALFRED: ...No...No...But she's surely there—lying in wait for me.

MONICA: In wait? For you?

ALFRED: You can't trust people like that—

MONICA: People like what?

ALFRED: Anyone not born in this city, with such an accent...They pretend to love children and then...

MONICA: And then?

ALFRED: Blackmail, blackmail, always blackmail! *(He takes an envelope from his pocket.)* Here's the envelope, before she appears again...ten twenty dollar bills—as you requested.

MONICA: *(Taking the envelope.)* Thanks! And think about my proposition. Ten years in advance and you'll be rid of us, of all your obsessions and fears.

ALFRED: *(Uncertain, struggling with himself.)* But I don't want, I don't want to get rid of you...to lose Frank...He's my son.

MONICA: Then give me money for Marta.

ALFRED: Later, perhaps, in the future... *(Having a sudden idea.)* A young girl from South America. They're the most loyal!

MONICA: No.

ALFRED: *Two* South American girls!

MONICA: No.

ALFRED: They work—from morning till night, they can only speak Spanish and…they're satisfied with a very modest salary.

MONICA: I want Marta, I'm set on Marta.

ALFRED: And it's very clear that South America has a great future. It's our new frontier.

MONICA: That doesn't interest me.

ALFRED: Spanish, you know, is fast becoming our second language. Sooner or later we'll have to learn it if we want to understand our servants. We'll have the "living" language right in our house! At no cost!

MONICA: *(Ironic.)* At no cost! Forget it! Marta or Europe!

ALFRED: *(Suddenly motionless, again, looking in another direction.)* There! There! There she is again, that spy! *(Trying to indicate with his eyes, without moving.)* There! There! *(With desperation, on the verge of tears.)* What does she want from me? What does she want?

MONICA: *(Trying to see her.)* Al, I don't see her…You're imagining all this…

ALFRED: There! There! She just moved! There! What is she after?

MONICA: Nothing, Al. Don't worry. What could she possibly want from us?

ALFRED: My son—that's it! To kidnap my son! She wants him! Do you have her address? I'll have her arrested!

MONICA: *(Patiently.)* Don't be afraid. I know her very well. I'm here to protect your son.

ALFRED: If she as much as touches him…I'll have her locked up for life! The electric chair, yes! She'll get the chair if I…

MONICA: *(Ironic.)* You're overreacting, Al!

ALFRED: Warn her! You better warn her! *(Reflecting.)* No. You better not! She mustn't suspect that he's mine…I'm leaving now, Monica. It's better if I leave…Goodbye, my dear…Take care of the baby. He's all that's left for me in life…You and the baby. Take care…I'll see you next Friday—same time, same bench. Everything the same…Goodbye!

MONICA: *(Waves at him tiredly, ironically.)* Next Friday…

(ALFRED exits. MONICA opens the envelope and divides the money. She puts five banknotes in the right pocket and five in the left pocket. She gets up and moves a certain distance from the basket. MARTA reappears, embarrassed and humble.)

MARTA: I'm sorry about what happened before but I was worried about Frank…I wasn't sure if he was warm enough…

(MARTA sits next to the basket and caresses the baby lovingly; takes a baby bottle out of her tote bag and proceeds to feed the baby. MONICA is depressed.)

MARTA: *(To MONICA.)* He's a handsome man…

MONICA: An idiot.

MARTA: A bit nervous, maybe…

MONICA: Terrified.

MARTA: Of what?

MONICA: Life, responsibility, everything.

MARTA: When I saw him taking snapshots—

MONICA: He saw you too!

MARTA: —It really got me.

MONICA: Why?

MARTA: I said to myself. Maybe he could be a good father...

MONICA: *(Taking out five bills from her right pocket.)* Here! Three for me. Two for you. *(She hands them.)*

MARTA: Thanks. *(A silence.)* I bet he's crazy for the baby...

MONICA: If nothing goes wrong...

MARTA: Nothing will go wrong. I promised—didn't I? *(Indicating the basket.)* We'll come here every Friday.

MONICA: And what will happen when he begins calling him "my son"?

MARTA: What's the difference? You know that Frank hasn't got a father. We'll get used to it, I suppose...It's a little cruel but...

MONICA: Why cruel?

MARTA: *(Slowly.)* It's not going to happen but...Suppose he finds out some day that it's not his son—that you killed his real son by choking him to death the night he was born?

MONICA: *(Tightens up, very upset. Aggressively, articulating each word.)* I had nothing to do with it! He choked by himself!

MARTA: *(Very apologetic.)* I'm sorry. I swore not to remind you, ever...I was just thinking out loud. Please, forgive me. What if he finds out that his son is dead?

(A silence.)

MONICA: *(Quietly, with sadness.)* He's never seen his son...For him, he does not exist...For me, it's different...I saw him alive.

(While MARTA smiles at her baby, MONICA stares ahead; her expression is blank; she knew how to kill her child; she is desperately alone.)

(CURTAIN.)

Suicide Club

The Persons:

DORA, the mother; in her early forties
STEFANO, her son; in his early twenties
ANNA, the friend; in her early forties

A modest living room. STEFANO is sitting at a table; he is reading a sports magazine. DORA is nervous; she's walking around; then she decides to interrupt STEFANO's reading.

DORA: What's new? *(Indicates the magazine; caresses STEFANO's hair.)*

STEFANO: Nothing.

(A silence; DORA stands behind him.)

DORA: Are you going out today?

STEFANO: In a little while.

DORA: Where are you going?

STEFANO: Out.

DORA: To Angela's house?

STEFANO: No.

DORA: To Frank's?

STEFANO: Maybe.

DORA: How is Frank?

STEFANO: Fine.

DORA: He used to come by here. That was nice when the two of you would be here, studying.

STEFANO: He gave up.

(A silence.)

DORA: Do you want me to fix something for you?

STEFANO: You just made me breakfast an hour ago.

(A brief pause.)

DORA: What are you reading?

STEFANO: Sports.

DORA: Who won?

STEFANO: Won what?

DORA: *(Timidly.)* There's always someone who wins…

STEFANO: You don't know the teams…

(A silence.)

DORA: Stefano…are you coming home tonight?

STEFANO: Why are you asking me?

DORA: Sometimes you don't come back, you disappear for two or three days. You worry me.

STEFANO: Don't.

DORA: What are you doing?

STEFANO: I hang out with my friends. Sometimes I find work.

DORA: I don't like you doing security work, especially at night.

STEFANO: Well, that's all there is right now.

DORA: It still worries me. There are all sorts of nuts out there.

STEFANO: You know me. I'm calm, I'm cool.

DORA: It's true, you're good in a crisis. And you have moral principles.

STEFANO: *(Ironical.)* Thanks to you. Now let me finish this article.

(A silence; DORA sits next to him and puts her hand on his hand.)

DORA: We never talk to each other...

STEFANO: Never?

DORA: You don't talk about yourself, about your plans, your dreams.

STEFANO: Dreams? There's nothing to dream about nowadays.

DORA: Mothers can't help but worry...I'd like to know, to talk, to share.

STEFANO: I'm here right now. I'll be here tomorrow.

DORA: You seem depressed.

STEFANO: Who isn't?

DORA: What do you mean?

STEFANO: Everybody I know, everybody I meet.

DORA: You've become a pessimist.

STEFANO: Like mother, like son. You too. What I see today is *your* pessimism. I watch you, I know you.

DORA: You watch me? I have the impression that you're avoiding me, that you do everything not to see me—really see me.

STEFANO: Sometimes it's easier to avoid the sad eyes of whom you love.

DORA: *(Moved.)* ..."Of whom you love..." You never said that before.

STEFANO: Never? At least one thousand times.

DORA: Perhaps, when you were a baby, when you pinched my cheeks and gave me big kisses. You haven't mentioned love for a long time. Never, as a grown-up.

STEFANO: You exaggerate. I don't think twenty-year-old sons often say that to forty-year-old mothers.

DORA: *(Pleased.)* A compliment. Thank you.

STEFANO: What did I say?

DORA: That you see me young, that you don't feel it's proper to hug me, to kiss me.

STEFANO: *(Staring at her.)* You're strange, today. You're saying weird things.

DORA: You see? This is what's missing in my life. *(Trying to make him laugh.)* The chance to say unusual things to my son...I feel alone.

STEFANO: We all feel alone. That's why I go out with my friends. And I can assure you that at times we don't talk to each other for hours.

DORA: That's strange...

STEFANO: You need girlfriends to talk to. You women like to talk.

DORA: *(After a brief pause.)* I have friends...at the club.

STEFANO: *(Interested.)* What club?

DORA: Where women, mothers abandoned by their sons, confide in each other.

STEFANO: "Abandoned?" Do you feel abandoned? I'm still living at home. I'm happy to live here with you.

DORA: You talk to me only when I force you to. Like today, now.

STEFANO: Is it worth talking? About what?

DORA: About everything. You see? We said new things.

STEFANO: "New"?

DORA: When one talks, one always says something new. Every word is different.

STEFANO: *(Thinking it over for a moment; with cordial irony.)* That's the wisdom of a mature person. *(Indicates her.)* Sometimes I don't talk to you because I feel I know everything about you.

DORA: You never know everything about a person.

STEFANO: *(Made curious.)* Do you have secrets?

DORA: *(Happily, mysterious.)* Of course!

STEFANO: Well, well...do you finally have—let's forget the "finally." Have you found a...companion, a man?

DORA: No.

STEFANO: Dad did leave you six years ago. It would be OK. I could handle it. Some sons might get jealous, but, honestly, I would be happy for you.

DORA: Do you miss him?

STEFANO: No. Yes. But he betrayed you. He betrayed us. Don't change the subject. What's your secret?

DORA: The club I mentioned. We tell each other everything.

STEFANO: You women...you talk about everything. Love, men, sex.

DORA: These are very special women. We never talk about sex.

STEFANO: What kind of club is this?

DORA: Lonely women, widows.

STEFANO: You are not a widow.

DORA: I feel like one.

STEFANO: How old are these new friends of yours?

DORA: My age and older.

STEFANO: And you never talk about sex? What do you talk about?

DORA: We talk about the past and the future. What will happen to us.

STEFANO: *(Thinking it over.)* Why are you there?

DORA: To be with women who feel lonely, abandoned by their families.

STEFANO: And you told them that you feel abandoned by me?

DORA: *(Avoiding a direct answer.)* I've discovered incredible, strange, sad things...

STEFANO: For instance?

DORA: Some of those women exaggerate.

STEFANO: What do you mean by exaggerate?

DORA: They think they have failed as mothers. They feel they have neglected their mission.

STEFANO: What's their mission?

DORA: To love and protect.

STEFANO: You always did that.

DORA: And some of those women lie.

STEFANO: They lie? Sounds like a bunch of women with too much time on their hands. What's it called: "Women with Woes"?

DORA: No. I'll tell you, but don't worry. It reveals nothing of me or my thoughts. I love life, I want to see you married, I want happy grandchildren with college degrees and faith in the future.

STEFANO: What's the name of this club?

DORA: *(Hesitating.)* Club...Suicide.

STEFANO: *(Alarmed.)* Mom. I had no idea.

DORA: None of us wants to commit suicide.

STEFANO: Then, why the name?

DORA: It was founded twelve years ago by a mother who had lost her son.

STEFANO: A suicide?

DORA: Yes.

STEFANO: What about the other women?

DORA: They all lost their sons the same way, and they don't understand why.

STEFANO: How do you fit in? Do you think I could do such a thing?

DORA: No.

STEFANO: I think like you, Mom. I want a family, children, and grandchildren. I was even thinking I should go back to school.

DORA: *(Happy and joyful.)* That's wonderful! I have some money stashed away. It's all yours. For that purpose. I am happy to know that you're going back to college. You're so intelligent, you'll succeed.

STEFANO: So we are both looking forward to the future. Why do you go to that club?

DORA: Because I feel alone, because I want to know how the other mothers who love their children cope. I want to learn.

STEFANO: To learn what?

DORA: How to avoid mistakes.

STEFANO: Why do they let you in? They accept your curiosity which is rather...morbid? It seems strange to me.

DORA: I taught you when you were a child not to tell lies, remember? But that if you confessed them, I would forgive you right away. Do you remember?

STEFANO: Yes. So what?

DORA: Well...I lied.

STEFANO: Lied? What did you tell them?

DORA: Don't make me tell you...I am ashamed...I feel you won't understand...

STEFANO: What did you tell them?

DORA: *(Hesitating, uneasy.)* I invented a name, the name of a son who doesn't exist, and...I told them he committed suicide.

STEFANO: *(Amazed, but almost amused.)* So, I have a "brother" who killed himself! Poor guy! What an imagination, Mom! You've got some imagination! You should write a novel to occupy your time. Write a diary. What's my brother's name?

DORA: He doesn't exist.

STEFANO: But if you just said...

DORA: I told them he was my only son and—

STEFANO: *(Interrupting.)* Great! So I am the suicidal son! Thank you! Knock on wood! Why? Why did you invent such a story? It must be true that my grandfather was dangerously loony!

DORA: I'm not crazy. I am alone, I feel alone.

STEFANO: I am here, I am here with you. And I am with you because you are a wonderful mother. You do so much for me. You do everything... *(Looking at her with love.)* I'll never find a great woman like you. *(Trying a joke.)* Maybe, that's why I didn't leave the nest for the illusionary freedom of a bachelor pad. My friends never understood it.

DORA: Promise that you will stay with me until you finish college.

STEFANO: I promise *(Thinking it over, amused.)* It's an intriguing blackmail...maybe it's in my interest to take less credits...Why should I rush my studies when I have a mother like you? *(Kisses his mother's hand.)* All right now, tell me everything about this story. I'll forgive your lie if you tell me everything. You must tell me *everything* or I'll come to the club and unmask you. Imagine for a moment. What would they say if your son's "ghost" appeared? *(He indicates himself.)*

DORA: *(Horrified at that thought.)* I beg you...

STEFANO: Did they believe you?

DORA: They did.

STEFANO: How did I kill myself?

DORA: Don't joke...

STEFANO: The way I did it. You must have invented something. Do you see me as a courageous man or as a coward? Was it a window or poison?

DORA: *(Timidly.)* A gun...I blamed your father...he had left it in a drawer and...

STEFANO: Poor Dad! You do hate him. He never touched a gun in his life!

DORA: I had to invent something.

STEFANO: Give me the details. In which room? My bedroom? Was there blood everywhere?

DORA: Please...

STEFANO: I'm sure that all the other..."widows" have mentioned gory details.

DORA: No. They avoid them. There is a tendency to wipe them out of your memory.

STEFANO: How convenient! So you could stop the outpouring flow of your imagination. Don't worry. Just add them to your novel. Details are important. Especially in detective stories. Do you have in mind writing a detective story? What kind of death have you in store for Dad?

DORA: Don't joke, please. None of my friends has ever given details.

STEFANO: What do you talk about then?

DORA: Guilt. They all feel guilty.

STEFANO: If I did that thing—an absurd thought—I would never do it—it wouldn't be your fault. It's never the mother's fault.

DORA: *(Pleasantly surprised.)* How can you be so sure? Do you talk about that with your friends?

STEFANO: Not about suicide. But I never heard a word against their mothers. Hatred for mothers is a story invented by psychoanalysts. All my friends adore their mothers.

DORA: "Adore"? You too?

STEFANO: *(Jokingly.)* You want too much, now. There are things one never admits, but...It's obvious, isn't it?

DORA: Obvious? Nothing should be obvious. One should use a word like "adore." It's a pleasure to hear it, it's encouraging.

STEFANO: I don't use that word.

DORA: You used it now.

STEFANO: It's a verb used by my friends. I'm against the concept of adoration.

What does it mean, after all, to adore someone?

DORA: What does it mean, in your opinion?

STEFANO: *(Thinking.)* All right...Adore means not to see faults. Love, however, is deeper. Speaking about mothers, it's easier to...say love. *(He looks at her with love.)*

DORA: That look of love is enough for me. Thank you.

STEFANO: *(Changing the subject.)* How come those mothers feel guilty?

DORA: When someone dies, a son, a parent, a grandparent, one always thinks: "I should have loved him more...I should have spoken with him more...I should have given him more..."

STEFANO: *(Incredulous.)* And you were able to invent, to make them believe such an incredible story. Or maybe...have you ever thought for a moment I could do...such a crazy thing?

DORA: No. Never. But I imagine being alone and wanted to know, to share, to console. We talk to each other a great deal, we console each other. And we discover secrets of the soul, hidden thoughts, atrocious doubts. I'm just preparing myself for—

STEFANO: *(Funny, interrupting.)* Not for my suicide!

DORA: No, absolutely not. I am preparing for the inevitable loneliness of—

(We hear the doorbell from downstairs. DORA goes to answer.)

DORA: *(Surprised and alarmed.)* Yes...Oh, Anna. Oh my God! Yes...I'm here, I'm at home... *(Very alarmed.)* No, it's OK. I understand, I understand...give me a few minutes...I'm undressed...and everything is in a mess here...take the elevator... *(Hangs up; to STEFANO.)* Please, I beg you, go to your room... *(Puts the magazine in his hand.)* and don't make a sound, don't come out, please, I beg of you. It's Anna, one of the mothers...She found a letter from her son and wants to show it to me...

STEFANO: The dead son?

DORA: Him, him. An old letter hidden somewhere. Please, I beg you. Don't show yourself!

STEFANO: One from the Club?

DORA: My best friend. She would die if she knew that you...if you show up. Think for a moment. I wept with her, I shared her pain...I beg you, I love you, I adore you, I'm thinking right now that I am the luckiest mother in the world...

(She pushes him toward the bedroom.)

DORA: Don't make a sound...You *don't* exist! I beg you.

STEFANO: *(Moves toward the bedroom with reluctance.)* But this is where the story has to end.

DORA: It will end, it will end, I promise! But not today, not in this way...Please! *(She's upset, distressed.)*

(STEFANO exits. DORA puts some objects out of the normal order, to indicate a mess. Doorbell. She goes to the door and opens it. ANNA comes in. She's beautiful, but distraught, tragic. The two women hug in silence. They go to sit at the table in silence. ANNA hands a letter to DORA, who reads it carefully.)

DORA: Where did you find it?

ANNA: Among his papers...I was straightening out his room, again, reliving special moments...

DORA: *(Continuing to read.)* See? He doesn't blame anyone.

ANNA: But he was so unhappy and depressed!

DORA: Aren't we all? Life is not easy.

ANNA: It's all pain.

DORA: Infinite pain, in our... *(She corrects herself.)* in your case... *(Rereads the letter and quotes.)* here he says, clearly, "lucky with a family like mine..."

ANNA: He adds "but." And then, he puts down that list of negative thoughts.

DORA: *(Reading.)* All young people say such things. It's fashionable now. It's a harmless trend.

ANNA: And then, why? Why did he kill himself? We all loved him. His father, especially. He loved his son more than me.

DORA: Did they get along with each other?

ANNA: Yes... *(She has a doubt.)* At times, he told his father, "Take her out for dinner, to see a movie. Give her a good time." He was talking about me.

DORA: You see? He loved you. He was thinking about you and your happiness. About your right to enjoy life.

ANNA: *(Thinking it over.)* Maybe...maybe he was reproaching his father, he hated his father because...because he was not affectionate with me...He was short tempered, absentminded...I don't think my husband loves me any longer...It's over between us.

DORA: You see? He was defending you, your life, your rights, your desires.

ANNA: Why, then? Why?

DORA: There is never an acceptable answer.

ANNA: What's yours? What kind of an answer did you give yourself?

DORA: *(Avoiding.)* Fate. Sometimes it's only a tragic fate...

ANNA: You told me that your son missed his father, that he hated him.

DORA: *(Aware that her son might be listening.)* "Hated"? Maybe not...

ANNA: But he blamed him for ignoring you, for abandoning you.

DORA: *(Vague.)* A little bit, yes, a little bit...

ANNA: You told us one day that your son disappeared, for weeks, at times. Maybe he was looking for his father...

DORA: Perhaps.

ANNA: But he abandoned you and made you suffer...

DORA: *(Correcting what she said at the Club.)* Temporarily, for a few days...His purpose was to find his father, to bring him back home.

ANNA: To bring him back to you.

DORA: *(Uneasy.)* Yes, yes...He was good, he loved me a great deal. It's not my fault. It's not your fault...

ANNA: Did he call you?

DORA: Every day.

ANNA: From where?

DORA: Other cities...where he was hoping to find his father.

ANNA: My son never called me. And sometimes he came back home at four in the morning.

DORA: He didn't want to wake you up, to disturb you.

ANNA: But I begged him to let me know at any hour, any time, if he was late.

DORA: When they're out with friends... they are embarrassed to show they still call Mamma, to justify, to explain...

ANNA: Was your son using drugs?

DORA: Never.

ANNA: How can you be so sure?

DORA: He was always the same, even tempered. Drugs excite and change you.

ANNA: And then, suddenly, one day your son killed himself...How can you explain that?

DORA: I can't explain it.

ANNA: I wanted to die.

DORA: Me too...We all feel like dying. They all say it, they all admit it. Even just the thought of losing a son makes one cringe... *(She instinctively looks at the door through which STEFANO is maybe listening.)*

ANNA: It wasn't your fault. If he called you, if he was just searching for your husband...

DORA: It's not your fault either. It's clear in this letter that he loved you. Sometimes you can't blame the family. Maybe the wrong friends, drinking...Did he drink a great deal?

ANNA: Now and then, but once... *(She hesitates.)*

DORA: Once?

ANNA: I found a white substance. I showed it to him. He wanted it back. He said it was a medicine. I threw it away. Maybe, that's the reason why...

DORA: Don't go wild with your imagination. Even if it was the thing you suspected, you don't kill yourself for just some white dust. Was it very much?

ANNA: Oh no! Maybe a spoonful.

DORA: How many days before the accident?

ANNA: One month. More than a month.

DORA: You see? There's no connection. If he was angry with you because of your action, your taking away his mysterious medicine, the accident would have happened the same day, soon after.

ANNA: *(Interrupting.)* You keep calling it an accident. Do you really think it was an..."accident"?

DORA: We lie to each other, don't you realize that? At the Club they all lie. We are all looking for justifications, excuses.

ANNA: *(Reflecting.)* Accident? No. You don't fall from a window, by mistake, at his age. Your son, did he shoot himself by mistake?

DORA: *(Uneasy.)* Maybe...It often happens...They try, they handle a weapon with curiosity, and they don't realize it's loaded...

ANNA: What did the police tell you? That it was an accident?

DORA: They also lie, sometimes, out of compassion.

ANNA: They all feel compassion for us poor mothers.

DORA: We have to accept that there are things we will never, can never understand. No matter how close you are to a child or a husband, there are always secrets. There is a part of everyone that is untouchable and sometimes that place is filled with pain. Pain so big that...All I am saying is that there are reasons beyond our understanding.

ANNA: That makes it sound as if it were reasonable.

DORA: No. That's not what I'm saying at all. I'm saying that we cannot understand how another person thinks, what another person wants out of life, or how lost they might feel.

ANNA: It's very hard to accept the fact that we cannot save each other.

(STEFANO enters. ANNA is surprised. DORA is petrified. STEFANO slowly moves toward DORA. He kisses her hair, her cheek. He sits next to her. A tense silence.)

STEFANO: *(Offering to shake hands with ANNA.)* My name is Roberto.

ANNA: *(Shaking hands.)* Anna.

STEFANO: *(Indicates his mother and speaks slowly, with extreme clarity.)* This treasure of a woman asked me to stay in the bedroom…She begged me to. Maybe she's a bit ashamed… *(To ANNA.)* I heard some of your words…It's easy through that door…Dora *(He kisses her hand.)* has found a solution for her grief…a young lover… *(He indicates himself; he kisses her hand again.)* A new love makes you live again…We have been lovers for six months…Love is miraculous…

(DORA's face is shining with joy. She shows love and gratitude.)

STEFANO: *(To ANNA.)* You too, Anna, you should look for a young lover, someone like me…A new love heals all wounds…all of them.

(IMMOBILITY. CURTAIN.)

Alessia

The Characters:

ALESSIA
MARK

ALESSIA is a beautiful young woman in her early twenties. She is in bed, half-naked; she is getting dressed. A man is talking to her from the bathroom.

VOICE OF THE MAN: You can't imagine my joy...When I'm with you I feel young again...You're wonderful...You're unique, divine. Thank you.

(A handsome man enters; he is in his early sixties, still strong, in good shape. He is only wearing a towel. He is surprised to see that ALESSIA is getting dressed.)

MARK: What are you doing, my love? It's early...please... *(He invites her to sit on the bed.)*

ALESSIA: We had an agreement, didn't we?

MARK: Yes...to be together...

ALESSIA: And we've been together. *(She indicates the bed.)* Therefore...

MARK: Oh no! We didn't say one hour, two, three. We said...together for a whole afternoon, an entire night...

ALESSIA: You know very well Mother's rule. I must be home by eleven. It applies to both of us. We are never out after eleven o'clock.

MARK: *(Consulting his watch.)* There's still time...Make me happy, please. This is the most beautiful day in my life...

ALESSIA: All right...a little while... *(She lies down on the bed.)*

MARK: Thank you...thank you, my love. *(He caresses her arm and kisses her hand.)* It may seem impossible to you...maybe you won't believe me...this is a precious, stupendous gift...the most beautiful day in my life...

ALESSIA: I think you're exaggerating, but thank you. One has often the impression of being happy, very happy. You think it's a unique encounter that can't be duplicated. Instead...

MARK: Has that ever happened to you?

ALESSIA: Yes.

MARK: *(With curiosity.)* Tell me. Have you had...a very "unique" encounter that turned out differently? You thought it was. And on the contrary...

ALESSIA: You remember my friend Frank? The first time, he was very sweet...tender...it was a very special night. I thought I never—

MARK: Night.

ALESSIA: Mother was traveling. I told her the whole story afterwards.

MARK: What did she say?

ALESSIA: She gave me good advice. She is a good mother.

MARK: Meaning?

ALESSIA: It would have been better if I had waited. But since it had happened...

MARK: She was right. It would have been better if you had waited.

ALESSIA: *(Ironical.)* Better for you, you mean? You men. You are children at any age.

MARK: Your night with that...boy? Why did it seem less beautiful, to you, later?

ALESSIA: The memory faded...far away...like a vague dream...there have been better days, more beautiful hours—

MARK: *(Flattered.)* You mean that...our being together this very sweet afternoon has been more romantic than... that night?

ALESSIA: I always tell the truth.

(A silence.)

MARK: Tell me the truth, my love.

ALESSIA: *(Hesitating, keeping him in suspense.)* Well...I must admit that...now, in this moment, this seems to me the most interesting, the most exciting experience...

MARK: *(All excited.)* My heart is melting away. You can't imagine what I feel. Thank you, thank you, thank you!

ALESSIA: Don't die on me now. You know, we need you.

MARK: Oh no! Oh no! I don't want to die on the most beautiful day of my life. Tell me—your sincerity is divine—why does this afternoon impress you as the most wonderful in your life?

ALESSIA: Maybe because I'm young and I've had very few experiences.

MARK: "Few"...and this divine afternoon seems to you to be the best?

ALESSIA: The most interesting.

MARK: Why? Tell me, please tell me. I feel you will make me happy.

ALESSIA: Whatever I say?

MARK: Whatever you say.

ALESSIA: *(Slowly, hesitating, looking for the right words.)* I think that...I hope this does not offend you...you obviously have your technique...you know a woman's body very well. All her secrets—

MARK: And my love? my adoration? my infinite admiration? Didn't you feel them?

ALESSIA: Sure, sure. But to that vibrant desire, to that passion, you added... technique.

MARK: Meaning? What are you talking about? What do you mean by "technique"?

ALESSIA: Intimate knowledge of what a woman wants...even if she didn't know that she wanted it.

MARK: *(Repeating almost to himself.)* "Even if she didn't know that she wanted it." Did I surprise you?

ALESSIA: Yes...and I surprised myself when...

MARK: When?

ALESSIA: When I felt what I felt.

MARK: Was it the first time?

ALESSIA: A friend of mine told me that it is always the first time. It was that, for me.

MARK: *(With curiosity.)* The first time that you...had an orgasm?

ALESSIA: I don't know. It's always different. It was more intense with you.

MARK: Yet, you don't want to spend the night with me?

ALESSIA: You know I can't.

MARK: *(Enjoying the words.)* ..."More intense," "different," "wonderful."

ALESSIA: Wonderful. You know how, and—where.

MARK: Have you discovered new things, with me?

ALESSIA: Sure. Frank was twenty. You are... *(She invites him with a gesture to tell his age.)*

MARK: Let's not talk about age. When one loves, he is always young.

ALESSIA: All right. I admit that you look fifty. But Mother told me your real age. I admire a man who is not ashamed of his age. Tell me, how old are you?

MARK: *(Uneasy.)* Why do you want to force me to...? I refuse to feel my age. I feel very young. With you, today, I am twenty.

ALESSIA: *(Insisting.)* I know what month you were born. You remember? We celebrated your birthday. You were...

MARK: *(Trying to avoid it.)* You know, you know. I remember it was written on the cake.

ALESSIA: ...And that you told Mother "Thank you, this is the most beautiful birthday of my life." "Of my life." It's an expression you use a great deal, an expression you love.

MARK: It was true...you know I live alone. No one ever remembered to celebrate my birthday.

ALESSIA: *(Insisting.)* Say it, how many?

(MARK indicates his age with his fingers.)

ALESSIA: Six plus one. Say it.

MARK: *(Quickly, almost imperceptibly.)* Sixty-one.

ALESSIA: But don't worry. Mother finds you very young. She likes you a great deal. She said, "A man like that can make you happy for thirty years."

MARK: Make you happy. She was talking about us.

ALESSIA: No. She was talking in general, thinking about herself.

MARK: *(Who always wants to avoid the subject "Mother.")* ..."Happy for thirty years"...Therefore, you too, found me...rather young.

ALESSIA: Yes. You're well kept. You're in good shape.

MARK: And in a way...I surprised you.

ALESSIA: In a way.

MARK: Tell me, make me happy. I love your voice, your love for sincerity, for truth...what things...what gesture, which one of my caresses surprised you most?

ALESSIA: A couple of things that...I did not know, or to be more precise...that Frank did not know.

MARK: *(Anxious.)* Which ones?

ALESSIA: Why do you need details? *(Vaguely ironical.)* Is it a characteristic of...older people?

MARK: I adore you, I worship you, I want to know.

ALESSIA: It's difficult for a woman to say...this way, that way, how...

MARK: *(Jumping up and taking a pen and a sheet of paper.)* Write it down. I'll keep this page, these words of yours, on my heart for the rest of my life.

ALESSIA: You are really a...child.

MARK: I am, I am! I'm born again with you. Please!

(He hands her pen and paper.)

ALESSIA: *(Reluctant.)* All right...I'll write it in caps so that no one—not even my mother will recognize my writing.

(ALESSIA writes a couple of lines; she looks at them; she smiles; she gives the paper to MARK.)

ALESSIA: And don't let Mother find it! No one must get hold of it!

MARK: *(He reads it; kisses the paper with joy and passion.)* Thank you, my love, thank you. And you said you don't want to spend the night with me! How can you give up the chance to relive these experiences? *(He indicates the paper.)*

ALESSIA: We have a very clear pact, a very clear agreement. An afternoon together if...

MARK: I said "One Day." I remember very well that I said: "One Day Together."

ALESSIA: Which excludes the night.

MARK: I'll ask your mother.

ALESSIA: What will you ask?

MARK: The permission to keep you with me for... *(Searching.)* a trip in the country, some excuse. She trusts me!

ALESSIA: She trusts me too. And look what we did, *(Indicates the bed.)* look how we took advantage of her trust!

MARK: She'll never suspect!

ALESSIA: No, probably not...I know she admires you and trusts you a great deal. And do you know since when?

MARK: Since when?

ALESSIA: You are very clever. When we were guests in your house, you said: "You fill up my home with warmth. My dream has always been to have a gentle wife, vulnerable like you, and a wonderful daughter like Alessia."

MARK: "Wonderful."

ALESSIA: From that moment on, you conquered her love.

MARK: And her trust. She will never suspect that we...

ALESSIA: And she must never know about it. *Never!*

(A long pause.)

ALESSIA: So, when will the ceremony take place?

MARK: *(Avoiding.)* Let me call her. You know she's happy when I call her.

ALESSIA: Not from here. It feels wrong. I feel guilty and have doubts. I am...a bad daughter.

MARK: You are a wonderful daughter.

ALESSIA: If she knew... *(She stares at MARK.)* You swore. Never! Never! She must never know about this!

MARK: Only if you spend the night with me.

ALESSIA: Ha! Are you trying to blackmail me? You said, a while ago, you repeated it: "One day." You see? I'm still here. I'll go away at sunset.

MARK: The sunset of my life.

ALESSIA: The beginning of your new life.

MARK: To lose you is to die.

ALESSIA: Don't play the martyr, don't be so tragic. I admire you, I accepted this—and I don't regret it—because you are a real man, a man who really knows how to keep his word. Therefore...no doubts, no blackmail! I kept my part of the bargain. I'm here... *(She offers herself with a feminine, vague gesture.)*

MARK: *(Who is uncertain and sad.)* You are right, Alessia. You kept your part of the bargain, but put yourself in my shoes. I'm crazy about you, I'm overjoyed, full of sweetness and tenderness, and...I'm about to lose you.

ALESSIA: Lose me? We will see each other practically every day.

MARK: Yes! "We'll see each other." Imagine what a torture it'll be for me!

ALESSIA: *(Mild and wise.)* I'm losing the esteem I had for you. I thought you were a real man. We had a clear and precise agreement. These special hours with me, and then...the beginning of a life which I guarantee you will be happy and serene.

MARK: You must see it...

ALESSIA: What?

MARK: That I am absolutely crazy about you!

ALESSIA: Don't exaggerate. A twenty-year-old in your life? It would be a big mistake, I assure you.

MARK: Do you remember the first time I met you?

ALESSIA: I remember.

MARK: To whom was I giving my attention, whom did I admire most?

ALESSIA: It's strange you are talking about that. I asked Mother about that. She assured me that you were admiring her and courting her.

MARK: Every woman believes that. Think about it. Why did you ask her that question? Why did you ask who was the object of my admiration?

(A brief silence.)

ALESSIA: Because...I had doubts.

MARK: Because you had noticed that I was staring at you, that I was falling in love with you.

ALESSIA: It seems impossible to me.

MARK: I love you, Alessia.

(ALESSIA ignores him.)

MARK: *(In a pleading voice.)* Alessia...

ALESSIA: Stop whining! *(With some defiance and irony.)* Come here. Prove to me you are a real man. A man capable of keeping his word.

MARK: You are right. You are right. But think about me for a moment, about what I'm feeling, about what I am experiencing now.

ALESSIA: *(Vaguely ironical.)* The most beautiful hours of your life.

MARK: Exactly. The most beautiful, divine hours. Tell me, have you ever seen your love, a great love of yours, take leave forever?

ALESSIA: Not yet. I'm only twenty.

MARK: *(Dramatic.)* The train is moving away. The handkerchief waving, the tears...

ALESSIA: My train is not going anywhere. I'm staying at home.

MARK: *(Sad.)* At home...

ALESSIA: Where only my mother and a "wonderful daughter" will live.

MARK: Do you think it would be easy for me?

ALESSIA: It *Must Be Easy*. Nothing is easy in life. Do you think it was easy for me to make this decision?

MARK: Which one?

ALESSIA: To be here with you.

MARK: Do you regret it?

ALESSIA: No...but you must admit that it was a courageous choice, a difficult choice.

MARK: A sacrifice?

ALESSIA: No.

MARK: But you don't regret it.

ALESSIA: No...I love my mother...You know, she divorced my father when I was two years old. She brought me up, she sacrificed herself for me. I owe her everything.

MARK: *(Who wants to know as much as possible.)* How did she behave with...the other men in her life? Did she send you away to the country, or were you in the house with them?

ALESSIA: She only had two relationships. She told you—I was there—one for six years, one for five; two good men. I was there in the house. Normal home, normal behavior. As if they were husband and wife.

MARK: The first one, the one who stayed for six years, who was he? What did he do?

ALESSIA: He was an accountant. A regular guy.

MARK: Boring? Accountants only talk about numbers.

ALESSIA: He was nice and quiet.

MARK: Did they often go out at night? Where did they go?

ALESSIA: They only went out Saturday nights. Dinner out. A show or a concert.

MARK: What about the night when...? *(Gesture.)* Did you hear them? Your room is near your mother's.

ALESSIA: No. They were...quiet and respectful.

MARK: Respectful? What a strange adjective! Respectful, meaning what?

ALESSIA: They didn't want me to hear and fantasize about...

MARK: About what?

ALESSIA: About their sexual activity.

MARK: "Activity." Was there a lot of it? Every night?

ALESSIA: Oh no.

MARK: How did you know? They were..."respectful." Therefore, you heard nothing.

ALESSIA: Mother told me. They did it only once a week, for a few minutes.

MARK: What about your mother? Did she complain?

ALESSIA: Oh no. She told me, she explained that what binds a woman to a man is not sex, it must not be only sex. What counts is to have someone near you. Companionship, love. *(A brief pause.)* You mustn't worry.

MARK: *(Hurt.)* Me worry? about what?

ALESSIA: Nothing, nothing. Mother is not demanding. She doesn't ask for much.

MARK: *(Boasting.)* With me...

ALESSIA: It's enough for her to have a companion, a man to love and respect.

MARK: How come she lost the accountant?

ALESSIA: He vanished. One day, I remember it well, he kissed my forehead, a strange kiss—I should have guessed it was a farewell kiss—and he left us.

MARK: And your mother thought right away that she needed a substitute. Who was the other one? The one who stayed five years?

ALESSIA: An unemployed artist. You must have seen a couple of his paintings. *(Ironical.)* "Masterpieces" in our dining room. Castles and angels floating into clouds.

MARK: Unemployed. Always at home. Always… "active."

ALESSIA: Active?

MARK: You used that expression before: "sexual activity."

ALESSIA: He was always at the bar. Disappointed and depressed. He drank a great deal, too much. From that time on, we never had any alcohol at home.

MARK: Would he come home drunk and beat up both of you?

ALESSIA: No. He'd fall asleep on the sofa.

MARK: And when did they make love, when did he use your mother?

ALESSIA: Use? What an ugly verb.

MARK: When did he take her, rape her, make what he probably called "love" to her?

ALESSIA: Seldom.

MARK: How do you know that?

ALESSIA: Mother always told me everything.

MARK: Did she complain to you? Why didn't she get rid of him?

ALESSIA: Because—as she used to say—the presence of a man in the house is important. It gives a feeling of… serenity, success, accomplishment.

MARK: With an accountant who was always half-asleep? with an artist who was always drunk? What kind of life was that?

ALESSIA: And, in fact, after a few months—

MARK: Years.

ALESSIA: —She convinced him to leave, to go to Europe. He never wrote to us, he never thanked my mother.

MARK: *(With a bit of jealousy.)* And, did you get a goodbye kiss from him, too?

ALESSIA: No. I avoided him. I didn't like him.

MARK: Why?

ALESSIA: It's obvious, isn't it? I didn't respect him.

MARK: And… those two men, did they ever notice you, try anything?

ALESSIA: I was a little girl… eight years old when the accountant was around.

MARK: And with the artist? You were at least fifteen…

ALESSIA: *(Slowly, uncertain.)* That was one of the reasons I was avoiding him.

MARK: Why?

ALESSIA: One night he grabbed one of my breasts.

MARK: *(With anger and jealousy.)* Pervert! Did you call the police?

ALESSIA: I avoided him. That's the best way.

MARK: *(Reflecting.)* Two bad experiences for your mother. Two men who lived with her as if they were husbands. And later? Did she have other men, other adventures?

ALESSIA: No.

MARK: Did she go away, disappear for a week or a weekend?

ALESSIA: No, we are always together. Like two sisters. We tell each other everything.

MARK: But you allowed her to make two grave mistakes!

ALESSIA: Which ones?

MARK: To live with two lovers.

ALESSIA: You're right. I learned from my mother's mistakes not to live with a man without a real commitment. I learned everything from her.

MARK: What else did you learn?

ALESSIA: Love, respect, tolerance, sense of humor. She's a perfect woman. You're a lucky man.

MARK: *(Looking at her with love.)* I am. I know…I'm very lucky…especially with you, today.

ALESSIA: And tomorrow will be the beginning of your new life. With us.

MARK: Both of you. Will it be easy for you?

ALESSIA: Of course. I have lied only once in my life. Today.

MARK: *(Alarmed.)* With me?

ALESSIA: No. I've been sincere with you. You know that. We lived these hours together with absolute sincerity. But I lied to my mother, not telling her about this. Not talking to her about our agreement. *(Decisive, precise.)* Never! Never! She must not know. *Never!* You promised. This will be my only lie—at least it's for a good cause.

MARK: Good cause? Whose good?

ALESSIA: All three of us. We'll finally have a family. My mother is crazy about you. She tells me every day. She dreams about you. She desires you, she knows you are the ideal man for her.

MARK: She's never said that, she never gives me a hint. She's all smiles. That's all.

ALESSIA: After two wrong experiences, a woman becomes cautious. She told me she loves you. She tells me everything.

MARK: When? Since when?

ALESSIA: I told you. When we were guests in your house. I'll never forget your words. You said "You fill up my house with warmth, my dream would have been a wife gentle and vulnerable like you, and a wonderful daughter like Alessia." *(Reflecting.)* Very clever…were you sincere?

MARK: Yes…sure…especially when I said "a wonderful daughter."

ALESSIA: And "vulnerable"? Mother does not seem vulnerable, but you knew. You guessed it. That is real love. An intuition of love…You'll be happy.

MARK: When?

ALESSIA: Starting tomorrow. You promised that you will talk to her tomorrow. Do you remember?

MARK: I remember.

ALESSIA: At what time may we expect you?

MARK: It depends…

ALESSIA: On what?

MARK: On the time we…wake up. *(She ignores it.)*

ALESSIA: At noon. We'll wait for you at noon.

MARK: Will you be there?

ALESSIA: At the beginning, yes. Then I'll leave you alone.

MARK: *(Uneasy.)* What am I going to tell her?

ALESSIA: That you understood her love, that you love her, that you want to marry her.

MARK: What will she say?

ALESSIA: She'll say yes. She loves you very much.

MARK: And she will never suspect that…?

ALESSIA: Never. She knows I've never lied to her. It would be inconceivable for her to think that…I did this for her. *(She indicates the bed; then she looks at her watch.)* It's getting late… *(She opens her arms.)* Come to me…Make me feel your passion.

MARK: Ours, once more. *(Sad, moving toward her.)* Before my sunset. *(He drops his towel, remaining naked in front of ALESSIA.)*

ALESSIA: *(Looking at his probable erection.)* The last one.

(DARKNESS. CURTAIN.)

The Piggy Bank

The Persons:

THE MAN: in his thirties
SHE: a beautiful woman in her mid-twenties
HE: the client, a timid man in his forties

Today. New York City. A modestly furnished room in a New York apartment. A bed. A table, three chairs, a washbasin, and a curtain that hides a corner of the room. A MAN is smoking and watching television. He hears footsteps approaching. He quickly puts out his cigarette in the ashtray; he turns off the television and hides behind the curtain. The light remains on. SHE and HE enter.

HE: *(Looking around.)* You live alone?

SHE: I do. I left the light on because I knew I'd be back right away.

HE: *(Surprised.)* "Right away"?...You didn't know you would meet me.

SHE: You or someone else.

(They study each other. He suddenly notices he cigarette, which is still burning.)

HE: *(Alarmed.)* The cigarette—there! Someone is here! *(He looks around, frightened.)*

SHE: That's mine. I always smoke a cigarette after that... *(She indicates the bed.)* I leave it here...It doesn't look good to smoke in the streets...

HE: Why?

SHE: Married ladies don't. I'm married.

HE: You are?

SHE: What made you think I wasn't? What did you expect? A virgin?

HE: No. I was just...Are you *still* married?

SHE: *(Vague.)* Aren't we all—somehow?

HE: Somehow... *(He looks around. He is still worried.)*

SHE: Does your wife smoke in the streets? Or in restaurants? Does she curse? Does she do *everything* in bed? She wouldn't be a well-brought-up lady if she did...

(A brief silence; SHE studies him; HE avoids her eyes.)

HE: She's away...a long vacation...

SHE: How long?

HE: Six weeks—

SHE: Twenty-five dollars for the first time. Twenty for the second.

HE: Why less the second time?

SHE: After the first time the novelty is gone. Isn't it?

HE: In a way—

SHE: It's as if I were your wife. In advance.

HE: What?

SHE: The twenty-five.

(HE hands her two bills. She indicates the piggy bank on her dresser.)

SHE: In there. I never touch the money. It would spoil the beauty of our…encounter. *(She studies him, vaguely sarcastic.)*

HE: *(Puts the money in the piggy bank. Admires it for a moment and notices that it cannot be removed. It is part of the dresser—stuck. Surprised.)* It doesn't…move.

SHE: Specially built. Part of the dresser. The money goes inside the first drawer. I locked it and threw the key away. I will use that money when I grow old. If I need it.

HE: *(Surprised.)* What about your living expenses?

SHE: Nice…You care.

HE: I care…How do you manage?

SHE: In the morning, the first two clients put the money near the piggy bank. I keep it covered. *(Shows a pair of black panties.)*

HE: The first two…

SHE: Only the first two. Fifty dollars a day is more than enough for me…I live modestly.

HE: *(Looking around.)* Modestly…

SHE: Would you like a cup of coffee?

HE: If it's ready… *(Timidly.)* Don't you want to wash me, first…?

SHE: *(After a short hesitation.)* Wash what?

HE: *(Timidly.)* …My…It's ready, full of desire…

SHE: Wash it yourself.

HE: *(Lost, disappointed.)* Where?

SHE: In there… *(Indicates the sink.)*

(HE meekly goes to wash himself. SHE ignores him completely. SHE prepares two cups of coffee.)

HE: Aren't you a bit curious?

SHE: No.

HE: *(Trying to joke.)* We are not created equal and…curiosity is human.

(SHE ignores him completely. The two cups of coffee are ready. SHE sits down at the table and waits for him. HE is puzzled. HE does not know what to do.)

HE: Aren't you in a hurry to…?

SHE: *(Signaling him to sit.)* No.

(HE sits down. SHE observes him and invites him to drink.)

SHE: Where did you send your wife?

HE: To California…

(A silence.)

HE: And your husband?

SHE: He's here.

HE: *(Jumping up, alarmed.)* Here?

SHE: In the city.

HE: *(Worried.)* You think he…could…? *(Indicates the door.)*

SHE: He comes home at midnight.

HE: *(Worried, studying her.)* He knows that you…?

SHE: I'm not sure.

HE: What do you mean? Does he or doesn't he?

SHE: I think he does. That's why he comes home late.

HE: *(Worried.)* You mean to say…He could…he could show up early.

SHE: He could.

(A silence.)

HE: What...what does he do until midnight? Does he work somewhere?

SHE: He doesn't work.

HE: And he...he accepts the profits of your..."encounters"?

SHE: I made him believe I was rich when I first met him. So he would marry me. When he sees the fifty dollars he takes for granted they come from me. He takes them and goes shopping.

HE: But he must know they come from somewhere. Friends or maybe—

SHE: —An inheritance. He's the quiet type. He accepts everything without ever asking a question. But let's talk about you.

HE: *(Still tense and worried.)* But he could come back, let's say—at nine o'clock?

SHE: He could. But he has never done it before.

HE: *(Nervous.)* There's always a first time...What does he do until midnight? Where does he go?

SHE: I don't know. He never tells me. Do you have any children?

HE: Yes and you?

SHE: He doesn't like them. How many do you have?

HE: *(Reluctant.)* Three.

SHE: Let me see their pictures.

HE: *(After a brief hesitation.)* I don't have them.

SHE: Too bad. I like children. *(SHE observes him.)* And I like men who have pictures of their children on them. I give more.

HE: *(Interested.)* What do you mean?

SHE: You know what I mean. I put all I've got into it.

HE: You mean—more passion? More...love?

SHE: You guessed. Let me see the pictures.

HE: *(After a silence.)* How do you know I have them with me?

SHE: You're the type.

HE: What do you mean—"type"?...

SHE: A good father.

(A silence; HE hesitates.)

SHE: What are you afraid of? That I'll contaminate them?

HE: Oh no!

(Another brief silence.)

SHE: Put them on the table. I only want to see them. I will not touch them.

(HE gallantly puts them in her hand.)

SHE: Beautiful. Especially the two girls. How old are they?

HE: Eighteen, sixteen, fourteen.

SHE: What's the boy's name?

HE: Vito. *(Indicating.)* Donata and Rosalia.

SHE: *(Vaguely ironic.)* Original.

HE: My wife chose them.

SHE: Do you have her picture too?

HE: I'm here to forget her. *(Pockets the pictures again.)* Why don't we...? *(Indicates the bed.)*

SHE: *(Pretending not to understand.)* Why don't we what?

(HE makes the gesture: SHE pretends to be nearsighted.)

HE: ...What I paid you in advance for.

SHE: *(Standing up, offended.)* Here I am! You want it on the table or standing up? I'm ready!

(HE is again uneasy.)

SHE: *(Kinder.)* Why the rush? Why ruin everything?

HE: *(Uneasy.)* I'm sorry...I thought—

SHE: What's wrong with you? Can't you control yourself? When was the last time you had sex?

HE: A few days ago. It's not that—

SHE: Why the hurry then? Let's get to know each other. It's in *your* interest.

HE: *(Curious.)* My interest?

SHE: That's what I said.

(They study each other; HE is uneasy.)

HE: Aren't *you* in a hurry?

SHE: No.

HE: The others...

SHE: The others?

HE: —They're all in a great hurry.

SHE: Because they don't like what they're doing. They don't feel anything.

HE: And you?

SHE: I like it. Especially when I know and respect my partner. I want to enjoy it too.

HE: *(Confused and flattered.)* Thank you...Thank you but...I'm not rich...I only had those twenty-five. I know the price and...Don't you lose money staying here—talking?

SHE: I already had thirty-one today. I don't need more. I like you. *(SHE smiles at him.)*

HE: *(Uneasy, shocked.)* Thirty-one...Are you sure?

SHE: I always count them; you want to see? *(SHE shows him a booklet; the page has thirty-one red x's; SHE adds another.)* And you make thirty-two!

HE: Does your husband ever see those x's?

SHE: Once. I told him they were kisses—kisses for him. He smiled.

HE: He believed you?

SHE: I think he did.

(They study each other.)

HE: With those..."partners" did you talk this much before...? *(Indicates the bed.)*

SHE: Only with the ones I like. Types I would have dreamt of marrying...Sex is awful without love.

HE: *(Confused, vaguely flattered.)* Thank you...Did they show you their pictures? Their children?

SHE: Only the best ones. Good fathers and husbands. Those I reward. The other ones, I punish.

HE: *(Worried.)* Punish? How?

SHE: There are a thousand ways.

HE: What ways?

SHE: *(Straight in his eyes.)* You know.

(A silence.)

HE: If I hadn't shown you the pictures... what would you have done to me?

(SHE studies him; an ironic smile.)

HE: Please tell me. I'm curious.

(A silence.)

HE: Please.

SHE: It doesn't pay to be curious at times... *(SHE is very mysterious.)*

HE: Please.

SHE: *(Mysterious.)* Some things are better left unsaid...Anyway...it won't happen to you.

(HE is uneasy. HE's afraid but at the same time curious. HE thinks with horror that if HE had not shown her the pictures, SHE might have...)

SHE: Tell me something...How old were you when you had your first woman? Was she a virgin?

HE: *(Studying her, annoyed by her curiosity.)* How come you want to know all these details about me?

SHE: I told you, I like you. I want to know everything about you.

HE: That would take hours...I obviously can't stay until your husband comes back.

SHE: We have three hours. We'll enjoy it all the way, like two real lovers, two passionate lovers who met again after—

HE: *(Interrupting.)* Three hours?

SHE: Or less, if you prefer. Until you get tired. Whichever way you like it. It's the man who chooses positions, intensity, duration. It will be up to you.

HE: To the other—the one before me. *(Indicates the ashtray.)* How much time did you give?

SHE: I didn't like him. A fat businessman. A nigger. Only a few minutes.

HE: *(Shocked.)* A ni—? You take them too?

SHE: If they pay.

(A silence.)

HE: Are they different?

SHE: Sexually, you mean?

HE: Sexually.

SHE: That's just a legend. They're just like you.

HE: How...how do you know?

SHE: They're often worse than you whites. They don't know the meaning of the word "tenderness." They never wait for the woman to... *(Vague gesture.)*

HE: For the woman to?

SHE: ...To come! They never did, with me. Don't tell me you're selfish too!

HE: Oh no, no! *(HE is perplexed.)* ...How many Negroes, today?

SHE: *(Opens the booklet and counts the first column.)* Twenty-one. They like me because I'm blonde and my skin is very fair... *(Keeps counting.)* two Vietnamese...a German tourist...a Brazilian cop...three French sailors...two Italian businessmen.

HE: *(Trying to hide his discomfort.)* All married?

SHE: Only nineteen.

HE: All with children?

SHE: Only fourteen.

HE: And how many...how many showed you their pictures?

SHE: Only nine.

HE: Then you...punished five.

SHE: I did.

HE: What did you do to them?

(A silence.)

SHE: *(Avoiding.)* Why ruin everything with depressing details? Let's talk about you. How old were you when you began to play with yourself?

HE: *(Lost.)* Play?

SHE: *(Indicating his crotch.)* When did you discover you had that toy, between your legs?

(A silence.)

SHE: You can tell me. I'll be your woman in a little while. More passionate and intimate than your wife ever was.

HE: *(Reluctantly.)* Eleven...eleven years old.

SHE: Quite early. Good!

HE: *(Who has not forgotten.)* Those Ne—those strangers who...Were they healthy?

SHE: How do you mean?

HE: Clean, I mean.

SHE: I think so.

HE: *(Alarmed.)* You "think" so? You didn't wash them?

SHE: You're not children, you wash yourselves, right?

HE: But...let's suppose one of them was sick?

SHE: I don't care.

HE: *(Frightened.)* You don't care?

SHE: Let's be frank. Forty a day for seven years...If I were afraid of diseases, I'd die of heart failure forty times a day! I wiped that fear out of my life. I don't think about it anymore.

HE: But...let's suppose the last one had something—

SHE: That's life, my dear! *(Melodramatic and funny.)* We must have faith in our destiny, amigo! *(Changing.)* How many times a week, with your wife?

HE: How many times a week, to your doctor?

SHE: Twice a year. And you?

HE: Twice a week.

SHE: *(Making fun of him.)* At the doctor's? With your hang-up about sickness, I don't think you'll like it.

HE: What?

(A silence; SHE observes him.)

HE: What "won't I like"?

SHE: If you're so afraid to catch a disease, how can you enjoy a woman?

HE: Tell me the truth. Are you sure you're not...?

SHE: *(Smiling.)* ... "sick"?

(A silence; they study each other.)

SHE: *(Maternally.)* Remember when I mentioned "punishment," for some clients?

HE: *(Eager.)* Yes—and you didn't explain what you meant. How do you punish them?

SHE: *(Slowly, friendly.)* When a client chooses me, I try to be kind...want to know him better, more intimately. I know you well now. *(A brief silence.)*

HE: Go on.

SHE: *(Deliberately.)* If he's a bastard and refuses to talk, communicate, relate... Or if he's a Commie, a troublemaker, a foreigner, well...

HE: *(Eager to know.)* Well?

SHE: ...I punish him.

HE: How?

SHE: I allow him...intimacy.

(HE is confused; HE does not understood.)

HE: You allow him...?

SHE: The bed. Whatever he wants...

HE: *(Lost, confused.)* And that's "punishment"!

SHE: *(Slowly, observing him.)* If he's instead a good man like you, a man who loves his wife and children, well...

HE: *(Eager.)* So?

SHE: I tell him the truth.

HE: *(Losing his patience.)* What truth?

(A silence; she studies him.)

SHE: I have AIDS.

(HE jumps up from his chair. HE does not know what to do. HE paces around for a few seconds. Then HE goes near the piggy bank in which he put the twenty-five dollars. HE stares at it, ready to break it. He thinks it over. HE is unsure. HE is debating his situation. HE lifts his hand, ready to break it. HE thinks it over. HE relaxes for a few seconds: looks at her.)

SHE: I was honest with you...Please don't break my piggy bank...It's a souvenir, very dear to me...From my mother.

HE: But my twenty five...

SHE: It could have been thousands, if I hadn't warned you...Thousands of dollars to cure you, your wife...Thousands...

(HE is finally convinced. HE suddenly decides to leave. Without looking at her, HE goes toward the door and leaves, slamming it behind him. THE MAN comes out from behind the curtain holding a butcher knife. A silence. No one moves. The audience will think for a few seconds that her husband has surprised her and is about to kill her. Their eyes meet. They explode into loud laughter.)

THE MAN: *(To the woman, who evidently knew that her husband was hiding behind the curtain.)* When he got near the piggy bank, I said to myself, "If he touches it I'll cut his balls!"

SHE: *(Amused.)* How can they? When I tell them the tender story about my mother leaving it to me...

THE MAN: *(Consulting the booklet.)* Thirty-two! Eight hundred dollars without even one pig laying a hand on you! Wasn't I right?

SHE: You're always right, darling! *(Coquettish, begging.)* Enough for today?

THE MAN: *(Looking al his watch.)* It's still early. Two more and then we'll go out to dinner.

SHE: Chinese food?

THE MAN: Italian, my love! *I need energy to make you happy!* (Indicates the bed.)

(They laugh. They hug with love.)

(CURTAIN.)

The Fourth One

Characters:

THE THIRD: thirty-five years old, a beautiful woman
THE FOURTH: twenty-five years old, a shy and insecure young woman

The present; a well-furnished apartment in New York. THE FOURTH enters timidly. THE THIRD stares at her. Silence. THE THIRD gestures for THE FOURTH to sit.

FOURTH: *(Sitting.)* Thank you...Thank you for taking the time to see me... You're very kind... *(Silence.)* I told you on the phone why...I pointed out the reason why...It's about Albert...I'd like to talk about him...

THIRD: Go ahead.

FOURTH: You know him well...

THIRD: That's true.

FOURTH: I'd like to know about him...

THIRD: *(Ironically.)* Good idea!

FOURTH: ...Men are so mysterious, so unpredictable...

THIRD: Unpredictable.

FOURTH: I never understood them...

THIRD: It takes time.

FOURTH: They change from day to day...from moment to moment.

THIRD: *(Vaguely ironic.)* Constantly.

FOURTH: Maybe it's because of his worries...

THIRD: He has only one.

FOURTH: What's that?

THIRD: Himself.

FOURTH: Is he really so selfish?

THIRD: He is.

FOURTH: In everything?

THIRD: Let's see... *(She counts on her fingers.)* In bed, of course...

(THE FOURTH turns her head, blushing.)

THIRD: His spare time—he prefers to enjoy it by himself...His money—he spends only on himself...

FOURTH: So does my brother. Men are used to that...The best, always...the lion's share...Their mothers are to blame...

THIRD: *(Ironically.)* Naturally! It's always the woman's fault.

FOURTH: *(Timidly.)* Not always...Sometimes...Many mothers spoil their children, especially the little boys...

THIRD: His mother is a monster.

FOURTH: *(Interested.)* Really?

THIRD: She always defends him.

FOURTH: He...speaks well of her...

THIRD: Of course.

FOURTH: He always says good things about women.

THIRD: All women.

FOURTH: It's a good sign, they say...A man who doesn't criticize women—

THIRD: *(Interrupting.)* —Paves the way for getting them into bed. It's an old trick.

FOURTH: And he loves animals, I noticed.

THIRD: *(Ironically.)* When did you?

FOURTH: A bug one day, on our table...I pointed to it with disgust...He didn't kill it to protect me and show his... gallant virility. He took it delicately between two fingers and put it on a windowsill...

THIRD: *(Ironically.)* ...Delicately!

FOURTH: A gentle man!

THIRD: Very gentle!

FOURTH: So, why...? *(A vague gesture.)*

THIRD: What do you want to know?

FOURTH: You two...are no longer... *(Puts two fingers together.)* together...

THIRD: Too...soft and gentle.

FOURTH: You don't like gentle men?

THIRD: He was gentle with...every woman.

FOURTH: Were you jealous?

THIRD: Human.

FOURTH: I know that he...has an eye for the ladies...It's a habit...many men...but he doesn't...

THIRD: He doesn't...?

FOURTH: He looks—intensely—that's all.

THIRD: *(Staring at her.)* Intensely. Before and after.

FOURTH: After what?

THIRD: After bed.

FOURTH: I don't believe that...not all the women...

THIRD: The fools. Twice and then he jilts them. *(Stares at her.)* Where do you stand? First time? Second?

FOURTH: *(Uneasily, after a pause.)* Excuse me for being...uneasy...He doesn't have the opportunity to speak to you anymore and—

THIRD: *(Interrupting and dodging the last statement.)* He called me the other day. In a great mood. Laughing heartily, happy. What happened to him? Speed?

FOURTH: Oh no! He feels great...He's happy.

THIRD: I should have guessed it. That animal never gets sick. He's eternal. Gymnastics every morning from 5:00 to 6:00; the usual jog through the park from 6:00 to 7:00...

FOURTH: *(Alarmed and confused.)* So early?

THIRD: *(Studying her.)* Without fail. *(Continuing.)* He showers from 7:00 to 7:15. Wolfs down breakfast at 7:16.

FOURTH: At 7:16—exactly?

THIRD: Exactly. *(Studies her.)* Strange... Aren't you familiar with these details? Haven't you spent a night in his bed yet?

FOURTH: *(Blushing, uneasy.)* No...Not yet...

THIRD: Where have you?... *(Gesture.)* On the desk, in his office?

FOURTH: No...

THIRD: On his green couch?

FOURTH: No...

THIRD: Intimate afternoons at the little hotel on the corner of Fifty-Ninth?

FOURTH: *(Shyly.)* No...

THIRD: How come?

FOURTH: I just came here because...

THIRD: Because he hasn't taken you to bed yet! You're right. This is serious.

FOURTH: No...As I mentioned on the phone...I'm in love.

THIRD: With whom?

FOURTH: With your husband.

THIRD: He's not my husband.

FOURTH: With your ex, I mean.

THIRD: Ex. I forgot him long ago. What do you want from me?

FOURTH: A favor, from woman to woman. I know you're kind...I want to talk...about him. Please!

THIRD: *(Ironically.)* Virginal and inexperienced?

FOURTH: No...I'm divorced, too. I don't want to make another mistake in my life.

THIRD: *(Ironically.)* So that's why you haven't gone to bed with him!

FOURTH: That too. I hope it's true love. Not just a sexual infatuation...

THIRD: And what do you want from me? Marital advice?

FOURTH: Sisterly advice. We're all in the same boat. Mistake after mistake...What do they want, these damn men?

THIRD: Ask them.

FOURTH: I tried. They don't know.

THIRD: Then how can I tell you?

FOURTH: You lived with him for four years. You're supposed to know him.

THIRD: I know him well, unfortunately!

FOURTH: So, then? Please...

(A brief pause.)

THIRD: What do you want to know?

FOURTH: ...He gets up at five, you said...Strange...Beth told me that—

THIRD: You spoke to that bitch?

FOURTH: And to Monica—

THIRD: *(Irritated.)* I don't want to hear those names in this house!

FOURTH: I'm sorry. I spoke with...the first one. She told me that she'd wake up early—at seven thirty—and would have this urge to hug him. He was furious to be awakened at that hour.

THIRD: He was twenty years old and didn't need gymnastics to stay in shape.

FOURTH: Is he...a health nut?

THIRD: The older he gets, the nuttier he gets. He skips dinner...not to get fat.

FOURTH: He skips it? Monica told me— *(Correcting herself.)* The second one told me that she used to prepare special treats for him...to excite him...to arouse him...

THIRD: Not anymore. *(Ironically.)* I'm..."number three." I know the bastard better than the others. I know the "old" Albert.

FOURTH: Forty-one is not so...

THIRD: Old and spoiled. The final version. Forget what the other two told you!

FOURTH: Maybe you're right...up to now...

THIRD: Up to now?

FOURTH: Nothing coincides.

THIRD: Of course. The first probably told you that they made love night and day. The second, only at night. I'm telling you that... *(She trails off.)*

FOURTH: *(Timidly.)* What?

THIRD: The final version... *(Ironic, ambiguous gesture.)*

FOURTH: You were divorced eleven months ago... How was he, those last few months?

THIRD: Zero.

FOURTH: Zero. You mean...?

THIRD: The last few months... he never touched me. Never.

FOURTH: The last months, generally... a certain resentment, preparation for divorce—

THIRD: And a young mistress. How old are you?

FOURTH: *(Surprised, vague.)* ...twenty-four...

THIRD: The little whore was nineteen. *(Stares at her.)* It wasn't you, obviously.

FOURTH: No... I only met him three months ago.

THIRD: And in three months, nothing?

FOURTH: He tried... he wanted... I was the one who...

THIRD: Poor kid!

FOURTH: I have a very wise mother. She told me: "If you're really in love, if you dream of marrying him, nothing! Don't allow him... the slightest intimacy!" Nothing...

THIRD: I bet she's... a good Catholic?

FOURTH: *(Nods. Surprised.)* How did you guess?

THIRD: Feminine intuition.

FOURTH: Moni— *(Correcting herself.)* His second wife told me that he's very... passionate... ardent and giving.

THIRD: He was.

FOURTH: *(After some hesitation.)* Anyway, it's not the most important thing...

THIRD: Good. So you won't be disappointed.

(A brief silence.)

FOURTH: You spoke about a young woman, a few months ago. Was he in love with her?

THIRD: The first time he's... ardent, full of vigor and passion. *"Real love!"* Then... *(Ambiguous gesture.)*

FOURTH: *(Uneasy.)* I'm not hard to please... Actually, I would prefer...

THIRD: What would you prefer, dear?

FOURTH: That he wouldn't insist.

THIRD: He insists?

FOURTH: Yes... He loves me... he desires me...

THIRD: *(Ironically.)* Poor guy! And you make him suffer!

FOURTH: A little... Only because Mamma... Is he really suffering?

THIRD: Don't worry about it. All men are like that. They pretend to be desperate.

FOURTH: *(Surprised.)* Pretend?

THIRD: They like to keep the flame burning, inside.

FOURTH: *(Confused.)* The flame?

THIRD: They desire desire.

(THE FOURTH does not understand.)

THIRD: They prefer the flame of desire to the consummation of desire.

(THE FOURTH is still confused.)

THIRD: They're like matches. Once you light them, they die quickly. Better the promise of the flame, than the flame itself.

FOURTH: *(Confused.)* Beth— *(Correcting herself.)* The first one told me that... *(Lowers her voice.)* he wants everything.

THIRD: Everything, the first week. But don't worry. Then, later, the main course is more than enough for him!

FOURTH: *(Naïvely.)* What's the... *main course?*

THIRD: *(Losing patience.)* Listen, my dear! Go to bed and find out!

(A brief pause.)

THIRD: *(Ambiguously.)* Maybe he's changed. Everyone changes these days.

FOURTH: Changed?... In what sense? What do you mean?

THIRD: Haven't you heard the news? Forty-two percent have admitted being bisexual.

FOURTH: *(Very surprised and alarmed.)* Bi—You're kidding!

THIRD: *(Pensive.)* To tell you the truth... I don't believe he... He always spoke with contempt about homosexuals.

FOURTH: Yes, that's true... To me too, once... That doesn't worry me at all... It's a subject he'd rather avoid. He doesn't like to talk about sex. It's better that way.

THIRD: Better?

FOURTH: I don't like implications, complications, confusion...

THIRD: I'm sure the other two—the first and second—have... described the infinite sexual details—

FOURTH: Everything! In great detail... *(Trying to change the subject.)* Now, please... You were the last...

THIRD: I wouldn't say that... *(Counting on her fingers.)* The nineteen-year-old Italian, a twenty-three-year-old Turk, two English sisters, his secretary, a black model, and now you.

FOURTH: *(Surprised.)* Two... how do you know that?

THIRD: Seven. I had him followed. My lawyer used the pictures to blackmail him. I bagged a queen's settlement; five thousand dollars a month, for life.

FOURTH: *(Pensive.)* He was alone, the last few months... Naturally he felt the need for women... But during... When you were married... did he have other...?

THIRD: Has he ever taken you to dinner on Friday?

FOURTH: *(Thinking.)* Truthfully, no...

THIRD: He never will.

(A silence; they study each other.)

FOURTH: Why?

THIRD: He's got an old flame—older than he is—the first love he can never forget. He sees her every Friday of the year.

FOURTH: Beth has hinted, vaguely...

THIRD: She's always vague. She never told the truth in her life!... I made the mistake of accepting the... *"old flame."* Are you ready to compromise?

FOURTH: *(Evasive.)* Only on Friday?

THIRD: *Every* Friday. For twenty-three years.

(A silence.)

FOURTH: By some strange coincidence, Friday is the day that I always spend with my mother...

THIRD: For reasons incomprehensible to me, you've indeed decided to marry him. It's more than clear. What do you want from me?

FOURTH: I made mistakes with my first...I don't want to make any more.

THIRD: What kind of mistakes?

FOURTH: I discussed them with my brother—he's a priest. He told me that he doesn't consider them sins. Only slip-ups. He would have tolerated them, had he been my husband.

THIRD: *(Ironically.)* An interesting family...

FOURTH: I'm a little lazy. For example, I wouldn't get up to fix breakfast.

THIRD: Don't worry. I got him used to making his own.

FOURTH: My husband was—he's a writer...Every afternoon he goes to see a film...I didn't go with him.

THIRD: Don't worry about it. Albert prefers to climb mountains. And he doesn't want "complaining females" with him—as he likes to call us.

FOURTH: Then in the evening, he'd go to the theatre or to a concert...I was usually tired and preferred to stay home.

THIRD: Don't worry. "Salami" prefers television.

FOURTH: "Salami?"

THIRD: That's what I called him. He looks like a big salami when he falls asleep in front of the TV.

FOURTH: What programs does he watch?

THIRD: Baseball.

FOURTH: Will he be offended if I go to read in bed?

THIRD: Don't wait up for him. It makes him nervous and he'll accuse you of being insatiable.

FOURTH: *(Surprised.)* "Insatiable"?

THIRD: Of wanting him every minute, silly! Pretend to be asleep when he comes into the room.

FOURTH: While he's watching baseball, where can I go to read my book?

THIRD: Anywhere. *(Stares at her with curiosity.)*

FOURTH: What other programs does he like?

THIRD: Everything but the news and political debates.

FOURTH: Good. I don't like them either. And the other shows I don't mind. Won't he be hurt if I go to bed without waking him?

THIRD: He prefers it.

FOURTH: Should I turn off the television?

THIRD: It's better not to.

FOURTH: Thank you, you're very kind. You're giving me valuable suggestions.

THIRD: *(Half-serious; it is not clear whether she is speaking seriously or pulling her leg.)* —Don't let him know you want him again; it makes him nervous.—Don't walk around nude; he'll misunderstand and insult you.—Don't stay nude in bed after...It seems like a request for more.

FOURTH: *(Naïvely.)* But I always sleep nude!

THIRD: Forbidden! You must cover yourself, somehow. At least with a sheet.—Don't embrace him first.—Don't caress him there, without being invited.—Don't smoke a cigarette afterwards—or get a glass of water; they are signs of dissatisfaction.—Tell him that you have a headache, Saturday night; he'll be glad to hear it.

FOURTH: *(Uneasy.)* Please, enough! Those details...They aren't important.

THIRD: They aren't?

FOURTH: Not to me.

THIRD: Because the other two already filled you in?

FOURTH: They mentioned...

THIRD: The same advice, I bet.

FOURTH: More or less...

THIRD: Tell me a difference.

(A short silence; THE FOURTH searches for words.)

THIRD: At least one, please!

FOURTH: *(Searching.)* ...the headache... Saturday and Sunday, they told me.

THIRD: Sunday too, of course! That's the day of rest! Tell me dear, why are you so...desperate?

FOURTH: *Desperate*, me?

THIRD: Why do you want to marry a guy like this?

FOURTH: *(Shyly.)* I'm in love...

THIRD: With what? There are thousands better than him.

FOURTH: Love is blind. You loved him too, years ago...

THIRD: But I didn't know him! You're fortunate to know, to have spoken to the three idiots that married him and...unmasked him, finally!

FOURTH: He has his good points...

THIRD: Where?

FOURTH: He's tall, attractive, sophisticated...

(THE THIRD grimaces ironically; she doesn't agree.)

FOURTH: And then he has... *(She hesitates.)*

THIRD: What's he got that escaped me?

FOURTH: Blue eyes. I always dreamed of a son with blue eyes!

THIRD: He doesn't want children! Are you blind? Three wives and a hundred mistresses! He never...goofed! He's afraid of the responsibility of children!

FOURTH: He promised me...He's decided now. He wants a son by me.

THIRD: And how will he support him? To me alone, he pays five thousand a month.

FOURTH: *(Smiling.)* When you mentioned that amount before, I felt like smiling. I spend at least twenty thousand dollars a month.

THIRD: Twenty thousand dollars? Where does he get it, that penniless bastard! We took him for everything! He doesn't have a cent to his name!

FOURTH: *(Slowly.)* I'll help him...Thank God... *(She crosses herself.)* We are very well off. We can afford anything.

THIRD: Anything?

FOURTH: Within limits, of course...My mother's already told him that...He can only have a million a year.

THIRD: A million...dollars?

FOURTH: Naturally...

(THE THIRD is amazed.)

FOURTH: Do you think that's enough for him?

THIRD: Certainly, yes...it depends... maybe...It's a reasonable amount... *(Suddenly.)* And your brother became a priest?

FOURTH: He lives in Rome now, at the Vatican. He hopes to become...at least a Cardinal.

THIRD: Cardinal? He'll become Pope if he pushes a little.

FOURTH: *(Naïvely.)* He's the type who insists and persists. He's a real charmer. Like Pius XII.

THIRD: *(Surprised.)* Pius XII. The one that made all his relatives rich?

FOURTH: That one. The Prince. Another thing...My brother is very concerned...

THIRD: About what?

FOURTH: Albert's political ideas...We investigated...He never votes. Why?

THIRD: *(Pensive, vague.)* Few people vote in this country...

FOURTH: It's not because he's a subversive and wants to sabotage our system?

(THE THIRD stares at her in silence.)

FOURTH: *(Continuing.)* My first husband—we discovered later, much later—was a Socialist...He used a lot of my money for...that cause...a newsletter, political literature, propaganda, organizing a strike...Imagine my brother! He almost had a heart attack!

(Silence; THE FOURTH begins to worry.)

FOURTH: Why aren't you saying anything?...

THIRD: *(Slowly.)* My dear...Unfortunately I have to... *(She hesitates.)*

FOURTH: *(Alarmed.)* Unfortunately?...

THIRD: I don't know if I should...

FOURTH: Please, I beg you!

THIRD: It is disloyal, in a way...

FOURTH: It's loyal, it's loyal! Between women!

(A brief silence.)

THIRD: Well...I have to tell you, unfortunately... *(She hesitates.)*

FOURTH: *(Very alarmed.)* Unfortunately?

THIRD: *(Hesitating.)* ...Well...

FOURTH: Please tell me!

THIRD: *(Hesitating.)* ...I found out that... *(She hesitates.)*

FOURTH: *(Tense and alarmed.)* What did you find out?

THIRD: ...something that...will displease you...upset you...hurt you...

FOURTH: *(Pleading.)* What is it?

THIRD: ...I understood from what you mentioned...your brother...politics...the Vatican... *(Hesitates.)*

FOURTH: What did you understand?

THIRD: ...His political background is important to you...

FOURTH: It is! Please tell me!

THIRD: *(Deliberately.)* Well...I'm sure... It's definite...I have proof that...

FOURTH: That?

THIRD: He's a Commie.

(THE FOURTH jumps to her feet, shaken and desperate. Her dream of love has come to an end. She opens her handbag and in horror and flings a key on the table. She runs out, crying. THE THIRD takes the key, recognizes it, smiles. She goes to the telephone and picks up the receiver. She dials a number.)

THIRD: Monica...Thanks for warning me...She was a hard nut to crack...The story about the million is true...Incredible! The bastard—after putting three wives through hell, he finds a fourth and...a million a year!...I was beginning to lose patience and hope...She believed only the last story...that he's a Communist...volunteer in Vietnam? I didn't think of it...We can always say that he volunteered to aid the enemy...Irrevocable decision...She even gave me the key to Albert's apartment...She'll never go there again...Tell Beth, too...a united front...If she calls, we must confirm—all three—that he's a Communist...I agree. Bye. Talk to you tomorrow... *(She slowly replaces the receiver; stares at the key; she smiles; she's finally gotten even with Albert.)*

(CURTAIN.)

Dolls No More

Characters:

SHE: lean, strong, good-looking, self-confident
HE: shy, sincere, emotionally restrained, optimistic
UNCLE SAM: A mime (invisible to the two actors; not needed in most productions)

Time:

Today in New York.

HE and SHE are talking. They are unaware that UNCLE SAM is weaving a very tight net around them.

SHE: Women are slaves.

HE: They are.

SHE: I mean: we're treated like slaves.

HE: That's what I meant.

SHE: Worse than slaves.

HE: No doubt.

SHE: No independence.

HE: True.

SHE: Woman's independence in economic life is viewed with distrust. Why?

HE: It shouldn't, I agree.

SHE: Why do you fear our economic independence?

HE: I don't. We shouldn't.

SHE: We want economic, social, and sexual self-determination. We want financial independence!

HE: Absolutely!

SHE: We want nurseries, maternity leaves, equal footing in the labor force. And housekeeping must be collectivized, to spare women its drudgery.

HE: Right.

SHE: It has been proved that all women would find happiness and fulfillment in work outside the home.

HE: Correct.

SHE: And key jobs. We want women in key jobs.

HE: No objection!

SHE: I am a woman. In a man's world, unfortunately.

HE: Unfortunately.

SHE: Man's ideology motivates and supports a nonproductive, subservient, voiceless role for women.

HE: I can't deny that.

SHE: He is proud of his mandatory role of breadwinner.

HE: True.

SHE: *(Ironical.)* ...Of being the "protector"... Who needs a protector today? We're no longer so naïve as to depend on a man for protection against famine or nuclear annihilation.

HE: Well put.

SHE: They're wrong, dead wrong.

HE: They are.

SHE: Who?

HE: Men.

SHE: You too then.

HE: Me too.

SHE: *(Ironical.)* Man imagines that his life is richer by keeping woman in a subservient position.

HE: He's wrong.

SHE: Time has come for women to redefine themselves, to break down the rigid and false concepts of sex roles that have limited their destinies.

HE: Absolutely right,

SHE: We must reexamine the crippling conditioning women undergo as children.

HE: Beyond any shadow of doubt!

SHE: The giving of dolls to little girls should be abandoned, just as many women have refused to give guns to their young sons.

HE: *(Puzzled.)* ...Dolls no more...

SHE: Woman's biological role has become passé in an overcrowded world.

HE: Passé, I agree.

SHE: Our bodies are now obsolete in an overpopulated world.

HE: *(Puzzled.)* Obsolete if you say so.

SHE: We have been finally freed from the cruel stigma historically attached to barrenness.

HE: Finally.

SHE: Being barren is a virtue today.

HE: I agree.

SHE: A sign of morality.

HE: I agree.

SHE: The best don't reproduce like rabbits.

HE: Right.

SHE: Women are no longer used as passive receptacles of semen—to reproduce the race. We're no longer inferior.

HE: No longer, I agree.

SHE: *(Ironical.)* The most popular explanations of the female's inferior status ascribe it to her physical weakness and intellectual inadequacy!

HE: It's absolutely wrong!

SHE: The heavier musculature of the male, a secondary sexual characteristic and common among mammals, is biological in origin but is also culturally encouraged through breeding, diet, and exercise.

HE: True.

SHE: Girls are neither allowed nor encouraged to explore their bodily strength through contest. To flex muscles, lift weights, climb trees.

HE: Right.

SHE: We *are* strong.

HE: Right.

SHE: More than men—often.

HE: Often.

SHE: Women have always worked. They have generally worked longer hours for smaller rewards and at less agreeable tasks than men.

HE: True.

SHE: Cruelly underpaid.

HE: Right.

SHE: *(Suddenly losing her patience.)* Right—shmight! You're agreeing too much, man! Why? Are you hoping I'll let you put your shoes under my bed?

HE: *(Calm and courteous.)* Only if you want to.

SHE: How come you agree with everything I say?

HE: I happen to think you're right.

(They study each other for a few seconds.)

SHE: And it's not true that the feminist movement runs the risk of becoming bogged down in hatred. I don't hate men.

HE: I don't hate women. I love them.

(They study each other.)

HE: Sorry, am I being too aggressive?

SHE: *(Ignoring him.)* In this society a girl has no alternative but to perceive her body as a prize, a prize that goes to the man who manages to throw a ring around her. That's why we often reject men. We're not prizes. We're human beings. Rejection must be preferred to submission. Sex should *not* involve surrender. Intercourse is *not* an act of submission.

HE: *(Timidly.)* I hope you agree that... chastity is the most unnatural of the sexual perversions.

SHE: Is that supposed to be a compliment?

HE: *(Puzzled and lost.)* No...I don't think so...

SHE: My chastity is temporary. The day will come when a man will consider me his equal!

HE: I do!

SHE: *(Ignoring him.)* Science has proved that we are different but equal. We know now. We can drop a painful burden of centuries.

HE: It's high time, I agree.

SHE: Every cell in the body of the female is chemically different from the cells in the body of the male.

HE: Vive la difference!

SHE: We are different. Down to the very marrow of our bones! But equal, as human beings!

HE: Equal.

SHE: We are not "deficient males" as Aristotle, Thomas Aquinas, and Freud said.

HE: "Deficient males"? Never!

SHE: You forced on us the false characteristics of "feminine" and "masculine." What's feminine?

HE: You. At times.

SHE: What's masculine?

HE: Me. At times.

SHE: *(Ironical.)* At times.

HE: When you let me.

SHE: What do you mean?

HE: *(Timidly.)* May I put a word in—edgewise?

SHE: You may.

HE: Should we make the man more feminine and the woman more masculine?

SHE: No. Let's change the educational system. We need the most sweeping changes in that field so that we may accomplish human growth and true reeducation.

HE: Reeducation. I agree. New education in a new society.

SHE: We have been taught systematically to distrust our own intellectual capacities. By men teachers.

HE: I had women teachers who suggested music and languages to my co-eds. And science to us boys.

SHE: Traitors! Brainwashed by centuries of serfdom.

HE: Most women—you must admit it—are basically conservative. Why?

SHE: Their marginal life frequently renders them conservative, because like all persons in their situation—slaves are a classic example—they identify their own survival with the prosperity of those who feed them.

HE: *(With admiration.)* That's an interesting thesis. You're a very intelligent woman.

SHE: It shouldn't surprise you. We are intelligent.

HE: And romantic. There's a romantic halo about you.

SHE: The concept of romantic love affords an instrument of emotional manipulation which the male is free to exploit, since love is the only circumstance in which the female is pardoned for sexual activity.

HE: I like you...

SHE: If a woman believes herself to be a worthy human being, she finds in sex a glorious affirmation of her own value. But if she perceives herself as inferior, as the sexual object of her social conditioning, she will experience a sense of degradation.

HE: And I read in your eyes that you like me too.

SHE: It's difficult being a woman. We have been taught to hide our feelings. Our inability to react spontaneously precludes our sexual fulfillment.

HE: You could be a fantastic lover...You like sex.

SHE: *(Slightly embarrassed.)* They are trying to brainwash us into believing that we dislike sex because men are inferior, sexually.

HE: Not inferior. Different.

SHE: If one is inferior, between us, it's man. All the best scientific evidence today unmistakably tends toward the conclusion that the female possesses, biologically and inherently, a far greater capacity for sexuality than the male, both as to frequency of coitus, and as to frequency of orgasm in coition.

HE: Tactful lovers never mention that...

SHE: *(Ignoring him.)* It has been proved that the human fetus is originally physically female until the operation of androgen at a certain stage of gestation cause those with Y chromosomes to develop into males.

(Meanwhile UNCLE SAM has woven around them a very intricate web. They are prisoners, but they do not realize it yet. He keeps weaving around them.)

HE: Why are you trying to frighten me? I—

SHE: I'm not. I believe in vaginal orgasm. But I may agree with you that the establishment of clitoral orgasm as a fact would really threaten the heterosexual world.

HE: You know a lot, I must admit.

SHE: Have you read Kate Millett's *Sexual Politics*?

HE: I have read it.

SHE: Then you should know that we know. And who our enemies are.

HE: Who are they?

SHE: *(With pride.)* When *I* read a book, it stays read.

HE: Who are your enemies?

SHE: Sigmund Freud. Dead. D. H. Lawrence. Dead. Henry Miller. Dead. Jean Genet. Dead. Norman Mailer. Half-alive.

HE: Half?

SHE: You know we're generous!

HE: You are! Jokes aside. They are not "enemies." They are victims. Like you and me.

SHE: Of what?

HE: "Brainwashing," as you well put it. They are the offsprings of this society, where a few pigs rule.

SHE: Men.

HE: Not because they're men but because they own the world.

SHE: Women should rule the world. We would never send our children to die in a war.

HE: Not only women. The best—

SHE: —Who happen to be women.

HE: Have you read *How to Make It in a Man's World* by...Letty...Something.

SHE: She's a fool. Brainwashed by men into believing that only whores make it big in this world.

HE: Well, she only says that—

SHE: —"You must be clever and pretend. Wear a mask and play their game. Be sneaky, crawling snakes." "Bait and switch."

HE: Men too must behave like that if they want to—

SHE: *(Interrupting.)* Nobody should be ever be forced to lie!

HE: I agree completely. But please don't force me to say that women are the best leaders. That Letty...she writes that her lady boss was an "entirely female nervous wreck. With maddening hot flashes which afflict many menopausal women."

SHE: That's an unmitigated lie. How many men—presidents and generals—are often "nervous wrecks"?

HE: I surrender again. You're terribly bright. And charming. A beautiful creature—

SHE: Thanks!

HE: Suppose I feel like buying flowers for you—I really do—should I refrain from it?

SHE: No.

HE: But I would never buy them for another man!

SHE: If you like him. When he's promoted or at his birthday.

HE: I feel like opening a door for you, sitting down after you, getting up first to help you, lighting your cigarette. Is that wrong?

SHE: No. If you like a person—regardless of sex—you should do things for her—or him.

HE: Do you believe in having a family?

SHE: You cannot abolish the family completely. But you have to replace it.

HE: What do you mean?

SHE: A new relation between man and woman. We are not domestic animals.

HE: You are not, obviously!

SHE: Today there's a whole sexual undercurrent that makes it impossible for men and women to talk to each other as people.

HE: We just did.

SHE: The undercurrent is still there—between us.

HE: So what? It adds spice to our conversation.

SHE: *(Sadly.)* Is it possible to love a person who doesn't quite view you as a human being? Who sees you as a domestic object?

HE: No. But I'll try to prove to you that—

SHE: *(Interrupting, with sadness.)* In this society we're programmed into domesticity as infants.

HE: Let's say: "Men and women are programmed into *obedience* as infants." That sounds better to my ears. More sensible.

SHE: To your ears. But I'm talking about *our* battle.

HE: Love.

SHE: Love we need. We're human.

HE: Thank you for admitting it!

SHE: But nothing has prepared us to accept the violence, the heat, the sweat, and the total tumult of coupling with authentic pleasure.

HE: *(Taken aback, studying her.)* You've an interesting feeling for the dramatic…

SHE: Unfortunately, forced penetration by the male penis is still an unspoken fear.

HE: *(Puzzled, timidly.)* I promise it isn't so bad…

SHE: Promise? What do you want from me?

HE: I'm your friend.

SHE: What kind of friend?

HE: I'm liberal minded. I understand you, I like you. Count me in—

SHE: In where? You've all got a one-track mind!

HE: I meant in your battle. I understand it.

SHE: I don't think so. There's a chasm between me and you. You're taught to use, exploit, discard. We're taught acceptance and adherence to the authority of male institutions.

HE: Male? Why don't you just say "these institutions," the world we're living in?

SHE: Our relationship is vitiated from the beginning.

HE: *Before* the beginning.

SHE: I don't like the fact that the female is continually obliged to seek survival or advancement through the approval of males.

HE: Let's say: "of those who hold power."

SHE: Who happen to be men. Authoritarian governments favor patriarchy. The atmosphere of fascist states depends heavily upon the patriarchal character. The Führer is the father of the country. Pater Familias. Kneel down before him.

HE: Men and women. Men too.

SHE: Women first. To each pater familias, husband, brother. To "man." The male symbol. The power symbol.

HE: It was true in the past. No longer. You're rebelling against all that. You're new and interesting. You're bringing a new excitement in the man-woman relationship.

SHE: *(Ignoring him.)* Unfortunately most women still think they must find a man to replace the paternal authority and, through marriage and their new keepers, recapture the security and warmth they knew as children.

HE: We men, we often recapture, in our wives, the warmth our mothers gave us. We are even.

SHE: *(Sadly.)* And often, too often, we have to confront the terrible realization that our lives have been wasted.

HE: Ours too. Wasted. Why don't you begin to realize that both men and women are in the same boat?

SHE: You've rocked the boat so far.

HE: It's only partially true. The few rulers of the world happen to be men becau—

SHE: That's what we're fighting!

HE: It's not the way!

SHE: *(Ironical.)* What do you suggest?

HE: Unity. A coalition of expropriated groups: blacks, youth, women, the poor—men and women together.

SHE: Together. You men will keep exploiting us, using us.

HE: We use each other. Please realize that.

SHE: That's what we want to avoid: the word "use." Love is much higher than using a body.

HE: Under the wings of love, everything is allowed!

SHE: That's another typical male slogan! It's for instance statistically proved that men prefer "back-scuttling" from behind—you know why?

HE: No.

SHE: Not to face us—never to face us. I'll never let that happen to me.

HE: All right. You'll choose the position—

SHE: *(Angry, cutting in.)* Vulgar again! You men think of nothing but that! We're objects in your eyes. Filthy objects into which you want to vent your neurotic steam. We need a sexual revolution that might at least accomplish its aim of freeing half the race—our fifty-one percent—from its immemorial subordination!

HE: —To free us—ninety-nine percent of mankind—from its immemorial subordination to the few selfish bastards who own the world.

SHE: Can we ever trust man after his innumerable crimes?

HE: We must. There is no other way. This is a sick society we can only reconstruct *together*.

SHE: *(With a gleam of hope in her eyes.)* First, you must recognize that we're equal.

HE: Who's denying it?

SHE: *All of you* must recognize it.

HE: All? It's like saying that we can make a revolution only when all mankind is ready to pee on this world at the same split second. We'll never be *all* ready to think like you or like me. *Never.* We're different, remember?

SHE: I know.

HE: Join us, the many of us who understand and love you.

SHE: —As equals.

HE: As equals! Damn it! Different but equal!

SHE: *(Studying him.)* You get up first.

(HE tries. It is impossible because UNCLE SAM has woven a tight net around them. He is there, happy, admiring his masterpiece.)

HE: I cannot. You try.

SHE: *(SHE tries. Impossible. She gives up.)* I cannot.

HE: Let's try together.

(They join hands. They try together. It is a difficult task. They struggle. They want to succeed. They finally succeed in breaking the net that was enwrapping them. They smile. Together they can win.)

(CURTAIN. THE END.)

Porno

Characters:

DORINE: the wife
DICK: the actor
PAUL: the husband

Time:

Today.

Place:

New York.

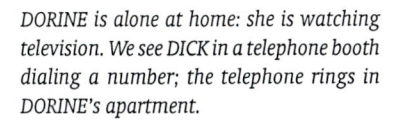

DORINE is alone at home: she is watching television. We see DICK in a telephone booth dialing a number; the telephone rings in DORINE's apartment.

DORINE: *(Picking up the receiver.)* Hello?

DICK: Dorine?

DORINE: Yes...

DICK: Are you alone? Can you talk?

DORINE: Who is it?

DICK: It's Dick.

DORINE: Dick who?

DICK: Dick Raffert...Don't you remember me?

DORINE: *(After a brief pause.)* I'm sorry, no.

DICK: Dick...May 1982...

DORINE: I'm sorry but...how am I supposed to remember someone I met in '82? And with a name like yours. I must have met at least ten...

DICK: Not like me, I hope. Not intimately like me.

DORINE: Listen. I am very busy and can't...

DICK: *(Interrupting.)* I know you're pretending. I'm sure you remember me...Dick, the man you loved with such passion and generosity...

DORINE: *(Skeptically, ironically.)* Me? Passion and generosity?

DICK: Do you want to deny it now?

DORINE: Listen, either you got the wrong number or you feel like joking. Sir, please let me...

DICK: *(Interrupting.)* So formal with me, after what we...

DORINE: Excuse me but I don't know you, I don't remember you. Honestly!

DICK: In '82...Fifty-Fourth Street...third floor...no elevator...

(A silence.)

DORINE: *(Perhaps remembering now.)* Third floor...

DICK: You remember now? Narrow, dirty stairs...

DORINE: *(Vaguely.)* Maybe. It's possible. Everything is possible. Listen, Dick, I'm married now. To a man I love. We're happy. Thank you for calling, good night.

DICK: No, no, wait...You must first remember who I am. It's impossible you've forgotten me.

DORINE: *(To end the conversation.)* Listen, Dick, I remember everything. You were great! You are...special, unique. A real master. It was a great pleasure to know you. I have pleasant memories of you, wonderful memories. Good night!

DICK: I never forgot you.

DORINE: That makes me happy. Thanks for the compliment. Good night!

DICK: No...You must first prove that you at least remember what we did together. Those precious hours...

DORINE: Crazy years. What we did was probably foolish.

DICK: Probably?

DORINE: Sure! For sure!

DICK: Tell me what we did together.

DORINE: What do you want? A list? I don't keep records. I don't take notes, I don't remember every detail! Please...

DICK: To be sure that you remember me, describe what we did together with a single word, four letters—only four: one, two, three, four...It's easy, isn't it?

DORINE: *(Thinking, without understanding what he is alluding to.)* Fine. We even did that. So what?

DICK: We made an F-I-L-M. We made a film together!

DORINE: *(Who has finally understood.)* Ah. You are the one who...Forgive me. They didn't introduce us. I didn't remember your name. Forgive me.

DICK: "Burning Lips," remember? A nice little film. I had almost forgotten it, but today I saw it again and...you and me together...Dorine. I have never met a woman more...sensual than you...generous, passionate, a real woman...I was very excited when I saw again how you...

DORINE: *(Interrupting, worried by this news.)* Where did you see it? They promised me they would destroy it!

DICK: And you trusted that low-life director?

DORINE: He swore to me he would! A few copies in the Orient were impossible to get back. Japan. Hong Kong and Taiwan. In America, not a single copy! All destroyed!

DICK: I saw it half an hour ago and my desire came back. You are fantastic. The best in the world! If you are alone, I'll come to your place and...

DORINE: No, no! I'm happily married. My husband is coming back any minute! Please! We get along. Don't ruin everything with... *(She hesitates; she is undecided and confused.)* Where did you see it? Tell me. Please...

DICK: I enjoyed every moment of it, horny with desire. You bring real passion to it. Your husband is a lucky man. Do you do to him what you did to me when—

DORINE: *(Interrupting.)* Where did you see it? I even paid that bastard five hundred dollars, so they would destroy every copy.

DICK: Five hundred! They only gave us one hundred to make the film. At least to me. And you…how much did they give you?

DORINE: Me too, just one hundred. I was broke then. I had to pay rent. Then things got better. Now I'm all right. Tell me where…I have some money now. We can buy it back.

DICK: "We"? Together? Together again?

DORINE: No, please…The past is past. I am older now, I am wiser.

DICK: More experienced, more passionate. A real woman.

DORINE: Where? Give me the address. I'll go there tomorrow and offer to buy it.

DICK: I already asked the lady in charge.

DORINE: What lady? Who is she?

DICK: She owns the place where I saw the film. I wanted a copy for me, to re-live those moments a hundred times. She doesn't want to sell it.

DORINE: Why? Where is she? Is she the manager of a movie theatre? Perhaps they'll show it for a few days and then…

DICK: She told me it's part of a cycle.

DORINE: What cycle?

DICK: A tape that lasts twenty-four hours. Twenty films put together, showed continuously.

DORINE: Where?

DICK: In this place.

DORINE: What place?

DICK: Private.

DORINE: What is it? A movie theatre? A club?

DICK: A club, in a certain sense; very private.

DORINE: Who goes there? What type of an audience?

DICK: Men, women…

DORINE: What kind of women? Why do they want to watch films like that?

DICK: They don't watch them, really… They just create atmosphere.

DORINE: Atmosphere?

DICK: Background, while the couples…

DORINE: Couples? What kind of place is it? Where is it?

DICK: At Fortieth Street. I went there a couple of times. And I noticed, this time I noticed…When I saw myself again—on the screen…

DORINE: What screen?

DICK: A TV, a TV screen…a VCR. I told my— *(He hesitates: regretting having said so much.)*

DORINE: "My"—who?

DICK: …A dear friend. You don't go to those places alone. I told her: "Watch, watch Dorine. Watch and learn." And I have to tell the truth. You women have spirit of competition. She tried to imitate you, she tried her best, but no one is as good as you, Dorine. Are you still called Dorine or have you changed your name?

DORINE: *(Ignoring him.)* Then that place is a kind of…?

DICK: Hotel for…"affectionate friendships."

DORINE: A whorehouse.

DICK: In a broad sense…There aren't any women. You bring the woman yourself…They offer only pink lights, a bed, two towels, television that runs constantly…And you were there, fresh as a rose, horny as a tigress. But your moans, were they real or for the director? for the audience? I've never understood. We never understand with you women.

DORINE: What kind of place? Elegant? Expensive? What kind of clientele?

DICK: Modest. Medium price. Managers with secretaries, mature women with studs. I was surprised to see such couples. Middle-aged women begin to like young boys. And they pay for the room, of course. Your husband, how old is he? I'm still in good shape. Thirty-six. One night with me, Dorine, and you'll feel like—

DORINE: *(Interrupting.)* What's the exact address?

DICK: Near Madison Avenue. Give me another opportunity, Dorine, and—

DORINE: No. Give me the exact address.

DICK: I'll give it to you when we see each other. I have an idea. We'll get together there, take a room and…try to recreate the film, the same energy, the same enthusiasm. It would be an original experience, unique. In life, before television, how many people had the chance to repeat—in front of a video—the unique situation. We are unique, you and I! No one, I bet! A perfect couple!

DORINE: Forget the past, please, and help me.

DICK: *(Gallantly.)* At your service, my love!

DORINE: Don't joke around. For the sake of the past, of what we did and enjoyed together—

DICK: Enjoyed? Then you really had orgasms!

DORINE: Yes…We were young, it was a beautiful, healthy experience.

DICK: But you ignored me immediately after, as soon as we were through. Why?

DORINE: A habit…Just like great actors. They kiss in front of the camera. And then "bye bye!"…As if they hadn't even met. I wanted to separate my screen life from my real life.

DICK: *(With desire.)* Let's get back to reality. After having seen that film, I have to do it with you again. I need you! *(With desire.)* Dorine, I want to give you the best I ever—

DORINE: *(Interrupting, pretending that her husband has arrived.)* My husband! He's at the door! Give me your number, right away! I'll call you tomorrow!

DICK: *(Uncertain.)* But I…

DORINE: Right away, he's opening the door! I'm hanging up!

DICK: *(Rapidly.)* My home number is 212-242-3317! *(Repeating clearly.)* 212-242-3317.

(DORINE hangs up. DICK does too, deep in thought. A brief blackout indicates the passage of time.)

—

(A few days later. DORINE is wearing a different dress. She is reading. PAUL, her husband, enters. His steps are slow and measured. He stares at her a long time, with hatred.)

DORINE: *(Timidly, affectionately.)* Do you want a cup of coffee?

(PAUL comes forward, furious. He stares at her. He takes the book. He reads the title. He throws it away. He bangs on the table. Furious with rage, he destroys several objects. DORINE is frightened.)

DORINE: What happened? What's the matter with you? Did they fire you?

PAUL: Yeah, sure. So you would starve! You deserve it!

DORINE: Why? What's happened? What have I done?

PAUL: You were used to it, weren't you? When you were an actress off, off—where I had the misfortune of finding you. You told me that they didn't pay you. Real starvation!

DORINE: Difficult times. But please, calm down. Tell me what happened!

PAUL: I saw you the first time, in that play...at the Café...

DORINE: Café La MaMa...*Madame Senator.*

PAUL: You were one of the whores.

DORINE: A role like any other. Completely dressed, remember? It was a musical. A political musical.

PAUL: Political, yes. It was about how to screw the next guy. In what other plays have you...performed?

DORINE: *(Running to a drawer which she opens.)* I have all the programs. *(She takes them and shows them.)* Off off...little theatres, clubs, schools...

PAUL: And they never paid you, eh?

DORINE: Seldom. Actors aren't paid in New York, you know that.

PAUL: How did you live? How did you pay your bills?

DORINE: Waitressing in several restaurants, remember? You even came as a customer to the Three Fools...

PAUL: I'm the fool.

DORINE: You didn't pay. You were a guest...They told me that you could eat there for free, now and then.

PAUL: Who told you?

DORINE: The owner.

PAUL: A friend of yours? An intimate friend? A lover?

DORINE: Oh no! A good man. In love with his wife. Deeply in love.

PAUL: Did you have an agent, for your... theatrical enterprises?

DORINE: It's difficult to find an agent. Only if you're well known.

PAUL: *(Staring at her, ironical.)* What a pity! *(Slowly.)* Perhaps he would have found you a chance to...make some films.

(A silence: they stare at each other.)

PAUL: How many films have you made?

DORINE: *(Vague, uncertain.)* One...a silly college film.

PAUL: What part did you play?

DORINE: One of the students.

PAUL: And what did this student do? Go to bed with the professor?

DORINE: Oh no! There were six or seven of us, at a party.

PAUL: What kind of party?

DORINE: A family get-together.

PAUL: What kind of family get-together? An orgy?

DORINE: No...But why are you asking me all these questions?

PAUL: ...I am curious about your... "movie career."

DORINE: All of a sudden?

PAUL: *(Breaking something else in rage.)* Yes, yes, all of a sudden. You never spoke to me about it. You never told me anything! How many men have been in your life! You never told me!

DORINE: We decided not to keep stupid lists. My past and your past don't count.

We were reborn when we met and fell in love.

PAUL: Very convenient, my friend. *(Correcting himself.)* Too convenient, enemy of my life!

DORINE: Men generally have a past that's more...intense. Dozens of women in your life, I'm sure. We, instead...

PAUL: We who?

DORINE: We women. Two or three mistakes. Sweethearts who deceived us, betrayed us, abandoned us.

PAUL: How many?

DORINE; I told you...Three...But why dig up the past?

PAUL: Because I want to know!

DORINE: Really? All of a sudden? What happened? Who have you seen?

PAUL: No one.

DORINE: Strange...You have never come home this furious. You must have seen someone, there must be a reason...

PAUL: There is a reason, but first...first I want the truth from you! The absolute truth! How many films have you made?

DORINE: ...Only that one...a big nothing of a film.

PAUL: How come you never showed it to me?

DORINE: It was destroyed, burnt. There are no copies around.

PAUL: Oh yeah? Are you sure? No copies! And what do you know about it? They make thousands of copies of films like that...

(A silence; they stare at each other.)

PAUL: You're not saying anything? Why don't you admit it was porno? That guy with you, the one you did...things with, was he one of your three lovers?

(A silence.)

DORINE: *(Staring at him.)* Where did you see it?

PAUL: See what?

DORINE: A porno film where you think you recognized me...

PAUL: *(Furious, interrupting.)* Recognize? What gall!

(He follows her because he would like to hit her.)

PAUL: You are there, with everything...open, wide open—obscenely!

DORINE: *(Calmly; by now she knows that her husband has seen the film in the "club.")* Where did you see it? Show it to me.

PAUL: Why? You never saw it? Weren't you curious to see yourself in action?

DORINE: Where did you see it?

PAUL: "Where" is not important. What counts is the fact that the film exists and that you are *admitting* you made it. It's you in that...incredible garbage!

DORINE: I don't admit anything. I want to see it with you.

PAUL: Are you crazy? That's absurd. How could I show up in that place with you, my wife, and...we watch it together...among so many?...

DORINE: So many what?

PAUL: ...Degenerates who go to see that type of...

DORINE: Just you and me. We'll see it alone, you and me, privately.

(A brief silence; PAUL is perplexed.)

DORINE: Let's go. If it's someone who looks like me...

PAUL: *(Furious, again.)* It's you! It's you! And you know it perfectly well!

DORINE: *(Calmly, continuing.)* We'll buy the film. We'll buy it back.

PAUL: And will those people sell it to you? Should I buy it back and pay for what you...for those horrible scenes?

DORINE: No. I will. After we've seen it together, we'll tell the owner of this...place that...Either he sells it or we sue.

PAUL: "We sue"?

DORINE: I have my father's inheritance now. I can sue, demand, buy.

PAUL: Look at your gall! Instead of weeping, being ashamed, sorry, and asking for forgiveness.

DORINE: Me? For what?

PAUL: For what you've done! For your horrible past!

DORINE: *(Stares at him calmly.)* Let's go and see this film, first. Then we'll talk about it.

PAUL: *(Hesitant.)* It's a depressing, squalid place. It isn't for women like you...

DORINE: Oh yes? *(Ironically.)* One of those dark, dingy little places where men go, alone and desperate, to watch the flesh market!

PAUL: Flesh market. Exactly! You know what I'm talking about. When I saw my wife doing such horrible things...I wanted to kill you!

DORINE: Did you tell anyone?

PAUL: Who? I was ashamed, I felt like a criminal! And the criminal was you! The culprit was you!

DORINE: *(Calm, vaguely ironic.)* Did you tell this person, this friend of yours—generally one goes to the movies with someone—did you tell *him*, this friend of yours, that that woman looked like your wife?

PAUL: Never! One doesn't tell a thing like that to anyone!

DORINE: Not even to your friend? Your intimate friend?

PAUL: No.

DORINE: Who is he? Do I know him?

PAUL: No! No one you know!

DORINE: So much the better. Otherwise, he too would have thought that the actress looked like me.

PAUL: Actress? What actress? That was a whore! And how she enjoyed it, that whore, the... *(Refrains; he is furious.)* what she had in her mouth. *(He is ready to hit her again.)*

DORINE: *(Calm.)* Let's go see this film. You made me curious.

PAUL: You've really got nerve. You know perfectly well what I am talking about and you are pretending to...

DORINE: I'm not pretending anything. But I know *perfectly well* what you are talking about.

PAUL: *(Confused.)* So?...you're admitting?

DORINE: First I have to see it together with you. Let's go.

PAUL: *(Who obviously does not want to go to the "club.")* First you have to tell me that you are the protagonist of "Burning Lips."

DORINE: Did you see my name in the credits?

PAUL: No. I missed them. I never read them.

DORINE: Didn't you watch the beginning again, after the shock, out of curiosity, to see the name of the actress?

PAUL: No...it's one of those places where...the film isn't shown again right away...It's a tape on a VCR that lasts twenty-four hours.

DORINE: *(Feigning surprise.)* Twenty-four hours? What time did you see it? We'll go back around that time and see it from the beginning. With the titles, the credits...

PAUL: I don't remember...

DORINE: At lunchtime? You often leave the office for a couple of hours...

PAUL: Perhaps...

DORINE: Let's go at lunchtime then. *(She takes the newspaper; consults the movie schedule.)* What's the name of that movie theatre? Is it near your office?

PAUL: Those obscene little places are not listed.

DORINE: What's the address?

PAUL: *(Vague.)* A side street near Third Avenue.

DORINE: Fiftieth? Fortieth? Thirtieth?

PAUL: *(Vague.)* Between Fiftieth and Thirtieth.

DORINE: Near Madison Avenue?

PAUL: Around there.

DORINE: Fine. Let's go there.

PAUL: *(Trying to avoid it.)* All right, if you admit that...you were in that film, and if you tell me that you are ashamed and sorry...

DORINE: *(Firmly.)* I don't admit anything. I am not ashamed. I am not sorry. *First I want the facts.* Let's examine the facts.

PAUL: *(Furious again.)* I'm going to kill you! You women are incredible! Even when you are guilty, caught with your hands in the till, or in this case with— Let's forget it—You women manage to turn the tables. I'm becoming the defendant now!

DORINE: Exactly.

PAUL: What do you mean by that?

DORINE: Nothing.

PAUL: No, explain yourself.

DORINE: Only that you shouldn't accuse anyone without proof.

PAUL: More proof than this? No one ever had more proof than me! It's...visual proof! A movie with incredible details: close-ups of morbid, clinical obscenity. It made me vomit.

DORINE: Fine. Let's go see it.

PAUL: *(Pretending to suffer.)* I can't, I can't...It would hurt too much...It's a disgusting spectacle. I can't see it again but I am ready to forgive you if...

DORINE: Forgive me for what?

PAUL: For your horrible past! I should torture you, beat you up, kill you, throw you out of the house, and instead it's me who...

DORINE: Who...?

PAUL: ...Who is almost apologizing.

DORINE: If someone doesn't have proof, he has to apologize.

PAUL: *(Incredulous, astonished.)* Are you serious? Should I apologize and ask to be forgiven?

DORINE: Exactly.

PAUL: For what?

DORINE: You know.

PAUL: What are you talking about?

DORINE: Apologize and perhaps, if I think you are sincere, I will forgive you, I am ready to forgive you.

PAUL: You mean you're ready to die!

DORINE: *(Calm.)* I said—to forgive you, We women know how to understand and forgive.

PAUL: *(Exploding.)* Bitch! Slut! Whore! First you do those things, in a film seen by millions of people. Your…parts exposed to the world, forever. And then you want me to apologize! This is the last straw! Out! Out of my house!

DORINE: *(Very calm.)* Yes, I'm getting out. *(Puts on a jacket; takes her purse, ready to leave; she speaks slowly, with great clarity.)* I…"betrayed" you, as you say, years ago, before I met you. *You betrayed me…today.*

(She goes out, leaving him astonished.)

PAUL: *(To himself, incredulous.) Today?* HOW DOES SHE KNOW? HOW DID SHE FIND OUT?

(IMMOBILITY—BLACKOUT. CURTAIN.)

Dina and Alba

Characters:

DINA
ALBA

Two beautiful strong women (preferably naked; Junoesque). They have just finished making love; they are caressing each other, tender and happy. DINA is in her late thirties. ALBA is ten years younger.

ALBA: When we make love, I see pink clouds...soft and warm...surrounding me...drowning in their tender softness...You, what do you see?

DINA: Your ecstatic face...your deep eyes.

ALBA: I always close them!

DINA: I see them all the same. They are as deep as the deepest of all lakes...I lose myself in them...It's all so mysterious...Love is always mysterious.

ALBA: It's magic.

DINA: When we start with our first kiss, I try to imagine the intensity of what we are going to feel...I can never guess.

ALBA: Never. It's always more intense, *more* mysteriously deep.

DINA: Magical. Unreal.

(They start to dress.)

DINA: Do you think you could live without me?

ALBA: *(Jokingly.)* Of course!

(They laugh.)

ALBA: I was alive last year, two years ago, three years ago, when I began to make love.

DINA: With a man. Could you still make love with a man?

ALBA: *(Jokingly.)* Certainly!

(They laugh. DINA's laughter is a little constrained this time; a silence, they stare at each other.)

ALBA: And you?

DINA: *(Trying a faint smile.)* Of course!

(They don't laugh this time.)

ALBA: Why do you ask? You brought this up yesterday too...

DINA: I don't know...

ALBA: Are you jealous? Because I was flirting with the bartender?

DINA: Oh no!

ALBA: I'm always like that. I like being friendly with everybody. It's my nature. It's easy for me.

DINA: I know, I know.

ALBA: You're jealous. I see sadness in your eyes.

DINA: I'm just a bit depressed...

ALBA: Why?

(A silence.)

DINA: I don't know...I'm tired.

ALBA: *(Smiling.) Post coitum fletum*...the Latin women used to say. Tears after sex.

DINA: *(Smiling.)* That's a good one. They never say "Latin women." They always say the Latins. Always men.

ALBA: They are still in charge.

DINA: It's true. How do you explain it?

ALBA: They control the economy, politics, the life of the country. They can buy anything they want. Therefore...

DINA: Some of them are poor, they live a modest life. But they still have power, charm. They attract...

ALBA: Who do they attract?

DINA: Women.

ALBA: From time immemorial. It's normal, some women would say. "It's a rule of nature."

DINA: *(Stressing the feminine subject.)* All women.

ALBA: Sure. Most women prefer men... *(She stares at her.)* You confessed to me that you like them. I confessed to you that I have slept with them.

DINA: What did you think of Mike—the guy I introduced you to at the theatre? A casual encounter after many months...

ALBA: *(Studying her.)* Pleasant...good looking...Do you still like him?

DINA: I must say it was nice seeing him again.

ALBA: *(Suspicious, studying her.)* And the flame started burning again.

DINA: Not exactly. Just a tiny spark.

(A silence.)

ALBA: Your relationship. How long...did it last?

DINA: Almost two years.

ALBA: That's a long time... *(With curiosity.)* You can't forget him, can you?

DINA: Aren't there relationships you remember?

ALBA: No. They were all forgettable.

DINA: Not even a special one...your first man?

ALBA: The first woman. She surprised me with her...moving passion. I didn't know, I was not prepared for that type of love...

(A silence.)

ALBA: That friend of yours...why was he unforgettable?

DINA: For many reasons.

ALBA: Which reasons?

DINA: It's difficult to pinpoint them...to analyze them...

ALBA: Try.

DINA: First quality...I was the center of his life.

ALBA: You're the center of my life.

DINA: I know, but we are talking about him now.

ALBA: OK. Talk to me more about it. Then maybe you'll understand it...

DINA: You're right...we'll understand more...

ALBA: *We.* You're including me. That makes me happy.

DINA: He was paternal...strong...I was at ease with him, I felt protected.

ALBA: Financially?

DINA: *(Reflecting.)* No...I was not talking about that...I felt protected as if he were a father who was leading me by the hand.

ALBA: How old is he?

DINA: Three years older than me...He's still young and virile.

ALBA: You mean the sex was good?

DINA: Yes...he's the only one who could give me...He is very good...When I was with him, I was the center of his life. I mean, he always thought of me first. He *is* not selfish.

ALBA: So you still think about him?

DINA: Sometimes.

ALBA: Maybe he's changed now.

DINA: I don't think so. A man who knows how to wait, a man who takes care of you first, does not forget how to make love.

ALBA: Do you miss him? Are you still in love with him?

DINA: *(Uncertain.)* No...

ALBA: You seem uncertain...Tell me the truth. We promised each other.

(A brief pause; DINA decides to confess.)

DINA: Seeing him upset me...Did you notice? I had to touch his shoulder...

ALBA: Why?

DINA: One relives the past...

ALBA: Which always looks better in retrospect. More romantic.

DINA: No...one thinks about the mistakes...what could have been and was not.

ALBA: Meaning?

DINA: My father always warned me about being a rebel.

ALBA: What did he want you to do?

DINA: Be a lawyer, a doctor, get married.

ALBA: Anyone specific?

DINA: A family friend.

ALBA: Did you sleep with him?

DINA: No.

ALBA: You sound regretful.

DINA: We all make decisions. It's gone. In the past.

ALBA: Those decisions brought us together.

DINA: You're right. But how do you stop your imagination?

ALBA: So what? The past is past.

DINA: I think about it all the time. And as a consequence...

ALBA: As a consequence?

DINA: Open the drawer.

(ALBA opens the drawer and takes out, with surprise, a gun.)

ALBA: Where did you get this?

DINA: It's my father's. It was in the attic.

ALBA: And why did you bring it here?

DINA: I don't know...

(ALBA studies her.)

DINA: Sadness, depression...I thought about giving up.

ALBA: Maybe it's real anger. You want revenge on a man that betrayed you.

DINA: He didn't betray me.

ALBA: Then what happened?

DINA: We changed.

ALBA: Did he hurt you?

DINA: No.

ALBA: Do you want me to kill him?

DINA: No.

ALBA: Do you want to…kill me?

DINA: No. You know I love you.

ALBA: With you I'm never sure.

DINA: Nothing has changed. I confided in you because you asked me. Because we promised to be true to each other.

ALBA: Why this gun?

DINA: I thought…for a moment…that it could be useful to me.

ALBA: That is?

DINA: Useful…

ALBA: That's a temptation, an enemy. When did you bring it here?

DINA: Four days ago.

ALBA: After seeing him again…

DINA: After seeing him again.

ALBA: And so you thought about killing yourself.

DINA: I thought. I admit it, to put an end to it…

ALBA: Killing our great love?

DINA: Facing the deep sleep, the eternal peace.

ALBA: And then? Why didn't you do it?

DINA: He called.

(A long silence; ALBA is surprised; she is reflecting.)

ALBA: So he called you.

DINA: Yes, he did.

ALBA: What did he say?

DINA: The usual…

ALBA: What? What did he want?

DINA: The usual questions. "How are you?" "What have you been doing lately?" "Where are you working now?"

ALBA: Is that all?

DINA: More or less.

ALBA: And then you started reminiscing. *(Exaggerating.)* "I miss you!"

DINA: Something like that.

ALBA: Which rekindled the fire.

DINA: …Which saddened me.

ALBA: Because the past is often more beautiful, more romantic than the present.

DINA: Oh no. I just felt a sense of melancholy, depression.

ALBA: I noticed it. It's all his fault!

DINA: Oh no!

ALBA: Then is it all my fault?

DINA: You know better than that. You know I love you.

ALBA: The word love finally! What's missing in our relationship? I adore you. You're everything to me.

DINA: I know, I know.

ALBA: *(Insisting.)* What's missing? Tell me?

DINA: Nothing…You are perfect.

ALBA: But if "He" the man from the past, reappears, doubts and nostalgia surface.

DINA: I have no doubts.

ALBA: What about nostalgia?

DINA: I don't know what to call my state of mind.

ALBA: It's called nostalgia, the reappearance of happy moments. You think fondly of those times with him…

DINA: Yes…you told me you feel that for some of your lovers.

ALBA: Only two, before you. But they didn't call me. They didn't ask "How are you? Are you happy?"

DINA: But if they had called…

ALBA: I would have hung up right away.

DINA: I don't believe you, it's not possible. You are instinctively cordial and gentle with everybody.

ALBA: I wouldn't have given them the chance to evoke the past. When it's over, it's over.

DINA: Because you fear the reopening of wounds.

ALBA: "Wounds"…well, well, we are in the middle of a tragedy now. You are confessing that he has reopened your "wounds."

DINA: Some images always come back into your mind. Some images cannot be wiped out.

ALBA: Which ones?

DINA: You admitted you loved those other two.

ALBA: A man and a woman, yes.

DINA: I'm sure you had special moments with them, happy moments—which you can't forget.

ALBA: I admit it.

DINA: If they spoke to you, the warmth of their voices—

ALBA: Oh you're admitting also the warmth of his voice. It's getting better and better.

DINA: I'm sure that some happy memories would have surfaced for you, too.

ALBA: Let's speak about your memories. What did he remind you of? What did he give you more than what my love is giving you?

DINA: I told you. It's all vague, strange…

ALBA: Why did you give him time to speak to you for a long time? You should have told him "That's enough, I'm busy, I'm in love with a woman. Goodbye."

(A silence.)

ALBA: I would have told him: —"Let's face it. What's the real reason for this call?"

(A silence. ALBA is studying DINA.)

ALBA: Did you ask him?

DINA: I did.

ALBA: And what did he say?

DINA: He hesitated…

ALBA: And then?

DINA: At first he denied that there was a precise purpose. Then…

ALBA: Then?

DINA: He told me.

ALBA: All right. What is this "precise purpose"?

DINA: Curiosity.

ALBA: Regarding?

(A silence.)

DINA: He asked me about you…

(ALBA is surprised.)

DINA: About you, about us.

ALBA: And I'm sure you denied that we are lovers.

DINA: *(Vague, uncertain.)* No…

ALBA: *(Ironical.)* Thank you! Congratulations! You really have the courage of your own convictions! You didn't deny our love.

DINA: No...He guessed it.

ALBA: *(Ironical.)* Well, well, let's add to his many qualities, intelligence and intuition. He's a real genius. He saw us holding hands!

DINA: He congratulated me on my choice. He finds you very beautiful.

ALBA: Another quality! He's not short-sighted. And he must have added "You always choose well, first a handsome Valentino like him, and then a sensual Venus like me!"

DINA: He mentioned Juno. He finds you Junoesque.

ALBA: *(Surprised.)* Is that a compliment?

DINA: It is.

ALBA: He must be a courageous man. Generally men run away from strong, Junoesque women like us.

DINA: You, how do you find him?

ALBA: What do I know? I just saw him for two minutes.

DINA: For the two hours of the show. I was watching you. You were staring at him, you were studying him.

ALBA: I was jealous at the thought that that man, those long fingers, had touched you, caressed you. He has the hands of an aggressor, of an enemy.

DINA: Friendly hands...

ALBA: *(Ironical.)* Unforgettable.

DINA: Please. Juno, the Goddess, was never jealous, she was only curious... *(Stares at her.)*

ALBA: *(Feeling the stare.)* "Curious?"... What are you trying to say?

DINA: That you are very beautiful. That he would like to know you better.

ALBA: Better? How?

DINA: To know you, to speak to you...I told him that you are intelligent, well read, witty.

ALBA: Is that all? And did you tell him that I am in love with the woman he fucked in the past?

DINA: He knows that.

(A brief silence.)

ALBA: Let's be clear here. In your opinion, what does he really want?

(A silence.)

DINA: To talk to you.

ALBA: What's his ulterior motive? To break us up?

DINA: No.

ALBA: What does he really want? Did he tell you he's still in love with you?

DINA: He was vague...

ALBA: Like all men who don't know how to face love. Did he tell you yes or no that he's still in love with you?

DINA: The tone of his voice...

ALBA: *(Ironical.)* The "warmth" of his voice!

DINA: That too...He would like to invite you to dinner.

ALBA: *(Surprised.)* Me?

DINA: You.

ALBA: And you would allow it?

DINA: Why not?

(A silence.)

ALBA: Let me get this straight. We decided always to be truthful. So...

(A silence; DINA does not say anything.)

ALBA: OK. Let's see...you would let me have dinner with him, just the two of us, alone?

DINA: I suggested dinner.

ALBA: *(Ironical.)* Very good, it's your initiative, it's your idea.

DINA: He wanted to speak to you. I suggested dinner as a possibility...

ALBA: *(Reflecting; almost speaking to herself.)* He wants to talk to me...why?

DINA: I told you. To get to know you better.

ALBA: Why?

DINA: Curiosity. He finds you beautiful and interesting. I told him other things about you.

ALBA: What things?

DINA: All your wonderful qualities.

ALBA: Make a list to remind me that maybe you still love me.

DINA: Intelligent, loving, tender, inquisitive, wisely aggressive.

ALBA: *(Ironical.)* And Junoesque, of course.

DINA: That's how he saw you.

ALBA: What else?

DINA: Many other qualities. All positive.

ALBA: And he convinced you to...

DINA: That there should be a meeting.

(A silence.)

ALBA: I see...He is persuasive, he has the power to convince.

DINA: *(Vague.)* His request seems reasonable...

ALBA: This is the way I see it...He saw you again. He fell in love again, he wants to meet me to convince me that our love is not a great love and that I am the wrong woman for you. That he is the only one who can make you happy, really happy. He is a man, therefore...

(A silence.)

DINA: That's not the way it is.

ALBA: All right. It's up to you now to be truthful. *(Ironical.)* Let's have it.

DINA: *(Uneasy, hesitating.)* He is incredibly intelligent...

ALBA: *(Ironical.)* "Incredibly."

DINA: He's a fortress.

ALBA: *(Ironical.)* What an expression! That's a real compliment for someone who has wide shoulders.

DINA: *(Ignoring her.)* He understood that I was happy with him.

ALBA: *(Hurt.)* ..."Happy with him..."

DINA: He admitted that he misses me...He's ready to come back.

ALBA: *(Surprised.)* Come back where?

DINA: Into our lives.

ALBA: *(Very surprised.)* "Our"?

DINA: Didn't we promise to be always sincere? I've finally found that strength. *(A brief pause.)* I miss him.

ALBA: Sexually?

DINA: No! Sex is never the most important part in a relationship. I've read many times that love and sex don't necessarily go together.

ALBA: What's missing, then, is his love.

DINA: I don't know…I don't know how to define it. I miss his person, his personality, his presence. With him, I always felt protected.

ALBA: And with me?

DINA: With you, too.

ALBA: *(Ironical.)* Just a little bit less, anyhow. After all, I'm not a…"fortress." So you want to…start again?

DINA: He would like to…

ALBA: "He would like"…what about you?

(A brief silence.)

ALBA: I see…he's going to try to convince me. You couldn't do it. He wants to intervene…OK? When do we do this?

DINA: There'll be a price to pay.

ALBA: *(Ironical.)* Very well, very well! What's the price? Who must pay?

DINA: I shouldn't have said…"Price"… There is a condition.

ALBA: Same difference. What's the condition he is imposing?

DINA: He's not imposing anything…He told me…He would do anything to know you…

ALBA: Meaning?

DINA: *(Uncertain.)* Also…

ALBA: Say it.

DINA: Also…I know it sounds crazy, but it is true.

ALBA: Tell me.

DINA: He's ready to see me again, when I want to, when I need him.

ALBA: He's ready to fuck you.

DINA: No. Only as friends. He wants to see *us*, now and then…

ALBA: *Us?*

DINA: Yes.

ALBA: *(Reflecting.)* The two of us. Together…the three of us…Why?

DINA: It's not what you're thinking… Help me by listening, please…

ALBA: Of course. Talk, talk. I want to hear.

DINA: Do it for me, for us…

ALBA: Sure, sure! In the name of our love. I should be convinced to…Clarify!

DINA: Can't you guess?

ALBA: No. Spell it out.

DINA: He wants…something else.

ALBA: What else?

DINA: After seeing you, after what I told him about you—

ALBA: What did you tell him? How we make love?

DINA: No…How you are…Your many qualities.

ALBA: And he concluded that…?

DINA: He's in love with you.

ALBA: *(Very surprised.)* With me?

DINA: With you.

ALBA: He's crazy.

DINA: He's convinced that he's deeply in love with you.

ALBA: *(Ironical; maybe flattered.)* It's your fault, all your fault. You described me too well.

DINA: He wants… *(She hesitates; does not know how to say it.)*

ALBA: *(Coming to her help.)* All right. He wants to meet me. You've made me curious now. *(Ironical.)* Where can you find a "fortress" today among so many spineless men? Where? When should I see him?

DINA: If you love me...Here.

ALBA: *(Surprised again.)* Here? In this bedroom?

DINA: If you love me...

ALBA: *(Amazed, unbelieving.)* I should...

DINA: Out of love for me.

ALBA: That's the price to pay...

DINA: I assure you...It's an experience—

ALBA: You're crazy! I hate men! I love YOU!

DINA: A unique experience.

ALBA: Oh yeah! The unforgettable giant!

DINA: Oh no! I'm not talking about sex. I'm speaking of something else.

ALBA: What? What else?

DINA: With him I felt...daughter, sister, mother...A complete experience.

ALBA: *(Ironical.)* And since you love me so much, you want to give me this...unique, unforgettable experience.

DINA: Because I love you, because I love him.

(A silence.)

ALBA: *(Studying her.)* And you...you're not going to be jealous?

DINA: No. It's the price I'm paying.

ALBA: The price *you are paying*?

DINA: My sacrifice of love.

ALBA: And after this...Are you thinking about "later"?

DINA: No...I've faith in the future, I've faith in you, in him...

ALBA: I see...you want him back so badly that you're asking me to make this sacrifice.

DINA: It will be a sacrifice for me too. Knowing that he will...be with you. But it's his condition, and I need him.

ALBA *(With sadness.)* ...You need him...

DINA: For a better future, our future.

ALBA: Do you really think we three have a future? Me, you, and him?

DINA: I do. All like before, better than before.

(A silence.)

ALBA: When?

DINA: He's downstairs, at the bar. I'll tell him to come upstairs.

(They hug in silence; DINA exits. ALBA takes the gun and puts it under the pillow. She lies down on the bed and waits. Maybe she's going to shoot him. Lights fade slowly.)

(CURTAIN.)

The Bridge

Characters:

PABLO, thirty-five years old; a Puerto Rican living in New York
JOSEPH, a policeman assigned to rescue work
A LIEUTENANT in the police force

The Place:

New York.

The Time:

Today.

The top of the Brooklyn Bridge, a place not too uncommon for suicide. PABLO is standing in the middle of the double span. He is looking down, apparently in a good position to jump. Down at the foot of the bridge, we imagine a curious crowd. PABLO, lost and bewildered, looks around. He is surrounded only by the blue sky.

PABLO: *(To someone who is evidently trying to reach him.)* It's no use. You're wasting your time, my friend...Don't! Or I will jump right away...No use...It's too late now. *(Backing up.)* I warn you...If you come close...Go away! Go back to them! *(He points to the crowd down below.)* or do you want this "show" to get going? *(He backs up to the very edge, wavering.)* I'm warning you...Don't come near or I'll...

(JOSEPH, the policeman, appears at the opposite side of the span. He is out of breath and sweating. He sits down to catch his breath.)

PABLO: I'm not joking. I mean it!

JOSEPH: I know.

PABLO: One more move and...

JOSEPH: I know.

PABLO: What do you know?

JOSEPH: That you're not joking.

PABLO: Then why are you up here?

JOSEPH: *(Shrugs his shoulders.)* Let me catch my breath.

PABLO: You have all the time you want.

JOSEPH: I know.

PABLO: If you don't move.

JOSEPH: I know.

PABLO: If you try to—

JOSEPH: *(Interrupting.)* I know.

PABLO: You know too much.

JOSEPH: That's my job.

PABLO: Then you know there's nothing you can do about me.

JOSEPH: I know.

PABLO: Then why are you up here?

JOSEPH: It's my duty.

PABLO: *(With some surprise and curiosity.)* Just duty?

JOSEPH: And the bonus. There's extra money for such trips.

PABLO: If you save me.

JOSEPH: That's not necessary. Just climbing up here is considered "special duty." And we get double pay.

PABLO: *(After a silence.)* How many have you seen up here?

JOSEPH: Nine.

PABLO: How many have you...saved?

JOSEPH: Eight.

PABLO: A good record. I'm sorry to spoil it. I've made up my mind.

JOSEPH: I know.

PABLO: Eight saved; two lost. It's still a good average. Eighty percent.

JOSEPH: Ninety percent.

PABLO: Why ninety?

JOSEPH: Nine saved; one lost.

PABLO: Why do you say "nine"?

JOSEPH: I always tell the truth.

PABLO: Do you think you can...? *(He includes himself with a gesture.)*

JOSEPH: Absolutely.

PABLO: *(Incredulous.)* Are you including me?

JOSEPH: Yes.

PABLO: Are you serious?

JOSEPH: I'm serious.

PABLO: Do you really think...you'll save me?

JOSEPH: As true as there's a God.

PABLO: You must be an atheist. It's unusual, for a cop.

JOSEPH: On the contrary, I'm very religious.

PABLO: *(Incredulous.)* And you're sure that—as true as there's a God—you'll save me?

JOSEPH: Don't take the name of our Lord in vain. *(He crosses himself.)*

PABLO: You started.

JOSEPH: I'm on the side of the Law.

PABLO: I forget. You're allowed everything.

JOSEPH: Not only because I'm a man of the Law but also because I'm not about to commit a mortal sin. I've just come from Church. *(He wipes off his perspiration.)*

PABLO: *(Ironically.)* I apologize if this trip made you lose the holy perfume of the incense. I'm so sorry you're perspiring because of me.

JOSEPH: It doesn't matter. Thanks to you, I get a day off tomorrow. There can be some advantage to a calamity.

PABLO: Am I the "calamity"?

JOSEPH: I'd say so.

PABLO: What a way of consoling one's fellow brother! Did you talk to the others like this?

JOSEPH: What others?

PABLO: Those nine— *(He does not utter the word "suicides" but he indicates with a gesture "jumping.")*

JOSEPH: Yes.

PABLO: *(More and more intrigued.)* To all of them?

JOSEPH: To all of them.

PABLO: Even to the one...you didn't save?

JOSEPH: That one too. A thick-skinned Jew.

PABLO: I see. You're one of those who consider the Jews to be different...An inferior race, maybe.

JOSEPH: Insensitive.

PABLO: *(Reflecting.)* Insensitive...to what? *(Ironically.)* To what you said?

JOSEPH: To that too.

PABLO: Which is what you're telling me.

JOSEPH: More or less.

PABLO: Maybe he was too sensitive and preferred to— *(He makes the gesture of jumping.)*

JOSEPH: Are you Jewish by any chance?

PABLO: No, I'm a Catholic. Like you, I guess.

JOSEPH: *(With tolerance.)* There's always something in common, alas!

PABLO: Alas?

JOSEPH: You can't avoid it.

PABLO: Is that bad?

JOSEPH: In a street, in an office, in a prison—people always find that they have something in common. Same religion. Political opinion, race...

PABLO: Same sex.

JOSEPH: You can't avoid it. The chances are fifty-fifty.

PABLO: *(Ironically.)* Yes we have two things in common. We are both Catholics and we are men.

JOSEPH: The only two things we have in common.

PABLO: The only ones I hope.

JOSEPH: I hope so too.

PABLO: *(Studying JOSEPH.)* Did you tell that Jew you're a Catholic?

JOSEPH: Of course.

PABLO: That's why he jumped.

JOSEPH: *(Looking straight in his eyes.)* Who told you he jumped?

PABLO: You said so yourself.

JOSEPH: Me? You're wrong.

PABLO: You said—"Eight were saved and one was lost."

JOSEPH: That's what I said.

PABLO: Well?

JOSEPH: Well what?

PABLO: If you saved eight of them but not the Jew, it means that the Jew jumped.

JOSEPH: You misunderstood me.

PABLO: Evidently. What did you mean?

JOSEPH: I meant—eight saved from the miseries of this world. One—the Jew—asked for a ladder.

PABLO: *(Surprised.)* So that's what you meant when you said that you'd save me.

JOSEPH: As true as there's a God. *(He crosses himself.)*

PABLO: *(Shaken; reflecting.)* You're right...I've made up my mind...But how can you be so sure?

JOSEPH: It's instinct. And experience.

PABLO: I always thought men like you could not be very smart.

JOSEPH: Never underestimate Men of the Law, remember that! We would never be trusted with keeping "order" if we weren't well schooled and prepared.

PABLO: What did they teach you?

JOSEPH: Everything.

PABLO: Even how to read the minds of other people?

JOSEPH: That's called "psychology." It's one of the most important subjects.

PABLO: And with that psychology you never made a mistake?

JOSEPH: With exception of the Jews. They're unpredictable.

PABLO: All of them?

JOSEPH: All of them.

PABLO: Including the...possible suicides?

JOSEPH: Also those. They pretend. They do it to attract attention. Then there's always a rich Jew who comes along and offers them a job at three hundred dollars a week, and they change their minds.

PABLO: *(Unable to hide his envy.)* Three hundred dollars a week...

JOSEPH: You'd spend every penny of it on whisky.

PABLO: How would you know?

JOSEPH: I know your kind. All I have to do is look at your face.

PABLO: What kind of face do you see?

JOSEPH: You Puer— *(He holds back.)* You're all bums.

PABLO: *(Sadly.)* You started to say—You Puerto Ricans.

JOSEPH: I admit it. Did you study psychology too?

PABLO: Is a Puerto Rican and a bum the same thing to you?

JOSEPH: *(Looking straight in his eyes.)* The same thing.

PABLO: Then why did you come to our country and take over?

JOSEPH: Me?

PABLO: Your people.

JOSEPH: If it was up to me... *(Scornfully.)* I wouldn't touch you people with a ten-foot pole.

PABLO: It's me who wouldn't let one of you touch me.

JOSEPH: Don't worry about that. I won't touch you. *(He "washes" his hands.)*

PABLO: Do all you cops feel that way?

JOSEPH: A man in uniform can only speak for himself. I, personally, wouldn't touch you with a ten-foot pole. My friends on the Force... *(He thinks for a few seconds.)* ...feel the same way. But that's their business. They can speak for themselves, if they wish. I believe in freedom of choice. *(A brief pause.)* How about you?

PABLO: So do I. *(Pointing below.)* Is there any freer choice than this?

JOSEPH: I mean, do you believe in Freedom, in our Democracy?

PABLO: Why do you ask me that?

JOSEPH: I don't trust your kind.

PABLO: What kind are we?

JOSEPH: Bums with many kids.

PABLO: What do you know about me? What do you know about my family?

JOSEPH: You're all alike. It's always the same story and complaint.

PABLO: Did I complain?

JOSEPH: That's because I didn't give you a chance to. Please don't tell me your story. I've heard it a thousand times.

PABLO: Then you tell me.

JOSEPH: You left your old parents starving in your little village—

PABLO: I'm an orphan.

JOSEPH: *(Ignoring.)* You came to New York full of hope. To make money. Instead, you began making children. The result—starvation for all. Big families always starve.

PABLO: How many children make a "big family," according to you?

JOSEPH: In your case? I saw four. But I'm sure you have more in some dump.

PABLO: *(With curiosity.)* Where did you see them?

JOSEPH: Down there, with your miserable wife. My buddies are holding them back. They trust me. They know I can "save" you single handed.

(A silence.)

PABLO: *(Slowly.)* Why did you say…she's miserable?

JOSEPH: Your wife? Not because you're about to die. That she will be widowed is not a misfortune. It might be a stroke of luck for her. I said she looks "miserable" because… *(He takes his time.)* you must know how she looks early in the morning! She just got up. And hasn't washed her face!

PABLO: *(Timidly.)* Did she say anything?

JOSEPH: Oh I forgot.—And I know it's unfair not to report the last words to a dying man.—She told me to tell you that… *(He is trying to remember.)* a certain man by the name of…Sanchez—I think I'm right—has a good job for you, with very good pay. And…she also promised not to complain ever again. She's swearing it by one of your Madonnas.

(A silence.)

PABLO: *(Sadly.)* They all lie…Always… *(To JOSEPH.)* Would you believe them?

JOSEPH: Believe what?

PABLO: In a job with "very good" pay, in all their promises…

JOSEPH: Sometimes they tell the truth. Sometimes they lie. It depends. There's freedom of opinion in this country.

PABLO: *(After a silence.)* What else did she say?

JOSEPH: *(Trying to remember.)* —That if I persuade you to come down, I'd be welcome into your family with gratitude and "love." *(With contempt.)* Who needs it? *(Reflecting.)* Maybe she also meant…in bed. Who wants that wreck?

PABLO: *(Hurt.)* You're a swine!

JOSEPH: *(Tense.)* Come over here and repeat that to my face.

(A silence.)

JOSEPH: Come on! *(He rises to his feet, aggressively.)* If you have the guts to do it…

(A silence; they stare at each other.)

PABLO: And what about my…? *(He indicates "children" with a gesture of his hand.)*

JOSEPH: Your brats? They weren't crying. You're a strange breed. Not even a tear. *(Staring at him.)* You tell me. Why do you suppose they don't cry?

(A silence; PABLO does not have the courage to reply.)

JOSEPH: Too exhausted maybe?

(PABLO gestures in the negative.)

JOSEPH: Sometimes hunger makes you react like that.

(PABLO gestures in the negative.)

JOSEPH: Or maybe you people beat them too often?

PABLO: *(Weakly.)* No...

JOSEPH: Maybe they're glad to be rid of you. A drunkard isn't a joyful sight to one's children.

PABLO: *(Who has not heard the last words; deeply moved.)* Maria is twelve...

JOSEPH: Who's Maria?

PABLO: My daughter. *(With a gesture he indicates her height.)* She's a real little lady. She promised me she wouldn't cry. She is not crying.

JOSEPH: *(Surprised.)* Promised?

(PABLO nods.)

JOSEPH: You spoke to her about—? *(He makes the gesture of "jumping.")*

PABLO: To a wife it's hard to say such things. She laughs in your face, she doesn't believe you...A daughter has more respect...She understands...

JOSEPH: What did you tell her?

PABLO: That it's better for them...

JOSEPH: What's better? Why?

PABLO: When a father dies in this way, everybody becomes generous.

JOSEPH: Who?

PABLO: Everybody...And my family will receive a lot of help, and many gifts...They'll be able to go back to San Juan.

JOSEPH: Bon voyage! But did she really understand? Did she understand that you—? *(He makes the sign of the cross in the air, meaning "death.")*

PABLO: She understood.

JOSEPH: And she didn't cry?

PABLO: When I first told her she cried. She held me tightly. With her hands clasping my shoulders. Then she began to understand and promised not to cry today...to encourage her little brothers.

JOSEPH: *(Incredulous, with irony.)* "To encourage."

PABLO: She has always obeyed me. She loves me.

JOSEPH: And you reward her with—

PABLO: *(Ignoring.)* She always keeps her promises...Always. My poor baby, not even a tear...

JOSEPH: Yes. You are a strange breed.

PABLO: Because we learn not to cry?

JOSEPH: Because you know how to exploit even death.

PABLO: What do you mean?

JOSEPH: Your blind belief that "everybody will become generous and will give money."

PABLO: It's true.

JOSEPH: That's why I said—"You know how to exploit even death." But after all, how can you be so sure that we aren't tired of giving you people charity? There's a limit to everything!

PABLO: In the presence of death...

JOSEPH: It's practically become a daily occurrence. A dead person on every street corner. No one is upset by it.

PABLO: I'm certain that—

JOSEPH: *(Ironically.)* "Certain!" You people are ridiculous! There's no such word as "certain" anymore.

PABLO: Two years ago a friend of mine attempted suicide and—

JOSEPH: *(Interrupting.)* Attempted. That's different.

PABLO: One of you convinced him to give up the idea. With a million promises.

JOSEPH: Not me!

PABLO: I believe that.

JOSEPH: Thanks!

PABLO: You speak your mind...

JOSEPH: Always, I call a spade a spade. And a bum a bum.

PABLO: You've already called me that.

JOSEPH: "Repetita iuvant."

(PABLO does not understand.)

JOSEPH: They even teach us a little Latin at the Police Academy. To impress fools. "Repetita iuvant" means: "Explain the truth ten times, to thick heads. Maybe they'll understand." That friend of yours, for instance, maybe he was convinced because the Police Officer repeated the same thing ten times. I have no patience.

PABLO: The promises weren't kept, of course...No job, no apartment...

JOSEPH: That's life...

PABLO: You say that as if it were an insignificant event.

JOSEPH: Is it perhaps a great international event?

PABLO: It's a man's life.

JOSEPH: *(Raising one finger.)* ONE man... Don't get carried away. ONE man.

PABLO: Do you know what they did to him, when he came down?

JOSEPH: Are you going to tell me they beat him up? With all those photographers around? I don't believe you,

PABLO: They put him in an insane asylum.

JOSEPH: A few weeks under observation to calm the nerves. But what are you trying to prove with the story of your friend?

PABLO: Six months ago, he finally did it. From here. His case made headlines. His family returned to Puerto Rico with a lot of money.

JOSEPH: It's the headlines that you want.

PABLO: If it helps my family, yes.

JOSEPH: The usual excuse. *(Ironically.)* "For the family." It's the publicity that you guys want. All of you!

PABLO: *(With sincerity.)* No! Please believe me. And please tell them. Everyone. Repeat our conversation. Tell them I did it only for my family, that I put my hope in the good hearts of...anybody who can...

JOSEPH: You Latinos have a strange mentality. The only thing you want is charity.

PABLO: Only when—

JOSEPH: *(Interrupting.)* You people are real parasites.

PABLO: It isn't me who created the world the way it is. They promise you the moon but—

JOSEPH: Not me!

PABLO: —But they don't keep their promises. If you die, everybody—

JOSEPH: *(Interrupting.)* Not "everybody." Only some with sins on their conscience. Maybe it's a way of feeling absolved. That's their business. But you, why do you pick the easiest way out?

PABLO: *(Sadly.)* The "easiest"?

JOSEPH: Why do you want strangers to support your children?

PABLO: It's the only way they can be happy. Unfortunately, only death brings pity. That friend of mine—

JOSEPH: You already told me.

PABLO: It's not my fault if that's the way the world is.

JOSEPH: But you're responsible for your children. You brought them into the world. Stop drinking and take care of them.

PABLO: I've never been drunk in my life.

JOSEPH: I'm sure you have other vices.

PABLO: Did you ever pay a hospital bill?

JOSEPH: Here come the complaints! Get hospital insurance!

PABLO: Do you know what it costs here in America?

JOSEPH: My wife takes care of that.

PABLO: It's half my salary! *(After a reflection.)* You have a wife too...

JOSEPH: Sure. Why?

PABLO: I think of you without a family...The way you talk...Cruel and hateful...

JOSEPH: Me cruel! You, who order a twelve-year-old not to cry. Are you the model father?

PABLO: Do you have children too?

JOSEPH: Of course. A boy and a girl. Like any respectable family, only two. When the good Lord *(He crosses himself.)* summons my wife and me to Heaven, they will take our place. We don't reproduce like rabbits—we real Americans. Overpopulation leads to Communism. *(A brief silence.)* Why did you have so many children if you knew you were going to finish up like this? *(He points down.)*

PABLO: I didn't know then...

JOSEPH: In bed people don't think of suicide, I know. You bums are all alike. Selfish. You're just in it for physical satisfaction—as long as you find your wife attractive. But when she is reduced to that state, *(He points down.)* with four brats hanging on, you decide to commit suicide. Is this your way of insuring their future? Depending on the charity of strangers? You're a coward!

(A silence.)

PABLO: I've read a lot about suicide... Some claim that it's cowardice; others say it's an act of courage. What do you think?

JOSEPH: *(Slowly.)* I have no desire to influence you, as you know. What you decide is your own damn business. I couldn't care less. But I do have an opinion on suicide.

PABLO: What is it?

JOSEPH: They go into it in our psychology course. We divided ourselves into two groups. Some insisted on calling it courage; others, extreme cowardice. I personally think that it does take courage that fraction of a second when you jump. On the other hand, it's cowardice because it's an escape from life. But let me make this clear to you. I don't want to influence you in one direction or the other. One suicide more, one less...

PABLO: *(Sadly.)* Why do you talk like that?

JOSEPH: Like what?

PABLO: With such contempt...

JOSEPH: It's my point of view. Don't I have the right? This is a free country!

PABLO: It's the way you say it.

JOSEPH: It's the truth. I always tell the truth, that's me. When a bum does away with himself, there's more room for us. It makes our society more secure. In Indonesia for instance, they executed nine hundred thousands bums in a few days. Nine hundred thousand Reds less. The world is a little cleaner and safer for that.

PABLO: I'm no Red!

JOSEPH: Unemployed with a big family? Who are you kidding? You can only be a Red.

PABLO: The Church would excommunicate me.

JOSEPH: You mean that's the only reason why you're not a Red? Because you're afraid of the Church? That's an interesting confession!

PABLO: And because I believe in the family.

JOSEPH: *(Ironically, pointing down.)* I can see that!

PABLO: And in freedom.

JOSEPH: What kind of freedom?

PABLO: *(Pointing vaguely around him.)* This...

JOSEPH: The freedom to jump?

PABLO: Democratic freedom...That's what I've always believed in. Man should be free to do what he wants.

JOSEPH: And women?

PABLO: Women too.

JOSEPH: Are you leaving your wife and daughter the freedom to do what they want?

PABLO: *(Hesitating.)* Yes...

JOSEPH: Complete freedom?

PABLO: *(Unsure.)* Yes...

JOSEPH: Even if they take to walking the streets, I suppose?

PABLO: *(Hurt.)* They will have money, lots of money and—

JOSEPH: Are you sure of it?

PABLO: I read about it every day in the paper. There's always some good soul who starts a collection...even Oswald's family. They have lots of money now.

JOSEPH: He killed a *President!* You're only killing a poor stupid nobody. Yourself. You want to make a bet? They won't collect more than five hundred dollars.

PABLO: Sure if you tell them I'm a Red. Which isn't true. Please don't—

JOSEPH: I won't. I'll only say that...you had a nervous breakdown.

PABLO: ...With debts and no job...

JOSEPH: That's social protest. That wouldn't be wise. Anyway, do you want to bet?

PABLO: I've made up my mind and I'm going to jump. Who will pay if I lose the bet?

JOSEPH: You can sign an IOU. If your family gets over five hundred dollars, I'll add a hundred. If they get less, your wife will owe me a hundred. *(He takes a piece of paper and pen.)* Here, sign here.

PABLO: *(Uncertain.)* Are you so sure they'll...get less than five hundred dollars?

JOSEPH: Positive. I can guarantee it. Yours is an ordinary case. There're ten a day like you. People have become callous to it.

PABLO: If you lie and tell them I'm a Red—

JOSEPH: *(Interrupting.)* Keep politics out of it! Do you want to take me up on it?

PABLO: Honestly—would you have the nerve to take their money if they received less than five hundred dollars?

JOSEPH: *(Ironically.)* My friend, you're beginning to have doubts, aren't you?

PABLO: My name is Pablo. What's yours?

JOSEPH: *(Bored.)* Joseph.

PABLO: Tell me, Joseph…Tell me seriously. Would you have the nerve to take a hundred dollars from them if—?

JOSEPH: I won't be the only one. They'll be at the mercy of everybody down there. Even your friends who loaned you money.

PABLO: No friend of mine ever—

JOSEPH: *(Interrupting.)* All right, enemies then. Like the grocer and the landlord. And don't forget the undertaker. Nowadays a decent funeral costs six thousand dollars.

PABLO: *(Alarmed.)* Six thousand dollars? Are you sure?

JOSEPH: Positive. Even gravediggers have families to feed!

PABLO: But that friend of mine, he didn't pay at all—

JOSEPH: *He* didn't, I'm sure.

PABLO: —His family didn't pay anything for the funeral. The City—

JOSEPH: *(Interrupting.)* With the new Mayor the rules are different. Too many of you guys took advantage of free burials. *(He studies him.)* But what's bothering you? Are you worried about something?

PABLO: Nothing. I'm sure you're just trying to frighten me and—

JOSEPH: *Frighten* you? Who gives a damn about you? Whatever you've decided, you've well decided. And I, after all, I don't think you should worry so much.

PABLO: Why?

JOSEPH: I'm sure you've considered everything…taken everything into account, thought about it.

PABLO: About what?

JOSEPH: Your daughter.

PABLO: What do you mean?

JOSEPH: She's just twelve and…already an attractive little figure…

PABLO: So what?

JOSEPH: She'll find some rich customers.

PABLO: You're a pig!

(JOSEPH instinctively draws his revolver.)

PABLO: Shoot! *(Stretches out his arms.)* This way we'll get it over with sooner!

JOSEPH: Nobody calls me a pig!

PABLO: I call you that again. Fat pig! *(He stretches out his arms again; offers himself as a target.)*

(JOSEPH raises his revolver and aims at PABLO.)

PABLO: Go ahead, shoot.

JOSEPH: *(After reflection, lowering his revolver.)* You'd like that, wouldn't you? That way the guilt would be on my shoulders.

PABLO: You deserve it.

JOSEPH: And you wouldn't have to take that final step. You're a coward.

PABLO: Because I haven't jumped yet?

JOSEPH: And for everything else. I told you Maria would find rich customers because it always ends up that way. I've come across more than one like her.

PABLO: What do you mean, "like her"?

JOSEPH: In a French whorehouse for instance. Years ago. I took a very young girl—same eyes as your daughter. After we were through we talked for a while. She was the daughter of a Red executed by the Germans.

PABLO: *(Angry.)* I'm not a commie. How can I make you understand?

JOSEPH: That's the way all daughters of radicals wind up. In a whorehouse!

PABLO: *(Furious.)* I'm no radical!

JOSEPH: All right then. All daughters of bums. Is that better? In a whorehouse.

PABLO: *(Upset.)* Not Maria...They'll go back to Puerto Rico and—

JOSEPH: *(Interrupting.)* She will find customers there too. They'll pay less but—

PABLO: That's enough, you dirty...! *(Does not find the right insult.)*

JOSEPH: What are you getting so excited about? You're dead and buried. You won't see anything, you won't feel anything.

PABLO: I've never met a bastard like you before!

JOSEPH: I'm the bastard? Look who's talking!

PABLO: Damn you! If I had— *(He wrings his hands.)*

JOSEPH: You want my gun? Here! *(He puts it down beside him.)* Only with a gun would you have the guts to face anyone.

PABLO Put it in the middle of the bridge and then go back to your place.

JOSEPH: I suffer from heights. That's why I sat down here. *(He points to the gun beside him.)* You're as good as dead anyway. So you can risk your useless life.

PABLO: I'm more useful than you! More honest! I've worked all my life!

JOSEPH: *(Ironical.)* That's great! And here's the result. Look at you!

PABLO: I...I... *(He can't find words.)* I can't believe that you...

JOSEPH: That I—what?

PABLO: That you can talk like that. It's inhuman.

JOSEPH: That's psychology. All I need is to look at your face. You, a typical bum. Your daughter, a typical—

PABLO: *(Violent.)* Leave my daughter out of this!

JOSEPH: *(Suddenly noticing that someone is climbing up.)* Take it easy, friend, take it easy! The Lieutenant is coming.

(He buttons up his shirt and puts away his gun. The POLICE LIEUTENANT appears near JOSEPH.)

LIEUTENANT: Well? Where do we stand?

JOSEPH: We were talking about his children, his wife... *(To PABLO.)* Right?

(PABLO does not answer.)

JOSEPH: He's very attached to his family...Especially his daughter.

LIEUTENANT: Should we bring her up here?

PABLO: *(Promptly.)* No!

JOSEPH: He's afraid that something might happen to her. He's coming down... *(He instinctively gestures a "jump"; he corrects the gesture to indicate "descent.")*

LIEUTENANT: Are you sure?

JOSEPH: I'm doing my best.

LIEUTENANT: Please. If you fail again, I'll be demoted.

JOSEPH: Leave it to me.

LIEUTENANT: Is he difficult?

JOSEPH: Yes and no...I'll achieve my purpose, don't worry.

LIEUTENANT: *Our* purpose!

JOSEPH: Of course!

LIEUTENANT: *(To PABLO.)* Hello, young man! *(He waves and smiles.)*

JOSEPH: *(To the LIEUTENANT.)* His name is Pablo.

LIEUTENANT: Hello Pablo! How're you doing?

(PABLO does not answer.)

LIEUTENANT: We have some Cokes down below! Nice and cold! And your family, they're all upset! Come on, like a good sport.

(PABLO ignores him. The LIEUTENANT whispers something to JOSEPH.)

JOSEPH: *(To the LIEUTENANT.)* You can depend on me.

LIEUTENANT: Please... *(He descends; disappears.)*

JOSEPH: *(To PABLO.)* He's only worried about being demoted. Hypocrite!

PABLO: Less hypocrite than you! You lied to him.

JOSEPH: Me?

PABLO: You made him believe that you were doing your best to...

JOSEPH: To what?

PABLO: To get me to come down.

JOSEPH: It's useless with a headstrong fool like you.

PABLO: Why did you lie to him?

JOSEPH: I told him that we talked about your family. That's no lie, is it? And that you're partial to your eldest child. Isn't that right?

PABLO: She isn't my first-born.

JOSEPH: *(Surprised.)* You never told me that! *(Reflecting.)* She seemed to be the tallest.

PABLO: My first-born is a boy. He's fourteen now.

JOSEPH: Your family keeps growing. You see? I was right. The only thing you people know how to do is manufacture children. Where is he? I didn't see him down there with the rest of them.

PABLO: I left him in Puerto Rico. With his grandfather.

JOSEPH: You should have all stayed there. Only ungrateful people and parasites leave their native country.

PABLO: Your Government made me an American citizen.

JOSEPH: Nobody asked for my advice.

PABLO: You come to us with your chewing gum, your Coca-Cola, you give us passports with your American eagle and then—

JOSEPH: What else do you want? New York City?

PABLO: The freedom you promise. The right to travel, to come to America.

JOSEPH: But why do all of you come here? Take a trip in your own country. You must have some interesting sights there too!

PABLO: If Rome conquers a neighbor, the neighbor goes to Rome. It's natural.

JOSEPH: Conquests would stop if all the slaves descended on the Capital.

PABLO: This is not the Capital.

JOSEPH: It is. This city pays the highest salaries in the world.

PABLO: For those who can get work.

JOSEPH: Specialize at something and you'll find work.

PABLO: How?

JOSEPH: That's *your* problem.

PABLO: You see? In this world nobody helps you.

JOSEPH: I'm not your brother! Go to the Police Headquarters if you need help.

PABLO: And there I'll find somebody like you. I'll be lucky if he doesn't beat me up.

JOSEPH: Have you ever gone to my precinct?

PABLO: No.

JOSEPH: Try before criticizing.

PABLO: If they're all like you—

JOSEPH: We're different. On this side of the bridge: those who believe in Law and Order. On that side of the bridge: your kind, bums full of hostility. Your suicide is the only contribution to Society. Happy landing, amigo! *(He points down; then he looks at his watch.)* It's getting late. I have an appointment…

PABLO: With the Ku Klux Klan, I bet!

JOSEPH: Not exactly. I'm going to the K.A.W.

PABLO: What's that?

JOSEPH: "Keep America White."

PABLO: Same difference.

JOSEPH: You Latins—and the Blacks, and the Yellows, you're mongrelizing us. We must fight to survive. That's why no pure Aryan ever commits suicide.

PABLO: You're a Nazi!

JOSEPH: Do you know that's almost a compliment?

PABLO: I bet you've got a picture of Hitler hanging on the wall.

JOSEPH: No. He's in a drawer. It's a good picture and I didn't want to throw it away.

PABLO: *(Incredulous.)* I can't believe it. Are you serious?

JOSEPH: Of course I am. I've always admired Hitler. He believed in the superiority of the Aryan race. I am for the superiority of the Aryan race. He was for a New Order. I am a guardian of Order. And if I had something to say about it…it would be a New and Total Order, I assure you!

PABLO: You're a fascist!

JOSEPH: That word is out. Commies like you have succeeded in making it sound like poison.

PABLO: I'm not a commie!

JOSEPH: What else can a bum with five kids be?

PABLO: I'll sue you.

JOSEPH: Postmortem?

PABLO: I'm still alive.

JOSEPH: For how long?

PABLO: As long as I wish.

JOSEPH: You heathen! You even dare to take the name of Our Lord in vain! *(Ironically.)* "As long as I wish." As long as Our Lord wishes! *(He looks up and crosses himself.)*

PABLO: I'm the judge of this day.

JOSEPH: And you've decided. Have a nice trip!

PABLO: I'll stay here as long as I want.

JOSEPH: *(Looking at his watch.)* It's getting late.

PABLO: I'll see to it that you don't keep your appointment. People like you should be forbidden from meeting.

JOSEPH: Are you forgetting that this is a free country?

PABLO: I'll keep you here as long as I like.

JOSEPH: That's not fair. What I told you is confidential…Please… *(He indicates he should jump.)*

PABLO: I'll stay as long as I like!

JOSEPH: You see? People like you can't be trusted! I was being friendly!

PABLO: Friendly? God help me!

JOSEPH: You can't trust anybody in this world!

PABLO: You're right.

JOSEPH: Especially half breeds… *(He studies PABLO.)* You don't look like you'd have any Jewish blood…Probably there's some Negro in you…In Puerto Rico you're all very dark.

PABLO: Nazi!

JOSEPH: Why? Because I'm honest and tell you the truth? Let's stop pretending with each other. There's a superior race and inferior races. We have only two children. They're educated to lead. You boast about having five, six. There is no limit to how many. Then you commit suicide. Those children are left to us. Ignorant and defenseless. "An inferior race."

PABLO: People like you shouldn't exist.

JOSEPH: Let's face it. We not only exist. We rule. And there is never a suicide among us. *(Looking again at his watch.)* Please, amigo, it's getting late… *(He looks below.)* and I'm beginning to feel dizzy…

PABLO: It would be very funny if it were you who lost your balance and… *(Points down.)*

JOSEPH: Funny? *(He crosses his fingers.)* You have a morbid sense of humor! I've got a wife and two children!

PABLO: Do you really think your family is superior to mine?

JOSEPH: Can you even doubt it? We have genetic, intellectual, and moral superiority.

PABLO: *(Incredulous.)* You must be joking!

JOSEPH: I'm definitively not joking! Now please… *(He points down.)* Bon voyage, amigo!

PABLO: You promised the Lieutenant to—

JOSEPH: "Promises." I'm fickle like a sailor. I was in the Navy. What about you?

PABLO: Infantry.

JOSEPH: That figures.

PABLO: Your Army was happy to get me.

JOSEPH: Who else would we send to the front line? You and the Negroes are ideal for cannon fodder.

LIEUTENANT: *(Offstage, his voice coming from below.)* Well, have you made up your mind? We're blocking traffic here!

JOSEPH: *(Shouting.)* He's coming right down! We're discussing our glorious Army! Our friend Pablo was in the infantry.

LIEUTENANT: *(Offstage, from below; rhetorical.)* Three cheers for the infantry!

PABLO: You hypocrite!

JOSEPH: Whatever you want, but make up your mind. Did you notice how subtle I was? I said—"He's coming right down!" I didn't lie. You're going down either way.

PABLO: I've never met anyone like you. Never. You're inhuman.

JOSEPH: Me, inhuman? You must be joking. Look. I'll prove to you that I'm not only kind but a friend. If you get it over with quickly, *(He points below.)* I'll make a deal with you.

PABLO: What deal?

JOSEPH: First of all, I won't tell a soul you're a Red. That way your family—

PABLO: I'm not a Red! You bastard—

JOSEPH: *(Ignoring him.)* —your family will get sympathy and help. There'll be more money for that mess of your wife and for the five brats. And…there's something else… *(He hesitates.)*

PABLO: What?

JOSEPH: You're so sensitive on this subject that I don't know how to put it… *(He hesitates.)*

PABLO: Go on.

JOSEPH: We're friends now, right?

PABLO: God help me!

JOSEPH: You must admit you've gotten to know me a little—

PABLO: Yes I know you. I thought they took care of your kind for good.

JOSEPH: We? The Master Race, born to lead? You're wrong.

PABLO: No, I'm not wrong.

JOSEPH: Well, do you want to hear the second part of my deal, yes or no?

PABLO: Go on Superman.

JOSEPH: Better superman than a Red bum and a suicide too! This is what I propose…If you jump now and let me get to my meeting *(He looks at his watch again.)* I promise you—my word of honor—that I'll take care of your daughter.

PABLO: *(Tense.)* What do you mean by that?

JOSEPH: She has a charming little figure and sad, sad eyes…Once she recovers from this shock, *(He indicates the jump.)* I'll protect her.

PABLO: From whom?

JOSEPH: From the world. You know how things are. Would you rather have her fall into the hands of some pimp? Isn't it better with somebody you know?

PABLO: *(Incredulous.)* Are you telling me…?

JOSEPH: She'll have a better start with a respectable man like me.

PABLO: You're a worm.

JOSEPH: Let's be reasonable. Try to be calm and objective. Not a Latin father. Surely you must face the fact that the man who will screw her up good not only exists but is waiting for her.

PABLO: Bastard!

JOSEPH: *(Ignoring him.)* She'll be better off with someone like me. At least you know me and…maybe admire me…

(PABLO spits.)

JOSEPH: Did you see? It dissolved halfway down. You won't dissolve halfway down. Would you prefer that?

PABLO: *(With determination.)* I'll sue you! You're a disgrace to the police, to America, to the white race! You're the most sadistic bastard alive! I'll tell them what you really are! *(He is now determined to have JOSEPH denounced; he has forgotten about his suicide and prepares to descend.)*

JOSEPH: *(Worried.)* But I was being friendly...What I told you is very confidential...

PABLO: As long as there are people like you around, no one is safe! It's true, only a coward gives up and kills himself. We must defend ourselves with every weapon. And life—even my life—is a useful weapon.

(He descends and disappears. JOSEPH is alone now. His face is relaxed and relieved. He has become human now. He takes out a small walkie-talkie.)

JOSEPH: *(Into the walkie-talkie.)* It's all right. He's on his way down...He'll accuse me of everything and call me every name in the book. Promise him that we'll have a confrontation tomorrow morning...I'm too tired today...

(The LIEUTENANT reappears beside JOSEPH. He has the same type of walkie-talkie. Evidently, he has heard everything.)

LIEUTENANT: You're great, Joe! You're the most valuable man I have! You save them all!

JOSEPH: *(With sadness and frustration.)* All?

LIEUTENANT: *(Ignoring.)* Your performance was perfect. Precise and effective. You were in top form today. You'd have convinced a corpse.

JOSEPH: Did you hear everything?

LIEUTENANT: From beginning to end. *(Indicates his walkie-talkie.)*

JOSEPH: Did I seem sincere?

LIEUTENANT: Completely.

JOSEPH: On every point?

LIEUTENANT: On every point.

JOSEPH: *(Almost to himself.)* It no longer sounds like an act...

LIEUTENANT: Not at all!

JOSEPH: *(Bitterly.)* When one lies professionally, one learns to lie well.

LIEUTENANT: By the way, what made you say nine hundred thousand Indonesians? I heard that only three hundred thousand were killed.

JOSEPH: I read it in a British newspaper. They always tell the truth.

LIEUTENANT: *(After a brief pause.)* It's a delicate subject. I don't think you should have—

JOSEPH: *(Sarcastic.)* Any other complaints?

LIEUTENANT: Oh no! The essential thing is to save a life. Saving nine lives out of ten is an impressive record. You're the only one in this city who can do it. I must admit your method is infallible.

JOSEPH: No method is infallible.

LIEUTENANT: Are you still thinking of that poor old Jew?

JOSEPH: *(Nods.)* I shouldn't have made him believe I was a Nazi. It was a tragic mistake. I can still see his eyes...There was terror in them...He saw a real Nazi in me.

LIEUTENANT: He was very old and very tired. Too many months in that concentration camp. It was hopeless. Nobody could have saved him.

JOSEPH: *(Bitterly.)* Maybe I'm too convincing. If you preach hatred, it gets into your blood.

LIEUTENANT: But you saved their lives! That's what counts!

JOSEPH: Do you think I'm really becoming a Nazi?

LIEUTENANT: Nonsense! It's ridiculous!

JOSEPH: They believe me. They hate me.

LIEUTENANT: You've learned your role well. That's all. And you've put your heart and soul into your work. That's why you've succeeded. You'll be getting another medal, your ninth... *(He studies JOSEPH.)* And there'll be a tenth too, I'm sure...

JOSEPH: *(Slowly, almost to himself.)* I reminded him of his past—a terrifying past...He was frightened... *(To the LIEUTENANT.)* Is it really the past? Behind us forever?

LIEUTENANT: Forever.

JOSEPH: Then why was he so terrified? Why did he kill himself?

LIEUTENANT: Forget it, Joe. Don't poison your life with the memory of an old man who was doomed anyway. Think of the young people you've saved. Nine lives! Think of those nine families that are grateful to you! And now let's go down...

(A silence; JOSEPH is far away in his own thoughts.)

LIEUTENANT: Aren't you coming down?

JOSEPH: Just a few more minutes...The air is so pure up here...

LIEUTENANT: As you wish. *(He pats JOSEPH'S knee with understanding.)*

(THE LIEUTENANT descends, disappears. JOSEPH remains alone. He closes his eyes and takes in the quiet and pure air of that height.)

(SLOW BLACKOUT. THE END.)

Confessions

Characters:

CONFESSOR
PENITENT

Action:

All action takes place in a Catholic church in the present.

A Catholic church. Stage right: a pulpit. Stage left: a confessional. A young woman crosses herself and kneels down at the confessional.

CONFESSOR: Jesus Christ be praised.

PENITENT: May He always be praised.

CONFESSOR: How long is it since your last confession?

PENITENT: I don't remember exactly.

CONFESSOR: Months?

PENITENT: Several months.

CONFESSOR: Not even at Easter?

PENITENT: Not even at Easter. I'm sorry, Father. I felt for a while that confession was...unnecessary.

CONFESSOR: Sacraments are indispensable for salvation. Didn't you know?

PENITENT: More or less...

CONFESSOR: More or less?

PENITENT: I'm sorry, Father. I forgot that confession was a sacrament.

(Pause.)

CONFESSOR: Do you go to Mass on Sunday?

PENITENT: Yes.

CONFESSOR: Regularly?

PENITENT: Regularly.

CONFESSOR: But no confession for several months...Why have you waited so long?

PENITENT: I don't know.

CONFESSOR: How long exactly?

PENITENT: Since the beginning of last year, I think...

CONFESSOR: Do you have any crisis of a spiritual nature?

PENITENT: I'm human...I'm confused.

CONFESSOR: We all are. What have you to confess since...that last time! What sins have you committed?

PENITENT: I'm confused about the meaning of...what you call "sin."

CONFESSOR: We all know what sin is.

PENITENT: I don't know any longer.

CONFESSOR: Tell me about your doubts.

PENITENT: I'm too confused, Father. And I'm shy. Please, you ask me questions about...those "sins." Remind me.

CONFESSOR: *(Interested, careful.)* Do you say your prayers at night?

PENITENT: I do.

CONFESSOR: Have you ever doubted the existence of God?

PENITENT: I heard an ex-nun on television. She said: "If you haven't doubted the existence of God before you're twenty, you're either an idiot or a liar."

CONFESSOR: *(After a beat.)* The existence of Heaven and Hell?

PENITENT: Same answer.

CONFESSOR: Is this your opinion or… that TV person's opinion?

PENITENT: Mine.

CONFESSOR: What about the meaning of "Trinity"?

PENITENT: I don't know, Father. It's all so confusing.

CONFESSOR: Do you ever lie?

PENITENT: I prefer to tell the truth. I'm telling you the truth.

CONFESSOR: Acts of impatience, intemperance?

PENITENT: No. I'm very patient. Too patient.

CONFESSOR: You seem upset…What have you done wrong? Why have you waited so long?

PENITENT: I don't know, Father, I really don't.

CONFESSOR: Have you committed sins in speaking?

PENITENT: What do you mean?

CONFESSOR: Imprecations?

PENITENT: No.

CONFESSOR: Gossiping about other people's affairs?

PENITENT: No.

CONFESSOR: Any…white lie?

PENITENT: Not to my knowledge.

CONFESSOR: Have you taken communion?

PENITENT: You know I couldn't.

CONFESSOR: Do you have…amusements that are not normal, permissible?

PENITENT: In what sense?

CONFESSOR: Forbidden shows…

PENITENT: I just see what happens to be around. It's all right, I guess. Normal.

CONFESSOR: Do you read indecent books?

PENITENT: No.

CONFESSOR: Do you read any good Christian educational books?

PENITENT: I read very little.

CONFESSOR: Bad words?

PENITENT: No.

CONFESSOR: Blasphemy?

PENITENT: No.

CONFESSOR: Do you say a few prayers, morning and evening?

PENITENT: A few. And then I cross myself. And then I fall asleep.

CONFESSOR: Do you get along with friends, people?

PENITENT: I think so. I like being with people…

CONFESSOR: Do you work?

PENITENT: I do.

CONFESSOR: What kind of work?

PENITENT: An office. Nine to five.

CONFESSOR: *(Careful, deliberate.)* You're lucky you have a job…

PENITENT: I count my blessings.

CONFESSOR: Do you feel that you work with...sufficient diligence and commitment?

PENITENT: I do, Father.

CONFESSOR: Have you ever...taken anything from your office? Pencils, envelopes...things?

PENITENT: No, Father.

(A brief silence.)

CONFESSOR: Your coworkers...do you like them?

PENITENT: I do.

CONFESSOR: Anyone bothering you with...compliments or..."advances"? "passes"?

PENITENT: No.

CONFESSOR: What kind of people are they?

PENITENT: Good people. Jewish.

CONFESSOR: *(Surprised, careful.)* Jewish...Do you think you're confused and upset because you're among Jews?

PENITENT: No, Father. They're all right.

CONFESSOR: *(Careful, deliberate.)* They're all right, you say...Yet they're different from us...Subconsciously, that could create confusion in a devout Christian...

PENITENT: Not at all, Father. They're OK.

CONFESSOR: ...They often mention that our Lord is...one of them.

PENITENT: Jesus was born where they come from. Isn't that true?

CONFESSOR: *(Avoiding.)* Are they trying to convert you?

PENITENT: *(Slightly amused.)* They never talk religion, never.

CONFESSOR: *(Deliberate.)* They usually don't...They're very clever...They are the only ones who deny our Lord's divinity.

PENITENT: Never a mention. Not even once.

CONFESSOR: What about politics?

PENITENT: What about politics?

CONFESSOR: Jews are usually...liberal, progressive, revolutionary...They want to change the world.

PENITENT: Maybe they should. *We* should.

CONFESSOR: You see? You already feel you should rebel and change things! They're influencing you, poisoning you. That's why you're confused, upset.

PENITENT: *(Eager to change the subject.)* Father, my problem is another one.

CONFESSOR: *(More sympathetic.)* What's your problem, child?

PENITENT: *(Shyly.)* I'm still young...I'm alive...My senses...

CONFESSOR: Devote your energies to your work and to prayers. Leave your senses alone.

PENITENT: Senses do exist. Our Lord has put feelings in us.

CONFESSOR: Good feelings.

PENITENT: *(Ignoring.)* You can't condemn a person who's still young and vital to a life of continuous self-repression, constant mortification of the senses, and...humiliation.

CONFESSOR: Look, my child, you're adopting a mistaken attitude due to bitterness and resentment.

PENITENT: There's no bitterness in me.

CONFESSOR: Weigh your situation carefully, examine your will power, your

Confessions

ability to dominate those...damnable stimuli.

PENITENT: When I try to control myself, the strain is too much and I feel...neurotic.

CONFESSOR: You must repress nature, my child.

PENITENT: Nature is life; you can't repress life. Our Lord put those physiological needs in our bodies. Your body too. You should understand.

CONFESSOR: *(Ignoring.)* Do you have...nervous outbursts?

PENITENT: At times.

CONFESSOR: How old are you?

PENITENT: Twenty-eight.

CONFESSOR: Twenty-eight...a mature woman...You're sensual, I understand...

PENITENT: Thank you.

CONFESSOR: Do you...often have repressed desires?

PENITENT: I do, Father.

CONFESSOR: Have you...committed impure acts?

PENITENT: Why do you consider those things "impure acts"?

CONFESSOR: "Those things" are acts against nature.

PENITENT: What do you mean by "acts against nature"? We're human. We're part of nature. Everything we do...

CONFESSOR: *(Interrupting.)* You know what I mean, child.

PENITENT: Stop calling me child.

CONFESSOR: I'll call you...sister...You're my sister, in a way...We're brother and sister...You may speak to me quite frankly...We hear everything. Just this morning a lady of fifty was very upset—telling me about an erotic relationship with a sixteen-year-old youngster, the son of her best friend...

PENITENT: Lucky boy.

CONFESSOR: Why "lucky"?

PENITENT: His chance to...be human. To start so early, living and learning.

CONFESSOR: *(Ignoring.)* She told me everything. We discussed it—both of us blushing...We had to. Her guilt, my need to know, so that I could understand and absolve...

PENITENT: Did you?

CONFESSOR: She repented, she promised never to tempt him again...She's now happy and relieved. You will be too, sister, after we...Tell me...Do you have repressed desires that torment you?

PENITENT: They torment me.

CONFESSOR: What do you do about them?

PENITENT: I try to control myself, at times...

CONFESSOR: "At times"?

PENITENT: Most of the time.

(There's a brief silence.)

CONFESSOR: *(Careful.)* Tell me...What do you do when...? I'm human too. I'm a sinner too. You can tell me.

PENITENT: *(Reluctant.)* I...do things.

CONFESSOR: Do you seek pleasure by yourself?

PENITENT: Yes.

CONFESSOR: How?

PENITENT: The way people do in such cases.

CONFESSOR: With caresses?

PENITENT: Yes.

CONFESSOR: ...What is it that you do—exactly?

PENITENT: I told you...caresses.

CONFESSOR: When do you do it? In the evening? In bed? In the spring? After reading indecent books or seeing immoral films?

PENITENT: When I feel alone.

CONFESSOR: Do you bring about sexual excitement by using your imagination or...other things too?

PENITENT: Other things too.

CONFESSOR: Touching your sex with...fingers?

PENITENT: Yes.

CONFESSOR: Mirrors?

PENITENT: Father...Must I...?

CONFESSOR: You can tell me. We priests...we're under a similar strain. We know, we understand...I imagine you take a bath and see your naked body reflected in a mirror, you feel the burden of not being able to give love to that body and...

PENITENT: At times.

CONFESSOR: And you must feel very excited and a desire to arrive at...How do you call that final moment? When...the earth moves?

PENITENT: What earth? What are you talking about?

CONFESSOR: There are different names for that...moment. Release, climax, orgasm. Do you reach it?

PENITENT: I do.

CONFESSOR: Does it happen the way I described? Bath, naked body, mirror...

PENITENT: More or less.

CONFESSOR: "More"...do you use gadgets?

PENITENT: What do you mean?

CONFESSOR: With your hand is a more natural thing...On the contrary, if you use gadgets that one sees advertised nowadays, one arrives at true sadism, which is horror to our Lord's eyes. Do you understand, my child?

PENITENT: I never used anything I ever saw advertised anywhere.

CONFESSOR: Good. Those are the devil's instruments. If you have ever sought pleasure, orgasm, with artificial objects pushed into your...thing, your vagina, then your sin is much more serious...

PENITENT: Don't worry about that.

CONFESSOR: And there is danger of serious physical consequences. Those...objects are dangerous to your health. A woman's womb is a very delicate thing. Our Lord has provided us with powerful biological principles for defense against bacteria, but with a foreign body, such an intrusion, you're in danger...

PENITENT: I never did anything of the sort. I never even thought of it.

CONFESSOR: I'm happy to hear that. That's saintly. I mean..."human," within human limits...We are all human...We are all sinners.

(A brief pause.)

CONFESSOR: Temptation is everywhere...For everybody...One sees beautiful women, beautiful bodies...Do you have a girlfriend?

PENITENT: *(Slightly puzzled.)* Yes...

CONFESSOR: How long have you known her?

PENITENT: From college...Years ago.

CONFESSOR: A particular friend?

PENITENT: Yes. I think so. A long friendship.

CONFESSOR: Do you ever discuss these things with her?

PENITENT: What things?

CONFESSOR: Sin.

PENITENT: I don't think we ever mentioned the word "sin." Not even once.

CONFESSOR: Sex?

PENITENT: Of course. We talk about everything. Sex too, at times.

CONFESSOR: Intimate...details?

PENITENT: Less intimate than what we're discussing here, Father.

CONFESSOR: It's my duty. To know you better, to understand you...Do you discuss your...desires?

PENITENT: We talk mostly about...ideas, thoughts, dreams.

CONFESSOR: What kind of dreams?

PENITENT: We all have dreams. You too, I hope.

CONFESSOR: Have you ever dreamt of sleeping with a woman?

PENITENT: ...I have. They say we all have those kind of dreams. Men and women. Is it a sin?

CONFESSOR: Have you ever been intimate with her?

PENITENT: What do you mean—exactly?

CONFESSOR: Have you ever taken a shower together?

PENITENT: We have.

CONFESSOR: Slept in the same bed?

PENITENT: We have.

CONFESSOR: ...Had a homosexual relationship?

PENITENT: *(Firm.)* No. Never!

CONFESSOR: *(Uneasy.)* I'm sorry if...I'm asking because you said you don't know what sin is...you're too shy to confess...I must therefore...

PENITENT: Your questions are unusual, Father. They are bizarre.

CONFESSOR: I know.

PENITENT: If you know, why do you ask?

CONFESSOR: You authorized me.

PENITENT: I did? When?

CONFESSOR: When you said: "I'm confused. You ask me questions. Please remind me." We have a checklist. I'm going through it.

PENITENT: I know that checklist. "THOU shalt not..." Ten times. You forgot to ask me one. No. I don't covet my neighbor's wife. I wouldn't know what to do with her.

CONFESSOR: No irony, please. Confession is a sacrament. May I proceed?

PENITENT: Why not? It's educational.

CONFESSOR: Humility, my child. We need humility when we approach the Church.

PENITENT: I'm sorry. I'm humble. Please do what must be done.

CONFESSOR: *(Very careful.)* I'm going to ask another..."bizarre" question, as you defined it. It's my duty...We must know...

PENITENT: I'm ready.

CONFESSOR: Did you ever do...those things with...?

PENITENT: *(Curious.)* With...?

CONFESSOR: ...Animals?

PENITENT: *No!*

CONFESSOR: Good! The subject is out of the way. Let's forget about it.

PENITENT: Where do you hear about such things?

CONFESSOR: In the confessional, unfortunately.

PENITENT: Look, Father. I'm a young woman. I am alive, I have strong desires. That's all. No crazy stuff. Just instinct. A healthy desire to love. I never heard about the things you're mentioning.

CONFESSOR: I have, unfortunately.

(A brief pause.)

CONFESSOR: You are a good woman. And your instincts are strong, by the look of things...You must repress them. They are too strong.

PENITENT: Only lately, since he is away.

CONFESSOR: *(Very surprised.)* HE?

PENITENT: He's been away six months.

CONFESSOR: I see...You have a husband...You know about those pleasures...It's more difficult. Where's he now?

PENITENT: I don't know. He works for the Government. They send him on special duties. For many months, at times.

CONFESSOR: He's serving our country...You must control yourself, make a sacrifice for him, for our Lord...

PENITENT: I'm trying.

CONFESSOR: You told me you haven't confessed for over a year...

PENITENT: Fifteen months.

CONFESSOR: Then we must also talk about him, your past with him...the last months...before he went away...Do you have children?

PENITENT: No.

CONFESSOR: How come?

PENITENT: We decided not to. Not now.

CONFESSOR: Saint Paul said in his letter to the Corinthians that... "It would be better for man not to touch woman..."—

PENITENT: That's what you priests decided. Not to touch women. We love each other. We touched each other.

CONFESSOR: Saint Paul added, "Sometimes it's better to marry than burn; and when you're married you should make children..."

PENITENT: I see...Well, Father. We're not saints. We make love. We're not ready to have children.

CONFESSOR: You risk losing the Grace of our Lord...

PENITENT: Why? When?

CONFESSOR: "Why," "when"...You see, you don't know...You may sin again if I don't tell you...For instance...if you douche or...if he withdraws...

PENITENT: I lose the Grace of God?

CONFESSOR: You're not supposed to do those things after...before...

PENITENT: After or before?

CONFESSOR: You know what I mean. After for you, before for him. Does he touch you with affection or...with lust?

PENITENT: *"Lust"?*

CONFESSOR: Our Holy Father mentioned it a few days ago. "Any man who looks at a woman with lust in his heart is a sinner. Even if it's the husband who..."

PENITENT: "Lusts."

CONFESSOR: Does he touch you with affection or...lasciviously?

PENITENT: With affection.

CONFESSOR: "Love play" for a long time?

PENITENT: For a long time. We love each other.

CONFESSOR: I suppose he caresses you...You caress him...

PENITENT: Come straight to the point. What do you want to know?

CONFESSOR: Some caresses are...forbidden.

PENITENT: Forbidden? How can a caress be a sin?

CONFESSOR: There are two thousand seven hundred fifty-three ways to sin...

PENITENT: And you studied them all?

CONFESSOR: A father must know how to protect his children, how to warn and save them. For instance, if a man puts his serpent into a woman's den without...

PENITENT: *(Interrupting.)* "Den"? You're talking to me as if I were a repulsive Hell. I'm just a woman and I don't want to hear about "serpents" and "dens"!

CONFESSOR: *(Calm and paternal.)* It was our language at the Seminary...You know what I mean. I'm just trying to point out that a few...caresses are permissible; others are not.

PENITENT: Don't make me a list, please. I don't want to know. My caresses are not hurting anyone, that's for sure, that's what counts!

CONFESSOR: The scattering of seed, for instance...

PENITENT: All right, Father. Let's hear about the scattering.

CONFESSOR: It's homosexual.

PENITENT: *(Surprised.)* It's what? I must hear this. It's new to me.

CONFESSOR: Many things seem new and unclear, my child. They are not.

PENITENT: Please make it clear for me. Why is that action...homosexual?

CONFESSOR: It's like saying what "they" say..."I want the chain to stop here. No children, no link to the future. I am the last one. I'll disperse my seed. I'll accept your seed and let it die in me." "I am the last one..." they say. Do you want to be the last one?

PENITENT: When you say "they," whom do you mean?

CONFESSOR: Homosexuals.

PENITENT: I just thought. It applies to priests too. You all decided to break the chain, to be the "last one." Didn't you? No family, no children, no link to the future...Are you afraid of the future, like "them"?

CONFESSOR: My mission is to save souls...and to remind you of the duty to procreate. A moral religious duty...

PENITENT: I will have a child, some day. Later.

CONFESSOR: Meanwhile...you do sinful things.

PENITENT: We did. When he was around.

CONFESSOR: When he was around... We're talking about that. But you must know. He'll be back soon and...

PENITENT: I hope so.

CONFESSOR: When he was around...I hope he didn't behave in a bestial way...I hope he didn't force you to do filthy things.

PENITENT: Nothing I ever considered "filthy."

CONFESSOR: I hope so, I hope so...I trust your judgment, your wisdom...Nothing "indecent"?

PENITENT: Nothing indecent.

CONFESSOR: That's good...Some couples, for instance, use mirrors...

PENITENT: We don't need mirrors.

CONFESSOR: It would be sinful...Other couples observe each other in the bathtub...

PENITENT: *(Vaguely ironical.)* Really?

CONFESSOR: "Modesty powder"...scattered in the bath water, to cloud its transparency; that would be wise.

PENITENT: I never heard of "modesty powder." Where do you buy it?

CONFESSOR: At Bendel's. Fourth floor.

PENITENT: Thank you.

CONFESSOR: *(Timidly, hesitant.)* ...To avoid children, some husbands use sadistic methods...

PENITENT: Sadistic?

CONFESSOR: Does he turn you over?

PENITENT: What do you want to know?

CONFESSOR: Nothing, my good woman...I want to help you...To give you absolution, I must know what...It's harder for a confessor, I assure you.

PENITENT: *(Ironically.)* I can see it's very hard on you.

CONFESSOR: Does he do it in your...vagina or in the back part?

(Silence.)

CONFESSOR: Where?

PENITENT: ...Somewhere else.

CONFESSOR: "Somewhere else"...I think I know what you mean...You touch him with everything...With your mouth, too?

PENITENT: Father!

CONFESSOR: Yes, my darling...

PENITENT: I have not come here to...satisfy your curiosity!

CONFESSOR: My dear woman, you're being...unfriendly. You're sinning again, this very moment.

PENITENT: I am sinning? What kind of sin, this time?

CONFESSOR: The same sin I'm trying to uproot from your soul. A sin that is obsessing and possessing you. The sin of the flesh.

PENITENT: I don't want to talk about...positions. And you say I'm the one obsessed with sex!

CONFESSOR: We were talking about "unfriendliness." The Holy Father Pope John Paul II has said it clearly—"The sins of the flesh are not only fornication, impurity, licentiousness, orgies, looking at a woman with lust—even if she is your wife—but also..."

PENITENT: But also?

CONFESSOR: I'm trying to remember the correct order, what our Holy Father said, exactly...also "discord, jealousy, dissent, divisions, factionalism, and unfriendliness."

PENITENT: I see...That's my destiny. Being a sinner everywhere. Even in a confessional!

CONFESSOR: Don't feel discouraged, my good woman. We are all sinners...all the time.

PENITENT: I sense...humility. Are you including yourself?

CONFESSOR: Maybe...

PENITENT: That's consoling!

CONFESSOR: I want to help...It's my only joy in life...When I was asking how, where...I was only trying to find out if there's dispersion of seed...a sin that makes the angels blush...

PENITENT: I was blushing too, Father, when you asked about those intimate details. What we do is our business! As long as we don't hurt anyone!

CONFESSOR: You're hurting the purity of your soul. That's why I'm asking, that's why I must know...I'm trying to find out how serious your sins are...I care about you...The pill, for instance...If you take it you're piling sin upon sin.

PENITENT: I'm not taking it.

CONFESSOR: Good. You must avoid all deviations...Some women allow men to drag them through mud...After those humiliations, a woman goes away... diminished.

PENITENT: "Diminished"?

CONFESSOR: Used. Flesh of his flesh. A slave to his lust. I want to find out—for your own benefit—if you're his accomplice.

PENITENT: Another accusation, another sin.

CONFESSOR: It's not an accusation. I just want to know if you...experiment.

PENITENT: "Experiment"?

CONFESSOR: Our Lord has not give us...genitalia for sexual experimentation. There is no need for that sort of thing. We're here to give Christian legitimacy to the sexual act, to procreation...If you explain a little bit what you do, I can tell you if you're an accomplice.

PENITENT: We love each other. We do everything.

CONFESSOR: It's a sinful relationship, then.

PENITENT: What can be sinful in love? Nothing!

CONFESSOR: Everything. And you know it. You instinctively know what's wrong. That's why you have come here.

PENITENT: Oh, really?

CONFESSOR: That's why you shun from revealing yourself. You know it's wrong what you both do, you want to protect him...You don't want to know the truth. That's why you don't tell me if his kisses are emotional or sadistic. You don't want to tell me if he exposes you to his lust, if he paws your body...

PENITENT: *(Exploding.)* Do you want to know why I've come here? Not because I want to be "pawed" by you—spiritually! It's because I felt lonely!

CONFESSOR: *(Hurt.)* We all feel lonely. We all...

PENITENT: *(Interrupting.)* Some women go to a bar, pick up a man, and talk! I don't drink, I don't like bars. I don't pick up men! Is that wrong?

CONFESSOR: It is not.

PENITENT: Other women go to psychoanalysts. I can't afford those bastards. They charge an arm and a leg—just to listen. You, at least, you talk.

CONFESSOR: Thank you. I care.

PENITENT: I was told you care. That's why I came here.

CONFESSOR: Who...who told you?

PENITENT: Someone who knows you well.

CONFESSOR: *(Alarmed.)* What do you mean? I don't know anyone...well.

PENITENT: That's my problem too. I don't know anyone "well."

CONFESSOR: My dear woman, you're implying absurdities...You're sinning again.

PENITENT: What kind of sin this time? Unfriendliness? Refusal to say it all, the way you want to hear it?

CONFESSOR: Arrogance...Discord... You're implying I have an intimate friend.

PENITENT: I only said "Someone who knows you well." You jumped to conclusions.

CONFESSOR: Who is this person?

PENITENT: My best friend. She comes to you every week. She told me about you. She made me curious.

CONFESSOR: A penitent.

PENITENT: Of course. She comes here every Thursday evening. The last one you take. She told me you care. You give more time to the last one. Because you like to talk. Because you're lonely.

CONFESSOR: She told you that?

PENITENT: She did.

CONFESSOR: A very sensitive woman. I'm happy she's your friend. Is she all right?

PENITENT: She is.

CONFESSOR: I haven't seen her...these last two weeks...

PENITENT: She's busy.

CONFESSOR: "Busy"...doing what?

PENITENT: She's with a man.

CONFESSOR: What do you mean... "with"?

PENITENT: You know what I mean. She's living with a man.

CONFESSOR: Oh my God! I warned her!

PENITENT: She told me. She told me everything.

CONFESSOR: He's the wrong man, the wrong relationship!

PENITENT: She loved someone else. He rejected her.

CONFESSOR: I told her to be patient, to think it over.

PENITENT: While YOU were thinking it over...

CONFESSOR: She told you that, too?

PENITENT: Everything. She's my best friend.

CONFESSOR: Talk to her, then...Make her understand...

PENITENT: What?

CONFESSOR: The mistake...The horror of living in sin!

PENITENT: I met him. He's all right.

CONFESSOR: What do you mean? Why doesn't he marry her then?

PENITENT: He can't...She won't.

CONFESSOR: "She won't"? Why?

PENITENT: You know why. She is in love with someone else. She still hopes.

CONFESSOR: There's no hope, tell her!

PENITENT: I can't. I don't want to hurt her. Hope heals wounds.

CONFESSOR: False hope? No hope at all? Please tell her!

PENITENT: Father, she has been talking about you for months. She loves your voice, the things you say, how you say them. She loves you.

CONFESSOR: It's ridiculous! Absurd! She misunderstood my words, my caring about her! I'm like this with everyone! Sometimes...fatherly, sometimes...friendly. I'm human, it's my mission, and I like it!

PENITENT: You're human...You're lonely...You need tenderness. She'll make you happy.

CONFESSOR: Let's change the subject, please! We were talking about your...

PENITENT: One seldom finds a woman like Grace. It's the chance of a lifetime. She adores you. Don't lose her!

CONFESSOR: I'm a priest! I could never be a good husband, a good father!

PENITENT: You're dying to have a child. Grace sensed it. I felt it too, today, when you were calling me "child," when you mentioned a "link to the future, to eternity."

CONFESSOR: I have the Church. She's my mother, my bride. She's everything to me. I could never leave the Church.

PENITENT: Many have. They're good husbands and fathers, now.

CONFESSOR: I could never dedicate my whole life to one woman, just one woman.

PENITENT: You mean, you need more than one woman?

CONFESSOR: I want to save one thousand, one million souls. One is not enough. I don't know how to love one person. I'm afraid to love...

PENITENT: Those who are afraid to love are always the best lovers.

CONFESSOR: Who told you that?

PENITENT: They care. They try their best to make a woman happy.

(A silence.)

CONFESSOR: Did she send you?

PENITENT: No...I was just curious...

CONFESSOR: You're sinning over and over again. Confession is a sacrament. You're desecrating it.

PENITENT: Is it a sin to tell the truth?

CONFESSOR: It is not.

PENITENT: To help a friend?

CONFESSOR: It is not.

PENITENT: To help a priest?

CONFESSOR: To help a priest leave Mother Church? That's a mortal sin! Unforgivable!

PENITENT: "Unforgivable"...My instinct tells me to do "unforgivable" things...

CONFESSOR: Instinct betrays.

PENITENT: Honestly, Father, I cannot tell any longer what's right and what's wrong. I was trying...

CONFESSOR: There is no clear division. That's why I must know about you...

PENITENT: And what about Grace? Don't you want to know how she feels? She loves you and—

CONFESSOR: Please, don't mention that name again. Don't be cruel...Let's talk about you. Do you ever take the initiative?

PENITENT: Is that a sin, too? She did. With you. She's being punished for it.

CONFESSOR: *(Ignoring.)* That's what I meant before when I mentioned the word "accomplice." A woman must not take the initiative. You must act passively when he's trying to avoid procreation.

PENITENT: She's thinking about you.

CONFESSOR: *(Ignoring.)* If you lend yourself as if you were an instrument of his lust, you're not sinning.

PENITENT: A "passive instrument." I'm sure Grace is being passive.

CONFESSOR: *(Ignoring.)* You mustn't get pleasure out of it. When he married you, he got absolute rights on your body. You cannot deny yourself. But if you show yourself to be a passive slave, your husband is responsible. He's the sinner.

PENITENT: *(After hesitation.)* Father...you mentioned the word "husband." I didn't.

CONFESSOR: *(Surprised, alarmed.)* What do you mean?

PENITENT: I met him four years ago. We fell in love. When he's in town, we live together.

CONFESSOR: In a complete and total way?

PENITENT: Total.

CONFESSOR: Is he married?

PENITENT: He's separated from his wife.

CONFESSOR: And you...Do you realize? Think of his poor wife.

PENITENT: She no longer exists in his life. She has another family. What counts is that we love each other.

CONFESSOR: You're no longer in God's grace...*(He stops short, regretting the word he has just used.)*

PENITENT: "Grace"...She told me you like names like "Grace" and "Mary." They have a very religious connotation...

CONFESSOR: You're playing with fire... Should you die, you would be banished to the flames of Hell.

PENITENT: I'm already in Hell, Father.

CONFESSOR: You're on hot coals and trying to ignore it. You're lying to yourself.

PENITENT: Many people lie to themselves. They are afraid to face reality. My name is Mary. What's yours?

CONFESSOR: *(Ignoring.)* You and that woman...

PENITENT: *(Interrupting.)* Grace.

CONFESSOR: ...You're transgressing the word of the Gospel.

PENITENT: If the moralists had ever loved, they wouldn't have written so many restrictions on morality.

CONFESSOR: Practicing abstinence makes you holy.

PENITENT: I don't want to be holy, I prefer being human. Like Grace.

CONFESSOR: *(Ignoring.)* Chastity brings balance.

PENITENT: Unbalance, to me.

CONFESSOR: Unbalance, now. It's our Lord's punishment for those who begin a relationship in sin...

PENITENT: My doctor practically ordered me to.

CONFESSOR: You went to a doctor, to ask...?

PENITENT: I did.

CONFESSOR: And he told you...?

PENITENT: That I needed a man, to keep my sanity.

CONFESSOR: Some doctor! What's happening to the world?

PENITENT: It's growing up. Grace loves you. She took the initiative and told you. What's wrong with that? Don't you like honesty?

CONFESSOR: Honesty is something else…

PENITENT: What else? She begged you for months. She warned you for weeks. You practically forced her to go with someone else. Second best.

CONFESSOR: Please, don't mention that…thing any longer!

PENITENT: You kill a great love and call it a "thing"!

CONFESSOR: *(With some hope.)* Did she really…?

PENITENT: I never lie.

CONFESSOR: I thought maybe…

PENITENT: I'm sorry, I never lie.

CONFESSOR: You women…you're so weak, so vulnerable…You make so many mistakes…

PENITENT: It's to *avoid* mistakes that the doctor suggested I should go to bed with him.

CONFESSOR: I don't understand. What do you mean?

PENITENT: …Some men are selfish. It's better to find out before…

CONFESSOR: *(Losing his patience.)* "Before"? How many men, before you find the satisfying one? Do you know that most men—ninety percent—don't know how to give orgasms to women?

PENITENT: I'm surprised *you* know…

CONFESSOR: We learn everything, here.

PENITENT: Maybe that's why you're afraid…

CONFESSOR: *(Angry.)* Answer me! How many men, "before"?

PENITENT: I was lucky. My man is all right.

CONFESSOR: Before finding the "all right one," did you have intimate actions with other persons?

PENITENT: No. Would that be better?

CONFESSOR: My child, we need humility in life…You're being arrogant, again…

PENITENT: Forgive me, Father.

(A brief silence.)

CONFESSOR: That first time with him… did you feel guilty?

PENITENT: I was too happy to feel guilty.

CONFESSOR: How many times did you sin, that first evening?

PENITENT: It was an afternoon. Grace too…

CONFESSOR: How many times?

PENITENT: I didn't count them.

CONFESSOR: I'm only asking because confession requires…

PENITENT: I'll start counting when he comes back. And don't worry about Grace's friend. He's no athlete, like mine. He's a weak man, a weak soul.

CONFESSOR: My child, *your* soul is in danger…You're persistent in your sinning. I don't see any sign of repentance.

PENITENT: Father, I have come here for three reasons…

CONFESSOR: Tell me.

PENITENT: To try helping a friend of mine…and you. To confess and feel better…To have your blessing, your absolution…

CONFESSOR: You must first repent and promise not to do it again.

PENITENT: What I did with him or what I'm doing to myself?

CONFESSOR: You must promise not to see him again.

PENITENT: Is it less serious to satisfy oneself alone than to have relations with a man?

CONFESSOR: *(After a brief hesitation.)* Yes, it is less grave, although it is against nature...

PENITENT: Another confessor told me it's better to do it with a man, if you really love him.

CONFESSOR: That confessor was wrong.

PENITENT: When will you get together and agree?

CONFESSOR: My child, I'm trying to help you...Is this man you love so much a relative?

PENITENT: No.

CONFESSOR: Are you a relative of his wife?

PENITENT: No.

CONFESSOR: You see? I'm trying to understand and forgive...It's not easy to sit in a confessional...You must help me...Say at least that you will try...

PENITENT: I never lie, Father.

CONFESSOR: If you want absolution you must...

PENITENT: Lie?

CONFESSOR: No...Just make a little effort...Promise at least, that you will try...

PENITENT: I'm sorry, I can't promise.

CONFESSOR: I like you, my daughter...I called you "daughter." Maybe you were right when you said...

PENITENT: Grace told me. She felt you're dying to have a child.

CONFESSOR: I would like a daughter like you...maybe.

PENITENT: A "sinner" like me?

CONFESSOR: Someone so...open, sincere, determined...

PENITENT: Grace is like me. She adores you.

CONFESSOR: Grace is dead, now, for me...

PENITENT: You know she is alive, waiting for you. *(Handing him a piece of paper.)* This is her new address. Five blocks from here. Her...friend works at City Hall. Nine to five. *(Ready to go.)* Can I have my absolution now?

CONFESSOR: If you pray for...

PENITENT: I'll pray. May I have my absolution, please?

CONFESSOR: Maybe...

PENITENT: Even if I don't promise anything?

CONFESSOR: Just tell me that you believe in your love and that you will never harm anyone.

PENITENT: That I can promise.

CONFESSOR: I understand you...We obtain our teaching from the word of Christ...We understand love...

PENITENT: Thank you, Father...I understand you, I like you now...Before, I didn't feel in you the humility of a servant of God...

CONFESSOR: I'm like you, daughter...We both forgot that word...humility...Maybe we're offending our Lord...

PENITENT: We're not. He's infinite Goodness.

CONFESSOR: *(He looks at her with admiration.)* For penance, say three "Our Fathers," four "Hail Marys," seven "Glorias" to Jesus...and the "Act of Contrition"... *(He blesses her.)*

PENITENT: Thank you, Father. He works from nine to five. She's waiting for you.

(He looks at the paper she gave him and caresses it gently. She exits, after crossing herself.)

CONFESSOR: *(Looking heavenwards.)* Forgive my arrogance, my curiosity, my intolerance, my lack of humility...I'm human, too...I'm a sinner, too...Mea culpa, mea culpa, mea maxima culpa...

(He looks at the paper with Grace's address. After hesitation, he starts to tear it, partially. It can still be read. SPOTLIGHT on the paper. He is thinking. Maybe he is going to visit her.)

(BLACKOUT. CURTAIN.)

Note:

Sometimes there is an Act Two—mostly ad lib—when the actor has good knowledge of religion and can face an audience, explaining his behavior and doubts. Some surprises. Very polemic. See the play *Ambush* (Samuel French, 2008) for useful information about how priests justify everything.

The Coffin

The Characters:

SANGUEMARCIO
PAUL
THE THIEF
THE PARRICIDE
THE SEDUCED
THE MODEL
THE OLD WOMAN (WIFE)

The time is the present; in Italy; the 1960s. The scene: A bedroom. The headboard of the bed is at stage left. Plainly visible underneath it is a coffin. At the foot of the bed, one part of the room is isolated by curtains: only the side facing SANGUEMARCIO is open. In the course of the action, the profile of THE MODEL will be visible to the audience through these curtains. SANGUEMARCIO, an irascible old man, is lying motionless in bed. THE OLD WOMAN enters from the only door, which is upstage left. She is dressed in black and has a hard impenetrable face. She escorts into the room: PAUL, an intelligent-looking student, two of his male friends, and a girl.

SANGUEMARCIO: *(Without moving.)* Welcome!

PAUL: Hi! How are you today?

SANGUEMARCIO: Fine! I haven't *moved*. I'm letting my blood circulate.

(He signals THE OLD WOMAN to leave. Then he asks PAUL, with a movement of his head, to identify the three visitors.)

PAUL: Let me introduce my friends. *(He points to each in turn.)* The Thief...The Parricide...The Victim. She was seduced...

(The three smile.)

SANGUEMARCIO: Fine! Do they know?

PAUL: Everything.

SANGUEMARCIO: Make yourselves comfortable.

(They sit in chairs at the foot of the bed.)

SANGUEMARCIO: *(Addressing the victim.)* What's new in the world? Paul told you, I never go outside.

SEDUCED: *(After suppressing her embarrassment at being singled out first.)* Our new Pope seems rather progressive. They say he is inclined to allow divorce in Italy. So much the better for unmarried women like me!

SANGUEMARCIO: A typically feminine point of view; characteristic of your own condition. *(Turning to PAUL.)* What else?

PAUL: All you read about these days is that the cold war is over. Good. We'll finally enjoy peace and serenity.

THIEF: Not to us. People are starting to have faith again. They're traveling more, spending more. That's bad for us because less money is kept in the house.

(SANGUEMARCIO turns to THE PARRICIDE to ask for his opinion.)

PARRICIDE: Me? I had only one father. If I had it to do over again, I'd still do it. I would kill him.

SEDUCED: *(Invited to express her opinion on the cold war.)* Cold war or not, it's all the same to me. I'm alone.

PAUL: The important thing is that we'll all die in bed.

THIEF: *(Facetiously, alluding to THE SEDUCED.)* She will, anyway. That's for sure.

(The smile disappears from THE THIEF's lips as he notices that PAUL is staring at SANGUEMARCIO with alarm. He fears he has made a faux pas.)

PAUL: *(To SANGUEMARCIO, excusing himself.)* Forgive me. What I meant is *we* won't die in war. I shouldn't have mentioned dying in bed to you.

SANGUEMARCIO: Why? To me you can. I'll die if I get out of bed.

PAUL: Good thinking...

(They all laugh.)

SANGUEMARCIO: Why are you laughing?

(They stop immediately.)

THIEF: No reason.

(The three gesture vaguely.)

SANGUEMARCIO: *(Indicating PAUL with a nod of his head.)* What has he told you?

(THE THIEF glances at PAUL, asking permission to speak. PAUL gives his consent.)

THIEF: That you're sick. You never get out of bed.

PARRICIDE: He said that you're afraid to move.

SEDUCED: He said your mother—all your relatives in fact—died after an operation.

SANGUEMARCIO: A blood clot. We have rotten blood. My grandfather—I think it was my great-grandfather, I can't remember...he wouldn't spend the money for a doctor. He infected himself. V.D. Rotten blood—all of us—from way back. After an operation, a blood clot forms. This clot can prevent the blood from flowing...from warming the heart, the hands, from nourishing the brain. They told my grandmother she could get up after nine days. She died after two steps. They told my mother she could get up after a month. She got as far as the door, and turned around to smile at us. She died with that smile on her lips. As for me, I had my operation months ago. A hernia. If you were in my shoes—cursed with such a past—would you risk getting out of bed?

ALL: *(In a chorus, agreeing with him.)* —Certainly not! You're right! Never! I agree!

SANGUEMARCIO: I am afraid...But I still love life... *(With rapture.)* The rustling of a gown, two large innocent eyes, the perfume of a woman's hair, the warmth of a handshake, the noises of the streets, the faces of people, the grimace on the face of the losers, the offer of a whore, the smile that turns to hate when you ask her if she is healthy, the insult you receive when you ask her to prove it. I didn't want to give up the pleasures of the world...Paul helps me by bringing here protagonists of life, people like you. Every type there, at the foot of this bed, those who have lived and suffered and hated the most... *(Counting them on his fingers.)* The Hero, the Coward, the Madman, the Pederast, the Prostitute, the Religious Fanatic...I know all there is to know about life—thanks to Paul... *(He glances at him gratefully.)* ...thanks to your confessions...

(He claps his hands and THE OLD WOMAN appears.)

SANGUEMARCIO: Bring in the drinks!

(THE OLD WOMAN leaves.)

SANGUEMARCIO: *(To THE THIEF.)* How old are you?

THIEF: Twenty-nine.

SANGUEMARCIO: When did you start?

THIEF: Very early. I don't remember the exact year. My mother used to lock everything. So I made a false key and stole fruit and cheese...

SANGUEMARCIO: That doesn't count. When did you steal the first time away from home?

(THE OLD WOMAN enters with glasses of wine. SANGUEMARCIO indicates that THE THIEF should wait before speaking.)

SEDUCED: *(Refusing to drink.)* Not for me.

SANGUEMARCIO: Why? Did your seducer make you drink?

SEDUCED: No.

SANGUEMARCIO: Then you knew what was happening. You wanted...

SEDUCED: Yes.

SANGUEMARCIO: You will tell us about it later. To good health!

(They drink. SANGUEMARCIO dismisses THE OLD WOMAN with a gesture. She leaves.)

SANGUEMARCIO: *(To THE THIEF.)* Tell us about your first theft.

THIEF: It was in a church. The priest posted me at the door with a plate to collect offerings. One man gave what looked like a fortune. Two gold coins. They seemed wasted there. I fought with myself. I'd never...In the end, I pocketed them.

SANGUEMARCIO: Did you confess in that same church?

THIEF: Yes.

SANGUEMARCIO: What did they say?

THIEF: Nothing. They didn't make a tragedy out of it in those days.

SANGUEMARCIO: Did you tell them the money was stolen from their plate.

THIEF: No. I mumbled something about "two gold coins"...Perhaps they didn't realize it was their money. Nowadays...

SANGUEMARCIO: Nowadays?

THIEF: They want to know the exact amount, and they won't give you absolution until you return the fruit of your labors to the one you took it from. Or else make an offering to the church for an amount not less than the sum you took.

SANGUEMARCIO: *(After a short pause, urging him to continue.)* Were there other thefts?

THIEF: Oh, here and there, in the army, at the marketplace. Sometimes only to show my friends I was quicker than the salesman.

SANGUEMARCIO: What was your biggest haul?

PAUL: That was why I asked him to come here. You may have read about it in the papers.

THIEF: *(To SANGUEMARCIO.)* Try to guess.

SANGUEMARCIO: I wouldn't know.

THIEF: What place would you choose?

SANGUEMARCIO: *(Slowly.)* A jewelry store, or a bank...

THIEF: You guessed it. The only place where a thief is more honest than the man who is robbed. *(Reciting with emphasis.)* "What is a pickpocket compared to a stockbroker? What is the robbery of a bank compared to the foundation of a bank?" The writer who said that is...

(He feels PAUL's gaze upon him and hesitates.)

THIEF: ...Is someone I shouldn't know, since I am a thief. I forgot...

PAUL: *(Interrupting.)* Brecht. A friend told you.

THIEF: Brecht. A friend told me. I chose an American bank.

SANGUEMARCIO: *(With interest.)* I heard about that. It was six or seven months ago. Tell me about it...Especially your frame of mind, your fears, the thoughts that went through your mind...

THIEF: There were two of us. Myself and a Frenchman. He is waiting for me in Paris. That's where we're going to split the cash. I had studied the layout. There's an apartment right above the bank. It's empty most of the year. The owner travels a lot. It was a cinch to get in.

SANGUEMARCIO: *(Itemizing the information he wants.)* Describe your frame of mind before going in, your fears of running into someone, your reflections. Did you take a drink before?

THIEF: Yes, but only to warm up. My fears of running into someone? No, as long as you're well dressed, and confident. When I go to the movies, I tell them: "Inspection," and walk right in. Self-confidence, that's the most important thing in life; assurance.

SANGUEMARCIO: What did you carry?

THIEF: Two suitcases and an umbrella.

SANGUEMARCIO: Why the umbrella?

THIEF: I'll tell you when the time comes. Everything went smoothly. We lost some time inspecting the place. Then we began drilling a hole...

SANGUEMARCIO: *(Deluded.)* They make holes everywhere these days.

THIEF: It's the safest way.

SANGUEMARCIO: But it's not as thrilling. People don't use guns; where is the adventure? Was the umbrella supposed to be a weapon of some kind?

THIEF: No, it was an ordinary umbrella. We hung it inside the hole, opened, to catch the rubbish and absorb the noise.

SANGUEMARCIO: Was that your idea or did you see it in the movies?

(THE THIEF solicits PAUL's approval.)

THIEF: *(Without conviction.)* It was our idea, our idea...

SANGUEMARCIO: *(Almost to himself.)* I went often to the movies before my operation. One can get all kinds of ideas...it's easier imitating them once you've seen them done by someone else. *(To THE SEDUCED.)* A girl like you, for instance, so young...I would have had scruples, fears...But in the movies, even younger girls than you have sex...It gives me courage... *(Turning again to THE THIEF.)* Go on.

THIEF: The hole took almost three hours. It was already daylight...

SANGUEMARCIO: Did your heart beat very hard?

THIEF: In the beginning. Once you get to work, you don't think about it anymore.

SANGUEMARCIO: What about your pulse?

THIEF: I tested that, once. It was over ninety.

SANGUEMARCIO: Mine goes up to a hundred and ten when I think I've made too quick a movement, or when I think about my cursed blood. Who climbed down the hole?

THIEF: My friend from Marseille. He is very slender.

SANGUEMARCIO: What did you think about while he did his job? Were you afraid he'd fall, make a noise, set off the alarm?

THIEF: No, we turned the alarm off with the foam of an extinguisher.

SANGUEMARCIO: *(With emphasis.)* That Frenchman, he's clever. Do you think he'll give you half of the money?

THIEF: I hope so. We're honest with each other.

SANGUEMARCIO: Describe your thoughts in detail. What were you thinking, feeling while he did the looting?

THIEF: How quick he'd be and how much he'd get.

SANGUEMARCIO: Were you afraid?

THIEF: No. It was a large comfortable apartment. I felt as if I were at home... *(Correcting himself.)* That is, I felt it was the way a home should be. I wasn't afraid.

SANGUEMARCIO: Nothing went wrong?

THIEF: *(Thoughtfully.)* Just one thing. He couldn't climb back up. He was too tired, and he hurt his hands.

SANGUEMARCIO: Where is he now?

THIEF: Paris.

SANGUEMARCIO: What are you waiting for?

THIEF: They won't give me a passport. Once—when I was unemployed—I went to Switzerland without one. They arrested me and now...no more rights...

SANGUEMARCIO: *(Considering the story finished.)* Do you want a drink?

(They nod. SANGUEMARCIO claps his hands. THE OLD WOMAN comes in with a tray of glasses which are filled. They drink in silence, staring curiously at THE OLD WOMAN, who doesn't bat an eyelid. SANGUEMARCIO makes a gesture and she leaves. They turn expectantly to THE PARRICIDE.)

PARRICIDE: *(Mechanically, as though repeating a lesson he has learned.)* During the period of suckling, even before realizing in rhythmic suction the erotic action of the oral zone, I experienced paternal hatred whenever I confronted him. Freud has said in "Dostoevsky and the Parricide" that the child looks upon the parent as a rival...

PAUL: *(Correcting him with promptitude.)* That's in "Three Contributions to the Sexual Theory"...

PARRICIDE: *(Confused, repeats.)* In "Three Contributions to the Sexual Theory"... that the child looks upon the parent as a rival. *(Resuming his story.)* He took my prolonged bed-wetting as a sexual desire for my mother and hated me. But the feeling was mutual. I hated him when he caressed my mother; I hated him when he struck her to prove his power, his..."ownership."

SANGUEMARCIO: *(Confused.)* Go back to the beginning, I don't understand. At what age were you *aware* of your hatred for him?

PARRICIDE: *(Uncertainly.)* Early... *(Controlling himself.)* Before adolescence, in the sexual period of infancy, before realizing in rhythmic suction the activity of the oral erogenous zone...

SANGUEMARCIO: *(Impatient with this pretentious language.)* Don't talk nonsense. You read those things later on, to justify your guilt, to understand what you had done.

(THE PARRICIDE glances at PAUL for his assistance.)

PARRICIDE: *(Agreeing.)* It's true, yes. I looked it up in Freud later, to understand.

SANGUEMARCIO: *(Suspiciously.)* How long ago did you kill him?

PARRICIDE: *(Uncertain.)* Two years ago, it's almost two years now.

SANGUEMARCIO: Show me your identity card.

(THE PARRICIDE takes out his wallet, ready to show the card, but PAUL prevents him.)

PAUL: I'm sorry. If we start this, you won't see anyone anymore. They agreed to make their confessions provided they wouldn't have to reveal their identity.

(The three nod in agreement.)

SANGUEMARCIO: *(Disappointed.)* Go on.

(After a pause, urged on by Paul, THE PARRICIDE continues in simpler terms.)

PARRICIDE: He denied me everything: food, new clothes, toys. He was constantly giving orders, the most ridiculous commands. He was a frightened, insignificant little man. He was given orders all his life from his bosses. He got even by making our life a hell.

SANGUEMARCIO: What kind of job did he have?

PARRICIDE: He did everything—which means nothing. The last job he had: a messenger.

SANGUEMARCIO: What kind of orders did he give?

PARRICIDE: *(Thinking hard.)* He made me weigh every piece of firewood we'd use in the stove. He made me count matches, nails... *(Again thinking.)* He made me look up difficult words in the dictionary and read him their meaning. Dozens of times over. So that I'd know their meaning, he said; in truth he wanted to learn them.

SANGUEMARCIO: Interesting...How did he treat your mother?

PARRICIDE: Like dirt! He wouldn't let her talk; then suddenly he'd get the urge to make love and I'd be pushed outside, in the courtyard.

SANGUEMARCIO: Some of the things you read in books are probably true. Who told you to read them? *(He looks at PAUL.)*

PARRICIDE: *(Confirming the fact.)* Paul did.

SANGUEMARCIO: *(Complacently.)* He'll make a brilliant lawyer. He reads everything. And he knows how to find what he needs. *(To THE PARRICIDE.)* What about you?

PARRICIDE: I kept silent. He had huge hands. He used to beat me until he saw blood. He ruined my lungs.

SANGUEMARCIO: When did you finally decide to kill him?

PARRICIDE: I'd been thinking about it for a long time. I chose Christmas Day.

SANGUEMARCIO: Why Christmas?

PARRICIDE: It gave me an excuse to offer him something to drink.

SANGUEMARCIO: Did your mother know about your plans?

PARRICIDE: I don't know, I still don't know.

SANGUEMARCIO: So, what happened?

PARRICIDE: I sold Christmas trees and made some money. I bought a bottle of wine and took it home. My mother watched me strangely while we sat waiting for him to come home. She stared at the bottle, then at me. I wanted to have dinner without him. My mother was terrified. I remember, she was so upset that she burned the dinner. He came back half-drunk; as I expected. I told him the wine was my gift; he patted me.

SANGUEMARCIO: A caress?

PARRICIDE: Almost a caress.

SANGUEMARCIO: Was it his first?

PARRICIDE: Maybe not. But it was the first time I felt some warmth from his hand. He was staggering. If it hadn't been for his insulting my mother again...

(A tense silence; they are waiting anxiously for the decisive moment.)

PARRICIDE: He invited me to join him in a drink. I pretended to...But my throat was locked, not a drop went down...He touched me, seized my hands, told me about his other women...Mama sat there, petrified. He trusted Mama. He knew she was good and faithful. It was his only claim to victory in an otherwise miserable existence: the loyalty of my mother. *(There is a lump in his throat as he relives the scene.)* The bottle was almost empty. I went to the door to get a breath of air. He followed me, latched onto me...He talked incessantly...I kept my eyes on the large moat that surrounded the house. The water glistened; there was half a meter of it. Suddenly, I freed myself and got away from him. I shouted: "Fool, bastard, cuckold" again and again, feverishly, hammering at his vanity. He followed me like an automaton, with his hands stretched out, ready to strangle me. I looked back for a glance from my mother. I saw her standing in the doorway, motionless. The moon was shining down on her pale face...I leaped over the moat; in following me, he fell in... *(With some repulsion.)* It was easy for me to get his head under water...I kept it down, counted to one hundred, two hundred...For an hour perhaps...or it seemed like an hour...That night my mother wanted me in her bed...She was shaking from head to foot...Her teeth shook with a metallic sound that made me think of my father's jaw—nailed down out there...under water and mud...

(There is a sigh of relief; the description has proved effective, vivid.)

SANGUEMARCIO: *(Enthralled, with an enthusiasm due to his excitement and emotional state.)* Bravo! I mean you told it well. I imagined myself there. What does your mother do now?

PARRICIDE: She has remained silent ever since. I often ask her if she remembers, if she understands why I did it. She runs her hand through my hair in silence. She trembles less in bed now.

(SANGUEMARCIO claps his hands, and THE OLD WOMAN comes in so promptly that one suspects she has been eavesdropping.)

SANGUEMARCIO: *(His hand on his heart.)* My medicine.

(THE OLD WOMAN carefully pours a few drops in a glass and hands it to him.)

SANGUEMARCIO: The bedpan.

(THE OLD WOMAN takes it from the bedside table and puts it under the covers.)

SANGUEMARCIO: You can go now.

(THE OLD WOMAN leaves. SANGUEMARCIO addresses THE SEDUCED.)

SANGUEMARCIO: You must forgive me. With this rotten blood of mine everything takes time...Forgive me...Now it's your turn.

SEDUCED: *(Conscious of their gaze, embarrassed.)* My story is like that of many girls. I haven't done anything special...

SANGUEMARCIO: Was he much older than you?

SEDUCED: Only by two years. He was in my class at school.

SANGUEMARCIO: A little behind?

SEDUCED: *(Surprised at his accuracy.)* Yes. By two years. He flunked.

SANGUEMARCIO: How long had you known him?

SEDUCED: Years. He lived in the same building.

SANGUEMARCIO: What I mean is, since how long had he been kissing you, necking with you?

SEDUCED: *(Embarrassed, timid.)* A few months.

SANGUEMARCIO: Had he tried previously, unequivocally, to...?

SEDUCED: Yes.

SANGUEMARCIO: Where?

SEDUCED: In several places.

SANGUEMARCIO: For instance?

SEDUCED: The first time, in a doorway. Then at a dance, at the house of friends, then again...Whenever he got a chance.

SANGUEMARCIO: And you?

SEDUCED: I tried to defend myself, I tried to resist.

SANGUEMARCIO: How? With your hands? Did you scratch his face?

SEDUCED: No. I defended myself with tears. Tears are effective. He respected me, he loved me all the more...

SANGUEMARCIO: When did you finally give in?

SEDUCED: In a field.

SANGUEMARCIO: How did it happen?

SEDUCED: A friend of mine had already...They were ahead of us. They stopped a few feet away. We could see them making love...

SANGUEMARCIO: Did you cry?

SEDUCED: A little.

SANGUEMARCIO: Tell me in detail—everything—what you felt...

SEDUCED: *(Timidly.)* You can imagine...

SANGUEMARCIO: I can't imagine anything. You're here to tell about it, to give facts. Well then...

SEDUCED: *(Confused.)* I think I've said enough. The rest is...

SANGUEMARCIO: Oh, no. I want details. Pain, pleasure, satisfaction, disappointment. *(Brutally.)* That's what you're getting paid for.

SEDUCED: *(Pointing toward the others and including the audience in her gesture.)* But they're here, listening...

SANGUEMARCIO: Fair enough! *(To the other three.)* Step back.

PAUL: Of course!

(The three men go downstage, while THE SEDUCED is seen whispering answers to SANGUEMARCIO's insistent questions. PAUL turns to THE PARRICIDE.)

PAUL: Congratulations! You did fine, even if it sounded awful at first. One would have thought you were the most diligent pupil in your class...You'll never make a good lawyer with such a boring voice. *(To THE THIEF.)* You're to be congratulated too. But you shouldn't have mentioned Brecht. That name is dynamite. Now listen to me carefully. Don't turn around to look. You'll see it anyway—if you haven't already...Underneath the bed there is a coffin.

(The two men are anxious to look, but refrain until a later moment.)

PAUL: It's a mania of his... He claims it keeps death away...a defense mechanism of sort, almost a challenge... *(Imitating the old man.)* "As long as I don't move, you won't see the earth. As long as I sleep *above* you, this filthy blood will flow. Once inside you, my blood won't flow anymore...never again...never again...I want you near me, I want to feel my blood flowing while I look at you..." His macabre monologues go on like that endlessly. He doesn't even stop when I come in. Sometimes they last for hours. He'll touch it, run his hand along it, strike out at it...it's within arm's reach. I know it all by heart. *(Repeating SANGUEMARCIO's words with emphasis.)* "Life is anxiety toward immobility; a lofty journey ending in the narrowness of a coffin...I want my last resting place to be familiar. I want to see it and touch it..." Then down come the tears...he makes sense, you know. If we had his courage to see it as it is...empty... *(He looks at them slyly.)* Do you really think it's empty?

(A silence.)

PAUL: It's not! That's his safe-deposit box. He's a practical man in spite of his manias, and since he doesn't trust anyone who lives here...

SANGUEMARCIO: Paul, give me ten thousand. *(He points to the coffin.)*

(As PAUL goes slowly to the coffin, all eyes are fixed on the unusual casket. He lifts the cover and takes out a banknote which he hands to SANGUEMARCIO. Then he turns back to his friends. SANGUEMARCIO is seen talking excitedly to THE SEDUCED, as he tries to make her accept the money.)

PAUL: *(To his two friends.)* Do you see? I'm the only one he trusts. Now, listen closely. In a few minutes he'll ask me to take out the money to pay you. I want you both to stay at the foot of the bed...I'll let one package drop on the sly—some extra for all of us—then I'll take out what he owes us, pretending to listen to all he says. One of you two... *(To THE THIEF.)* ...your reflexes are quicker—you'll drop your handkerchief on the floor, and pick it up with the money. Then we'll walk out very calmly. Calmly, I said. The last time Foffo was in such a damned rush he almost let the cat out of the bag. I beat him up when we got outside. *(Menacingly.)* So, watch your step.

SANGUEMARCIO: *(To THE SEDUCED, gesturing broadly.)* Go to the foot of the bed, behind the curtain. No one will see you.

SEDUCED: *(Turning to PAUL with anger.)* Do you know what he wants?

SANGUEMARCIO: I want her to get undressed, like Cicci did. I won't even touch her. There, behind the curtain...

SEDUCED: *(Almost in tears.)* What is he talking about? That wasn't part of our agreement.

SANGUEMARCIO: *(Waving the banknote.)* You won't get this, after. What have you got to lose? I just want to look. *(Pleading.)* Tell her to, Paul...

PAUL: *(Shrugging.)* If she doesn't want to...

SANGUEMARCIO: *(With senile wrath.)* Stupid! Stupid! A stupid bitch!

(He suddenly feels sick, and can hardly clap his hands to summon THE OLD WOMAN. She appears. Breathless.)

SANGUEMARCIO: Eupa-verina, quick! My injection, quick!

(THE OLD WOMAN takes away the bedpan, which she replaces in the night table, and gives him an injection. He speaks when he is feeling better.)

SANGUEMARCIO: Take her out, that silly bitch, take her out with you!...

(THE OLD WOMAN takes the girl out. With difficulty, breathless.)

SANGUEMARCIO: I don't understand these women, Paul. First they sleep with whoever comes along—for nothing—then...then they refuse something as innocent as undressing...Unless she was ashamed because you were here... *(Gleeful, thinking he has found the reason for her behavior.)* She's out to hook one of you, that's why...she was playing coy to land herself a husband... *(His hand makes contact with the banknote on the cover of his bed.)* Take out another...

(PAUL obeys, kneels, and takes the cover off the coffin.)

SANGUEMARCIO: They'll stop at nothing...They are whores...but ask them to undress when you aren't even going to touch them...

(While he is talking, PAUL lets a package of banknotes slide between the feet of his two friends, who are waiting tensely.)

SANGUEMARCIO: Maybe that's the reason...I didn't think of that...Maybe it's because I don't want to touch her...

(He laughs falsely and is imitated by the others who breathe a sigh of relief now that the first step in their plan has succeeded.)

SANGUEMARCIO: I didn't think of that. It could be the reason...but I... *(He makes a grimace of disgust.)* If you had been the one to propose it, Paul, instead of me...Tell me the truth. Is there anything between you two? *(He holds two fingers up together.)*

PAUL: *(Ambiguously.)* Oh, you know how it is, we're young...

SANGUEMARCIO: *(Angry.)* But for me, that stupid bitch...

(At this moment THE THIEF drops his handkerchief to disguise his motive in bending to retrieve the money.)

SANGUEMARCIO: What about the two of you?

PARRICIDE: *(To cover the confusion of THE THIEF.)* Not me... *(Indicating THE THIEF.)* Not him, either.

THIEF: Not me, either.

SANGUEMARCIO: But if you were in the mood...

PARRICIDE: Perhaps.

PAUL: You never know with women.

SANGUEMARCIO: *(To PAUL.)* I didn't even trust my mother. That was her fault. She made me distrust women by her behavior, by all the things she...

(THE THIEF bends down and retrieves the money. SANGUEMARCIO includes him in his conversation and looks at him unsuspecting.)

SANGUEMARCIO: She was always making promises she didn't keep. She kept saying: "Tomorrow...tomorrow...tomorrow..." And then, when tomorrow came...Nothing. *(To THE PARRICIDE.)* Does your mother keep her promises?

PARRICIDE: When she has to buy me something, she just buys it without promising.

SANGUEMARCIO: An exceptional case! There are some exceptions, I believe you, I've never met one, but...

(He senses that the three are anxious to leave.)

SANGUEMARCIO: But maybe you... you're still young... *(Trying to be funny.)* I guess you want to get out so you can sniff down the neck of some pretty girl. *(With sadness.)* I used to think humanity stank. But now—now I envy you that luxury...So long...

(SANGUEMARCIO shakes hands with PAUL and then with the others.)

PAUL: I'll see you soon.

PARRICIDE: Good luck.

THIEF: Thank you...

(They move away with deliberate slowness.)

SANGUEMARCIO: *(To PAUL before he leaves.)* Send the old lady in.

PAUL: I will.

(They leave. THE OLD WOMAN enters. The action takes place in silence. She puts the chairs in order, gives the old man his medicine, tucks in the covers. THE SEDUCED and THE MODEL appear at the door. THE OLD WOMAN looks at them harshly, then leaves. There is a taut silence.)

SANGUEMARCIO: *(Staring at them.)* Well?

SEDUCED: This is a friend of mine. I told her about your proposition. She accepts to...

SANGUEMARCIO: An intelligent friend.

MODEL: Yes.

SANGUEMARCIO: *(To THE MODEL.)* No objections to undress?

MODEL: Away from you. Why not?

SANGUEMARCIO: *(To THE SEDUCED.)* You see? She knows she's not giving up anything. On the contrary...

MODEL: How much?

SEDUCED: *(Seeking confirmation in SANGUEMARCIO's eyes.)* I told you.

MODEL: I want it in advance. *(She looks around for a place to undress.)* Where? *(She goes behind the curtain and starts to undress; we can see her profile distinctly. She is still awaiting confirmation that she will be paid in advance.)* In advance, I said.

SANGUEMARCIO: Paul will pay you.

(THE MODEL, in doubt, stops undressing.)

SEDUCED: *(Standing beside the bed, her back to the audience.)* He'll pay. Don't worry.

SANGUEMARCIO: That's right. We need faith in life. She has it...Look...

(He begins to caress her hand. THE SEDUCED does not have the strength to withdraw it.)

MODEL: *(Continuing to undress.)* That Paul is pretty smart! He found a gold mine here!

SANGUEMARCIO: *(Surprised.)* Do you know him?

MODEL: I know him. *(Continues to undress with grace and professional skill.)*

SANGUEMARCIO: *(To THE SEDUCED.)* Look at her...how graceful, how beautiful... What has she got to lose by showing her nudity?

MODEL: For a price.

SANGUEMARCIO: Are you ashamed? Tell us, are you ashamed?

(He waits for an answer. There is none.)

SANGUEMARCIO: No...She knows how to do it...Perhaps it's not the first time... Were you also...seduced?

MODEL: That's none of your business.

SANGUEMARCIO: Are you engaged?

(He waits uneasily for an answer that doesn't come.)

SANGUEMARCIO: Lusted after, yes... you're beautiful...Are you a student? *(To THE SEDUCED because he gets no answer from THE MODEL.)* She's so absorbed in what she's doing, you can see...she doesn't even answer...What does she do in life?

SEDUCED: She's a model.

SANGUEMARCIO: *(Disappointed.)* Oh, that changes everything.

MODEL: *(Aggressively.)* What's changed? *(She stops undressing and stands defiantly, her hands on her hips.)*

SANGUEMARCIO: Hundreds have seen you.

MODEL: Thousands. *(Paraphrasing him.)* So what did I give up?

SANGUEMARCIO: I'll tell Paul.

MODEL: What? If you have something to say, tell me.

SANGUEMARCIO: *(Intimidated, evasive.)* Nothing, nothing...Continue...

MODEL: I want an explanation first. Am I worth any less because that idiot told you I'm a model?

SANGUEMARCIO: No, but Paul...

MODEL: *(Showing herself, half-undressed.)* What has that delinquent done to you? Has he hypnotized you?

SANGUEMARCIO: *(Nervous and uneasy.)* Why delinquent?

(THE MODEL manages to control herself as THE SEDUCED tries to calm her.)

MODEL: I know what I am talking about. *(Unnerved, she starts to get dressed.)*

SANGUEMARCIO: *(To THE SEDUCED.)* What has he done? What is she saying? He's a good boy, a real friend...

MODEL: Tell him what kind of friend he is.

SANGUEMARCIO: *(Very nervous.)* You're a couple of bitches. He probably doesn't want anything to do with you and so...

MODEL: *(Violently, shaking his bed.)* Be careful what you say, you old degenerate. I may be a bitch but no one has ever said so to my face. Besides, that girl is still a virgin.

SANGUEMARCIO: *(Shocked.)* What? What about the story she told me?

MODEL: That's all it is—a story invented by Paul to pay his way through law school.

(THE OLD WOMAN appears in the doorway and stands there like a ghost.)

SANGUEMARCIO: *(With anguish.)* And the others? What about the Hero, the Parricide, the Pederast?

MODEL: They're all stories. Foffo's might be true. I'm not sure...I think he is bisexual.

SANGUEMARCIO: *(Clinging to THE SEDUCED.)* Is it true? Is it true? Is it true?

SEDUCED: Calm down, please. There now...Yes, it's true...He offered us money...We decided ahead of time what confessions we'd make. He told us what you like to hear...

SANGUEMARCIO: *(Gesticulating, furious.)* No, no, no...It isn't true! You're both liars...Jealous...Jealous of his intelligence, envious, wicked...

MODEL: *(Staring at THE OLD WOMAN whom she sees only now.)* Who is that?

SANGUEMARCIO: *(Hoarsely.)* No, no...Tell me it isn't true...you're lying...Paul is sincere, he's loyal to me...he's the only one who... *(He wheezes terribly.)*

MODEL: *(More forcefully.)* Who is that?

SANGUEMARCIO: *(Aware of the question for the first time.)* My wife. A madwoman who has been persecuting me for thirty years, insane like you...

(THE MODEL, impressed by the ghostly presence of the wife, goes toward the door.)

SEDUCED: *(On her knees, trying to open the coffin.)* Look inside, look inside there...He's robbed you of everything...every time he visited you he snatched as much as possible.

SANGUEMARCIO: No, no...Don't touch it, no...It isn't true...

(THE SEDUCED, seeing that her friend is leaving and the eyes of the wife are on her, gets up and slowly goes out, while SANGUEMARCIO continues ranting.)

SANGUEMARCIO: No, no, no...not true, impossible...

(Seeing that her husband is trying to get up, the wife, very moved and encouraged by this unexpected effort to get out of that "cursed bed," tries to help him. The husband continues to bemoan his fate, shaking his head and saying "no," while he forces himself to rise from bed.)

OLD WOMAN: Come on! Come on! I'll help you...

(She tries to help him, he pushes her away; she encourages him instead with inviting movements of her hands.)

OLD WOMAN: All by yourself; be strong...That's it...that's it...One foot at a time...Be brave. Courage, there...Now the other foot...Support yourself...yes, against the bed...that's it...Fine, fine... Take one step...another step...head high...breathe deeply... now another step...

(The man sinks to his knees beside the coffin. With all his strength he pulls it to him. There is a silence. The wife is motionless, her back to the audience. He manages to get the cover off with difficulty, and he reaches inside with both hands.)

SANGUEMARCIO: No, no, it isn't true... Paul is my friend...a real friend...the only one...

(Discovering that the coffin has been emptied, he dies, his head inside the coffin, his face against the wood of his final resting place. The wife falls on her knees and lifts her arms toward heaven.)

OLD WOMAN: Have pity on him now, God. Now.

(CURTAIN.)

A.I.D.S.

The Persons:

OTTO, a victim of AIDS
EVAN, his best friend

The scene: today, in New York; a hospital room; the window is open. OTTO is looking with curiosity outside, through a glass door; he is very sick, very weak; he suddenly turns to go back to his bed; he moves with difficulty, with pain: he must have seen someone approaching the door. EVAN, his best friend, enters the room and, alarmed, helps him.

EVAN: What are you doing? Why are you up? You shouldn't, you know that... You are too weak...

(He succeeds in helping him back into the bed; a silence.)

EVAN: How do you feel today?

(A vague gesture: OTTO indicates that he feels "so-so.")

EVAN: You're so pale, breathless. Why did you get up? Just call the nurse, if you need something... (Kindly.) Do you need anything? Water, orange juice?

(OTTO indicates he needs nothing; a silence.)

EVAN: I'm late today because of the traffic, because of our Parade... Do you remember last year? We were together, hand in hand, happy, proud of being in that Parade, of our relationship, of our... *(He takes his hand: he hesitates.)* ...love.

OTTO: Who was there?

EVAN: Everybody...a group of senior citizens, some couples—proud parents of "gays"—...policemen, soldiers—men and women—...A poster read: "Protect Our Embassies With Gay Soldiers. You Can Trust Only Them."

(OTTO smiles.)

EVAN: They were all amused by it and they applauded with enthusiasm. You see? Our sense of humor is not dead.

OTTO: *(With a touch of sadness.)* That will never die, fortunately.

(A silence.)

OTTO: Who was in the Parade—from our bunch?

EVAN: Couples...Jim and Rudolph, Tony and Pablo, Mark and Phil...Fat Rose and her new girlfriend...

OTTO: David?

EVAN: I didn't see him.

OTTO: Art?

EVAN: Yes...In a wheelchair...Moses was pushing him...

OTTO: Bill?

EVAN: *(After a hesitation.)* I was told he went home...to his mother.

OTTO: How is he?

EVAN: *(Carefully.)* Not too well...They say it's the end...One more week, maybe...

OTTO: What about Conrad? Is he with him? Was he allowed to—?

EVAN: *(Interrupting.)* I went to his funeral, yesterday...

OTTO: Why didn't you tell me?

EVAN: It's not easy to tell a friend that—

OTTO: —That we are all dying, one after the other, implacably?

EVAN: It's not true...I'm still negative.

OTTO: For how long?

(A brief silence.)

OTTO: I'm sorry...

EVAN: Forever, I hope.

OTTO: I hope so too. For me...It's over. *(Suddenly.)* What was that doctor telling you, in the corridor?

EVAN: *(Surprised, hesitating.)* Hah...He is the hospital director...

OTTO: What did he want from you?

EVAN: The kind of guy who knows everything and likes to talk. Medicines, complications, costs, last gossip from Europe...

(OTTO studies him.)

EVAN: It seems a huge number of heterosexuals are getting it now. More and more. Especially in Africa. More than thirty percent are heterosexuals there. Thirty percent, drug addicts...Prostitutes, two out of three...The pimps are furious. No business. They beat the poor girls up. One of them—just sixteen—was found with her throat cut—

OTTO: *(Interrupting.)* What did he say about me?

EVAN: He knows all the details, every case. He told me the poor fellow in the next room is in bad shape. Ten more days, at most...

OTTO: *(Insisting.)* What did he say about me?

EVAN: Your case is not as desperate as—

OTTO: How long?

EVAN: ...Much longer. He was telling me that—

OTTO: *(Interrupting.)* One month? Two months?

EVAN: *(Avoiding.)* ...He was mentioning prices, costs...The hospital is spending more than twelve thousand dollars for the ten days your neighbor has got—

OTTO: What about me? How many more weeks?

EVAN: Months...He said you've got months, many—

OTTO: How many?

EVAN: *(Hesitating.)* ...Eight, at least...

OTTO: Are you lying to me?

EVAN: No...I'm not.

OTTO: Out of friendship?

EVAN: Out of love, you mean? *(Kisses his hand.)*

OTTO: Are you lying to me, "out of love?"

EVAN: No...We have always been honest with each other...

OTTO: I know. *(He studies him.)* But I know you too well not to sense that you're hiding something...

EVAN: Why? If you had only ten days or ten weeks, why would I lie to you? It's always better to know.

OTTO: It's better. Tell me everything.

EVAN: I swear it on our relationship, on the wonderful memories we share.

OTTO: Eight months?

EVAN: At least—he said. Cross my heart.

(A silence.)

OTTO: You're hiding something else, then...What?

EVAN: *(Uncertain.)* No...I don't...

OTTO: Who else died?

(EVAN hands him a newspaper, open to the obituaries.)

EVAN: *(While OTTO is reading.)* Three more.

(OTTO reads carefully.)

EVAN: A strange trio...A priest, a dancer, and a doctor...Read the one about the doctor.

OTTO: Someone we know?

EVAN: No.

OTTO: *(Reading carefully.)* Are they blaming us?

EVAN: No.

OTTO: *(Still reading.)* We are lucky this time...They blame us for everything... *(Discovering something.)* Hah.

EVAN: He showed guts, didn't he?

OTTO: He is not the first one. *(He thinks; reflects.)*

EVAN: *(Curious.)* What are you thinking about?

OTTO: How he did it. Just a plunge into nothingness.

EVAN: He wanted to avoid the agony of the last days...You should see the guy in room 911...Frightening.

OTTO: To whom?

EVAN: *(Uneasy.)* To those who see him...Orderlies, friends...

OTTO: Does he still have friends? I never saw anyone visiting him.

EVAN: He's not from around here. He comes from Texas.

(A silence: they stare at each other.)

OTTO: What are you thinking about?

EVAN: *(Vague.)* Nothing.

OTTO: If you're getting bored, just go.

EVAN: Me, bored? With you? Never!

OTTO: Maybe you've something to do, something urgent.

EVAN: Nothing, absolutely nothing. I can stay here the whole afternoon. For as long as they allow me. Until they kick me out.

(A pause.)

OTTO: I *know* you're hiding something from me.

EVAN: You know? What do you know? Who told you?

OTTO: I saw.

EVAN: What did you see?

OTTO: Outside, in the corridor.

EVAN: What did you see?

OTTO: That doctor—the director—gave you an envelope. What kind of envelope? Another bill?

EVAN: Oh no! They know we can't afford it any longer. You've sold your apartment, paintings, your furniture. They can't force me to sell anything... *(Smiling bitterly.)* I am not—according to the law—a relative. What an irony! I am your most intimate friend and I'm not considered part of the family!

OTTO: Maybe they're blackmailing you. Either you pay or...?

EVAN: Or...? What can they do to me?

OTTO: Nothing to you. Maybe to me...

EVAN: What? *(Joking.)* Poison you?

OTTO: Throw me into the street. There are so many sick people...Homeless, in the streets of New York.

EVAN: They can't do that to you. I'm around. I'll defend you. The ones they kicked out had no one to protect them, to defend them.

OTTO: *(Suddenly, again; a precise question.)* What's in that envelope?

EVAN: *(Vague.)* Figures, statistics. He explained that each one of you costs more than one thousand dollars a day to the Hospital. They are afraid to go bankrupt. *(Ironical.)* They deserve to. They should. They are only interested in "profits."

OTTO: *(Thinking it over, calculating in his mind.)* Six months...If it's true, it's over two hundred thousand dollars...

EVAN: It's what they say. They always exaggerate.

OTTO: Do *you* agree on that figure?

EVAN: *(Uncertain.)* Well...Many papers mention that figure. It must be true...One thousand a day, at least.

OTTO: All right. Show me those statistics, that envelope. You know I love numbers.

EVAN: *(Trying to change the subject.)* What's *our* number?

OTTO: *(With a touch of sadness.)* Eight...I should have at least eight months. If there were any justice in this world...

(They smile.)

EVAN: We met on the eighth—your birthday...We were both born in August—the eighth month. When traveling, we always asked for the eighth floor—a room containing number eight...The first months we always exchanged gifts on the eight—

OTTO: Only the first months.

EVAN: Then we decided together—full agreement—to stop...Too many neckties, shirts, underwear, chocolates...We decided to lose weight, remember?

OTTO: *(With a sense of humor.)* I succeeded, look at me. I've lost forty-nine pounds.

(EVAN, moved, kisses his forehead.)

EVAN: You told me: forty-eight.

OTTO: That was yesterday.

(A silence.)

OTTO: *(Insisting.)* What's in that envelope?

EVAN: *(Hesitating.)* It will seem strange, to you...A check.

OTTO: *(Surprised.)* A check? What happened? They feel guilty, all of a sudden, and they are reimbursing us? You see? There is some justice in this world! And I should be ashamed of myself I was in such a hurry to condemn hospitals and society! How much are we getting back? Did they admit they overcharged?

(A silence; EVAN is motionless.)

OTTO: Let me see. I'll figure everything in three minutes. How much we paid, how much we are getting back; and if they are shortchanging us.

EVAN: *(Hesitating.)* It's no reimbursement.

OTTO: What is it, then? Some award for good behavior? I'm no trouble here. I'm as quiet as a little tiny mouse.

EVAN: *(Carefully.)* An unusual, weird... proposal.

OTTO: Is it money or a proposal?

EVAN: Both.

OTTO: That is?

EVAN: A certain amount if... the proposal is... acceptable.

OTTO: How much?

EVAN: ...Twenty thousand.

OTTO: *(Very surprised.)* That's a fortune, for us. What kind of proposal? Did you accept it? Say "yes" right away. We need that money.

EVAN: The proposal is... absurd.

OTTO: Accept it all the same. What's important today is that money. In my will there is nothing left for you. What do they want from us? What must we do?

EVAN: The money is not for us. It's for the AIDS Foundation.

OTTO: *(Surprised.)* Hah... That's strange... His personal gift? Who caught AIDS? His son? His brother?

EVAN: It's not a personal gift... It comes from a bank. Some special fund...

OTTO: For what? What purpose? A moral crisis? Guilt? Are they ashamed they're charging one thousand dollars a day for a dump like this?

(A pause.)

OTTO: Explain the proposal.

(A pause.)

OTTO: Am I part of it?

EVAN: *(Nods. He finally shows the envelope: he is ready to tear it up.)* Let's tear it up and forget the whole thing.

OTTO: *(Intervening.)* No! You can't throw away twenty thousand like that... I must know. I'm involved in this. It's about me too—you said so.

EVAN: *(Slowly, carefully.)* You know how they think—these hospital directors... They're just accountants... They figure out the best budget, they are afraid to be fired if they don't make a profit...

OTTO: What did he tell you?

EVAN: *(Uncertain, slowly.)* That... as a rule... because of... considering... *(He cannot express himself clearly.)*

OTTO: Tell me something. Did he give the same proposal to the guy next door—the one who has just ten days left?

EVAN: No.

OTTO: *(Slowly.)* I begin to understand... That proposal is only for the ones who have eight more months to live.

(EVAN does not dare look into his eyes: he knows OTTO has understood.)

OTTO: The pills? Did he give you the pills?

EVAN: What pills?

OTTO: The poison you're supposed to give me.

EVAN: Oh no! The situation is... optional, absolutely optional.

OTTO: All right. I'll volunteer for it! Where are the pills? I'll take them voluntarily.

EVAN: No pills. He doesn't supply anything.

OTTO: *(Ironical.)* What a gentleman!

EVAN: He does not want to be involved in...

OTTO: Naturally!

EVAN: He is being... correct, in a way.

OTTO: Very correct.

EVAN: He explained—with polite detachment—advantages and disadvantages.

OTTO: Tell me about the disadvantages.

EVAN: The last days are...terrible.

OTTO: *(Bitterly ironical.)* I know. An infernal agony. I thought about it.

EVAN: About what?

OTTO: The agony. How to avoid it.

(A silence: they look at each other.)

OTTO: As you can see, they have read my thoughts, they have guessed.

EVAN: Guessed what?

OTTO: That I don't want that agony...That doctor— *(Indicates the newspaper.)* his method—a sudden jump from the tenth floor...I thought about that a thousand times...

(They both stare at the window; a painful silence.)

OTTO: Show me the check.

EVAN: *(Handing him the envelope.)* Here it is...

(OTTO opens the envelope and stares at the check.)

EVAN: Tear it up.

OTTO: It is not made out to anyone...

EVAN: Tear it up!

OTTO: To whom should we...make it out, in his opinion?

EVAN: Give it to me. I'll tear it up myself.

OTTO: *(Insisting.)* To whom?

EVAN: *(After a pause.)* To the AIDS Foundation.

OTTO: *(Slowly. Staring at EVAN.)* No...

EVAN: Let's destroy it!

OTTO: He gave you a choice, obviously.

EVAN: What choice?

OTTO: *(Slowly, studying him.)* You could put your name, here...

EVAN: No! Never!

OTTO: *(Calm; determined.)* It is my last desire...You cannot say no to my last wish...You *must* put your name here...it is for you...

EVAN: *(Tears in his eyes, shakes his head.)* No...No...

OTTO: *You must*...It's my last gift, to you...

(They hold hands tightly, desperately. EVAN kisses OTTO's hand. They both stare at the open window. A spotlight illuminates the window. Tableau. Blackout.)

(CURTAIN.)

Brothel (The Doorbell)

Characters:

THE WIFE: in her early twenties; beautiful and sad
THE HUSBAND: mature; in his early sixties
THE OLD WOMAN: in her late sixties, concierge of the former brothel

Time:

Today

Place:

A former brothel, in Venice

We hear the doorbell at regular intervals. The curtain goes up and we see the interior of the house. Stage left and stage right: two small parlors—very "brothel" in feeling; there are mirrors from floor to ceiling. They are in semi-darkness. Center stage: a comfortable dining room. There is a wood-burning fireplace with the fire going. Sitting in the armchair at right is THE HUSBAND. THE WIFE sits a few feet away. She is beautiful and young. She is gazing into the fire as if she were submitting her body to the warmth of the flames. There is a silence. Then we hear the doorbell. They both "feel" and react to it. But neither one moves. It is a routine that they pretend to be accustomed to but cannot ignore. A silence, broken only by THE HUSBAND's hesitant typing.

WIFE: *(Monotone.)* It's time for bed.

(A silence. He ignores her. Doorbell again.)

WIFE: Time for bed...

HUSBAND: *(Staring at her with suspicion.)* Because of the doorbell?

WIFE: *(Avoiding his eyes.)* Because I'm tired.

(A silence. Doorbell again. The OLD WOMAN opens the door, mutters something, slams the door. A silence.)

HUSBAND: Go to your room.

WIFE: Not alone.

HUSBAND: I'll come soon.

WIFE: I'll wait.

HUSBAND: You can't hear it in your room.

WIFE: Hear what?

HUSBAND: The doorbell.

WIFE: It doesn't disturb me.

HUSBAND: It does.

WIFE: No. It doesn't.

(A silence.)

HUSBAND: *(Indicating his typing.)* It'll be a while. I must finish this.

(A silence. Studying her.)

HUSBAND: What are you thinking?

WIFE: Nothing. I'm just tired.

HUSBAND: Go to your room. I won't be long.

WIFE: Not alone. It frightens me.

HUSBAND: Why?

WIFE: I don't know why.

HUSBAND: There's always a reason.

WIFE: I just don't know.

HUSBAND: Don't you feel protected?

(Doorbell.)

WIFE: *(Wearily.)* I feel protected.

HUSBAND: You're a married woman. You shouldn't be afraid.

WIFE: True.

(Doorbell.)

HUSBAND: Are you afraid?

WIFE: I just don't like to go "there" alone.

HUSBAND: "There"?

WIFE: To bed. I don't like to go there alone.

HUSBAND: Why?

WIFE: I have to pass eleven doors, on the way to my room. Eleven empty rooms.

HUSBAND: I filled them up for you.

WIFE: A string of parlors.

HUSBAND: Would you prefer bedrooms?

(Doorbell; a silence.)

WIFE: *(Looking directly at him.)* We already have one too many.

HUSBAND: *(Hurt.)* What do you mean?

WIFE: Nothing.

(A silence.)

HUSBAND: Which one?

WIFE: You know which one.

(A tense silence.)

HUSBAND: You agreed with my idea to have separate rooms.

WIFE: *(Ironically.)* Did I?

HUSBAND: It's vulgar to make love just because you share the same bed.

WIFE: Not again! It's an obsession with you.

HUSBAND: I just talk about it. You *think* about it!

WIFE: About what?

(Doorbell.)

HUSBAND: *(Referring to the doorbell.)* And even if you didn't think about it…that damn doorbell would remind you!

WIFE: *(Ironically.)* Of the postman, the grocery man, the milkman?

HUSBAND: Always men.

WIFE: Should I please you and say the seamstress, the laundress, the maid? I don't weigh my words!

(A silence.)

HUSBAND: You need some distraction. Why don't you invite somebody?

WIFE: *(Ironically.)* Wouldn't they love coming here?

HUSBAND: You could invite your relatives…

WIFE: *(Interrupting.)* —And take them on a tour of the house! Giving them the morbid details. No. Thank you. Those details make me uncomfortable.

HUSBAND: *(Ignoring her words.)* Receive them in this room.

WIFE: They'd want to know if it was like this before! As if I'd been here *before!*

HUSBAND: *(Annoyed, edgy.)* Don't even joke about that!

WIFE: I have to be careful with what I say!

HUSBAND: Why?

WIFE: I'm forced to. *(She stares at him.)*

(A silence.)

WIFE: *(She is now gentler.)* They'd ask questions. It's human to be curious...

HUSBAND: Only because women think of nothing else!

WIFE: *(Ignoring his words.)* ...Parlors, mirrors...

HUSBAND: Haven't they ever seen a mirror?

WIFE: *(Looking straight in his eyes.)* Not like these.

HUSBAND: A mirror is a mirror.

WIFE: Not in a place like this. They'd ask "Why up here?" "Why so many beds?" You still see the marks from the headboards. Many. For all those who—

(Doorbell.)

HUSBAND: —Ring the doorbell!

WIFE: Let them ring!

(Doorbell.)

HUSBAND: *(Embarrassed, getting back to the subject of the house.)* It's just a big house with many rooms. Anyone else would give anything to have such a home...

WIFE: "Anyone else." Who?

HUSBAND: Any girl. A beautiful spacious house. It's everyone's dream.

WIFE: I didn't know about it then. I thought they were staring at me because of you.

HUSBAND: What do you mean?

(A silence.)

WIFE: You do look older than me.

HUSBAND: *(Pretending to ignore.)* —You really hate this house then?

WIFE: *(Thinking about it.)* I'm not sure...

HUSBAND: Not sure?

WIFE: It's the first home I ever had. I'd like it perhaps, if you weren't...

(A brief pause; she stares at him; he is tense.)

WIFE: I mean...If you would stop tormenting me. You chose this house. *You* should ignore its past.

HUSBAND: I do.

WIFE: Set an example by your silence.

(Doorbell.)

WIFE: Even if it's broken—now and then—by an innocent ring.

HUSBAND: "Innocent"?

WIFE: And ridiculous. How many times a day do you hear the church bells ring? And the music from the radio? Or the children playing in the street? It doesn't bother you. *You* give a special meaning to that doorbell!

HUSBAND: *You* can't forget or ignore what's in front of that door. I can see it in your eyes.

WIFE: *(Aggressively.)* You can see *anything* in someone's eyes.

HUSBAND: For instance?

WIFE: *(Vague.)* …Sickness, depravity, impotence.

(He is about to strike her.)

HUSBAND: *(Upset.)* What are you insinuating?

WIFE: *(Looking at him with pity.)* I'm sorry. I only meant the impotence I see in your eyes when you're angry and…when you want to hit me. I realize now that *that* word has another meaning. I don't know or think about such things! I really don't!

HUSBAND: *(After reflection.)* You don't know the meaning of certain words… You don't read… You just stare at the fire.

(Doorbell; THE HUSBAND is discouraged again; he is tired. A silence; he waits for her to speak; they look at each other; doorbell again.)

WIFE: *(Referring to the doorbell.)* I don't hear it, I assure you! I could even grow to love this house. I—I don't hate your work. It's only your twisted way of thinking, of talking, of accusing that I hate—

(Doorbell.)

WIFE: Forget it! Ignore it! The way you ignore the sound of the rain, of the wind—or the beating of your heart!

(Doorbell.)

WIFE: Ignore it! They are not there! They don't exist.

HUSBAND: They exist. They ring the bell.

WIFE: All right then. They exist. They are alive. What can you do?

HUSBAND: *(Sarcastic.)* "Alive"…

WIFE: Whatever you say. Whatever you want.

(Doorbell.)

WIFE: For me—they are not there.

HUSBAND: "They." Your eyes tell me that you feel the strength of their presence. This house is getting into your blood. You're obsessed.

(Doorbell. THE HUSBAND makes gestures of annoyance.)

WIFE: Please, *try* to ignore it!

HUSBAND: *(Losing control.)* How can I? It's impossible! It's here—to remind us—

WIFE: *(Interrupting.)* To remind *you!*

HUSBAND: —To remind *us*, relentlessly!

(A brief silence.)

WIFE: Why don't you invite your sister to stay with me?

HUSBAND: *(Surprised.)* My sister?

WIFE: Find some excuse. But please tell her not to ask questions about the house. Make up some kind of story. Tell her I'm stupid—naïve. I promise to get along with her. I don't mind being dominated.

HUSBAND: That I know.

WIFE: When you're not here. Please ask your sister.

HUSBAND: I don't want relatives in my house. The old woman can keep you company.

WIFE: I need a friend—someone I can feel close to, someone I can trust.

HUSBAND: You can trust the old lady. She's—

WIFE: *(Interrupting.)* I never go near that door.

HUSBAND: Why?

WIFE: I just don't.

HUSBAND: She's the only one who will never ask questions.

WIFE: She doesn't have to. But I can't be close to someone who… *(She holds back.)*

HUSBAND: "Someone who"?

WIFE: Nothing.

HUSBAND: Say it.

WIFE: You know what I mean. Besides—

(Doorbell.)

WIFE: "You can read into my eyes." Why don't you?

HUSBAND: "You can't be close to someone who has seen so much."—

WIFE: That's right.

HUSBAND: …Someone who has seen hundreds of men. This is what's really bothering you.

WIFE: *(After a hostile silence.)* I have a right to dislike her.

HUSBAND: *(Slowly.)* You should get to know her better. If you were friendlier you might even learn a few things.

WIFE: *(Looking at him with contempt.)* So that's why you kept her! So you could satisfy your sick curiosity. You're always talking to her.

HUSBAND: So you saw me. You go near that door after all. Did you stop to listen?

WIFE: *(Calmly.)* When my father would leave for work, my mother always waved goodbye to him from the window. When you leave for work I go over to the window and wait for as long as a half hour—sometimes—while you talk to her. When you finally leave, you don't even bother to look up.

HUSBAND: *(Ignoring her words.)* She's a decent woman who works for a living. She knows how to handle those men. And in a few months,

(Doorbell.)

HUSBAND: When they stop ringing—

WIFE: They'll never stop.

HUSBAND: —When that bell becomes…meaningless—I'll dismiss her, to make you happy and to please you, I'll ask my sister and my—

WIFE: *(Sarcastically.)* Will you ask your sister to guard the door?

(A silence. He stares at her severely.)

HUSBAND: *(Slowly.)* I'll invite my sister and my mother…

WIFE: Why are you staring at me? Is it something I said? The day will come when they too will have to answer to that door. It's inevitable.

HUSBAND: That day will come for all of us. I got this house for half the original price because of this annoyance.

(Doorbell.)

HUSBAND: We must try to endure it.

(Doorbell.)

WIFE: That day will come for all of us. Your mother and sister will learn…

HUSBAND: We'll all learn how to handle those…people. It will be easy.

WIFE: *(Ironically.)* …And regular.

HUSBAND: To remind you… *(He holds back.)*

WIFE: To remind me?

HUSBAND: How fortunate you are to have a husband. That the family is precious…

WIFE: You're right. A family is something very precious. That's why one must defend it. That's why your wife shouldn't be forced to stay by the door of a... *(THE WIFE holds back. She cannot continue.)*

HUSBAND: Say it. By the door of a...?

WIFE: Of your house. This house.

HUSBAND: You were going to say something else.

WIFE: Do you really want me to say it? You'd be furious, I know. Because it's a word you hate.

HUSBAND: You're afraid to say it.

WIFE: Brothel! Everyone knows. But it's *our* house now. *You* chose it, not me. I'm here because of you!

(Doorbell. He stares at her.)

WIFE: Why are you looking at me like that?

HUSBAND: You *feel* that doorbell. You—

WIFE: *(Interrupting.)* What I *feel* is that look of yours—sick! And if I am blushing, I'm not ashamed of it.

HUSBAND: But you're trying to control yourself.

WIFE: It's human. I say to myself: —He's staring at me again, tormenting me again, I must defend myself.

HUSBAND: By avoiding my eyes.

WIFE: *(Without looking at him.)* But I can feel that cold look, I can guess your...depraved thoughts. You resent those young men.

HUSBAND: Most of them are old!

WIFE: *(Cuddled up in the armchair, gazing into the fire.)* One remains young if he still... *(She hesitates.)*

HUSBAND: *(Tense.)* If he still—what?

WIFE: *(Really defying him, for the first time.)* If he still desires.

HUSBAND: You—whore!

(A silence. She regrets her indirect insult.)

HUSBAND: Wives don't "desire." Honest women don't demand. They wait.

WIFE: I just want to be left in peace. Please! If you didn't torture me, I would be happy. Let's go to... *(She holds back.)* You see how careful I must be? Let's go to..."sleep."

HUSBAND: Life isn't just—

WIFE: *(Bored.)* I know, I know. It's also working, competing, accounting. Are you finished for the night?

HUSBAND: I don't like the way you said that.

(Doorbell.)

WIFE: It's the atmosphere...

HUSBAND: What do you mean?

WIFE: *(Ironically.)* Maybe I was inspired by the women who dominated here.

HUSBAND: *(Sharply.)* It's the men who paid. It's the men who gave orders.

WIFE: *(Ironically.)* You're paying too...

HUSBAND: How imaginative of you!

WIFE: Isn't that what you want to hear?

HUSBAND: *(Humbler now.)* If you loved me, you wouldn't have said that.

WIFE: What did I say?

HUSBAND: That I pay. Like those men paid. I *married* you.

WIFE: And you're paying all the bills. It's my duty to recognize your merits and rights.

(Doorbell. A silence.)

HUSBAND: *(Humble.)* What do you want of me? What more can I give you? This house—

WIFE: —Was a great bargain, I know. But no one else wanted it.

HUSBAND: That's not true! They were just trying to get the price down.

WIFE: The real reason was the doorbell. A disturbing symbol of life. *(Aggressive, pinning him down.)* But you—being shrewd—you did away with the doorbell! And no concierge for a while. Very shrewd! But the forces of life overcame the obstacle by breaking down the door!

HUSBAND: "Life overcame the obstacle." You call a crowd of drunken sailors "life"!

WIFE: Yes. Life.

HUSBAND: It won't happen again.

WIFE: It will. And you'll be found trembling, clutching my skirt while "they"—bewildered—wander through the rooms. Making all kinds of obscene gestures in front of the mirrors that you insist on keeping.

HUSBAND: I'll get rid of them, when I get a good price. And that incident won't happen again—I assure you. *(Tenderly.)* The day will come when no one rings that bell—

(Doorbell.)

WIFE: That ring will always be with us.

HUSBAND: That's a strange confession…

WIFE: You made it intriguing and meaningful.

HUSBAND: It's your indecent imagination.

WIFE: It's your hatred. You resent youth—you really do. You know they're strong.

HUSBAND: They're dirty!

WIFE: Bursting with life.

HUSBAND: Cowards!

WIFE: Bursting with desire.

HUSBAND: Liars!

WIFE: Burning with passion!

HUSBAND: *(Convulsively.)* Blind animals, frustrated failures, frustrated and blind like you!

WIFE: *(Reflecting, hurt.)* "Frustrated"…

HUSBAND: Yes—and blind!

WIFE: You're right. I was blind not to see…And to think that it's to that doorbell that I now owe my—

HUSBAND: Your what—?

WIFE: That doorbell—and your reaction to it—they're making me realize…

HUSBAND: What do you mean?

WIFE: …Making me aware.

HUSBAND: Of what?

WIFE: Of many things.

(Doorbell.)

HUSBAND: *(In a fury.)* I'll get rid of it! You'll see, I'll get rid of it!

(Doorbell.)

WIFE: It's too late. We can't turn off what we will always hear and feel.

HUSBAND: That sound should remind you that this was a place of sorrow.

WIFE: "Sorrow"?

HUSBAND: What these walls could tell you! They're permeated with despair. Would you prefer to say…"Joy"?

WIFE: I'd say…"life."

HUSBAND: *That?* A life!

WIFE: Yes. Even *that* is life. A texture of…feelings!

HUSBAND: Only anguish.

WIFE: Desires…

HUSBAND: *(With hatred.)* Only tears!

WIFE: Tears too are life.

HUSBAND: Tears negate life. They are shed over wounds.

WIFE: Weeping is an outburst of sincerity.

HUSBAND: It's suffering.

WIFE: It's love.

HUSBAND: *(Sharply.)* This is no place for love.

WIFE: You brought me here.

HUSBAND: It's no longer a place for love. After what you said.

WIFE: You made me say it.

HUSBAND: Those words were conceived in you! Offsprings of your kind of thinking!

WIFE: …Projected by you—day after day, insinuation after insinuation.

HUSBAND: It was in your blood before!

WIFE: *(Ignoring his words.)* …Suspicion after suspicion.

HUSBAND: Now you belong to this house.

WIFE: I belong here only because I'm your wife. Only for that reason. And a man's house—wherever it may be—belongs to his wife too. If I feel the way I do—you're to blame.

HUSBAND: It's in your blood.

(Doorbell.)

WIFE: *(Emphatically.)* Yes. It's mine now! With all its memories and sounds and tears, with all the moans and desires that these walls suggest!

HUSBAND: In this sad market of human shame there was only misery, grief, and disgust. They sold themselves here.

WIFE: Selling, buying…Isn't that the law of life? *You* taught me that. What do other men do? How do they behave? Do they pay for the satisfaction of showing off how much they own or how much they *can* give?

(Doorbell. She realizes that he has not understood the insinuation.)

WIFE: And after all they don't pay so much. If they paid a lot—as much as you do—they would be consumed by a fever of love. They would want to possess the woman until she hurts. Until her whole body burns with passion!

(She looks at him with defiance again; he avoids her eyes.)

HUSBAND: *(Calm.)* Do you know why they paid so little here?

WIFE: Because love costs nothing. Love is in one's blood.

HUSBAND: Because a whore is cheaper than a wife.

WIFE: Then why didn't you buy one?

HUSBAND: Because I could afford a wife.

WIFE: *(After a brief silence.)* Thank you for your sincerity. Now I know why you married me.

HUSBAND: It's a cruel law of life. If you marry for love when you're young and poor, you're bound to lose her. If you're sly, you enjoy other men's wives until you can afford the extravagance of having your own wife.

WIFE: *(Hurt.)* "Other men's wives," "the extravagance of a wife"…How disgusting!

HUSBAND: You were nothing—before I gave you my name.

WIFE: *(Sharp.)* I had my own.

HUSBAND: Your name was as fragile as crystal. Anyone could have soiled it. With money.

WIFE: *(In a rage.)* You—!

HUSBAND: Not a small sum. Money like this… *(He indicates the house and its possessions.)*

WIFE: *(Upset.)* …I married you because…I thought I was in love with you…That's the only reason…

HUSBAND: You know I could give you a secure future. That's why a girl gets married.

WIFE: Not always…There was a man who loved me—the way every girl dreams of being loved…If something hadn't happened.

HUSBAND: The "Brazilian."

(The WIFE is surprised that he knows.)

HUSBAND: *(With irony.)* What happened to him?

WIFE: He died.

HUSBAND: I had you investigated. He didn't send after you because he didn't want to spend the money. He didn't think you were *worth* it. He found someone else there. The first one to share his bed. It was cheaper that way. And now he's happily married.

WIFE: You're lying!

HUSBAND: I have pictures and documents in my safe. Do you want to see them?

WIFE: You would soil your own mother not to lose what you own.—I don't believe you.

HUSBAND: I'm telling the truth now.

WIFE: *Now?*

HUSBAND: I can afford to. *(A brief pause; freely.)* A poor man lies to survive. I don't have to now… *(With genuine sincerity.)* If you want to succeed, you must learn how to struggle, how to speculate, how to deceive. Even your best friend, if necessary. Within the letter of the law, of course. Our laws allow it. They give you plenty of liberty. More than one normally expects.

WIFE: You mean it?

HUSBAND: I bought this house for a fifth of its real value. And you want to know my plan? An honest girl like you and a serious businessman like me live here a couple of years. By that time the stigma of this house will be forgotten, and I'll be able to sell it at a big profit.

WIFE: So you speculate on me?!

HUSBAND: No. I speculated so I could get you. There's a difference.

WIFE: *(Sadly.)* Also on my home…

HUSBAND: Yes. So I can buy a better one later.

WIFE: At the cost of my serenity and my honor.

HUSBAND: Here they only sold the superfluous. It was a simple give-and-take. One doesn't lose one's honor in a place where "good honest work" was done!

(Doorbell.)

HUSBAND: Those girls were here to help poor unfortunate men who couldn't afford a wife.

WIFE: *(Wearily.)* I didn't feel horror when I first found out that this house was a…In every room, in every corner, I heard the cry of a tragedy—

HUSBAND: *(With irony.)* Don't romanticize! It was nothing more than an exchange of merchandise.

WIFE: I wasn't speaking of the passion of the men who paid—if they paid—

HUSBAND: *(Cutting in.)* Don't be naïve! Whores are never generous. I'll never forget the first one I had. She told me: —"You think you screwed me? *I* did. I screwed you out of your money."

WIFE: *(Ignoring his words.)* I've wondered about them when they were young and pure. I try to understand these tragic women…They can never forget—I'm sure—the happier days in their lives, when they had a man to defend them—

HUSBAND: *(Interrupting again.)* Why did they lose their men?

WIFE: This is what makes me think of them with compassion and understanding. Their tragedy—

HUSBAND: *(Interrupting again.)* It's not at all a tragedy, be sure. They sold themselves so that they could give alms—instead of receiving them—when they get old.

WIFE: How do you know that?

HUSBAND: Some I guessed. Some I learned from the old lady. I pay her also to talk.

WIFE: *(With contempt.)* You reduce everything to money.

HUSBAND: Life taught me to. There's no love, no compassion, no kindness—believe me. Everybody is selfish and calculating. In every act of his existence.

WIFE: Not in love though. Love is a desire to kindle a new flame in the heart of the person you love.

(Doorbell.)

HUSBAND: I could tell you that I brought you here to destroy all your dreams about "love." It would be in my interest. I would seem much more intelligent to you.

WIFE: Intelligent enough to guess my words and reaction?

HUSBAND: Intelligent enough to provoke those words. *(Deliberately, staring at her.)* To provoke is the best way to make someone react—a way to find out what they really feel about you.

(A silence; THE WIFE—astonished—looks at him with hatred.)

HUSBAND: My dear, man's only drive is self-interest. Even love is self-interest.

WIFE: To love is to give all of yourself!

HUSBAND: It's self-interest. Physical satisfaction. The joy of complete possession.

WIFE: Love is the desire to make someone happy.

HUSBAND: When a man reaches my status,—I agree. When he has a big house like this—

(Doorbell.)

HUSBAND: —Notwithstanding its past.

(Doorbell.)

HUSBAND: *(Trying to convince himself, nervously.)* The day I sell it, I'll buy you anything you desire!

WIFE: We were talking about love.

HUSBAND: Love—yes. But only if you're rich, you can afford a young beautiful wife!

WIFE: If that were true—life would be unbearable!

HUSBAND: Unbearable yes—for those who are weak and poor. They must accept and endure the will of the strong and powerful. It's their destiny.

WIFE: Not any longer.

HUSBAND: The world doesn't change, my dear. Life is beautiful for me only because I found a way to marry a girl like you. *(With utter sincerity, humbly.)* I'm happy with you. And I'll be happier when you realize what I did for you. It took a lifetime to reach my goal—they were years of hell. You should admire me for those years of struggle. I was ruthless to everyone. It wasn't easy. I did it for you. *(He approaches her and is about to touch her hand.)* Can you understand?

(She pulls her hand away.)

HUSBAND: *(A sigh and a shrug.)* As you wish. I'm going to bed now. In my bed. Tonight you don't want me…you don't need me…A man loves the girl who makes him feel strong. You were too hostile today. The duty of a wife is not to antagonize her husband…But I'll try to understand you and forgive you…It would be an act of violence if I tried to kiss you…And you know—I'm not violent…I respect your desire to be left alone… *(He hesitates; he exits stage right.)*

(THE WIFE is gazing at the fire. The doorbell rings. She reacts, reaches for a cigarette, and lights it. Doorbell. THE OLD WOMAN appears at stage left.)

WIFE: *(Surprised.)* The doorbell.

OLD WOMAN: It's midnight.

(Doorbell.)

WIFE: But they're ringing.

OLD WOMAN: I never answer after midnight.

WIFE: Who's supposed to answer?

(A silence; THE OLD WOMAN wants to embarrass THE WIFE, in her silent way. THE OLD WOMAN seems to ask—"Why not you?" Doorbell.)

OLD WOMAN: *We* always closed. They know.

(Doorbell.)

WIFE: But…Can't you hear?…There…

(Doorbell.)

WIFE: There it is again…

OLD WOMAN: They know we close at midnight. They'll stop.

(Doorbell.)

WIFE: What if they don't? What if they keep insisting?

OLD WOMAN: They won't, Signora. I know men. They give up easily.

(They wait for the doorbell; complete silence.)

WIFE: *(She accepts THE OLD WOMAN's wisdom; with kind concern.)* How old are you?

(The OLD WOMAN is surprised by her sudden warmth and desire to talk to her; she considers this a personal victory which she intends to enjoy, and not in a servile manner.)

OLD WOMAN: I'm sixty-seven.

WIFE: How long have you…?

OLD WOMAN: Have I—what?

WIFE: …Been at the door?

OLD WOMAN: Eighteen years.

WIFE: Always here?

OLD WOMAN: No.

WIFE: …Doing the same work?

OLD WOMAN: Yes. But it was easy before.

(A brief silence.)

WIFE: Why?

OLD WOMAN: I let them in; they were welcome...No longer, now...I have to reject them...

WIFE: Did you ever...go upstairs?

OLD WOMAN: Yes. To clean the mess.

WIFE: I mean...when you were younger—did you...?

OLD WOMAN: I've had a few men. I even have two daughters.

WIFE: Same father?

OLD WOMAN: Of course.

WIFE: I'm sorry. But you said...men.

OLD WOMAN: That was before. Later you settle down with the first man who agrees to marry you. I found one. He was a good man.

WIFE: Is he dead?

OLD WOMAN: For me he is. *(With pride.)* But he gave me two beautiful girls. I was happy with them.

WIFE: "Was"?

OLD WOMAN: When we were together.

WIFE: Where are they now?

OLD WOMAN: ...I'll tell you some other time.

WIFE: *(After a silence.)* Do they know that you...? *(THE WIFE refers to the door.)*

OLD WOMAN: They know.

WIFE: And they don't mind...?

OLD WOMAN: *(Smiling.)* Why should they mind? *(A brief pause.)* I even took them with me.

WIFE: ...To a place like this?

OLD WOMAN: I had to. They were behaving stupidly; giving it away for free.

WIFE: *(Shocked.)* With you here doing...

OLD WOMAN: What we women do, yes. I saw them every day. We liked being together.

(A silence.)

WIFE: How old were they when you told them to...? *(Indicates the house, the brothel.)*

OLD WOMAN: They were in their early twenties. *Your* age.

WIFE: Were they the youngest, here?

OLD WOMAN: No. Some were younger. But my daughters were the best.

WIFE: You mean—the most beautiful?

OLD WOMAN: I said—the best.

(A silence.)

WIFE: Were they...Were you...tired, busy?

OLD WOMAN: Yes. We had clients all the time. This was the finest house in town. All the girls were beautiful and smart. Like you.

WIFE: You mean...There were girls...like me?

OLD WOMAN: Lots of them. Men like your type.

WIFE: *(Unbelieving.)* My type, my age...

OLD WOMAN: Even younger. You couldn't be over twenty-five here. This was the rule of the house.

WIFE: *(Doorbell.)* My God! You couldn't be...

OLD WOMAN: No exception to the rule. You know, after twenty-five...

WIFE: *(With interest.)* What...?

OLD WOMAN: Something fades in a woman...the pleasure of giving, of living...

WIFE: *(After a brief silence.)* Did they seem...happy?

OLD WOMAN: Who?

WIFE: The girls in the house.

OLD WOMAN: Very happy. The house echoed with laughter. These young men gave with passion. They made them happy.

WIFE: *(Interrupting.)* Did the older girls have mothers who...?

OLD WOMAN: Yes. And some had husbands too. Like you. Husbands they didn't love.

WIFE: *(Ignoring her words.)* And their mothers...came to visit?

OLD WOMAN: No. Only men were allowed. This house was always full of men. In every room. In yours, in mine...

WIFE: Did the girls go out, for a walk?

OLD WOMAN: More often than you. Usually around noon.

WIFE: And...and were they...embarrassed to go out, in the street?

OLD WOMAN: *(Surprised.)* Why?

WIFE: Weren't they stared at? People must have known...

OLD WOMAN: A real woman is *never* "embarrassed." They were young and daring, don't forget. Under twenty-five. Like you.

WIFE: Didn't they want to avoid people...or escape from prying eyes?

OLD WOMAN: Never. They were proud of being *women*. Every girl should take pride in herself, in being a real woman... You're a beautiful woman...You should be proud...Of your beauty, of your youth...The way they were...Take pride in yourself, Signora...In being alive...young...ready to love...

(Doorbell. THE OLD WOMAN watches THE WIFE with curiosity. She is trying to see how she will react now. Doorbell again. THE OLD WOMAN notices a change in THE WIFE's reaction and smiles with ironic satisfaction. Doorbell again.)

WIFE: *(In control and calmly.)* Well...I think it's time to...Good night.

OLD WOMAN: Will you be using your room tonight, Signora?

WIFE: That'll be all.

(Immobility for a few seconds. They study each other. THE OLD WOMAN turns off the light and exits from stage right. The room is dark now except for the fire which is still burning. THE WIFE is staring at the fire. Doorbell. THE WIFE "feels" it. Doorbell. THE WIFE gets up slowly. Doorbell. THE WIFE steps forward. Doorbell. THE WIFE steps toward the door and opens it.)

(BLACKOUT. CURTAIN.)

The Letter

The Characters:

DINA: in her early twenties; beautiful and tender
HUBERT: in his late thirties; a successful businessman; suspicious

Today in New York. DINA's apartment. A low wide bed, candles, liqueurs, a fireplace. DINA is nervously waiting for HUBERT to arrive. She is worried and tense. Doorbell. Surprised, she looks through the peephole. She opens the door. It is HUBERT.

DINA: *(Kissing him.)* My love…

(He avoids her; she studies him.)

DINA: Why didn't you use the key?

HUBERT: I forgot.

(A silence; they study each other.)

DINA: Did you bring the envelope?

HUBERT: And the letter too. Unopened. As promised.

DINA: Thank you. May I…?

HUBERT: Here it is. Addressed to me. No return address. Anonymous, no doubt.

DINA: *(Observing the envelope.)* The date isn't clear.

HUBERT: It is. Mailed three days ago. From your hometown.

DINA: *(Putting the envelope on the fireplace and giving him a glass of white wine.)* To our love!

(They drink in silence; DINA sits on the bed.)

DINA: *(Tenderly.)* Come closer.

(HUBERT turns the light on and blows out the candle that is near him. The other candle will be lit throughout the action.)

HUBERT: Let's talk about the letter, first.

(A silence.)

HUBERT: Who do you think wrote it?

DINA: *(After reflection.)* It could be my mother.

HUBERT: To my address?

DINA: It's easy to get your address.

HUBERT: Why to me? What does she want?

(A silence; DINA prefers not to answer.)

HUBERT: Does she know about us?

DINA: No.

HUBERT: What would she want from me?

DINA: I don't know.

HUBERT: What do you suspect?

DINA: If my mother wrote it…she would just ask you not to hurt me.

(A silence.)

HUBERT: Perhaps it's not your mother…Perhaps it's from your… "sportsman"…A threatening letter! "I was her first man. She belongs to me for life. Leave her alone or I'll break your bones."'

DINA: I never told you he was the first man in my life.

HUBERT: *(Hurt.)* You implied that... Well...I'm always discovering something new about your past. So, he wasn't the first one...Who, then, was this mysterious—?

DINA: *(Interrupting.)* I'd rather not talk about him.

HUBERT: Of course! Then the letter could be from him. A mysterious lover who writes, with morbid jealousy, "She's mine; forever mine! Don't touch her!"

DINA: Impossible.

HUBERT: What's impossible?

DINA: That he wrote the letter.

HUBERT: Why?

DINA: He's dead.

HUBERT: *(After a silence.)* May he rest in peace! Now that we've eliminated your mother and the two seducers...who's left? Who do you suspect?

(A brief silence.)

DINA: *(Gently.)* Frank.

HUBERT: The great love of your life, I see...And...what would he write? That he's sorry he let you go?

DINA: We let ourselves go.

HUBERT: And you have moments of regret and pain, I know. Why would he be writing to me? What about?

DINA: ...To take care of me. I seem strong. I'm not.

HUBERT: *(Ironical.)* How noble! And since he's so noble he might want to warn me that *you* are to blame for his sexual complex. A generous warning, I must admit!

(DINA ignores him.)

HUBERT: Incidentally, what sort of complex did he have? You never told me.

DINA: How would you like it if I discussed any of yours?

HUBERT: *(Outraged.)* Mine?! Do I have a complex? You must be crazy!

DINA: You're special. I'll never talk about your..."differences."

HUBERT: What do you mean by "special"? Is that better or worse than the others?

DINA: You're different. The way you talk, the questions you ask. You're unique—one in a million.

HUBERT: *(Flattered.)* Unique. I take that as a compliment. It's true, I'm one in a million. Irreplaceable! But you're not going to make me forget that letter by flattering me!

DINA: That was not my intention.

HUBERT: Interesting that you never bothered to look at it! If you could only make it disappear—you would feel free and relieved. You want to forget your past.

DINA: My past is past.

HUBERT: There must be significant reasons why you want to bury it forever. But someone is trying to warn me about you. Who do *you* think it could be?

DINA: *(Slowly.)* No one...There's no one who would want to hurt me...I have many friends...They respect me...

HUBERT: *(Ironical.)* Many friends...And why would they send an anonymous letter?

DINA: Maybe it's signed.

HUBERT: Those who sign put a return address too. Who would write an anonymous letter? A letter against you?

DINA: *(Softly.)* Jerry…

HUBERT: Who's Jerry?

DINA: My closest friend.

HUBERT: The one you never went to bed with?

DINA: Right.

HUBERT: And never kissed you?

DINA: Never.

HUBERT: What reason would he have to write an anonymous letter, if he's your best friend? Why? Because he's jealous? Or maybe because he didn't succeed in going to bed with you?

DINA: We never thought of that.

HUBERT: Why?

DINA: There's a difference between friendship and love.

HUBERT: *(Sarcastically.)* No love, in a friendship?

DINA: Companionship, fun together, liking the same things. It's like having a girlfriend.

HUBERT: Is he queer?

DINA: Could be. *(Smiling.)* Once I felt like asking him to be my bridesmaid.

HUBERT: Did you ask him?

DINA: I did.

HUBERT: What was his reaction?

DINA: He wept.

HUBERT: Is that why you didn't jump into bed with him?

DINA: No. Physical intimacy always spoils a friendship. Ours was a beautiful one. I would have lost him.

HUBERT: Friendship, love…You girls are so confused. I don't believe friendship can exist between a man and a woman.

DINA: I know you don't.

HUBERT: We're friends only because we're lovers.

DINA: I know that too.

HUBERT: Don't you prefer it that way, with me?

DINA: I do. You're special to me.

HUBERT: Maybe he didn't agree with your theory. Maybe he wanted to go to bed with you. To try to…

DINA: To try what?

HUBERT: To see if he could…make love.

DINA: It's possible.

HUBERT: What would he write in that letter?

DINA: We've known each other for years…He knows everything about me…He was around when I was at my worst…

HUBERT: What's your worst?

DINA: *(Gently.)* It would be much better for you to find out for yourself, by living with me…

HUBERT: *(Suspicious.)* Living with you? What do you mean?

DINA: What we're doing now. Meeting when you're free. Knowing each other more and more.

HUBERT: What would your "best friend" write? "Watch out, Hubert! She's unfaithful, fickle, a liar. She's the kind of girl who doesn't want to miss a thing!"

DINA: That's what *you* think of me. He would say other things.

HUBERT: What other things?

DINA: There was a kind of rivalry between the two of us…Because of our different backgrounds, maybe…If I was popular, he took it as a…personal defeat…He has already lost his battle with life…He'd like me to give up too…He wants to see a loser in me.

HUBERT: Why would he want to tell me all this?

DINA: To let you know that I'm ambitious…He would tell you that I don't love you…that I pretend to, so that you can help me with my career…

HUBERT: Is it true?

DINA: What?

HUBERT: That you're pretending to love me just because I am in a position to help you with your career?

DINA: *(Sad, tired, and resigned.)* Can't you tell? Can't you feel if I'm sincere or not?

HUBERT: I must admit, I can't. It's difficult to understand women. They all seem sincere in bed. All of them! But before and after…

DINA: Before and after?

HUBERT: You know. Reluctance, games…

DINA: I thought you knew and understood me.

HUBERT: I only know what I see. I don't know everything about your past.

DINA: Because I don't like the way you ask me. Demanding it. Feeling it's your right to know. I'll talk when I feel like talking. Later, when it's easier…

HUBERT: *(Ironical.)* When the right moment strikes you!

DINA: When there isn't this sadistic pressure of an inquisitor. I've loved, yes. I'm not ashamed of it. I am what I am because I've loved. I am a child of my past. Better, perhaps, for having loved.

HUBERT: *(Ironical.)* You have learned a few things, I know that. From everybody except, of course, your "best friend."

DINA: Let's forget that letter, please! What should have been a wonderful afternoon is becoming ugly. And all because of that silly letter. Come here.

HUBERT: *(Ignoring her invitation.)* No…I don't think that letter is from your "best friend"…He may be a jealous bridesmaid but there's a limit to how much one can hate…Maybe it's from those two brothers you played around with. *(Ironical.)* First with the younger one, then with the older one, then back to the young one! Yes—and they probably wrote: *(Rhetorical.)* "She was ours. She belongs to the family, to *our* family. Hands off!"

DINA: *(Hurt.)* I was fourteen years old and there was nothing between us! Nothing at all, I told you! At fourteen—one just wants to run and play. It's *you* who sees something sick in it!

HUBERT: *(Covert and sly.)* Tell me, could you do it with two boys at the same time?

DINA: At the same time?

HUBERT: Same month, two lovers.

(A brief silence.)

HUBERT: Have you ever done it?

DINA: *(Hurt.)* No.

HUBERT: This is the first reassurance I've had today. And I know you're not lying because you promised you would always be sincere with me. *(He studies her.)* Are you really being truthful with me? You wouldn't be unfaithful to me without telling me first?

DINA: I wouldn't…For my sake.

HUBERT: What do you mean—"for your sake"?

DINA: I couldn't...It would destroy me...I believe in being loyal...Being disloyal would kill any respect I have for myself, for my real self...I would feel unclean...Indecent...A person who adds wounds to wounds...who creates ghosts in the lives of other people...in the life of two men, in this case...I couldn't...I respect myself too much.

HUBERT: Selfishly, then. For yourself. Struggle for survival...

DINA: *(Resigned.)* I suppose so. If he doesn't accept the way you want to be, then you must be what he wants.

HUBERT: *(Confused.)* What do you mean?

DINA: I would rather be sincere on my own terms. A confidence at a time, when I felt more in love with you, when I felt you deserved it. Not like this...

HUBERT: Like what?

DINA: Not when you're demanding it, pressuring me, using that stupid letter as an excuse.

HUBERT: That you'd rather tear up! So that the ghosts of your past—and your sense of guilt—would die with it, forever!

DINA: *(Exploding.)* What could be so scandalous in that letter? That I have a child? That I was an addict selling dope to pay for my habit? That I've slept with my father? Or with women?

HUBERT: *(Deliberately.)* No...I don't think you had a child...physically you're still rather... *(Gesture.)* Drugs? No...You would have asked for it. You know it's no problem for me to get them...With your father...No...I hardly think so...You described him with disgust...Old, tired, passive—a failure as a man... *(He studies her with suspicion and curiosity.)* As for women... *(A brief silence.)* Yes that could be from Sylvia...a hysterical letter, overflowing with jealousy...Yes, from Sylvia...You always speak of her with adoration and emotion...Intensely...Your traveling to Mexico together...the showers you took together...Locked up—together—in that small hotel...I always wondered about her...I always found it strange the way you caress me when we're in bed...Tenderly, as if I had skin of satin...soft and smooth—like hers... I always suspected that...you like women.

(DINA has a tragic smile, sad and resigned. HUBERT steps back, slowly, with disgust. He exits. DINA gets up slowly, mechanically. Picks up the letter. Looks at it with sad irony. This letter has destroyed her love. She would like to read it. She is uncertain. She decides not to. She brings it to the candle that is still burning. She burns it.)

(CURTAIN. THE END.)

Mothers and Daughters

Characters:

MOTHER, in her early fifties.
PEGGY, her daughter, twenty-seven.
EMILY, another daughter, twenty-one.
BOBBY, her son, twenty-five.
ANN, his wife, twenty-four.
FATHER, a handsome man in his early fifties.

Time:

The present.

Place:

New York City.

An elegant apartment in New York City. MOTHER is alone, on the phone.

MOTHER: ...All right...I see your point...If you insist...All right, I believe you...

(PEGGY, using her own key, opens the door and enters. MOTHER signals that she is talking with "him." PEGGY walks slowly, avoiding any noise.)

MOTHER: ...I understand...I always understood everything, you know that...I've been accepting everything for years!...Too much...Yes, I said too much, and I repeat it. You know very well what I mean! All right, all right. I need the contract by Friday. Don't forget...Impatient? Of course!...Yes, Yes...Sure! *(MOTHER hangs up. To her daughter PEGGY.)* It was *him*. *(MOTHER starts to knit a white sweater.)*

PEGGY: And you called, of course!

MOTHER: You were late.

PEGGY: *(Annoyed.)* Couldn't you wait another half hour? He'll get suspicious. Every time I go to his place, you have to call. Did you ask about me?

MOTHER: Oh no! I just asked about the new contract for the Madrid house. *(Anxious.)* What did he tell you?

PEGGY: *(Lighting a cigarette.)* Sit down and relax.

(They both sit down. MOTHER tries to relax.)

PEGGY: He lives alone, like a monk.

MOTHER: Where did you read that monks sleep alone?

PEGGY: No trace of a female presence.

MOTHER: Are you sure?

PEGGY: I looked everywhere. Bedroom, bathroom, closets, even in the paper basket.

MOTHER: Kitchen? Laundry bag?

PEGGY: Even in the kitchen, even in his laundry. I tell you, he lives alone.

MOTHER: He's clever. The bitch arrives at midnight and gets out at dawn.

PEGGY: I gave ten dollars to the elevator man, to ask a few questions. No woman, ever. Just the old maid.

MOTHER: Same one?

PEGGY: Same one.

MOTHER: *(Unconvinced.)* The elevator man…he gets twenty to shut up. He knows how to bribe people.

PEGGY: Everything is possible. If you want to know more, hire a detective.

MOTHER: Never! I'll never stoop to that. I won't have my husband shadowed.

PEGGY: Then, what do you want from me?

MOTHER: Were you direct? Clear?

PEGGY: Not initially. I didn't want to be obvious, brazen…We first chatted a little bit. About the good old times in Paris, Rome, Madrid…

MOTHER: *(Sarcastic, bitter.)* The "good old times." Did *he* call them that?

PEGGY: He did. He mentioned we were a happy family.

MOTHER: That's what he said?

PEGGY: I sensed…a little bit of nostalgia.

MOTHER: He's a hypocrite! He knows how to convince and flatter! And you believe him! That man is incapable of nostalgia! Incapable of feeling anything!

I'm the past for him! Gone forever! He doesn't even know I exist!

PEGGY: You should have heard him. He was praising everything about you.

MOTHER: What do I do with "praise"? I need facts!

PEGGY: *(Carefully.)* Let's be realistic…

MOTHER: I am! I am! And look where I find myself! Alone! After thirty years of service!

PEGGY: I've had the impression…just the impression…

MOTHER: *(Hopefully.)* What?

PEGGY: …That he's all right alone…he likes it, he's happy…He needs it…he lives well, he writes more, he writes better.

MOTHER: "Better"?

PEGGY: It's easier for him. He gets up early, no problem…He just writes.

MOTHER: What do you mean, "no problem"? I served him breakfast in bed!

PEGGY: *(Careful.)* Breakfast, newspaper, letters, family matters…It killed his morning. Now he just gets up and writes.

MOTHER: That's what he told you! He resented my breakfasts, my presence! But he never had the guts to tell me to my face!

PEGGY: *(Avoiding.)* He has almost finished a new novel. He read me a chapter. Great stuff!

MOTHER: Does he write about *her*?

PEGGY: No. It's about a writer who—

MOTHER: As usual. Just himself! Nothing new there!

PEGGY: With some…humility this time.

MOTHER: *That's* new!

PEGGY: Some feeling, pathos, a very human sense of resignation.

MOTHER: What did he say about *her?* Did he mention her?

PEGGY: He tried to avoid the subject. I brought it up a couple of times. He had to...

MOTHER: What did he say?

PEGGY: The usual justifications. He rationalizes about the old theory—it's in his novel too—that we're eternally young, inside; he feels eighteen, in his heart.

MOTHER: The old goat! What did he say about *her?*

PEGGY: *(Carefully.)* His desire—I stand corrected—his *need* for a woman at his side, when—

MOTHER: He had three in this house! Three devoted servants! Three stupid slaves!

PEGGY: He has told me, he seemed sincere, that it's over! Gone and forgotten! He swears to it!

MOTHER: He swore on his mother's grave that he was faithful to me just the time when he was fu—. Forget it! You know who I'm talking about!

PEGGY: I'm telling you—he seemed honest this time.

MOTHER: A father like him can wrap a daughter like you around his little finger!

PEGGY: That's not true! I hated him for what he did to you, to the whole family! And I told him to his face, many times!

MOTHER: And then you begged for his forgiveness.

PEGGY: I just apologized. He's my father, after all. And this time I really felt he was sincere.

MOTHER: *(Sarcastic.)* More sincere than other times. That's easy! He's never been sincere in his life!

(We hear the doorbell.)

MOTHER: It's Bobby and Ann. I invited them to discuss the whole story.

(PEGGY goes to open the door. ANN enters.)

MOTHER: *(Surprised.)* Where's Bobby?

ANN: You know your son. He forgets everything. He had another appointment. Maybe—he said "maybe"—he'll pick me up.

MOTHER: *(Angry and bitter.)* Are you sure he had another appointment?

ANN: *(Uncertain.)* I think so. Why?

MOTHER: He's like his father. He lies. He wants to avoid all responsibilities.

PEGGY: He knew this was an important family get-together.

ANN: It's not his fault. He had to—

MOTHER: Call him. I want to talk to him.

ANN: *(Looking for it.)* I have his phone number...where he is now, but I don't know if I should—

MOTHER: I'm asking you. I'm his mother.

ANN: *(Dials the number. On phone.)* Hi...It's Ann...My husband, please... Bobby, I'm sorry to do this to you, but your mother—

(MOTHER grabs the receiver.)

ANN: Here she is.

MOTHER: Bobby, I told you it was most important for all of us to get together and you...I told you last week. You knew... All right, all right...Come as soon as possible. You're the man of the house now. You can't run away from your responsibilities!

(MOTHER hangs up. A silence.)

ANN: *(Timidly.)* Bobby doesn't run away from things. He prefers to—

MOTHER: *(Interrupting.)* I have known him twenty-seven years. You, eighteen months.

ANN: Three years. A wife sees and feels things a mother could never perceive.

MOTHER: What's that? Tell me about these *feelings* I could never perceive.

ANN: *(Timidly.)* He told me...he doesn't like being called "man of the house." Not here. He left because—

MOTHER: *(Angry, interrupting.)* He is the man here! From the moment his father abandoned us! *He is* the man of the house! Our man! *(She turns, trying to hide her tears.)*

PEGGY: *(Consoling her.)* Calm down, Mama. He's coming later. He promised Ann.

MOTHER: He promised *me*!

PEGGY: *(Ignoring, jokingly.)* And if he doesn't show up, we'll keep Ann here—as our hostage!

ANN: *(Jokingly.)* Oh, please, don't tell him, or he'll never show up again!

MOTHER: *(Turning to face her again.)* Does he know why we're meeting here today?

ANN *(Uncertain.)* I think so...He told me...

MOTHER: What did he tell you?

ANN: ...You're going to talk about his father, your future...

MOTHER: Does he know about his father?

ANN: ...He does...

MOTHER: What does he know?

ANN: We've seen him...

MOTHER: *(Curious.)* Where?

PEGGY: *(Simultaneously.)* With whom?

ANN: *(Cautiously.)* We were at the restaurant...across from Lincoln Center...He passed by...He went to the concert...

MOTHER: With whom?

ANN: ...I prefer Bobby to tell you...

MOTHER: Was he with a woman?

(A silence.)

MOTHER: With that slut?

ANN: Bobby told me she is his secretary.

MOTHER: Secretary, my foot! She's a cow! Have you followed them?

ANN: I haven't...Bobby did...He waited for the end of the concert, he took a taxi and...

MOTHER *(Tense.)* Where did they go?

ANN: *(Uncertain.)* ...Bobby will tell you...

MOTHER: The hypocrite! That's why he didn't want to come here tonight! I know him well! He can't face reality! *(To ANN.)* You tell me! Women have more guts! Where did they go?

PEGGY *(To ANN, who is confused.)* It's nothing new...Mama knows...

ANN: Why does she want to hear it from me, then?

PEGGY: She wants a confirmation.

MOTHER: They went to her hotel, didn't they?

(ANN nods.)

MOTHER *(Tense, to PEGGY.)* I told you! They're still doing it! In that whore's hotel! That's why you found no trace of the bitch in his place!

(ANN looks at them with surprise. She did not know these details.)

MOTHER: *(Almost to herself.)* In her hotel…where everybody can see them!

PEGGY: Mother…you must accept the fact that he sees her because he needs her—

(MOTHER looks at her ferociously, with hatred.)

PEGGY: As his secretary. You know his habits. He writes late, as late as four o'clock in the morning—

MOTHER: "Writes"? In a bedroom?

PEGGY: You told me that when you were young and poor, he used to—

MOTHER: *(Interrupting.)* He's not poor any longer, that bastard! He can afford ten secretaries! In his office, at any time!

PEGGY: He told me that… *(She hesitates.)*

MOTHER: What else did he tell you?

PEGGY: He admitted he still sees her—as secretary, only as secretary. She is useful to him. She corrects his spelling.

MOTHER: She corrects something else, that whore!

PEGGY: He also told me about…sex.

MOTHER: Sex?

PEGGY: He told me he doesn't need it any longer. Writing is his sublimation.

MOTHER: Don't tell me! I know his habits and appetites. That…rabbit!

PEGGY: He's older. Years go by.

MOTHER: Not for him! Didn't he tell you he feels eighteen?

PEGGY: Spiritually.

MOTHER: That bastard doesn't even know where the spirit is. He screws, selfishly. And that's it!

PEGGY: *(Careful.)* …"Selfishly," you say…Then…good riddance! He's not such a big loss!

ANN: *(Curiously.)* What do you mean by "selfishly"?

MOTHER: This one wants sexual tips now!

ANN: *(Confused.)* Tips? *(To PEGGY.)* You tell me. What does Mama mean?

MOTHER: *(Mocking her.)* "Mama"…Bobby is not like him, I hope!

ANN: *(Lost.)* He's not. He's younger, taller…

MOTHER: *(To PEGGY.)* Tell her to shut up.

PEGGY: Shut up.

ANN: *(Hurt.)* Why? You're talking about my husband. Bobby is not selfish. He buys me things all the time. Look at this scarf. He found it—

MOTHER: And where did he find you?

ANN: You know. I was skating and—

MOTHER: And fell on your ass. He noticed it—men like blue asses—and—

ANN: Why blue? Mine is—

MOTHER: Pink like your brain, I know! *(Turning, trying to control herself.)* I'll kill her! I'll kill her!

ANN: Who? *(To PEGGY.)* She's in a foul mood today.

PEGGY: *(Signaling her to shut up.)* The slut we were talking about.

ANN: *(Insisting.)* We were talking about sexual selfishness, I think. I don't think I'm selfish. I—

PEGGY: *(Stuffing a cookie in her mouth.)* Mama made them. They're tops!

ANN: Oh, thank you! May I have another cup of coffee?

PEGGY: Help yourself!

MOTHER: And wake up! Men take advantage of ducks like you! They can smell them!

ANN: *(Hurt.)* I'm no duck and Bobby loves me. He's the best possible husband.

MOTHER: So much the better for you. What does Bobby say about all this? You speak in bed, don't you?

ANN: Also at breakfast, and during dinner.

MOTHER: What does he say!

ANN: *(Careful.)* He's a realist…He says…when a couple doesn't get along anymore, why stay together?

MOTHER: Do you understand what he's trying to say?

ANN: …That if you and your husband—

MOTHER: *(Interrupting.)* A couple. You and him. He's preparing the ground.

ANN: *(Vaguely worried.)* For what?

MOTHER: To drop you like a hot potato! No conscience, like his father! The years spent together! The family! What people say! Like father, like son!

ANN: Bobby is faithful. I'm enough for him!

MOTHER: More than enough! And the humiliation! You'll feel what humiliation is, when he dumps you!

PEGGY: Mother!

MOTHER: *(Ignoring.)* And the gossip! Neighbors staring at you, smirking!

ANN: *(Taking another cookie.)* We have no neighbors. How do you make these, Mama? They're great!

MOTHER: With my feet!

ANN: Really? Bobby always tells me that you're the best cook in the world. I'll never please him with—

MOTHER: *Never!* I'm sure of that. Tell me. What do Bobby's friends say behind my back?

ANN: We have no friends. Don't worry so much, Mama. Nobody knows. I haven't seen it in any paper! Not even the smallest item, like this!

MOTHER: "Not even!" That's what we need! A few tiny items, like that! *(Mimes her—mocks her.)* And all because of that little whore!

PEGGY: *(Alarmed.)* Mother!

(A silence. MOTHER was about to reveal some secret ANN is not supposed to know.)

ANN: "Little" whore! The one we saw was tall and strong. Some kind of Amazon.

PEGGY: "Little" intellectually…Amazons have no brains.

ANN: Just big teats, I know. I mean, all the exercise, the horse, bow and arrows…I'm sorry…

(They stare at her. ANN feels ill at ease.)

ANN: Forgive me…But when you said "little," I immediately visualized… *(Gesture of large breasts.)*

PEGGY: Forget what Mother said. Tonight she's a bit—

ANN: A bit—what?

PEGGY: That outburst. She didn't mean it.

(Another silence. PEGGY and MOTHER stare at ANN.)

ANN: You're hiding something from me...There's another woman in his life...

MOTHER: *Ten*, before that fat slob! But he used to dump them after a few quickies! With this one...they've been whooping it up for three years!

PEGGY: Good riddance, Mother! You don't need him.

MOTHER: I don't need him in my bed. I need him at home.

(We hear a key in the door. It is EMILY, the other daughter. She is four years younger than PEGGY.)

ANN: Hi, Emily.

EMILY: Hi.

(PEGGY smiles at her faintly. MOTHER ignores her. A silence.)

EMILY: What were you talking about?

PEGGY: Guess.

EMILY: I've guessed.

ANN: Good girl. Want one of Mama's cookies?

EMILY: No, thanks.

PEGGY: Ann and Bobby have seen him with his..."secretary."

(MOTHER turns to study EMILY's reaction. No reaction. A silence.)

MOTHER: *(To EMILY.)* You don't seem surprised.

EMILY: It's nothing new.

MOTHER: *(Aggressive.)* Today, two hours ago, he swore to Peggy—she went to his place—that he doesn't see her any longer! He lied, that snake! He doesn't live alone.

EMILY: He lives alone.

MOTHER: How do you know?

EMILY: We all know.

MOTHER: Who's "we"?

EMILY: Family—you always talk about it. The others.

MOTHER: Who are the others?

EMILY: *(Vague.)* Gossip-mongers. They've nothing else to do. *(She looks at ANN, inadvertently.)*

ANN: *(Who is still eating cookies.)* Why look at me? I didn't even know he had ten, before Olga!

MOTHER: *Never say that name in this house!*

PEGGY: Never.

ANN: I'm sorry...

EMILY: Ten, Olga...

(They all stare at her. They can feel defiance.)

EMILY: You know a great deal...

ANN: They told me!

MOTHER: *(Ignoring ANN.)* When did you see him last?

EMILY: A couple of months ago.

MOTHER: Where?

EMILY: My office. He dropped by.

MOTHER: What did he want?

EMILY: Talk.

MOTHER: What about?

EMILY: The usual.

MOTHER: What's the usual? Be specific.

EMILY: *(To PEGGY.)* What do you talk about, when you're with him? Like today.

PEGGY: About Mother.

EMILY: *(To ANN.)* What do you talk about, when you see Daddy?

MOTHER: *(Before ANN can answer.)* What's the "usual"?

EMILY: *(Without turning.)* His life. I was talking to Ann. *(To ANN, again.)* What do you talk about?

ANN: ...Bobby, his work, our place...when we'll give him a grandchild.

MOTHER: *(Interrupting.)* Don't!

EMILY: *(Still ignoring her mother, to ANN.)* When?

ANN: ...Mama thinks...Bobby too... We'll wait...

MOTHER: "Grandfather"! He would choke the baby who makes him a grandfather, revealing his real age! He'll drop your baby in the bathtub and drown him!

PEGGY: Mother!

MOTHER: And you know that too. You know what your father is capable of!

ANN: In my opinion—

MOTHER: I have no interest in your opinion. *(To EMILY.)* Did you have lunch together?

EMILY: That day? Let me think...We did.

MOTHER: Did you talk about me?

EMILY: *(Deliberate, trying to remember.)* ...Well...Yes, of course...We spoke about everything.

MOTHER: What's "everything"?

EMILY: *(Losing her patience.)* Do you see why I seldom come here? And why I never see Daddy! Because you're both obsessive!

MOTHER: *(Studying her.)* ...Both of us...obsessive...In different ways, I guess...

EMILY: Of course! You're different!

MOTHER: He's obsessive, in what way?

EMILY: You know him.

MOTHER: I don't, obviously. I've lost him.

PEGGY: Good riddance!

ANN: Good...

(MOTHER looks at her with a fulminating stare. ANN is ill at ease.)

ANN: ...Riddance...as they say...When a man doesn't deserve a great woman...like you...or like me...

MOTHER: *(Ignoring her, to EMILY.)* Obsessive, how?

EMILY: Questions, curiosity...

MOTHER: What kind of questions?

EMILY: You see? You've a lot in common!

MOTHER: We have nothing in common! Nothing! What kind of questions?

EMILY: Morbid ones.

MOTHER: The bastard! Is he still jealous?

EMILY: All fathers are.

MOTHER: He's a "special"...one! Any mention of..."sexual morality"?

EMILY: You know his boring theory.

ANN: What's his boring theory?

MOTHER: *(To ANN.)* Men can fuck anyone! Women must not. *(To EMILY.)* Did he mention his sexual "needs"?

(ANN is following with great curiosity. PEGGY is worried and intervenes.)

PEGGY: Mother…we have a guest: Ann.

ANN: A guest?

MOTHER: She married that coward of your brother. What he knows, she knows. *(Ironically.)* They talk in bed!

ANN: What am I supposed to know?

MOTHER: Everything. You're part of the family!

(PEGGY is very worried. She signals her mother to control herself and not to say everything.)

ANN: Tell me.

MOTHER: Learn to listen. If you were not so dumb, you would understand.

ANN *(To PEGGY.)* What does she mean? I always listen! What am I supposed to understand?

PEGGY: Nothing special. You know about Father. It's not easy to forget and forgive. Mother cannot. You try.

ANN: Try what? I'm confused.

PEGGY: Forget and forgive. Mother is angry.

ANN: With me? Why?

PEGGY: Please shut up.

ANN: No! I've the right to know!

PEGGY: *(Trying to save the situation.)* Father sees that woman—

MOTHER: And other ones! *(Looks at EMILY with hatred.)* And it's her fault!

(We hear a key in the door. BOBBY comes in. He is wearing a white sweater, the type his mother is knitting.)

MOTHER: It's all her fault!

(ANN runs to BOBBY and kisses him.)

ANN: How are you, love?

BOBBY: *(Who has heard MOTHER's last line.)* What's going on here?

(ANN shrugs. She does not want to make another mistake.)

BOBBY: *(To MOTHER.)* What do you mean by saying it's Emily's fault?

(A silence—immobility.)

(The same apartment, a few days later. Bobby and Peggy are alone. Peggy is very nervous; she is smoking. Bobby is questioning her. He is wearing the white sweater his mother was knitting before.)

BOBBY: Ann told me something was going on among you three…Something unusual, that evening.

PEGGY: Some tension, yes. You know how nervous Mother is.

BOBBY: Something more…Something new…Emily was being accused of…I don't know what. Ann was feeling it in the air. What was it? Why did Mother tell her: "It's all your fault!" What did she mean?

PEGGY: Mother always accuses everybody. Sometimes me, sometimes you. Now it's Emily's turn. What she was trying to say is that we're all guilty, the three of us. We should have kept the family together.

BOBBY: How? I stayed here until I was twenty-six! A good son, nice and patient, the victim of her hysteria!

PEGGY: Don't let her hear you. You've insulted her enough, with hints like that. And you've fought a lot with Daddy. Mother has mentioned it a few times. She says Daddy wouldn't have left her if we had more harmony in this family.

BOBBY: Wonderful! It's my fault now if they don't get along! My responsibilities are becoming…vaguely clear. What about you? You didn't fight with Daddy.

PEGGY: I've hurt him a lot—she says... My first affair—

BOBBY: That's true. He was furious.

PEGGY: My running away with his best friend.

BOBBY: That was even worse. I thought he would never speak to you again.

PEGGY: He didn't, for a couple of years. Mother thinks that was the beginning of the end.

BOBBY: What do you mean?

PEGGY: She thinks I poisoned their relationship, by falling in love with...the wrong men.

BOBBY: They were the wrong men.

PEGGY: Like father, like son.

BOBBY: But why would your escapades affect their relationship?

PEGGY: The old story. When I was a good girl, they were both vying over me. When I became a rebel and started to screw—

BOBBY: I don't like that language.

PEGGY: I'm sorry. I forget you're my brother. When I...fell in love, the accusations started. "She's like you!" said Daddy. "No. She's like you!" retorted Mother.

BOBBY: All right. I spoke too much. You did too much. What about Emily? The baby, the angel in the family. What's she guilty of?

PEGGY: More than us, in a way...

BOBBY: In what way?

PEGGY: She left home early...Younger than me. Mother has never forgiven her. In her opinion, it was the last straw...

BOBBY: Why?

PEGGY: The youngest...Daddy's "treasure," do you remember?

BOBBY: Of course, I remember, and I didn't like being ignored. Then I learned how to live with it. All fathers prefer the baby.

PEGGY: When she left, everything went downhill, according to Mother.

BOBBY: That's a nice compliment for the two of us. We were still around when she went. We don't count!

PEGGY: We count a little bit. That's why she's blaming us too.

(ANN enters; she was in the bedroom with MOTHER and EMILY.)

ANN: They're calmer now. A few tears, a big hug.

PEGGY: Thank you. They listen to you.

BOBBY: Because Ann is the wisest woman in the world!

ANN: *(Ironical.)* The best. But also because I am a "guest."

BOBBY: A "guest"? My wife!

PEGGY: Mother has used that word a couple of times. Ann can't forget and forgive.

BOBBY: Of course she can! She forgives me all the time!

PEGGY: Really? What's there to be forgiven? What Mother mentioned?

BOBBY: What did she mention?

PEGGY: That you're like Daddy. A great Casanova.

BOBBY: That's the first compliment I ever got from my mother. Unfortunately, it's not true.

ANN: Unfortunately?

BOBBY: I'm joking. You know me.

ANN: I know you. Your mother doesn't joke though. Her words are like knives. *(She indicates the bedroom.)* She called

Emily some ferocious names. Then she burst into tears…

BOBBY: My mother? I never saw her crying.

PEGGY: You don't need tears with a son.

ANN: I guess you saw her crying when your father—

PEGGY: A few times. But after a while she hugs you and forgives.

(We hear voices from the bedroom. MOTHER and EMILY are fighting again. We hear some fragments of conversation.)

VOICES:…You should have…guilt…fault…shame…to be blamed for…family…inconsiderate…love…not again…you don't love…you should…

(EMILY bursts into the room, angry and upset. She is followed by her mother.)

MOTHER: Come here! It's an order! And don't leave a room before I tell you!

(EMILY tries to talk.)

MOTHER: Don't interrupt me when I'm talking! You owe me respect! I'm your mother!

(ANN and PEGGY try to calm MOTHER. EMILY goes to BOBBY, who is ready to protect her somehow.)

BOBBY *(Holding EMILY.)* You're right, Mother! I'll take care of Emily!

(Signals the two women to control MOTHER.)

MOTHER: She's ungrateful! The most ungrateful of my children!

PEGGY and ANN: Yes, Mama…You're right…

BOBBY: I'll talk to Emily…I'll remind her what having a mother means…

(ANN and PEGGY take MOTHER away into the bedroom.)

MOTHER: *(Before exiting.)* Tell her how much she owes us! I want obedience and respect in this house! It's still my house! It will always be my house!

BOBBY: It's our duty, I know…I'll tell Emily… *(Pretending to admonish her.)* You, Emily… *(Waves his finger.)*

(The three women go into the bedroom. BOBBY and EMILY are left alone.)

BOBBY: *(Nice and gentle.)* What's going on now? What does she want from you?

(A silence: EMILY needs someone to talk to; she hesitates: she changes her mind.)

BOBBY: Tell me. You know I am your friend.

EMILY: I know.

BOBBY: What's she accusing you of?

EMILY: The usual complaints…She's alone, unhappy…She has to blame somebody. She blames me.

BOBBY: *(Playing cat and mouse.)* Peggy told me.

EMILY: Told you what?

BOBBY: She explained.

EMILY: *(Tense, alarmed.)* Explained what?

BOBBY: The reasons why she resents us…

EMILY: "Us"?

BOBBY: The three of us…

EMILY: What…would these reasons be?

BOBBY: We left home…We have, according to Peggy, destroyed family harmony.

EMILY: According to Mother.

BOBBY: And to Peggy. What do you think?

EMILY: *(Cautiously.)* Mother mentioned that a few times…

BOBBY: Mentioned what?

EMILY: The three of us, selfish, leaving home, creating problems...

BOBBY: What problems?

EMILY: Ask Mother. She created them, by accusing us.

BOBBY: *(Still playing cat and mouse.)* Peggy told me something else...

(A silence; they study each other.)

EMILY: Let's have it.

BOBBY: You already know what she's going to say.

EMILY: Maybe.

BOBBY: It's about you.

EMILY: Naturally.

BOBBY: According to Peggy—you're more responsible...

EMILY: What's new?

BOBBY: Mother is more aggressive with you, blames you more because you left before us...You were younger.

(They study each other.)

BOBBY: The baby...the youngest...Do you think Mother might be jealous of his love for you? He cared a great deal about you...You always got more attention than all of us together.

EMILY: And I am to blame, of course. Thank you!

BOBBY: Do you think she is jealous?

EMILY: Ten minutes ago she was telling me to ask him back here. All of us together. She's not jealous.

BOBBY: You'll never convince him. Peggy tried. I tried. Nothing doing. He's stubborn. With the excuse he's a writer, he gets away with murder. He needs...

(Sarcastic and bitter.) "Variety, relationships, women!" He'll never come back to Mother.

EMILY: That's what I think too. This reunion will be a sad flop. I told her. He's coming out of duty. Maybe pity.

BOBBY: I'll ask him too. Just to try. Just to please Mother. It's going to be damn embarrassing. He won't budge. He won't give up his freedom. Why should he?

EMILY: Not today. But when you have a chance, later, try to convince Mother...

BOBBY: What about?

EMILY: That she should accept...

BOBBY: We need patience. She's the typical martyr. The betrayed abandoned wife who must scream at somebody. We happen to be around.

EMILY: I wasn't, for a while. She tracked me down. *I am* the victim.

BOBBY: Let's hope it's for the last time. Father will say no in front of everybody. She'll be forced to accept it.

EMILY: She has a plan for tonight.

BOBBY: What plan?

EMILY: It's a trap. She'll entice him back by promising... *(She hesitates.)*

BOBBY: By promising what?

(PEGGY enters. She was in the bedroom with MOTHER.)

PEGGY: *(To EMILY.)* What the hell did you tell her? She was hysterical!

EMILY: *(Avoiding.)* We're going out for a while.

(EMILY takes BOBBY's hand. He is surprised.)

BOBBY: We are?

PEGGY: *(Surprised.)* Daddy will be here any moment now. We promised the whole family would be here.

EMILY: Just ten minutes.

BOBBY: Five minutes. We'll be back right away.

PEGGY: Buy Father's favorite. Strawberry ice cream.

EMILY: *(Vaguely ironical.)* Strawberry. Are you sure?

PEGGY: *(Puzzled.)* I'm sure.

EMILY: *(Smiling.)* Strawberry it will be.

(EMILY and BOBBY exit. PEGGY hesitates for a moment. She then dials a number on the phone. She waits. No answer. MOTHER and ANN enter.)

MOTHER: *(Alarmed.)* Where's Emily?

ANN: And Bobby?

MOTHER: Where did they go?

PEGGY: Just for ice cream, Mother.

MOTHER: On a day like this, ice cream?

PEGGY: For Daddy. You know how much he likes it.

MOTHER *(Suspicious, to PEGGY, who has still her hand on the phone.)* Who were you calling?

PEGGY: Daddy. To see if he has left his place.

MOTHER: *(Upset.)* He won't come, he won't come.

ANN: He will. He promised.

PEGGY: He always keeps his promises.

MOTHER *(Bitterly.)* Does he?

PEGGY: Promises like this. Dates.

(A silence; PEGGY has used the wrong word; MOTHER stares at her. The doorbell. MOTHER is nervous and fixes her hair.)

PEGGY: *(To MOTHER.)* Watch it now. Control yourself. Only if you show you're calm and rational, there is some hope.

(PEGGY goes to open the door. It is her father. A very handsome man. He has a winning smile and is at ease, very sure of himself. He is wearing the same white sweater his wife knits.)

FATHER: Hi, everybody. *(Kisses PEGGY's cheek.)*

MOTHER: Why didn't you use your key?

FATHER: I'm sorry, my dear. Forgive me. It just slipped my mind. Habit...Lately... *(He senses he must not insist on that subject.)* Where are Emily and Bobby?

PEGGY: They went to buy ice cream. Your flavor.

FATHER: Heavenly hash. How nice of them?

PEGGY: *(Puzzled.)* Heavenly...

FATHER: You remember too. The only flavor I can't resist. *(Kisses ANN's cheek.)* How can Bobby manage to stay away from you? Even if it's for five minutes only. *(He caresses her belly.)* When will you give me my first grandchild?

ANN: In two years' time.

FATHER: *(Joking, pretending to be alarmed.)* What are you going to deliver? An elephant? You are more beautiful every time I see you. Someone is going to kidnap you soon.

(He moves, slowly, cautiously, toward his wife, who is motionless. He hesitates, studying her. He kisses her cheek.)

FATHER: And your mother is getting younger...You look like sisters.

(A silence. No one dares to speak. Everyone is ill at ease. He sits down on the sofa.)

FATHER: Well, well...Tell me everything...What's new?

ANN: *(Breaking the ice.)* Bobby got a raise. They like him at the office. He gets along with everybody now.

FATHER: Good. He learned.

ANN: We're happy.

FATHER: What about your plans? You mentioned you wanted to go back to college.

ANN: In September. I want to take anthropology.

FATHER: Good choice. "Anthropos." The more we know about man, the better it is.

MOTHER: Man—the beast.

FATHER: In every man, a beast. And vice versa.

PEGGY *(Confused.)* And vice versa?

FATHER: Let's drop it. What about you, Peggy? Have you written any new short story?

PEGGY: After the way you criticized the last one? Never again!

FATHER: I'm sorry I discouraged you. I really thought my criticism was constructive. I liked the beginning a great deal. And I told you. It was almost perfect.

PEGGY: "Almost."

FATHER: Do you want me to lie? I'm your father; I love you. He who loves must always tell the truth.

MOTHER: *(Ironically and bitter.)* Ha!

FATHER: *(Ignoring.)* I wasn't trying to discourage you. On the contrary. You've got talent.

PEGGY: How come you said the ending was horrible?

FATHER: I didn't say "horrible." I said...unclear, uncommitted, uninteresting, Un—

PEGGY: *(Cutting.)* That's enough! Thank you.

FATHER: Don't give up! You'll make it. Any new poems?

PEGGY: *(Reluctant.)* ...A short one...

FATHER: Show it to me.

(PEGGY hesitates. FATHER smiles encouragingly. She goes slowly to a book, opens it, takes a sheet out, and hands it to her father.)

FATHER: *(Reading it.)* Interesting...Come tomorrow morning to my studio. We'll discuss the details, a couple of wrong words...Minor changes.

(He puts the poem in his pocket. A silence. They are uneasy again.)

FATHER: *(To his wife.)* What about you, darling? What's new in your life?

MOTHER: I'm waiting.

(An uneasy silence.)

FATHER: We are all waiting, more or less...In different ways...I just delivered the first three chapters of my new novel. I'm waiting for reactions...

(An uneasy silence.)

FATHER: *(To PEGGY.)* Did you tell Mother about my new novel?

PEGGY: I told her.

FATHER: *(To his wife.)* Darling, please... let's try to be civil, human, cordial...You invited me for an important family reunion. Here I am. I've come with anticipation and joy. You know how much I care about you all...Emily and Bobby, where are they?

PEGGY: *(Looking outside the window for a moment.)* They said they would be back right away. Any minute now...

ANN: Any minute, I'm sure. Bobby is never late.

(An uneasy silence.)

FATHER: *(Trying again, to his wife.)* And you, darling? Do you go out a great deal?

MOTHER: No.

FATHER: You should. Plays, concerts, to have some fun...

MOTHER: I prefer to stay home. Waiting.

(We hear someone opening the door: it is EMILY: FATHER is very happy to see her; he gets up, welcomes her by kissing her forehead.)

FATHER: Emily, finally! I was beginning to worry. Where's my ice cream?

ANN: Where's Bobby?

EMILY: He didn't feel well. A headache. He's waiting for you at home.

ANN: *(Utterly surprised.)* A headache? How come? Never before! Never in his life! *(Rushes toward the door, waving to everybody.)* Bye! Bye! Goodbye! *(Kisses FATHER; exits.)*

(Another uneasy silence.)

PEGGY: Where did he go?

EMILY: I saw him heading toward Grand Central.

FATHER: *(Surprised.)* Grand Central?

MOTHER: *(To EMILY.)* What did you tell him?

(They look at each other. A silence.)

EMILY: Everything.

(A silence. Tension.)

FATHER: What does that mean?

EMILY: He knows everything now. He'll never set foot in this house again.

(A silence.)

MOTHER: So much the better. Two men in the same family...Egos, conflicts. It would have created problems.

FATHER: Two men?

MOTHER: We had a family reunion...Ann doesn't know anything yet...Bobby did not know until a few moments ago... *(A pause.)* We *(She indicates her husband and PEGGY.)* all know why Emily left this house at eighteen...

FATHER: *(Tries to say something.)* I must...I really want to explain—

MOTHER: I am not accusing you of anything...It's all forgotten, all forgiven...Tell him, Emily.

EMILY: *(Uneasy.)* Mother thinks...She hopes that you will come back to live with us, here, if...

MOTHER: If...Tell him.

EMILY: It's your idea. You tell him.

MOTHER: *(To FATHER.)* You admitted one day you wouldn't have left this house if Emily had not run away...Didn't you?

FATHER: Well...it was painful, a surprise, a delusion...the baby in the family...Our little Emily...running away like that.

MOTHER: Admit it.

FATHER: In a way...it was a determining factor...the last straw...I admit it.

MOTHER: *(To EMILY.)* Did you hear? Tell him about our proposal.

(PEGGY is observing the scene in silence, as tense as an arrow.)

EMILY: Mother knows everything...We spoke about it...

PEGGY: *(To EMILY.)* You always denied it.

EMILY: I denied it to save the family. I'm admitting it now, to save the family.

MOTHER: Tell Daddy.

EMILY: *(Uneasy, reluctant.)* I'm ready to come back here...to live at home...

FATHER: *(Uncertain.)* ...to come back...

MOTHER: *(To her husband.)* If you come back too...to live with us...

(A silence. Tension.)

MOTHER: *(To EMILY.)* Tell him...

EMILY: Mother knows about us...She accepts...everything...like before.

MOTHER: Everything like before. For the family.

(A silence. All eyes are now on FATHER.)

MOTHER: Everything...Emily accepts too. Everything like before. You need her...You can have her.

FATHER: *(Touched, hesitating.)* Well...if it is for the family...for all of us...for the world...I understand... *(Looks at EMILY with love.)* I accept...I'll come back.

PEGGY: *(Turning suddenly; she has a gun in her hand.)* Now!

(PEGGY shoots her father. A red spot on the white sweater. He dies.)

PEGGY: *(To EMILY.)* You've paid enough, Emily. It's my turn now.

(They hug desperately, with love. MOTHER is motionless, frozen. Tableau.)

(THE END.)

Beata, the Pope's Daughter

The Persons:

BEATA
GUSTAV: her boyfriend; a Swiss guard at the Vatican
TEOFILA: Beata's mother
PIOTR: Beata's father
THE HOLY FATHER (John Paul II)
AHMET: Turkish; a member of the "Grey Wolves"
ZEKI: Turkish: a member of the "Grey Wolves"

Place:

Rome

Time:

Act One takes place in 1981, before the attempt on the Holy Father's life; Beata is in the third month of her pregnancy. Act Two takes place six months later; Beata is in the ninth month of her pregnancy.

Ten a.m. A modest bedroom upstage. Downstage left, the papal throne. Religious music in the background.

VOICE OF THE HOLY FATHER: *(From stage left.)* God created man in his own image. Man and woman he created…Man and woman, in the context of their beatificating principle. They are free in the liberty of their gift…A reciprocal gift of love, disinterested…Woman finds herself in giving herself through a sincere gift of herself…And they were both naked, the man and his woman, and they were not ashamed.

(Lights up on BEATA and GUSTAV, who are in bed, half-naked. They have just finished making love and are exchanging tender kisses in the afterglow. BEATA slides off her side of the bed and kneels down, hands united in a prayer. GUSTAV imitates her and kneels beside her.)

BEATA: I thank you, dear God…

GUSTAV: I thank you, dear God…

BEATA: Our Lord, generous and loving…

GUSTAV: Our Lord, generous and loving…

BEATA: For giving us…

GUSTAV: For giving us…

BEATA: The gift of love…

GUSTAV: The gift of love…

BEATA: When one wants to procreate…

GUSTAV: When one wants to procreate…

BEATA: To create a new soul for the glory of Heaven...

GUSTAV: To create a new soul for the glory of Heaven...

BEATA: We don't sin.

GUSTAV: We don't sin.

BEATA: As the Holy Father says...

GUSTAV: As the Holy Father says...

BEATA: "Eve's body was the arena and origin of temptation and sin..."

GUSTAV: Of temptation and sin.

BEATA: "Mary's body was the arena of redemption and saintliness..."

GUSTAV: Redemption and saintliness.

BEATA: I don't feel like Eve.

GUSTAV: *(Absentminded.)* I don't feel like Eve.

(BEATA stares at him reproachfully.)

GUSTAV: *(Correcting himself.)* I don't feel like Adam, the sinner.

BEATA: But like Mary. Her body was a temple of redemption.

GUSTAV: *(Vaguely confused.)* ...Redemption.

BEATA: *(Sits on the bed again.)* How do you feel?

GUSTAV: *(Joining her in the bed.)* Great!

BEATA: Do you feel the joy I feel?

GUSTAV: Sure, sure, love is redemption...love is joy...joy and redemption.

BEATA: And also when we make love only out of desire, tenderness—not to procreate—there is a feeling of joy, redemption, beauty. *(Stares at GUSTAV.)* Do you think the Holy Father is against our love, now that I am expecting a baby? Do you think he disapproves of us when we make love only because we desire each other?

GUSTAV: No...He loves you...He forgives you.

BEATA: He said once: "Whoever looks at a woman with desire has already committed adultery with her in his heart." Was he talking about you when you look at me with lust?

GUSTAV: No. He was talking about sinners, those who only want pleasure...We want a baby...we are expecting our heir, our child.

BEATA: Expecting... *(With love and tenderness.)* Touch here...I think I feel it...a new life, a new soul...

(BEATA puts GUSTAV's hand on her belly.)

GUSTAV: ...Nothing now...He must be asleep. *(Deciding to speak on a new subject.)* Beata...

BEATA: Yes, love. Tell me.

GUSTAV: This plan of yours...to go away...

BEATA: You're coming with me.

GUSTAV: Of course...but...I don't understand...I don't agree...This baby...*(Indicates BEATA's belly.)* should be born in Rome... There are one thousand reasons why...We both know why...we should stay here.

BEATA: No. They wouldn't understand. We have to elope, disappear for a few months...Don't worry about the expenses...I have some money put aside. And you said you have some...

GUSTAV: Sure, sure. I have some savings. I can help.

BEATA: We only need some money for a room and food. Hospitals are free in those countries.

GUSTAV: Poland or England—...Have you decided which one?

BEATA: I'll let *him* decide. It's all the same to me.

GUSTAV: *Him*... *(Reflecting.)* What will you...you tell him, if you succeed in seeing him?

BEATA: Everything. The whole truth. You don't lie to him...him who knows how to read your thoughts, to him who knows everything.

GUSTAV: And...will he understand?

BEATA: He will. And he'll be happy we're expecting a child.

GUSTAV: *(Incredulous.)* I hope so.

BEATA: You know how he feels. A fetus is sacred. Life is sacred. At any stage, even if it is just a glimmer of life. He said—about parents—that they are the ministers of the design established by the Creator. He was talking about us too: "Ministers." I like that word. It makes me feel important. What about you?

GUSTAV: Me too, me too.

BEATA: Because you are with me. A "minister" like me.

GUSTAV: Because of that, sure. But...

BEATA: *(Encouraging him.)* Tell me, love.

GUSTAV: We are not married and He—

BEATA: He'll understand. He will marry us.

GUSTAV: *(Doubtful.)* Maybe...And I probably will not be allowed to stay in Rome.

BEATA: He'll decide. He'll help us.

GUSTAV: You are so confident...

BEATA: I have faith. Faith in him, in his goodness, in his understanding and wisdom.

GUSTAV: *(Hesitatingly, cautiously.)* Maybe it would be better if...

BEATA: *(Curious.)* Better if? What are you trying to say?

GUSTAV: *(Cautiously.)* You see, if we started from scratch...

BEATA: What do you mean from scratch?

GUSTAV: As if we didn't know each other—

BEATA: As if we didn't know each other? We've been seen together for months.

GUSTAV: I mean...as if we didn't have this... *(Indicates her belly.)* intimate relationship.

BEATA: What are you trying to say? What do you really mean?

GUSTAV: I'll ask your father for your hand, formally we will ask for *his* permission; we will get married.

BEATA: *(Perplexed, thinking it over.)* "As if we didn't know each other..." *(Caresses her belly.)* and this baby?

GUSTAV: *(Cautious.)* We could—as I said before...start from scratch.

BEATA: How? Explain.

GUSTAV: It is not a sin if...one has the intention, the honest intention of having another baby, later...

BEATA: *(Incredulous.)* Another baby, later...

GUSTAV: If we plan on having other children...

BEATA: Are you suggesting an abortion? Killing this baby of mine? *(She caresses her belly.)* Never!

GUSTAV: *(Trying to explain.)* It's only because—

BEATA: Never! He would never allow it! Life is sacred to him! Even the first week, even the day of conception! *(She caresses her belly.)*

GUSTAV: *(Timidly.)* We don't need to tell him. We can...

BEATA: You would lie to him?

GUSTAV: At times lies, the little ones, the ones that have a good, sacred purpose...

BEATA: *(Ironically.)* "Sacred"?

GUSTAV: What's most important is not to hurt anybody. What you don't know can't hurt you.

BEATA: Lying? Never!

GUSTAV: It wouldn't be a big lie. It would be forgivable. We are honest, we want to get married, we want a child...

BEATA: *(Caressing her belly.)* We want this one!

GUSTAV: By the way, did you tell your mother?

BEATA: Not yet.

GUSTAV: You see? That's a white lie, a forgivable sin...

BEATA: I'm just waiting for the right moment.

(Someone approaches the door and tries to open it. A moment of panic. GUSTAV takes his clothes and shoes and flees through the window. Enter TEOFILA, BEATA's mother. She looks around suspiciously. She stares at the open window.)

TEOFILA: How come you are still in bed?

BEATA: *(Starting to dress.)* I was about to get up.

TEOFILA: Was that window open all night?...You could catch a cold.

BEATA: You too, leave it open all night.

TEOFILA: Because your father insists. Men are stronger. They don't catch colds the way we do... *(She looks around suspiciously. She goes to the window.)* It's easy for someone to climb in...or out. You should be more careful... *(Stares at her and touches the sheets; she senses the presence of a man in the room, a brief pause.)* Anyone could come in through here. Don't you agree?

BEATA: We're safe in here. With all those guards monitoring whoever comes in or goes out.

(A brief silence; TEOFILA stares at BEATA; she studies her.)

TEOFILA: Do you still see that guard, what's his name? *(She pretends not to remember his name.)*

BEATA: Gustav. I do.

TEOFILA: When was the last time you saw him?

BEATA: *(Lying easily.)* A couple of days ago.

TEOFILA: Where?

BEATA: In the city.

TEOFILA: Be careful. You can't trust men. They only want one thing.

BEATA: Gustav loves me. He was just telling me— *(She corrects herself.)* days ago, that last time I saw him—

TEOFILA: You said "just."

BEATA: I meant—not a long time ago—I told you I saw him recently! Well...he was telling me he wants to ask Father for my hand in marriage.

TEOFILA: Pointless! Your father will say no.

BEATA: Why?

TEOFILA: He already asked. They don't allow marriages, here. They would send him back to Switzerland.

BEATA: *(Jokingly, happy, while she finishes dressing.)* They say that Switzerland is a beautiful country...People live well there.

TEOFILA: He wouldn't allow you to follow him there.

BEATA: *(With curiosity.)* Who?

TEOFILA: Father.

BEATA: I'm not a minor. He can't stop me.

TEOFILA: Laws are different here. We are...guests, in a way...servants of the Holy Father.

BEATA: Servants? We are not servants.

TEOFILA: I meant—we have special duties. Where is your gratitude for this great chance to work...near him?

BEATA: If I want to travel, no one is going to stop me!

TEOFILA: Travel? Where?

BEATA: I was thinking of going to Poland, to see your mother.

TEOFILA: Granny.

BEATA: And all our cousins.

TEOFILA: No. There are problems in Poland now. They would persecute you.

BEATA: Melania and Kinga went. Nothing happened to them. They came back healthy and happy.

TEOFILA: Don't mention Kinga. You know why she went there.

BEATA: *(Naïvely.)* No. Why?

TEOFILA: Because hospitals are free there.

BEATA: Was she sick?

TEOFILA: Don't play dumb. You know very well that she was pregnant.

BEATA: Ha. For that. *(Teasing; pretending she is shocked.)* That's a very grave sin! That's why I don't talk to her any longer.

(A silence; they study each other.)

TEOFILA: Tell me the truth. You can tell your mother. You must tell your mother... *(A brief pause.)* Did you go to bed with...? *(She avoids his name.)*

BEATA: At my age?

TEOFILA: What do you mean "at my age"?

BEATA: I'm not sixteen.

TEOFILA: So what? At any age one waits for the sacrament of marriage.

BEATA: At the end of the twentieth century?

TEOFILA: What kind of attitude is this? The rules of honesty and morality never change.

BEATA: Don't you know what's happening in the world? Don't you watch TV?

TEOFILA: What other people are doing should not influence you. It must not influence you. *(Stares at her.)* What are you trying to tell me? That you are no longer... *(She does not dare say the word.)*

BEATA: *(Slightly ironical.)* A virgin?

TEOFILA: Yes. I meant...that.

BEATA: A recent poll has just revealed that only ten percent of women are virgins when they get married. I am not among them.

TEOFILA: *(Who hopes she has misunderstood.)* Among them? Among whom?

BEATA: Those who wait.

TEOFILA: *(Crossing herself.)* Oh my God! Oh Lord! In this sacred place! If your father only knew!

BEATA: Don't tell him.

TEOFILA: So, you and that, that…

BEATA: Gustav, yes. He's my man.

TEOFILA: Are you at least being careful?

BEATA: Of course.

TEOFILA: Where have you learned… those things?

BEATA: From books. I like reading.

TEOFILA: Where do…? Where do you meet to…?

BEATA: To make love? In his friend's apartment. In via dei Serpenti. *(Defiantly.)* Street of the Serpents.

TEOFILA: That man… *(Avoids his name again.)*

BEATA: Gustav.

TEOFILA: …You…how can you do this to us, to yourself?

PIOTR'S VOICE: *(Offstage.)* Teofila! Where are you?

TEOFILA: *(Blocking the door for a few seconds.)* I'm here, I'm here!

(PIOTR pushes, trying to open the door.)

TEOFILA: Wait! Wait a moment! Beata is getting dressed.

(Motions to BEATA to hurry; BEATA is now ready.)

TEOFILA: All right…You can come in now.

(She opens the door and PIOTR enters.)

PIOTR: *(To TEOFILA.)* Where have you been? I've been looking for you for an hour! And you, Beata! Lazy, as usual! *(Looks at his watch.)* Is this the time to get up?

BEATA: I went to bed late.

PIOTR: Why?

BEATA: I was studying… *(Shows him two books.)*

PIOTR: *(Taking the books.)* What are you studying?

BEATA: Languages. Didn't you want me to study Polish?

PIOTR: *(Reading the two covers.)* "Polish Grammar"…"English Grammar"…How many languages do you want to learn?

BEATA: *(Mildly ironic.)* Polish, because it's the language of your parents—

TEOFILA: Your grandparents.

BEATA: *(Continuing.)* —English because it's a very useful language.

PIOTR: *(To TEOFILA.)* You, what are you doing here? I can't find the sugar! Where did you put it?

TEOFILA: Third drawer left, where it always is.

PIOTR: You must put it on the tray, near my coffee. You know I can never find anything. We need some order in that kitchen. Does Beata help you?

TEOFILA: Yes…often… *(Finding the courage to talk to her husband.)* Beata was telling me before that she would like to take a trip…

PIOTR: Where?

TEOFILA: …To Poland.

PIOTR: *(Surprised.)* Alone?

BEATA: Alone.

PIOTR: Never! It's too dangerous. They hate us there.

BEATA: Why?

PIOTR: Because we are friends of the Holy Father. Because he invited us to come to Rome, to work for him inside these sacred walls.

BEATA: Who knows about us?

PIOTR: Everybody.

BEATA: I would only visit your friends, your relatives.

TEOFILA: Our relatives.

PIOTR: That's worse! They are the ones who know everything. In our village we are famous for our friendship with the Holy Father. And they watch us carefully for that reason. Police are everywhere. I'm sure our phone is bugged. That's why I never call them.

BEATA: Then, I will go to England.

PIOTR: What's this mania for traveling, all of a sudden?

BEATA: To see the world, to practice English. You can learn a language well only where they speak it.

PIOTR: Who puts these crazy ideas into your head? That slut of a friend?

TEOFILA: Kinga.

PIOTR: *(To his wife, stern.)* Don't even mention that name in this house!

BEATA: I don't see her any longer. I don't even talk to her. I have obeyed you.

PIOTR: With whom would you go? When?

BEATA: Alone. When we have *his* permission.

PIOTR: *(Surprised.)* Whose permission?

BEATA: The Holy Father's.

PIOTR: *(Furiously.)* I told you never to bother him. Do you realize how busy he is? He has the weight of the world on his shoulders!

BEATA: I sent him a note.

PIOTR: A note? Saying what?

BEATA: Asking to see him.

PIOTR: *(Furiously.)* You are crazy! He has no time for you! For us! He has already done too much for our family.

BEATA: He is always very kind. He loves me.

TEOFILA: He loves us.

PIOTR: That's why he invited us to Rome. Because he loves us. Because he loves all mankind! Not only us! Not us especially!

BEATA: But he didn't invite all mankind here!

PIOTR: Idiot! You always say stupid things!

BEATA: *He* sends gifts and birthday cards only to me.

PIOTR: That's not even his signature. I noticed but I didn't want to tell you. He gives orders to one of his secretaries to send you something on that date.

BEATA: Because he is generous, caring, divine!

TEOFILA: *(As if she were in a trance.)* "Divine"…

BEATA: He is.

PIOTR: *(Furious.)* He is, he is! And look at the result of too much generosity! People take advantage of him!

TEOFILA: *(Justifying herself.)* Not me. Never.

PIOTR: *(Ignoring her.)* You can't help people in this world. He helped us! *(To BEATA.)* You are taking advantage of him! I'm your father. I'm good to you. Patient, tolerant…

BEATA: *(Ironically.)* Naturally.

PIOTR: You take advantage of it! I give you a chance to study. I have given you everything you need. And look at the results! You take advantage of our goodness!

TEOFILA: It's true. *(Tries to intervene.)* Beata, you should—

BEATA: *(To PIOTR, ignoring TEOFILA.)* You never keep your promises. We were supposed to go to Poland two months ago and—

PIOTR: We'll go, we'll go...

BEATA: I begged you to ask the Holy Father for an audience.

PIOTR: *(Angry.)* An audience? He gives them to kings, princes, presidents! Who do you think you are, a princess?

BEATA: You see? You promised you would do it. It's obvious you didn't. That's why I sent him a message.

PIOTR: What message?

BEATA: Just a note.

PIOTR: Asking for what?

BEATA: To see him.

PIOTR: Why? What do you want to tell him?

BEATA: I love him, I worship him. I like his voice, warm and fatherly. He lets me kiss his hand. *(Ecstatically.)* He caresses my hair...

TEOFILA: *(After a hesitation, curiously.)* When?

PIOTR: When?

BEATA: *(To TEOFILA.)* Don't you remember? You were there.

PIOTR: Where was I?

BEATA: You were there too. Many times with Mother, a couple of times just with you...And on some other occasions.

TEOFILA: *(Vaguely suspicious, worried.)* What other occasions?

BEATA: I met him in the gardens. I know what time he goes there to meditate and pray.

PIOTR: And you spy on him!

BEATA: No, I love to be near him. He never rejected me. He always has a gentle word and a caress for me.

TEOFILA: On your hair...

BEATA: He caressed this cheek once... This one... *(She caresses it herself.)* and he always gives me good advice.

PIOTR: *(Alarmed.)* Advice? You never ask me for advice!

BEATA: There is a huge difference. He knows everything. He is wisdom incarnate.

PIOTR: *(Who does not know the word.)* ..."Carnate"?

BEATA: You see, you don't even know the meaning of that word!

PIOTR: *(Ignoring the point.)* What type of advice?

BEATA: Good, comforting, holy words.

PIOTR and TEOFILA: *(Together.)* Like what?

BEATA: He tells me to be good and obedient, to read a great deal, to study, to pray.

TEOFILA: The same things Papa and I tell you.

BEATA: When he says them they become holy, sacred. His words are like caresses...I would throw myself into a fire for him.

PIOTR: All right, all right. We all adore him. We love and respect him. He is doing wonderful things for Poland, for mankind but... *(Worried.)* What would you ask him this time if he answers you, if he received and read your message?

BEATA: Different things.

PIOTR: What things? Tell me.

BEATA: For instance...What he'd advise me about Polish or English. Which language I should study more.

PIOTR: I can tell you myself. English. America is the greatest country in the world. They rule the world. We must learn their language. What else would you ask him?

BEATA: If he advises me to travel to America or—

PIOTR: America? Are you crazy?

TEOFILA: *(Surprised.)* You never mentioned America before. You only said you wanted to go either to England or to Poland...

PIOTR: What's this new fixation about traveling? And the money? Who is giving you the money?

BEATA: I've been saving. He could give me some suggestions about where to stay...He certainly knows inexpensive places. Perhaps he could even find them for free...

PIOTR: I know the best places in Poland! For free! With families of our friends, if I allowed you to go. If! What else would you ask him for? Money?

BEATA: Oh no! I wouldn't dare. I know he has taken a vow of poverty. Christian poverty. Absolute poverty.

PIOTR: What else then?

BEATA: I'm curious about his ideas.

PIOTR: You want to talk philosophy with the Pope?

BEATA: I always read the *Osservatore Romano*. They write interesting things. Some, I don't understand. So I thought I would ask the Holy Father to explain to me the reasons why—

PIOTR: *(Furious, interrupting her.)* Those are big problems, philosophical, deep and difficult. It's none of your business. What do you want to know? Why? Are you crazy?

BEATA: *(Showing him a page from a notebook.)* Here, you see. I have prepared some questions—

(PIOTR takes some pages from her hands violently, and starts reading.)

PIOTR: *(Reading each word without understanding them.)* ...The breaking of the first alliance fructifies in the triple concupiscence...Desire as the actualization of the concupiscence of the flesh...The man of concupiscence is completely determined and controlled by libido...Concupiscence obfuscates and darkens the meaning of life...—appe-ti-tus con-cu-pi-sci-bilis *(Amazed.)* What's this? An obsession? *(Keeps reading aloud.)* ...Biological rhythms...spousal meaning of the body...prophetism of the body...scatological approach...ontological truth...giovannean expression...lex orandi...What the hell is this? Greek?

(TEOFILA crosses herself at the word "hell.")

BEATA: It's Latin. You see? These are his words. You wouldn't be able to explain these principles. He can. He knows.

PIOTR: And, according to you, he'll find the time to explain all this to you?

BEATA: A little bit at a time...He is patient... He is sweet...He is divine.

PIOTR: But he hasn't got the time for a stupid little pest like you!

BEATA: He has time for everybody. He is infinite goodness.

PIOTR: He will not have the patience to spoon-feed—

BEATA: *(Ironically.)* "Spoon-feed"?

PIOTR: *(Losing his patience.)* Yes, yes! To put spoonfuls of knowledge into you; small, patient doses of culture, *(Looking for the word.)* theo-sophic culture.

BEATA: *(Correcting him.)* Theological.

PIOTR: *(To TEOFILA.)* We have raised a monster.

TEOFILA: A serpent.

BEATA: Thank you! *(To TEOFILA.)* And we both know why you mentioned "serpent."

PIOTR: *(Who misses the nuance: "love nest in Serpent Street.")* You'll see. He will not find time for you. I hope not, I do hope not! He is terribly busy!

BEATA *(Calm and confident.)* Those who are terribly busy always find time for those they love.

(They stare at her; they study her. Religious music in the background. As the lights fade stage right, lights up on stage left on the papal throne. BEATA approaches the throne timidly. She touches it. She looks around. Sits on it for a few seconds. Jumps up as if she had committed sacrilege. Stares at the throne, fascinated. She sits again, enjoying this unique experience. HOLY FATHER enters and observes her benevolently.)

HOLY FATHER: *(Reproaching her sweetly.)* Beata, Beata...

BEATA: *(Descending from the throne, humble and sweet.)* Forgive me, Holy Father.

(She kneels down; HOLY FATHER helps her up. He allows BEATA to kiss his hand.)

HOLY FATHER: They told me you have some questions, for me...Curiosity in the young...is admirable.

(A brief pause.)

BEATA: *(Mustering up her courage.)* I'm in love...

HOLY FATHER: *(Smiling.)* Do you know how a woman in love is described in *Cantico dei cantici*? *(Reciting with a poetical flair.)*

"You are a closed garden,

my sister, my bride,

a closed garden, a sealed spring."

BEATA: *(After a brief pause.)* I feel this desire to hug him, to be near him...

HOLY FATHER: Woman was made out of the rib God-Jehovah took from man. "Made He a woman and brought her unto man." She is bound to come back to man. Is he a good youth? Does he respect you?

BEATA: *(Vague.)* He is a good man...I love him.

(A brief pause.)

HOLY FATHER: The capacity to abstain is a virtue...There is nobility in continence...There is virtue in chastity.

BEATA: *(Timidly.)* At times...he kisses me.

HOLY FATHER: Chastely. You must treat your body with sanctity and respect... *(He studies her.)* You must not allow concupiscence to prevail over spirituality...They told me you don't understand that sinful word.

BEATA: I understand it, Holy Father...I fight it.

HOLY FATHER: And you must win that battle. *(Quoting Saint Paul's words to the Romans—Romans 8:12–13.)* "Only if you let the deeds of the body die, you shall live!" You must let the deeds of the body die with the help of the spirit, my child...

(BEATA listens humbly, feeling guilty.)

HOLY FATHER: The flesh has desires contrary to the spirit and the spirit has desires contrary to the flesh. These are words of Saint Paul in his letter to the Galatians.

BEATA: It's difficult to kill desire when one is in love. How do priests do it?

HOLY FATHER: They have learned not to give themselves to lust or concupiscence, not to uncleanliness but unto holiness. *(Quoting Saint Paul, 1 Thessalonians 4:3–5.)* "They will have sanctification and honor only if they abstain from shamelessness..."

BEATA: *(Repeating mechanically.)* ...Only if they abstain...

HOLY FATHER: *(Quoting Saint Matthew.)* "It is voluntary continence, for the Kingdom of Heaven. It is the fruit of a charismatic choice."

BEATA: *(With admiration.)* Saying no to desires makes priests...true heroes.

HOLY FATHER: It is a voluntary choice, taken by those who know how to be humble, strong and dedicated. *(Quoting Matthew 19:11–12.)* "Many have chosen to be eunuchs for the Kingdom of Heaven."

BEATA: Eun... *(She does not find the courage to say the entire word.)* That word is frightening...I never thought that priests were, defined themselves as...eunuchs. It is as if they said: "I give up the future; the future of one thousand children dies in me, with me."

HOLY FATHER: *(Quoting Matthew 19:11–12.)* "All men cannot receive this saying, save they to whom it is given." Not everybody can understand it but only those who received the gift of grace.

(A silence. HOLY FATHER stares at BEATA. He knows she's about to say something important.)

BEATA: *(Hesitating, shy.)* Holy Father...I have sinned.

(A silence. HOLY FATHER crosses himself. Then he blesses her. BEATA kneels down. HOLY FATHER helps her up.)

HOLY FATHER: *(Quoting John 8:7.)* "Let he who is without sin, throw the first stone!" Our Lord forgives real love.

BEATA: If I had...had the strength to say no...If I could punish this sinful body of mine...

HOLY FATHER: *(Quoting Matthew 5:29–30.)* Christ said: "If thy right eye offends thee, pluck it out, and cast it from thee. And if thy right hand offends thee, cut it off, and cast it from thee because they are the causes of scandal." Not in your case. You're not lost. Love, true love, redeems. Does your family know about it?

BEATA: Teofila knows.

HOLY FATHER: *(Correcting her.)* Mother Teofila, that saintly woman. Does she know the young man who...?

BEATA: She knows him. But she is not happy that...it happened.

HOLY FATHER: Naturally. Is it true love?

BEATA: A great love.

HOLY FATHER: It will be therefore blessed by our Lord. *(Quoting Genesis 2:23.)* "In the mystery of creation woman has been given to man who enriches her and is enriched by her. The sacrament of marriage will give virtue to your reciprocal disinterested gift and will give dignity to your personal gift of love."

(A silence. They look at each other. BEATA is about to add a new truth.)

BEATA: *(Deciding to speak.)* I am with child.

(A long silence.)

HOLY FATHER: *(Crossing himself; quoting 1 Corinthians 7:9–9.)* "If they cannot contain, let them marry: for it is better to marry than to burn."

BEATA: A child, our heir...

HOLY FATHER: To have an heir is fidelity to the divine plan.

BEATA: We should have avoided...

HOLY FATHER: *(Quoting Genesis 2:24–25.)* "In the language of the body the conjugal act means not only love but also potential fecundity."

BEATA: It would have been better, maybe, not to...

HOLY FATHER: *(Quoting Humanae vitae II 12.)* "The church teaches that any conjugal act must remain open to the transmission of life. The role of the woman is concretized into motherhood, into expansion of herself, into new lives." We must now hasten the holy moment of the sacrament of marriage.

BEATA: We are both ready.

HOLY FATHER: *(Quoting Genesis 3:16.)* "Your instinct and desire will be toward your man and he will rule over thee." You must respect him and obey him.

BEATA: *(Uncertain, vaguely surprised.)* ..."Obey him"...

HOLY FATHER: Yes. If you have chosen him, he is a just man. *(Quoting the letter to the Ephesians 5:22–24.)* "Wives must submit themselves unto their own husbands, as unto the Lord for the husband is the head of the wife, even as Christ is the head of the church: and He is the Savior of the body. Therefore, as the church is subject unto Christ, so let the wives be to their own husbands in everything." Wives must be subject to their husbands in everything.

BEATA: *(Unconvinced.)* In everything?

HOLY FATHER: Subject the one and the other to the fear of Christ.

BEATA: *(Crossing herself.)* To his fear...

HOLY FATHER: *(Quoting Isaiah 54:5.)* Your bridegroom is your creator, Lord of the armies..."

(A silence. They stare at each other. BEATA is about to add a new element, a new reality.)

BEATA: *(Timid, daring.)* Holy Father, do you know why I told you, only you, first?

HOLY FATHER: *(After a brief hesitation.)* Because...you are Poland for me...your family is part of my country...your family is my family. I am—

BEATA: *(Interrupting.)* —A father, to me.

HOLY FATHER: Precisely.

(A brief pause. BEATA stares at him and speaks slowly, with determination, with great clarity.)

BEATA: I know everything.

(A long silence.)

HOLY FATHER: *(He may want to avoid unpleasant revelations.)* Well, my dear...it's time to say goodbye...may our Lord bless you! *(He blesses her.)*

BEATA: I know that Teofila and Piotr are not my parents...I know that my mother is dead...I found my birth certificate, the baptismal one...You baptized me...Then I was adopted...I was born in Poland when you, Holy Father, were only a...priest. I know that you brought us here, to Rome, to be near me...I am grateful to you, Daddy...

(HOLY FATHER cannot find words. He blesses her again. BEATA kisses his hand which he tries to withdraw.)

BEATA: *(Caressing her fertile belly.)* Flesh of your flesh, Daddy.

HOLY FATHER: May our Lord forgive this dream of yours, *your imagination*, my child.

BEATA: Your child. Thank you, Father.

(Freeze. Three shots. We see the film of HOLY FATHER being shot in Saint Peter's Square.)

ACT TWO

Spotlight stage left on the papal throne. HOLY FATHER is pale, recovering after the attempt on his life, May 13, 1981, when Ali Agca shot him three times. Religious music in the background.

HOLY FATHER: *(Speaking to the audience, with a sweet but firm tone.)* I am not stern, I am sweet by nature, but I defend the rigidity of principles. We must be intrepid and intransigent in defense of the family, of mankind. An important principle: Jesus has entrusted only males with the task of administering the duties of priesthood. The Church does not discriminate against the woman, does not put her into an inferior condition, doesn't deprive her of her right to equality. The church has recognized and respected her dignity. And has offered a model: the Madonna. Who was never a "priest."

(TEOFILA and PIOTR kneel down in front of HOLY FATHER. PIOTR hands him a letter. HOLY FATHER reads. He is upset by it.)

HOLY FATHER: *(Speaking again to the audience.)* Another important principle: Evil is present in our lives. Satan is not the mythical personification of the evil that is in the world and in men, but he is a personal being, an enemy of God and man, who tries to destroy the design of salvation that God has for man and the world, and who, out of hatred against God, tries to ruin and destroy man, tempting him to rebel against God, to put himself in his place and tear out from his heart the Word of God, so that it does not bear fruit. *(Insistently, with conviction and determination.)* Satan is not an abstraction. He is not the dark and horrible side of the heart of man. He is a spiritual, personal being. A presence that is a concrete power.

(Spotlight stage right, in a modest room where BEATA and GUSTAV are kept prisoners of the Turkish "Grey Wolves." There is a door upstage. BEATA is in her ninth month of pregnancy. She is in pain. She seems about to give birth. GUSTAV holds her hand and consoles her.)

GUSTAV. How do you feel, love?

(No answer. BEATA breathes with difficulty.)

GUSTAV: They told me they already warned the midwife...a friend of theirs...they'll surely call her if...

BEATA: If...?

GUSTAV: ...You sign this paper.

BEATA: *(With determination.)* No!

GUSTAV: *(Worried.)* It's only a formality...to make them happy...what's important now is your health, our baby's future...think of him.

BEATA: I will not sign.

GUSTAV: I read you the letter, it's harmless, they only want a confirmation...

BEATA: Confirmation of what?

GUSTAV: The truth.

BEATA: What truth?

GUSTAV: You know very well. You must just admit that the Holy Father is your father.

BEATA: Why? Why do they want such a document? What do they want to do with it?

GUSTAV: I don't know...I swear I do not understand them, I don't see their motives...

BEATA: They are negative, wicked, perverse motives! They want to hurt him.

GUSTAV: He is much better now. He is recovering. You saw him on television. His wounds were superficial.

BEATA: They wanted to kill him.

GUSTAV: Perhaps...It's possible.

BEATA: Why? He is a saint! Why do they want to kill a saint?

GUSTAV: I swear it is incomprehensible to me too. I don't understand them, I don't want to understand them. Let's think about us now. We must be logical and smart. You sign, the midwife helps you. We escape to Switzerland. Look. I have the number of the safe deposit box. There is a lot of money. It will be enough for at least ten years.

BEATA: Why did they pay you?

GUSTAV: I don't know. I don't understand them...Something to do with politics, international politics...you know I never understood that stuff.

BEATA: They paid you to betray me.

GUSTAV: Who could have imagined that this could happen to us? They invited me for an interview about life in the Vatican. It was an excuse, obviously. They insisted you should be present. You know what happened. They forced us to come here.

BEATA: It was a trap. A real kidnapping. Where are we?

GUSTAV: Not far away from Rome, I think... *(Beseeching her.)* Please sign!

BEATA: No!

GUSTAV: Why not? This is a question of life or death.

(BEATA cries out in pain; she moans.)

GUSTAV: You see? You see? We must be realistic. What's a signature? Nothing! You are not saying in this letter that you agree with the shooting. You just say the truth.

BEATA: What truth?

GUSTAV: Again? I told you. You just say that you have the proof he is your father. The truth is always the best choice. I always told you, remember? If you had told the truth to your mother—

BEATA: *(Correcting him.)* To Teofila.

GUSTAV: To Teofila. We wouldn't be in all this trouble.

BEATA: You put me here. You brought me to the "interview."

GUSTAV: It's my fault. I've been naïve. Forgive me. But now that we are in this situation, let's try to get out of it. Only your signature can save us.

BEATA: I won't sign.

GUSTAV: *(Losing his patience.)* Why? Why? It's the truth!

BEATA: They want to use that signature against him. They want a scandal.

GUSTAV: *(Cautiously.)* I think they have a different purpose.

BEATA: *(With curiosity.)* Which one?

GUSTAV: It seems to me that... *(He hesitates; he wanted to say something else; he changes his mind.)* It's a question of religious conflicts. They are not Catholics.

BEATA: You see? They want a scandal against the Catholic Church. I will not allow it.

GUSTAV: It's a question of saving our child. If you don't sign... *(Hesitates.)*

BEATA: If I don't sign? What will happen?

GUSTAV: They will not call the midwife.

BEATA: You will help me.

GUSTAV: *(With horror.)* Me? What are you saying? I can't help you with this. I hate blood. I would faint.

BEATA: I won't sign. They want to blackmail my father.

GUSTAV: How can they blackmail a pope? He's so powerful!

BEATA: Very easy! They just use his daughter.

(Spotlight stage left on the papal throne. TEOFILA and PIOTR are delivering a letter to HOLY FATHER.)

PIOTR: It's the third one, Holy Father.

TEOFILA: Please do something, Holy Father, we beg you.

HOLY FATHER: *(Paternal and sweet, worried.)* I told the authorities, they are doing their best...

TEOFILA: Did you give your favorable opinion, Holy Father? Did you suggest that they should accept their conditions?

HOLY FATHER: Naturally... Have faith, my child. *(Blesses them.)*

(Spotlight stage right on BEATA and GUSTAV. BEATA is in a lot of pain and is moaning.)

GUSTAV: Calm, try to stay calm... Should I tell them to call the midwife?

BEATA: *(Suffering.)* Yes, yes! Right away!

GUSTAV: Then, are you going to sign?

BEATA: No!

(BEATA is in a lot of pain and GUSTAV is very worried.)

GUSTAV: You really are stubborn! And those guys are more stubborn than you!

(AHMET enters. GUSTAV is aware of it, but pretends he does not see him. BEATA, on the contrary, is unaware of his presence.)

GUSTAV: *(Softening his words, using compliments for the sake of the kidnappers.)* They are persistent... good brave young men... they are very religious.

BEATA: Religious people don't kidnap a woman in this condition!

GUSTAV: They're religious activists with a cause—

BEATA: —Which is not ours!

GUSTAV: But it's still for a cause, a religious purpose—

BEATA: Against us! Against the Catholic Church!

GUSTAV: You are wrong, you see? Ahmet explained to me that religions are sisters. They should help each other, they should collaborate. Even the Holy Father, your fa—

BEATA: *(Stopping him.)* That's enough! Don't say anything! The less you talk, the better it is!

GUSTAV: *(Pretending to notice AHMET only now.)* Ha! Here is Ahmet—

AHMET: *(Going to BEATA, cordially.)* The more you talk, the better it is. We must communicate, exchange opinions. The more we talk, the more we understand each other. Don't you trust us? We gave you whatever you needed...

GUSTAV: She's feeling terrible...Please call a doctor.

AHMET: *(Calling his friend.)* Zeki!

(ZEKI enters.)

AHMET: My friend Zeki has studied medicine. He will help if...

GUSTAV: If...?

AHMET: We told you. We agreed. She must sign that paper.

GUSTAV: She doesn't feel well...she's unable to...

AHMET: *(Ironically.)* Poor little girl! But signing is not difficult. We can guide her hand, if she wishes...Do you wish it, Beata?

(BEATA does not answer.)

AHMET: What a beautiful name! Religious and holy...did your papa choose it?

BEATA: *(Strong and determined.)* No!

(A brief pause.)

AHMET: It's true, isn't it? *(To GUSTAV, accusing him ironically.)* You told us.

GUSTAV: *(Fearful.)* I didn't, I don't really... *(He does not know what to say.)*

AHMET: *(To BEATA.)* Born in Poland...your mother is dead, father unknown...now we know who he is; we are going to tell the world.

BEATA: It's not true!

AHMET: *(Always calm and slightly ironical.)* What's not true? That we are going to tell the world?

BEATA: It's not true that he is my father!

(A silence. AHMET and ZEKI stare at GUSTAV, who is timid and fearful.)

AHMET: Gustav told us he has the evidence.

BEATA: What evidence? It's not true!

AHMET: Tell us, Gustav. What evidence?

ZEKI: Where is it? We want to see it.

GUSTAV: I prefer to have Beata explain. *(To BEATA, begging her.)* Tell the truth, Beata. Please!

BEATA: I said it. He is not my father.

GUSTAV: But you always told me—

BEATA: You shut up! I told you stories! You believe everything!

AHMET: The birth certificate, the baptismal one, the signature of the Pope, where are they?

GUSTAV: *(Timid, confused.)* I only know that she told me that...

AHMET: Have you read those documents?

GUSTAV: I haven't read them, but I am sure that...

BEATA: *(Intervening.)* Sure of what? You believe everything and anything!

ZEKI: Gustav told us that he saw you together. That the Pope was kissing you and calling you "my child."

BEATA: He calls everybody that. Priests always say "my child." It's a habit. We are a united family! The family of Catholics. A real family!

AHMET: *(Who is trying not to lose his patience.)* We too, we too... *(Indicates ZEKI.)*

AHMET and ZEKI: *(Together.)* Alhamdulillah!

BEATA: *(Aggressively.)* Why do you want that signature? So you can create a scandal? I'll never allow it!

ZEKI: *(Threatening.)* That's why you don't want to tell the truth; to avoid a scandal.

That's why you don't want to admit that...*that* man is your father.

BEATA: He is the Holy Father. Father of all of us.

GUSTAV: *(Who is beginning to be really afraid.)* I beg you, Beata. For our child...Tell the truth. Sign and—

BEATA: *(Stubborn.)* No! I won't sign false documents!

AHMET: False? This is a simple declaration. I was born in...my mother was... my father is...

BEATA: It's not true!

(AHMET and ZEKI stare at GUSTAV, who is terrorized.)

ZEKI: You are getting your cute little husband in trouble...

GUSTAV: *(Trying to exculpate himself.)* I wasn't the first to tell you. You told me you knew...

AHMET: You confirmed the rumors we heard in Poland, Turkey, Greece. Now she must confirm it!

(BEATA does not react. She is silent and stubborn.)

ZEKI: *(To GUSTAV.)* Did you tell her what is in store for both of you if she doesn't sign?

GUSTAV: Yes...

BEATA: The scandal, that's what you want! Just the scandal!

AHMET: It's not the first time a Catholic priest has a daughter...

GUSTAV: It's true...It's not unusual any longer...Everyone is used to it by now.

AHMET: You see? Gustav agrees with us.

BEATA: He always agrees with anything and anybody!

AHMET: Listen, Beata, we are not interested in a scandal...we want to... humanize your father...we want to make people see he's just like everyone else...

BEATA: How dare you say that?

AHMET: *(Ignoring, continuing.)* —We want to tell the world that—notwithstanding the pomp, the ermine and the precious stones on his fingers—he is a human being, with the weaknesses of all human beings...

(Spotlight on stage left, on the papal throne. Religious music in the background.)

HOLY FATHER: *(Sweet, humble and sincere, to the audience.)* Pray with me... *(Quoting SIR 23:4–6.)* "Lord, Father and God of my life, don't allow sensuality and lust to become my masters...Don't abandon me to shameful desires!"

(Spotlight again on BEATA and GUSTAV's prison.)

BEATA: He is pure! He is a saint!

AHMET: We don't doubt that...

(He stares at her; he tries to mesmerize her, paternally.)

AHMET: And falling in love...having a daughter...is no crime. Many of our...priests—as you call them—get married and have children...we venerate and respect them all the same. I could even say, we respect them more because they honored the laws of nature, they respected the natural, divine gift of procreation.

BEATA: Not him! Not him! He is a saint!

AHMET: *(Always calm and paternal.)* Your desire to defend him is noble, but think for a moment...you could be very useful to your church...

(A silence; BEATA stares at him with curiosity.)

GUSTAV: *(Interested.)* How? Tell her! *(Correcting himself.)* Tell us.

AHMET *(Staring at BEATA.)* As you well know, many Catholic priests are leaving the church—a great loss for your people—because priests too need a woman in their beds...Telling the world will show that the pontiff had that very natural, human desire to—

BEATA: It's not true!

AHMET: *(Ignoring her.)* —Desire to love. You might influence the Vatican to finally allow those poor young priests to love, to build a family...

GUSTAV *(To BEATA.)* Think about it. Maybe—

BEATA: *(Furious with GUSTAV.)* Brainwashing! *(To AHMET.)* You see? It works with him! But not with me! Never with me!

ZEKI: *(Losing his patience, threatening.)* Think about it...Reflecting is good for your health.

BEATA: *(Stubborn.)* I said no, it's no! I will never betray the Holy Father!

ZEKI: *(Ironical.)* ...Your Holy Papa.

BEATA: It's not true! I'll never betray him!

(ZEKI moves toward her, threatening. He is ready to hit her.)

AHMET: *(Stopping him.)* Zeki has studied medicine. He knows how to dislocate arms, legs...Make up your mind, Beata...It's in your interest...

(Stares at GUSTAV, who is terrorized.)

AHMET: In the interest of your sweet little husband...in everybody's interest.

BEATA: I swear, I swear it's not true!

AHMET: We sent letters to your family, the press, to him! Do you realize that he knows you are our prisoner and he has not lifted a finger to save you?

(A brief silence.)

BEATA: *(Shaken, uncertain.)* He knows... He knows what's in the interest of the Church.

AHMET: You're naïve. He is only thinking about his personal interest. To save his reputation.

BEATA: It's not true! And I'm not naïve!

AHMET: *(Still calm and patient.)* Then you are a very moving martyr...ready to die to defend your church. We admire your faith...We too, have many martyrs, ready to die for our faith... *(Slightly threatening.)* and, of course, we are ready to kill for our cause...we've proven it in Saint Peter's Square.

BEATA: *(With defiance.)* And you failed! Our good Lord protects him!

AHMET: *(Calm and precise.)* But he does not protect you... *(With a cold threat.)* You are here...It would be easy for us to...punish you. To eliminate you.

GUSTAV: *(Very worried.)* Please, Beata! Sign, sign that stupid paper!

BEATA: *(With defiance.)* I will never betray the Holy Father. If I signed, I would feel like a coward, as if I stabbed him in the back!

(A threatening silence.)

AHMET: *(To ZEKI.)* Take them to Sami. He'll take care of them.

(To GUSTAV, grabbing him by the lapels of his jacket, clearly threatening him.)

AHMET: This is the last generous chance we are giving you. If you don't succeed in convincing her, you know what's going to happen. You die, she will end up in a whorehouse. We'll put her there. Did you ever hear of the white slave market?

(ZEKI takes them to the next room. Spotlight stage left on the papal throne. Religious music in the background.)

HOLY FATHER: *(To the spectators with grief, sadly.)* Dear children… *(Quoting from his Encyclical "Splendor Veritatis.")* I am deeply grieved by the contempt for human life, the permanent violation of the fundamental rights of human beings…I see a grave crime in acts that are intrinsically evil…And there are so many…Any kind of homicide, genocide, abortion, euthanasia, and even suicide; all these violate the integrity of the human being, like mutilations and tortures inflicted on the body and on the mind, efforts to violate the intimacy of the spirit; all this offends human dignity: subhuman living conditions, unlawful incarcerations, deportations, slavery, prostitution, the selling of women and young people…

(Spotlight stage right, on AHMET and ZEKI.)

ZEKI: What do you think, will that idiot succeed in convincing her?

AHMET: I don't think so. She feels like a heroine now. She's a stubborn bitch. She won't give in.

ZEKI: What are we going to do, then?

AHMET: Let's give him this last chance… If he makes her understand that she's going to lose her child…who knows? Maybe he will succeed.

ZEKI: I would eliminate him right away. I can't stand him. We don't really need him.

AHMET: No, we don't.

ZEKI: And we'll save a lot of money.

AHMET: What money?

ZEKI: The money we put in Switzerland for him.

AHMET: *(Laughing.)* You believe that? You're as naïve as he is sometimes. You see? Give them the number of a safe deposit box in Switzerland. Tell them it contains millions, and they'll do anything for you.

ZEKI: *(Joining the laughter.)* I see…That Gustav is a real idiot. He was born stupid, he'll die stupid. *(A brief pause.)* This story about the signature…why are we insisting on it? Do we really need it?

AHMET: It would be useful…to show the world what he really is. Just a man.

ZEKI: A man? He tries his best to appear…"divine." Did you notice how he poses on TV?

AHMET: He behaves like a Roman God who loves preaching from morning to night. He even thinks he can convert us and the Jews! What a delusion!

ZEKI: Listen, I was thinking…It's easy to forge a signature. I've done it many times…It's easy. I could forge her signature.

AHMET: We'll see…

ZEKI: But…tell me the truth. We went through hell to find that idiot husband of hers, to convince him about the interview, to kidnap them. We threatened to torture both of them. All this just for a signature?

AHMET: The orders are very clear. We want freedom for our brother Ali in exchange. If they let him go, we'll let the stubborn bitch go back home, signature or no signature.

ZEKI: *(Laughing.)* Who does she think she is? I hate her heroics. A bitch who might give birth any minute…A real slut.

AHMET: I don't think you should call her a slut. After all, she's married and she's going to be a mother.

ZEKI: *(Amused.)* Married to that Swiss idiot who is so gullible he believes anything.

AHMET: *(Continuing.)* She seems loyal and faithful...a good girl, after all.

ZEKI: But she sure is giving us a lot of trouble being such a heroine!

AHMET: She must have Sicilian blood. You can't get a word out of them, not even under torture.

ZEKI: If she were not pregnant, I would torture her my way, a very special way...

AHMET: *(Ironical.)* The daughter of a pontiff? You really are an infidel.

ZEKI: Why do they call us "infidels"?

AHMET: Because, according to them, there is only one true religion, theirs. Everyone else is an "infidel," godless people, people who don't obey the big chief in Rome.

(Telephone rings. AHMET picks up receiver.)

AHMET: *(In Italian.)* Si...Si...Certamente...Tutto in ordine, tutto sotto controllo...Come previsto......Ci vuol pazienza...Certo, certo......Ma, Eminenza, lei dovrebbe—...Noi non possiamo—Abbiamo anche noi...i nostri ordini...Ali deve essere rilasciato......Siete potentissimi, voi...Se date un ordine, a Roma, vi ubbidiscono tutti...Certo, Eminenza...D'accordo. *(Puts the receiver down.)*

ZEKI: Who was it?

AHMET: *(Ironical.)* Our Italian friends...

ZEKI: What do they want?

AHMET: I think they're sorry they started this...They're worried.

ZEKI: They should be.

AHMET: They're pretending now they don't have any power...Hypocrites! They control Italy...

ZEKI: Maybe they prefer...

AHMET: What?

ZEKI: That everybody dies...

AHMET: It's possible... *(Looking at his watch.)* Bring the Swiss here. I want to have some fun with him. I feel like frying him a little bit. *(Shows an electric tool that sends out sparks.)*

ZEKI: My pleasure!

(He goes out and comes back with a very frightened GUSTAV.)

AHMET: Tie him to that chair.

GUSTAV: *(Terrorized.)* Why? Why? What are you going to do?

AHMET: Where is the signature?

GUSTAV: She's very sick, very upset. She's incapable of making decisions in this situation...She will sign for sure later, after she has the baby, when she's happy and relaxed.

ZEKI: *(Threatening.)* We want the signature now!

GUSTAV: *(Trying to find a solution.)* I was thinking this is one of her letters... *(Shows it.)* here is her signature. I know how to copy it perfectly. I'll sign the letter myself.

(AHMET and ZEKI laugh heartily at a proposal that coincides with theirs.)

GUSTAV: *(Worried, not understanding the laughter.)* Why are you laughing? I think it's a good idea...

ZEKI: Excellent! The solution of a genius!

AHMET: Tie him down.

(He shows the cathodes that are sending out sparks.)

GUSTAV: *(Trying to resist.)* No! No! I'll tell you everything! Anything you want to know! Absolutely everything! I'm no hero. I am Swiss!

(AHMET and ZEKI are amused. They laugh again.)

GUSTAV: I mean we Swiss, we're neutral. We don't believe in war, in torture, in anything *violent!*

AHMET: *(Stopping ZEKI.)* All right. Don't tie him down. *(Puts down his torture tool. Ironically.)* If he really wants to tell us…everything… *(To GUSTAV.)* Start.

GUSTAV: *(Trying to calm down, sitting down.)* Thank you…What do you want to know?

AHMET: Everything.

ZEKI: Everything.

GUSTAV: For instance?

AHMET: Start wherever you want.

GUSTAV: *(Searching.)* If you want…I can tell you which room he sleeps in…what time he goes to bed…what time he gets up…where he goes…when he is about to leave the Vatican…when he goes to Castel Gandolfo.

AHMET: *(Ironical.)* Really? What else?

GUSTAV: All his moves. They could be useful to you.

AHMET: For what?

GUSTAV: *(Uncertain, he's afraid to say something wrong.)* I am a farmer's son… I am a—

ZEKI: —A Swiss, we know.

GUSTAV: I was born in a very small village. We're all pacifists. We have no interest in politics. I don't know what you want to do, what your intentions are…

AHMET: But you want to give us details on where, when, how. Why?

GUSTAV: *(Uncertain; he's afraid to make a mistake.)* I had the impression—maybe I'm wrong—that you want… *(Hesitates.)*

AHMET: We want what?

GUSTAV: That friend of yours…the Turkish one…

ZEKI: Like us.

AHMET: Our brother Ali Agca.

GUSTAV: Him, yes, well, we all know that he tried to…you know, don't you?

AHMET: We know. And he is now a prisoner of war. Like you and the Polish heroine.

GUSTAV: War?

AHMET: War.

(A silence.)

GUSTAV: *(Daring.)* Out of curiosity, just curiosity. I told you I know nothing about politics and religion…Why? Why do you want to kill him?

AHMET: Because he is a symbol.

GUSTAV: Symbol of what?

AHMET: *(Ironical.)* A Swiss guard at the Vatican and you don't know?

GUSTAV: No! It's just a job…They don't explain "symbols"…They never told us.

AHMET: He is the symbol of Western civilization.

ZEKI: Of Americanism.

GUSTAV: *(Confused.)* I understand "Western civilization."

AHMET: Do you know what it is? Tell us.

GUSTAV: *(Uncertain.)* Italy, Switzerland, England—

ZEKI: —America.

GUSTAV: Yes, the white people…it's a bad thing…Italy discovered America…

AHMET: *(Ironical.)* Italy, a country with many ports on the Atlantic.

GUSTAV: *(Confused.)* Oh yes! Italy has many ports; it is surrounded by many seas…

AHMET: What about the other countries that have colonized the world?

GUSTAV: England and France have brought…civilization to…they have helped Africa.

ZEKI: Helped?

GUSTAV: You spoke of civilization before…it means of course…civilizing, helping…

AHMET: And what do you think about the results?

GUSTAV: Good *(Correcting himself.)* so so…some are good some are less good…

AHMET: Describe the good results, where you see them.

GUSTAV: There were savage tribes in Africa…now they are like us they live like us, more or less…

AHMET: More or less?

GUSTAV: *(Careful.)* Less…but they are improving.

AHMET: *(Ironical.)* "Western Civilization"…have you looked around? Do you see signs?

GUSTAV: Sure I live in a big city and I watch TV.

AHMET: And you are surrounded by what?

GUSTAV: *(Uncertain; he does not know what they want to hear.)* Good things bad things…

AHMET: Tell us about the "good" ones.

GUSTAV: Nice houses, large, clean streets, rich people…

AHMET: And the starving ones?

ZEKI: And the prostitutes?

AHMET: And the drugs?

ZEKI: And the transvestites?

AHMET: And the porno films?

ZEKI: And the shamelessness of women?

AHMET: And the greed?

ZEKI: And the exploitation?

AHMET: And violence against everything and everybody?

ZEKI: And the crazy feminists who want absolute equality with us!

GUSTAV: You are right, you are right. There are many ugly things, wrong things. But it's not his fault. He is a good man, he is a saint.

AHMET: He is a symbol.

GUSTAV: Of what?

AHMET: Of…the Christian Empire.

ZEKI: Of the American Empire.

AHMET: Of a country where violence, ferocity, corruption, pornography, and drugs prevail. Where disorder rules.

GUSTAV: Why blame the Holy Father! He always speaks against pornography and Communism.

AHMET: What do you know about Communism?

GUSTAV: A dreadful system. No freedom at all. Millions of starving people, free love.

ZEKI: *(Amused.)* Free love? There?

(AHMET and ZEKI laugh.)

GUSTAV: Why are you laughing? It's true. I have read it in many books. They copulate everywhere freely. They don't get married. And if children are born, they give them to the state. No family. A total hell.

AHMET: *(Ironical.)* Bravo! You know a great deal. You are a genius.

GUSTAV: *(Encouraged.)* And the Holy Father is doing his best to destroy Communism, to bring back freedom to Poland and to all the other satellites.

AHMET: To bring back what kind of freedom?

GUSTAV: The one, the one we know here.

AHMET: Like in the West.

GUSTAV: Yes…

ZEKI: And in America.

GUSTAV: Sure…

AHMET: Freedom to do all the things we mentioned before…

GUSTAV: Those, yes…

AHMET: Tell us again. Which things?

GUSTAV: Some are good, some are bad…

ZEKI: Which ones are the bad ones?

GUSTAV: *(Searching.)* …Prostitution, drugs, corruption, pornography…

AHMET: Bravo! And what religion prevails in that American world? Tell us…

GUSTAV: *(Uncertain and confused.)* What prevails is… *(He hesitates, he does not want to make a mistake.)*

AHMET: Christianity!

GUSTAV: *(Relieved, agreeing.)* Christianity! That's true, very true!

AHMET: And he, your master, is the symbol of all that!

GUSTAV: *(Trying to defend HOLY FATHER.)* But he is against all those things! He's always preaching against Communism!

AHMET: And in favor of the American dream.

GUSTAV: *(Uncertain, surprised.)* You…I hope you don't prefer Communism to the American way of life…I had the impression you were anti-Communists like all of us…One must choose in life…our Holy Father has chosen.

AHMET: Listen, you Swiss. There are three great ideologies. Islam—chaste and very moral. It attracts millions because it's based on precepts of love and morality. Family and respect for authority. Second. Communism that used to attract so many with its promises to create the "new man," a lover of social justice, a protector of the poor. It's losing ground.

GUSTAV: *(Intervening.)* Thanks to the Holy Father.

AHMET. Agreed. It's the only useful thing he has done. And it is to our advantage. Third ideology: Yours.

GUSTAV: Mine?

AHMET: The corrupt, rotten, decadent Western civilization, where there are no rules. They're all after money and pleasure. And your women…they are aggressive and obscene, looking only for…you know what.

GUSTAV: The Holy Father is always condemning all that. He preaches purity and chastity.

ZEKI: *(Ironical.)* Chastity?

GUSTAV: *(Ignoring him, continuing.)* He always declares that women must be faithful wives and good mothers. My wife can bear witness to that... She reads the *Osservatore Romano*, she knows a great deal about her duties. And she will be a good mother, I know, I'm sure of it.

AHMET: One woman out of a thousand is moral and honest. And the other nine hundred ninety-nine?

GUSTAV: Let's not exaggerate. Many are good Christian women, religious, honest, and faithful. More than fifty percent, I'm sure of it.

AHMET: And the other fifty percent? Who has corrupted them? The so-called Western civilization, your world. And it's clearer and clearer that your master—

GUSTAV: The Holy Father.

AHMET: *(Ironical.)* Holy, yes! Most Holy! He is the symbol of that ideology!

GUSTAV: And, in your opinion, he should be murdered?

AHMET: When your Mussolini died—

GUSTAV: I'm Swiss.

AHMET: —Fascism died. When Hitler died, Nazism died. You must cut the head to kill the body.

GUSTAV: But our Holy Father is not the founder of the church! When a Pope dies another one is elected.

ZEKI: A less political one. The world could finally find some peace.

AHMET: *(Interrupting, wanting to change the subject.)* But let's go back to the signature. What do you really think? Why doesn't she want to sign?

GUSTAV: As I was telling you before, she's faithful, loyal, very religious. She feels she cannot betray the Holy Father.

AHMET: ...Who happens to be her father, too.

ZEKI: A double treason, in her opinion...

GUSTAV: Double, I agree. She's a good Christian woman, she loves the family, she cannot betray the family.

(A silence; they stare at him; they study him.)

AHMET: You are sure—one hundred percent sure that he is your...father-in-law?

GUSTAV: *(Uncertain.)* Yes...she told me many times...she found her birth certificate in Poland, the baptismal one. The dates coincide.

AHMET: When your master lived there, as a bishop...

GUSTAV: As a cardinal, I think...

AHMET: And you saw those documents?

GUSTAV: In a way she waved them in front of me, triumphant, all excited, when she found them...

AHMET: So, you have no doubts. You are one hundred percent sure?

GUSTAV: *(Doubting, reflecting.)* In my opinion, one hundred percent does not exist...it never exists, under any circumstance...Let's take this situation, for instance, my situation here...we are the same age, more or less...I like you, I consider you my friends...at times, I am one hundred percent sure...at other times, a bit less...

ZEKI: *(Smiling.)* Congratulations! Your brain works now and then.

AHMET: Survival instinct.

GUSTAV: *(Alarmed.)* What you say proves it. What do you mean? That I can trust you one hundred percent or only ninety-five percent?

ZEKI: Less, much less. It's always better to have doubts in life.

GUSTAV: *(Confused, alarmed.)* Meaning what?

AHMET: *(Ignoring the question.)* So? Are you or aren't you sure he's your father-in-law?

GUSTAV: "Father-in-law," it sounds strange. I never thought of it that way...I didn't think of it before...The Holy Father—my father-in-law?

ZEKI: *(Ironical.)* You are so absentminded! He married you himself!

GUSTAV: Because my wife's family is Polish. The Holy Father loves the Poles.

AHMET: So? Are you or aren't you sure?

GUSTAV: *(After a hesitation.)* Ninety-five percent...*(Looks at ZEKI.)* There is always some doubt...

AHMET: Good! And for this reason, maybe she does not want to sign that paper...

GUSTAV: I don't know...it's possible.

AHMET: So, you have doubts after all...

GUSTAV: As Zeki said, there is always some doubt.

(We hear BEATA screaming in the next room.)

GUSTAV: *(Worried.)* Please, help her! Call someone...

AHMET: Don't worry. Women are always like that. They always scream.

GUSTAV: But she's about to—

AHMET: *(Interrupting him, ignoring.)* So, there is a chance this baby is not the Pope's grandchild...

GUSTAV: I don't know, I don't know!

(We hear BEATA screaming.)

GUSTAV: Everything is possible... *(He is listening to BEATA's screams; he is very worried.)*

AHMET: Your wife, does she ever lie?

GUSTAV: Sometimes, like everybody else...small things...white lies...

AHMET: Did she ever lie to Teofila?

GUSTAV: *(Who is still trying to listen to all the sounds coming from the next room.)* Yes...

AHMET: And to Piotr?

GUSTAV: Yes...sometimes.

AHMET: And to you?

GUSTAV: Silly, unimportant things...we all lie a little bit, isn't that true? Everybody...me, you...

(A silence; they stare at him.)

GUSTAV: *(Daring.)* That lie about the interview, for instance...it wasn't true...

AHMET: One must be Machiavellian in politics.

ZEKI: Your Machiavelli. Part of your world!

GUSTAV: Why should my wife be Machiavellian? No reason...

(We hear screams again; BEATA is about to give birth.)

GUSTAV: Listen, listen...

(They ignore him.)

GUSTAV: She's just a daughter who found, discovered who her parents are, and is enthusiastic about it!

(BEATA keeps screaming.)

AHMET: She doesn't seem so enthusiastic and happy now.

GUSTAV: Because she is in pain! Help her, please! Let me see her and—

(They stop him; they do not allow him to go to the next room.)

ZEKI: *(Stopping him.)* Be quiet! Calm and quiet...

(Loud moans. BEATA is giving birth to her baby.)

GUSTAV: *(Very alarmed.)* The midwife! Call the midwife! Please, I beg you!

(Tries again to go toward BEATA; they stop him; they do not allow him to go.)

AHMET: Calm, my dear friend...everything will be all right...Sami is in the other room with her. He too has studied medicine...

(Moaning. A scream. First cry of the baby.)

GUSTAV: My child! He is born! He is born! *(He tries to run toward the door.)* I want to see him! Please let me see him! Please, I beg you!

(AHMET gives a gun to ZEKI. GUSTAV does not see it because he is facing the door.)

AHMET: *(To ZEKI.)* Let him see it, *before* you shoot him.

(GUSTAV exits into the other room, followed by ZEKI, who has gun in his hand. After a few seconds, we hear a shot. A silence. ZEKI comes back, triumphant; the gun is in his belt. He raises the newborn baby who still has some traces of blood on his little body. He is raising the child as if it were a trophy.)

ZEKI: A boy!

AHMET: An orphan...

ZEKI: An orphan.

AHMET: Blood of a Pope.

ZEKI: *(Still raising his trophy.)* A grandchild of the Pope! A new warrior for Islam!

(Spotlight stage left, on the papal throne. Religious music in the background.)

HOLY FATHER: *(Looking heavenwards.)* Have pity on them...Forgive them, Lord! They know not what they do.

(FREEZE. BLACKOUT. END OF THE PLAY.)

Notes:

If a director wants to be polemic, this is a possible second ending: Pope John Paul II will be in full armor, dressed like Pope Julius II, leader of the League of Cambrai against Venice. He will say: "I pledge allegiance to the Christian Flag and to the Savior, for whose Kingdom it stands, one Savior, crucified, risen, and coming again, with life and liberty for all who believe."

Many elements in this play are based on historical facts: (1) There was an attempt on Pope John Paul II's life. (2) A Polish couple was invited by the Holy Father to the Vatican. (3) Their daughter was adopted. (4) She was kidnapped by the "Grey Wolves," a Turkish political organization. (5) Many letters were sent to the Holy Father, the family of the kidnapped young woman, and Italian and foreign newspapers; the letters asked for an exchange between the young woman and Ali Agca, the man who tried to kill the Pope. (6) The young woman has not been found; the Italian police have put the research on the back burner, believing that the young woman is probably dead. (7) Even as recently as 2007, articles were written about this kidnapping; the police have been accused of inefficiency.

The Wish

Characters:

GRANDMA: a sweet lady; vague, confused, bizarre

HONEY: her little granddaughter; inquisitive, precocious (but not in the sense of ever being obnoxious)

Time:

The present

The action takes place in a large living room which resembles a storeroom: old chairs, a table, a sofa, stacks of newspapers everywhere, boxes of all sizes, plants, birds in a cage, a bowl with fish, a cat, and a dog. These last two have brightly colored leashes which have been tied one to a chair, the other to the sofa. Stage left: the door of the bedroom. Stage right: a door leading to the street. In the background: a window. As the curtain rises, an old clock strikes six p.m. GRANDMA, a sweet old lady, has just finished watering her plants. She distributes various rations to her "friends" after sampling them. They taste all right. She reassures her pets by telling them how tasty they are.

GRANDMA: Very good...Perfect... Exquisite...Delicious...For a "gourmet"... Here I come... *(Etc., ad lib.)*

(We hear a sudden noise coming from the bedroom. GRANDMA hides behind the boxes. HONEY, a pretty girl clutching a huge doll, is pushed into the living room. The door is slammed and locked behind her. HONEY is hurt, angry, sad. She stares at her doll with her arms clasped around it.)

HONEY: *(Mimicking someone by kissing the doll on its mouth with fury; in a changed voice.)* "Listen doll, let's make a baby!" *(She drops the doll on the floor with contempt.)*

GRANDMA: *(In surprise; coming out.)* What did you say?

HONEY: *(Pointing to the bedroom.)* Did you see? She just kicked me out. And I didn't do *anything!*

GRANDMA: That's your side of things. What did you *try* to do?

HONEY: Cross my heart, Granny. I don't have the faintest idea...

(A short pause.)

GRANDMA: Is Mommy busy?

HONEY: She is. *(HONEY moves slowly to the door, as if she wanted to eavesdrop.)*

GRANDMA: Get away from that door. Your Mommy has the right to do as she pleases.

HONEY: I know that. Grown-ups are entitled to anything. They're allowed to do everything! It's no cinch being a child, I assure you.

GRANDMA: Be patient and keep your voice down. Mommy loves you…She told me you're the prettiest girl on earth.

HONEY: *(A sly smile on her face.)* Did she?

GRANDMA: She's always so busy…

HONEY: I know that.

GRANDMA: Unfortunately grown-ups have little time for children…

HONEY: You have, when you're in the mood for it.

GRANDMA: *(Smiling.)* I try my best… *(A short silence.)* I heard you talking to your doll…What did you say before you threw her down?

HONEY: Nothing important.

GRANDMA: Don't you love her any more?

(A short silence.)

GRANDMA: Pick her up.

HONEY: No.

GRANDMA: Don't be stubborn.

(A silence. GRANDMA decides to pick up the doll herself. She slowly steps over the doll, ready to bend down.)

HONEY: *(Alarmed.)* Don't step over her! Or you'll stunt her growth! *(HONEY picks up the doll and hugs it with love.)*

GRANDMA: That's a good girl. You still love your baby. How is she feeling today?

HONEY: She's thriving. Don't you think so? *(HONEY shows her doll.)*

GRANDMA: Yes, she is. And I'm happy for her.

HONEY: Look. She's smiling.

GRANDMA: Good. If an infant smiles in its sleep, that's a sign that he is communicating with good angels.

HONEY: *(Looking at her doll with some sadness.)* She's still an infant, she'll always be an infant. She'll never talk to me.

GRANDMA: But she understands you perfectly. And you're right to talk to her. As you did just a while ago…What were you saying?

(A silence.)

HONEY: Granny…Am I going to have a baby brother?

GRANDMA: No…I don't think so…

HONEY: Aren't you sure?

GRANDMA: I am. No baby brother.

HONEY: Why not?

GRANDMA: Because your daddy left long ago and…

HONEY: Is he coming back?

GRANDMA: *(Uncertain.)* Of course…And if he comes back, you can have a little brother…

HONEY: Only if he comes back?

GRANDMA: Only in that case, yes.

HONEY: Why?

GRANDMA; Because babies grow only in married people.

HONEY: Isn't Mommy married?

GRANDMA: …In married people who live together.

HONEY: Aunt Kate isn't married and…

GRANDMA: She *was* married.

HONEY: I never saw her husband.

GRANDMA: She got married in town and…

HONEY: Now she lives alone!

GRANDMA; They lived together at the beginning…a month…

HONEY: Even Mommy got married in town. And Daddy lived with her for years. Is it possible to have a baby brother without a daddy?

GRANDMA: Impossible.

HONEY: Are you sure?

GRANDMA: Positive...No baby without a daddy.

HONEY: *(Thinks it over. She seems very happy.)* Granny...Could you please put that in writing?

GRANDMA: Why in writing? Don't you trust me?

HONEY: I want to be sure.

GRANDMA: I will, Honey. Later. Now I'm busy feeding our friends.

(She goes back to feed her animals. HONEY is happy now. Hugging her doll, she goes to the window.)

GRANDMA: *(To her pets, tasting their food first.)* Here I am...Delicious...Just right...Real savory...Here it is...Very good...

HONEY: *(Looking outside the window with fervor; in the attitude of prayer.)*
Star light, star bright
First star I've seen tonight;
I wish I may, I wish I might
Have the wish I wish tonight.

GRANDMA: What's your wish tonight, Honey?

HONEY: The same as ever,

GRANDMA: What is it?

HONEY: I want Daddy to come back...My Daddy...

GRANDMA: That's a beautiful wish. *(A short pause.)* Is it only because you want a little brother?

HONEY: I miss Daddy... *(With disarming candor.)* Can he be the father of my babies?

GRANDMA: He cannot.

HONEY: Why not?

GRANDMA: Because he cannot...A daddy is only a daddy. That's final.

HONEY: He's the best daddy in the world...He's the most handsome... Where is he now?

GRANDMA: He had to leave.

HONEY: Why? Because Mommy is naughty?

GRANDMA: Mommy is *not* naughty. He had to go because...We need money and...

HONEY: I'll be better than Mommy. Can't you write and tell him that? Cross my heart! I promise!

GRANDMA: I lost his address.

HONEY: Lost his address?

GRANDMA: Yes...It's somewhere...I don't remember now...I've forgotten where...

HONEY: When he writes again, I'll copy it for you...in all my notebooks...

GRANDMA: That's a good girl...

(A silence.)

HONEY: Will he write again?

GRANDMA: *(With some doubt.)* He will...

HONEY: I love him...I'll be good to him...I want him to be the father of my babies.

GRANDMA: Don't say that. It's a deadly sin.

HONEY: Why is it a deadly sin?

GRANDMA: Because...He's your daddy...Because he's married to Mommy...and because...married men are married forever...to one mommy only.

HONEY: *(Ironical.)* You don't say?!

GRANDMA: What do you mean? Married once, married forever.

HONEY: So they say.

GRANDMA: You have to believe your Grandma...I'm over sixty...I know a lot.

HONEY: I hope so. But don't you know that many daddies leave and marry again?

GRANDMA: Who, for instance?

HONEY: All of them... *(A silence.)* Except my daddy. My daddy is good...My daddy loves me...I'll tell him things and he'll marry me.

GRANDMA: What things?

HONEY: I know.

GRANDMA: Tell me.

HONEY: Only to Daddy.

GRANDMA: What sort of things?

HONEY: You name it.

GRANDMA: What do you mean?

HONEY: You're so busy with good deeds, Granny, that you see nothing! Mommy is naughty.

GRANDMA: How *dare* you? She isn't! She breast-fed you for over seven months. Don't you ever forget it!

HONEY: All mothers use their breasts. But that doesn't change the fact that...

GRANDMA: You're a naughty, naughty girl. Beware of the bogeyman!

HONEY: *(A sly smile on her face.)* Granny! Do you still believe in the Bugaboo?

GRANDMA: *(Trying to frighten her.)* I certainly do believe in the bogeyman! He's capable of doing harm to disobedient little girls like you. Lurking in dark corners, devil incarnate. Beware of him!

HONEY: Are you serious, Granny?

GRANDMA: Of course I'm serious!

HONEY: Granny, that's a white lie. Everyone...

GRANDMA: Take that back. I'm not a liar. Apologize!

HONEY: *(After a short silence.)* If you insist, Granny...

GRANDMA: Your Mommy will just be heartbroken if you don't.

HONEY: ...So be it.

GRANDMA: Be it what?

HONEY: ...I apologize. But in all honesty and frankness...

GRANDMA: Say no more.

HONEY: But...

GRANDMA: Not another word! Don't ever argue with grown-ups. For your own sake.

HONEY: For my own sake, as usual. You grown-ups, you just can't take any criticism...

GRANDMA: Grown-ups have the last word.

HONEY: ...And the upper hand, I know.

GRANDMA: That's a time-honored custom. There's a set of rules, in life, and we must live by them.

HONEY: Granny, you know I love you. I was only saying that Mommy...

GRANDMA: Love for Mommy is a must.

HONEY: And love for Daddy?

GRANDMA: Is a must too.

HONEY: Am I allowed to love Daddy more than Mommy?

GRANDMA: It's not fair...Your mommy is a real angel...

HONEY: *(Ironical.)* You don't say?! Is that a fact?

GRANDMA: It is!

HONEY: If you say so, Granny, I'll settle for it.

GRANDMA: Good girl.

HONEY: *(With a straight face.)* It was so silly of me not to notice that she's an angel...I wonder why she doesn't fly...

GRANDMA: *(Almost to herself, while feeding her dog.)* That little imp...This is what happens when a child is raised in a broken home...

HONEY: "Broken"?

GRANDMA: It's a figure of speech...When a daddy leaves, the home is broken.

HONEY: Were you raised in a broken home?

GRANDMA: Not me...not your mommy...We were lucky...

HONEY: Daddy is coming back. I'll be lucky too.

GRANDMA: You will...You deserve happiness.

HONEY: Have you always been happy?

GRANDMA: Always...In the good old days, it was easier...

HONEY: Why easier?

GRANDMA: We knew...We knew everything...

HONEY: Everything about what?

GRANDMA: How to behave...It was easier...Life's no longer a bowl of cherries.

HONEY: Why?

GRANDMA: I don't know...We were taught the rules. We lived by them.

HONEY: What rules? Teach me.

GRANDMA: Easy ones...From the beginning...

HONEY: What beginning?

GRANDMA: When you marry, the bride must wear...something old, something new, something borrowed, something blue...I did. And I married on a Wednesday.

HONEY: Why?

GRANDMA: "Monday for wealth
Tuesday for health
Wednesday's the best of all;
Thursday for crosses,
Friday for losses
And Saturday no luck at all."

HONEY: I want to be lucky, I'll get married on a Wednesday. Like you. Was your dress white?

GRANDMA: *(Thinking back with nostalgia.)* White, yes...The good old days...He carried me across the threshold, the proper foot entering first...

HONEY: Which proper foot?

GRANDMA: The right one, I think.

HONEY: Why did he do that?

GRANDMA: Carrying the bride across the threshold brings good luck. If the proper foot enters first. He did that. We were happy...

HONEY: I love you, Granny. You're such a kind lady, you're so gentle...I want to become a plain lady like you.

GRANDMA: "Plain"?

HONEY: ...And lucky like you. You're always so happy...

GRANDMA: It's more difficult today but I manage...I have Mommy, I have you, I have my pets...I try to forget that life is so full of anxieties...I feel lucky all the same.

HONEY: Daddy told me once that I'm lucky because I was born with a silver spoon in my mouth. Is it true? Where's that silver spoon now?

GRANDMA: That's a figure of speech... There is no silver spoon...But you'll really be happy and lucky. I saw you being born. You were born with a veil. Which means that you're especially gifted, especially favored...

HONEY: *(Surprised.)* "With a veil?" How? What do you mean? A veil around me?

GRANDMA: *(Regretting the detail, embarrassed.)* Around you, yes...Some babies are born with a veil...Only a few...The lucky ones...You'll be lucky...

HONEY: You really saw me..."with a veil"? Under cabbage leaves?

GRANDMA: *(Evasive.)* ...Under cabbage leaves, yes.

HONEY: Granny...I think it's high time you tell me...the truth.

GRANDMA: What truth?

HONEY: I'm so confused...You tell me "under cabbage leaves." Mommy told me that the stork brought me...Daddy told me that the doctor brought me in a bag...Alina told me other things...

GRANDMA: What things?

HONEY: A few...strange facts...

GRANDMA: The facts of life...

HONEY: That's what Alina called them, yes!

GRANDMA: Did Mommy tell you any...? *(Vague gesture.)*

HONEY: She just says: "Live and learn," when she is in a real hurry. And the stork story when she has two minutes. But it's a lie, I know!

GRANDMA: Mommy is always so busy... but she does nor lie. Mommies never lie. They just take their time...

HONEY: And grandmothers? Even the story of the cabbage leaves is a lie—according to Alina!

GRANDMA: *(Flustered, all confusion.)* It's a little white lie that...Try to understand...We grown-ups, we...On the other hand...Well...As a matter of fact...It is not in my line of duty but somehow...Besides, for your own sake.

HONEY: *(Who has been studying her with curiosity.)* Even Daddy began hemming and hawing like that one day. And nothing came out. This is a strange house. Everyone talks in riddles.

GRANDMA: Well...It's an issue we have to face...I've more time than Mommy...

HONEY: Oh Granny, thank you. Let's face it. How do we...?

GRANDMA: Well...To unfold the miracle of birth is most delicate...a complicated subject...

HONEY: Confusing, I'd say. What's the sober truth?

GRANDMA: *(Embarrassed, with difficulty.)* Well...the sober truth and reality...is simple...We want to keep your heart pure...

HONEY: My heart is pure. I love the whole world.

GRANDMA: That's beautiful and moving...Altruism is not an instinct. It has to be taught, they say. But in your case...

HONEY: Daddy taught me.

GRANDMA: He's a good daddy. Well, let's start from the real beginning...As you well know, our Lord is generous. He gave life, he created flowers and trees, water and grass—everything that is nature, including people... *(She goes to her flowerpots and indicates them.)* Let's begin with these flowers...Look how beautiful they are...Our Lord created them...Now...How should I put it?...Our Lord is very busy, you know, in protecting everyone, in loving everything...So, He gave these flowers—and all creatures on earth—some independence...A choice, the chance to reproduce...And gave them means, a way to...do it.

HONEY: What way? How?

GRANDMA: Well, you saw it in some books, I guess...It's a question of seeds—as always.

HONEY: As always.

GRANDMA: You plant a seed in the ground, flowers sprout.

HONEY: And if we are not around to plant seeds—who does the job?

GRANDMA: *(Unsure.)* That's a good question...They just fall, I suppose...Somehow, somewhere...

HONEY: "Somehow, somewhere..."

GRANDMA: From some tree, I suppose, into the earth...

HONEY: Flowers should only grow around trees, then. And how about the ones which grow in the middle of a field?

GRANDMA: Oh yes, I remember...It just slipped my mind because it's a difficult word...Anemosomething...It's the wind which sends, carries, and fertilizes...

HONEY: Just like that? At random?

GRANDMA: At random...You know the wind—south, north, west...Who gets it gets it. Nature is very liberal and democratic...

HONEY: I see...Black seeds, red seeds, green seeds...Flying around at random...

GRANDMA: And no one complains. It's real democracy. Our Lord thinks of everything...

HONEY: To sum it up. The wind "gives." It's the masculine partner. The earth "receives." It's the feminine partner.

GRANDMA: *(Rather shocked.)* ...You can put it like that...I never thought of it that way but it sounds reasonable...Wind-masculine. Earth-feminine.

HONEY: It's as simple as that. Let's go on, Granny.

GRANDMA: All right...That's a good start...Next step. Fish. *(She moves to the fishbowl.)*

HONEY: I go for that. It has always made me curious. Who gives what to whom?

GRANDMA: *(Puzzled.)* Let me stress just one fact. It's not a question of "giving what to whom." Nature is harmony, melody, agreement, understanding... *(She tries to find other words but fails to find them.)*

HONEY: *(Ironical, aware of GRANDMA'S caution.)* Keep trying.

GRANDMA: *(Indicating the fish.)* Well, they swim around...They meet... *(She thinks.)* The trouble is...Big fish eat small fish... *(She thinks it over. She is confused.)*

HONEY: That's life.

GRANDMA: That's life...I lost the thread of my story...

HONEY: When fish of the same size meet...

GRANDMA: Yes, they must be the same size and color. Yes, they're very tribal and conservative...Only if the same species...

HONEY: Fish are like that too!

GRANDMA: The point is...When they meet,—if they are in a mood for...They smile at each other, woo each other...kiss each other...

HONEY: How?

GRANDMA: That's something confusing...I'm not a specialist and...

HONEY: The seed must go from somewhere to somewhere else.

GRANDMA: Something like that, I guess...I think they kiss on the mouth...I think I saw them kissing like that...Then they lay their eggs...Those are their seeds...And they plant them at the bottom of the ocean...or of the bowl...There...The miracle of birth takes place.

HONEY: *(Disappointed.)* Up to this point, nothing is clear. What else? Who else?

GRANDMA: Birds, now. *(She moves to the cage and indicates the two birds.)* Even birds lay eggs.

HONEY: Where? When? How?

GRANDMA: *(Searching.)* Practically everything that lives grew from some kind of egg or seed.

HONEY: Us too? What kind of seed?

GRANDMA: Later. I'll tell you later. Step by step.

HONEY: Today?

GRANDMA: Today.

HONEY: Cross your heart!

GRANDMA: Cross my heart.

HONEY: At last! Thank you, Granny. You're a darling! And make the short story long, if that helps you find yourself.

GRANDMA: *(Studying her.)* Of course. One thing leads to another...We are facing a very important issue...delicate and most important...

HONEY: *(Seriously.)* We are.

GRANDMA: To elaborate...Different kinds of seeds grow differently...The seeds of plants and trees grow in the ground. The seeds of chickens and birds are hidden in their eggs...

HONEY: What comes first? Chicken or egg?

GRANDMA: That's an ancient issue...Rather mysterious...Our Lord's ways may sometimes seem mysterious but...

HONEY: They sure are mysterious!

GRANDMA: So, they lay eggs...They sit on them...Miracle of birth again.

HONEY: Just a moment! What about the rooster? What's his part?

GRANDMA: The usual.

HONEY: Meaning?

GRANDMA: *(Hesitating.)* Wooing...kissing...

HONEY: How? Like fish?

GRANDMA: More or less...

HONEY: Oh no! I saw hens being jumped on!

GRANDMA: Oh yes, of course. That's the way. They jump on each other, they play, roll, fight...They call that love play.

HONEY: *(Savoring the word.)* Love play...I like those two words. I really do. I go for that sort of playing...What about us, now?

GRANDMA: *(Trying to find the right words.)* "Us"...They call us the mammals because of...You know what... *(She timidly indicates her breasts.)* What you used to call the "bumps," the "lumps," the "things"...

HONEY: The bosoms.

GRANDMA: That's the word. Do you know what bosoms are for?

HONEY: To wear a bra.

GRANDMA: Yes, of course, But the purpose is...To store milk for new babies...

HONEY: Alina told me. First I was told mothers have milk in their tummies. What a lie!

GRANDMA: Some misunderstanding, I suppose. Looking at cows you may think milk comes from the tummy.

HONEY: Amateurish!

GRANDMA: Who?

HONEY: The explanation.

GRANDMA: Well, now...The cow is a mammal and breast-feeds her calves. The sow is a mammal and breast-feeds her piglets...

HONEY: What about dogs and cats?

GRANDMA: They are mammals too. Mother-dog breast-feeds her puppies. Mother-cat breast-feeds her kittens.

HONEY: *(Indicating them.)* What's wrong with these two? No puppies, no kittens! Why not?

GRANDMA: This is a special case. Animals living in a house all the time...

HONEY: Let them out! Free to love play! They'd like it!

GRANDMA: Not really...I don't think they would, now...I was explaining... Animals that live in a house all the time...are normally...altered...

HONEY: "Altered"? What's that?

GRANDMA: My Lord, we are getting into trouble...Never mind. It's difficult enough when nature goes straight...Let's skip it. We were talking about the miracle of birth. *(Indicating the dog and cat.)* That "alteration" is beside the point.

HONEY: I want to know. Is that another of our Lord's mysteries?

GRANDMA: Oh no. He has nothing to do with this innovation. We did it...

HONEY: You did it?

GRANDMA: I mean men, in general. But I think that's enough for today. Play with your doll and...

HONEY: Oh Granny! You promised! Let's face the facts once and for all. What about "us"? Do men "alter" us too?

GRANDMA; Oh no! What are you saying? Only animals...

HONEY: What for? How?

GRANDMA: Sometimes—...to avoid too many puppies...—they stop the internal seeds from...growing.

HONEY: The "internal seeds"...

GRANDMA: Yes, we all have them...inside...

HONEY: Me too?

GRANDMA: All of us. In a special place near the tummy.

HONEY: *(Caressing her tummy with joy.)* You mean I'm ready for...I might...

GRANDMA: *(Quickly.)* Seeds are not ripe in children!

(HONEY is very disappointed.)

GRANDMA: We all grow from seeds, darling...Everything that lives grew from some kind of seed...Animal babies and human babies...We all get started the same way...famous people and poor people and everybody.

HONEY: *(Still holding her tummy.)* When will I be...ripe?

GRANDMA: When you grow up.

HONEY: How old must I be?

GRANDMA: Around twenty...

HONEY: How old were you when Mommy was born?

GRANDMA: I was twenty-seven.

HONEY: Why so old?

GRANDMA: You have to meet a daddy first...

HONEY: A daddy?

GRANDMA: A husband, I mean.

HONEY: Must he be a real husband or just a boyfriend?

GRANDMA: It's a deadly sin if he's only a boyfriend.

HONEY: But the seed, inside, works all the same.

GRANDMA: It's a deadly sin, I told you.

HONEY: Suppose we repent?

GRANDMA: Who?

HONEY: The boy and girl we are talking about. Do they still get the baby?

GRANDMA; If they get married, yes. They get the baby, the blessing, and everything.

HONEY: It figures.

GRANDMA; What do you mean?

HONEY: They told me a story about people who did "that deadly sin"...And they're now happy and blessed. I couldn't figure it out. Now, let's suppose I'm twenty and I've found a daddy for my babies. How do we make them?

GRANDMA: He'll know.

HONEY: Let's face the issue, Granny. I must know it too.

GRANDMA: Well...You already know a few things, I'm sure...

HONEY: A few. But they're rather confusing...You have more experience than Alina. You should know

GRANDMA: A bit more. How old is Alina?

HONEY: She's ten. But she seems to know a lot. If she is not bluffing.

GRANDMA: All right. Well...Even before you and Alina talked about birds and bees...You knew that men and women are constructed differently...There are some differences in boys' bodies. You have no brother and you never saw... But maybe you know that boys...tinkle from... *(She cannot find the word.)*

HONEY: ...The wee wee, I know.

GRANDMA: Very well... *(She does not know how to go on.)* Well...They have the little... *(Another pause.)*

HONEY: Be practical, Granny. And describe what you have on your mind.

GRANDMA: Well...in life...We all search for our soulmate...Boys search for girls. Girls search for boys...

HONEY: I'll be very good at it. How did you meet your soulmate?

GRANDMA: *(Thinking of the past with tenderness.)* I was already twenty-five, I began to feel alone...Many things frighten a lonely girl... *(She looks at the bedroom. She thinks of her daughter too.)* ...I wasn't old, really, but I began to worry...

HONEY: You're always worried. You worry too much.

GRANDMA: That's the right attitude. Never worry. Never feel it's too late...I met him at the library.

HONEY: I like libraries. Where did Mommy meet her soulmate—Daddy?

GRANDMA: At a party.

HONEY: I like parties... *(A sudden thought on her mind makes her sad again.)* Can you meet *two* soulmates?

GRANDMA: Only one is the real soulmate.

HONEY: *(Who is thinking of her mother.)* That's good. Only my daddy. Go on, Granny. Suppose I've already met my soulmate. What do we do?

GRANDMA: If he is the real boy our Lord has chosen for you... You feel something, inside...

HONEY: Stirrings.

GRANDMA: Something like that... And between the two... There is tenderness, kindness, warmth, affection, gentleness... A desire for...

HONEY: Sex.

GRANDMA: Not yet, no... Before sex one longs for a little romance and idealism... and caresses...

HONEY: That's true. Daddy was always patting Mommy's ass...

GRANDMA: *(Horrified.)* That word, Honey!

HONEY: I'm sorry. Mommy's fanny... or behind, if you prefer.

GRANDMA: ...a desire for clean caresses...

HONEY: What are "clean caresses"?

GRANDMA: ...Above the waist...

HONEY: Up to here? *(She shows her waist.)*

GRANDMA: Not really... Above the shoulders, I should have said... All right... Now... *(She has lost the thread again.)*

HONEY: Clean caresses. Above the shoulders. What comes next? Please be clear.

GRANDMA: I'm really trying... To the best of my ability but... You're my first grandchild and I never thought I was going to... Let's wait for your mother to finish up!

HONEY: She's too busy. You tell me. You've got more time.

GRANDMA: *(Looking at the bedroom.)* What's she up to? Was she alone?

HONEY: Don't change the subject. What comes next?

GRANDMA: Well... Our Lord constructed our bodies so that we have a special place, near the tummy, for the babies to grow...

HONEY: I know which place you mean.

GRANDMA: Good. Babies grow inside there until they are big enough to get along outside... They're strong and ready after nine months...

HONEY: Is it nine months for everybody?

GRANDMA: It depends on the size of the babies. It doesn't take a rabbit nine months. The babies are tiny. It takes a mother elephant nearly three years to have a baby elephant. But look what she gets!

HONEY: And for women it has to be nine months?

GRANDMA: As a rule, yes.

HONEY: That's a long time. You couldn't hurry it up, could you? Eat more or something?

GRANDMA: Nature can't be hurried.

HONEY: Nine months from *what* day?

GRANDMA: "From what day"...That's the whole question...Well...

HONEY: Well?

GRANDMA: Women have seeds, inside...

HONEY: We know that.

GRANDMA: And men have, too.

HONEY: Where?

GRANDMA: Inside.

HONEY: Inside where?

GRANDMA: Somewhere, in their blood...They're called...It's a long and difficult word...

HONEY: It's difficult all right. I knew it. it ends...z-o-o-n. Twelve letters. It's the longest word in the dictionary.

GRANDMA: That's the word...It's a tiny cell which must join the tiny cell in our bodies...

HONEY: How?

GRANDMA: When two people feel very close and loving...they caress, they embrace, they...

HONEY: ...Neck. Tell me one thing, Granny. I once saw two dogs doing something...Love play, I guess...They were taking turns biting each other's neck. Was that "necking"? Do they call it "necking" because they bite their necks?

GRANDMA: *(Reflecting.)* I suppose so...Maybe you're right...I never thought of it...Maybe...

HONEY: Does it hurt?

GRANDMA: What kind of question is that?

HONEY: I heard Mommy moaning, one night, while...

GRANDMA: Do you eavesdrop by chance?

HONEY: No. I just heard her moaning. Loud. Does it hurt?

GRANDMA: Not really.

HONEY: Count me out, if it hurts. I don't like pain.

GRANDMA: It doesn't hurt. Love is a combination of strength with delicacy...The man is strong...The girl must pretend to be delicate and very feminine...

HONEY: Pretend?

GRANDMA: It may sound a little scheming and conniving but that's the rule...We women have to pretend a lot of things...softness, delicacy, pain...

HONEY: I get it. I'm very good at lying.

GRANDMA: Are you?

HONEY: Don't get me wrong, Granny. Only when necessary. With my boyfriend.

GRANDMA: Husband.

HONEY: I'll be the best at love playing! I'll caress, kiss, pet, neck, moan...

GRANDMA: Just a moment. Let's not confuse the terms...You must never make the first move. You mustn't take any initiative. Never!

HONEY: Why not?

GRANDMA: Men object when their wives show initiative. They resent it. They want a soft, yielding woman...A wife must be tender, patient, tolerant, submissive, resigned, uncomplaining, long-suffering...

HONEY: *(Disappointed.)* And what else? Is it worth all that fuss?

GRANDMA: *(After a silence.)* It's worth it. A woman must know how to behave, how to win, how to convince, how to make a man happy...

HONEY: I know what you mean. Tricks in bed.

GRANDMA: *(Shocked by this.)* Where on earth did you hear *that* expression?

HONEY: Alina heard it.

GRANDMA: That Alina...You shouldn't see her any longer.

HONEY: That's why my gentle Granny should explain everything; clearly. How do the two seeds join?

GRANDMA: *(After pondering a while.)* When the two people feel...

HONEY: The two lovers, you mean?

GRANDMA: Husband and wife, yes... When they feel happy, close and loving...When they feel extra warm...

HONEY: "Extra warm?"... *(She thinks it over.)* That's why!

GRANDMA: Why what?

HONEY: That's why they get undressed!

(A silence.)

GRANDMA: How do you know? *What* have you seen?

HONEY: You mean...*Who* have I seen?

GRANDMA: Yes, whom did you see undressing?

HONEY: *(After a silence; sad again.)* I was playing in the bedroom with my doll... *(She indicates the door.)* Near the mirror, in the corner...They didn't see me at first...

GRANDMA: *(Looking at the door; very worried.)* They!...Who?

HONEY: He was kissing Mommy on the mouth...with his hands here... *(She indicates her behind.)* ...Then he said: "Listen doll, let's make a baby!"...And he began to undress her...

GRANDMA: *(With anguish.)* Who began to...?

(A silence.)

HONEY: *(In a whisper, lowering her voice.)* Uncle Bill...

(A silence. GRANDMA is shocked at what she has just learned. She goes over to the door and pounds on it.)

GRANDMA: Open the door!

(From inside, no sound. She tries to open the door. It is locked. She pounds again, with more force. No answer.)

GRANDMA: Open, please...She saw you...Do you understand...? *(She cannot find the right words. She pounds again and again.)* Open! Open! *Open!*

(Meanwhile HONEY has gone to the window and looks outside with her back to the audience. GRANDMA is pounding with insistence and desperation.)

GRANDMA: Open, open! Do you realize she saw you! Do you understand what you've done...? *(She cannot find words.)* Open! Do you—

MAN'S VOICE OFFSTAGE: *(Sudden, strong, violent.)* Shut up, old witch!

(A chilling silence.)

HONEY: *(Looking out the window.)* Star light. Star bright...

(GRANDMA moves slowly to HONEY and puts her arm around HONEY's shoulder. Born out of this is a new understanding between them. We feel warmth and closeness.)

HONEY: The star I love tonight;
    I wish I may, I wish I might
    Have the wish I wish tonight...

(The stage slowly darkens as the curtain falls.)

(THE END.)

Erotic Adventures in Venice (Promises)

The Persons:

GUIDO, the musician
ALFIO, in his late twenties
ELENA, in her early twenties
THE SENATOR, in his late fifties
THE MANICURIST (the lover, ROSETTA)
ROSETTA, the Senator's lover
DORA, Guido's wife
THE GHOSTS (the available actors)

The Place:

St. Michael's Cemetery in Venice

The Time:

1991–1992 during Tangentopoli ("Bribestown"—Corruption in Italy)

Downstage, GUIDO plays his [saxophone] for the audience. He stops; he smiles at the audience.

GUIDO: You recognize me, don't you? I was the [saxophonist] in the band at the Café Chioggia in St. Mark's Square...I was happy, popular, and everybody applauded...One evening, a sexy, smiling American woman sat down right in front of me...red hair, very sensual. I felt her smile caressing my soul, caressing me everywhere, especially where she kept staring...First night, second night, third night, she would enjoy one ice cream after another... Finally, at the end of one of my performances, at one o'clock in the morning, she introduced herself and began telling me the story of her life... Then one night, courage overtook her, and she took the initiative. She grabbed me and kissed me passionately, seducing me on the spot...A few weeks went by. She continued to sit there paying homage to my musical prowess. Then, an incredible attractive proposition: would I go to New York with her? I would have a new life amidst the glamour of the most exciting city in the world... Broadway. Perhaps even Hollywood one day. Well, what would you have done in my place? How can you say no to a woman like that? How can one refuse her exciting promises?...and so, I went to New York, to live in the heart of Manhattan. I got a quick tour in a taxi, and then...Do you know how we used to spend our evenings? I had to play for her. For hours. She would fall in a trance at the sound of my playing. She would close her eyes, touch herself, lost in her own world, ecstatic in a paradise she called "Venetian"...And what about me?...I am playing today, and tomorrow, and the next day, every day of the week. I began to feel like an accessory, an instrument, only there to enhance her experience. I suggested we tape my playing when I wanted to join her in her erotic Venetian paradise. Well, she would explain how she needed to be alone with herself and my playing. "No, no, I want to see you there, in front of me, erect, vibrant, alive, magnificent, in your Venetian fullness." She's nuts about Venice, a real fanatic...I reminded her she had tempted me with a promise of life, real excitement in New York. We never went out. She was tired, busy, under the weather.—Always a new excuse. In the end, I discovered that the American women who kidnap European lovers promising them glory, never keep those promises. They're afraid that the man, their lover, their prisoner, will escape if he has any success...This went on for three and a half years. I felt trapped, a victim, her sexual toy...I decided to come back to Venice...So, I'm here again...I tried to get my old job back with the orchestra...it was too late. They had found someone better—which is impossible—but that's what they told me. True, he is younger than I am, full of energy, but he is rather ugly. I wonder if perhaps they chose a less attractive guy so as not to tempt an American tourist who would pretend to fall in love with him. Same fate as mine. New hiring for the orchestra. Fortunately, when I was in New York, I was invited to a couple of parties given by Senator "M," a nice Venetian politician with a very subtle instinct for special evenings where he felt like a new seducing Casanova... Very exciting parties with the most beautiful women of New York, all attracted, I think, by the political power of Mr. "M"... *(Reflecting.)* "M"...why do I call him just "M"? To protect him, but it sounds too Mussolini-like, and he does not deserve that insult. He's serious, intelligent, well informed, a well-rounded person. Plus he had this unique rare quality of keeping his promises. In New York, he told me—just a casual remark—he said "If you return to Venice, come to see me. I'll find you a good job." A good job? This promise, made by a powerful politician, was reassuring. So when the orchestra would not give me my old job in Venice, I knocked at the door of his office. I stand corrected, there was a doorbell. His secretaries were beautiful, but they were real bitches. All secretaries are like that. Loyal and overprotective, and they stop everyone from disturbing their bosses. To safeguard them. Bitches nonetheless. The only solution was for me to wait outside with infinite patience for many many hours. I was about to fall asleep, when I saw him going out with two of the bi—secretaries. I screamed "Your Honor Saint— *(Interrupts himself and corrects himself.)* All right, in Venice, they call him Saint Michael because...he's good to his people. After a brief hesitation, a moment of panic, he recognized me, he apologizes for the behavior of his overzealous secretaries, and made an appointment for the next day. The next day, when I returned, he asked: —"Do you want a job?"—There is a crisis in Italy today, a serious crisis because they have discovered that...you know what I'm talking about...about the so-called 'Bustarelle'—bribes." He looked through a pile of papers and finally found what he was searching for—a note written on a scrap of paper. He told me in a calm and convincing manner "This is an unusual position...original, unique well paid...besides, it's a romantic job on a beautiful, restful island. Are you interested?" "Sure," I answered. "All right. You'll be the custodian in the most beautiful cemetery in the world...San Michele...an island of peace, an idyllic spot where, among saints and angels, great men are resting. Stravinsky, Diaghilev, Ezra Pound...a peaceful island where very few will disturb you...only a few rare visitors who talk softly because they are afraid of the inhabitants, and they just whisper prayers..." In reality, San Michele is very famous, as it is the final resting place of some great men. *(Addressing the audience.)* Actually, a pleasant job, interesting and poetical...With many extra benefits...foreign visitors give you good tips to show them the tombs of the great men, to take photos and short films in bizarre situations and positions...One who plays the violin, another one who is pretending to play the cello, dancers in tutus jumping or kneeling down...a job that I must confess, gives me a sense of power. It's completely up to me to let the mausoleums be used by homeless friends of mine or some young couples in need of a cozy, romantic corner to make love...I realized another resource or, shall I say, advantage. There are many spacious chapels that can house more than their residents. Suddenly, I became a landlord. After all, real estate is everything.

(He indicates the curtain that opens or the spotlights that are illuminating the set now. We see an elegant chapel with an ornate coffin in the center. On top of the coffin there is a telephone. Downstage, we see a young couple, ALFIO and ELENA. GUIDO exits stage left.)

ALFIO: Try again...

ELENA: Yes, darling, it's me...how are you? I'm always thinking of you—

ALFIO: *(Interrupting.)* No! No! Your voice must be sweeter, more maternal.

ELENA: Maternal? Give me a break. I am twenty, your mother was sixty!

ALFIO: Try again. It's getting better.

ELENA: *(Trying a more maternal approach.)* Yes darling, it's me, how are you? I'm always thinking of you, and I feel so close—

ALFIO: No, No! It sounds fake!

ELENA: Stop it! I've tried this a million times! You're always complaining, I can't take it anymore!

ALFIO: She's my mother. I know her voice, don't I? I want your voice to be perfectly identical.

ELENA: It will never be perfect and identical. I'm not your mother. I am your...your what? You tell me! I have agreed to live here like two gypsies because you promised—

ALFIO: *(Interrupting.)* And I will keep my promises! I adore you, and I will marry you. But first we need my inheritance.

ELENA: Get a job. That's the best way to start a new life together.

ALFIO: A job in Venice? What kind of job would you like me to find? Thousands are unemployed!

ELENA: Be a gondolier. They make a lot of money.

ALFIO: You're joking! It's like taxi drivers in Rome. Jobs go from father to son. *(He starts to sing the song "Tradition" from Fiddler on the Roof.)*

ELENA: Then go work for your father. Apply to be...his deputy director. How can he say no?

ALFIO: I wish it were possible! You know he kicked me out of the factory. He can't stand me! He's an intolerant son of a bitch.

ELENA: Well, so are you. It's stupid to be rebellious. You have to learn how to handle parents. I've been forgiven at least ten times. Go to him, be humble and apologize. Ask for forgiveness. He'll give you a big office in the factory. Just mark my words.

ALFIO: He swore he'd never forgive me.

ELENA: That's what my father always said. Then I'd kiss him tenderly on his cheeks. He smiled and melted like ice cream in August. Try it sometimes.

ALFIO: Kissing my father? You're kidding. You are a woman. Sweet little kisses from a daughter to a father are a bit different. It's easy for you to butter people up.

ELENA: Try, try! Anything is better than this!

ALFIO: I've tried. He humiliated me in front of everybody, calling me an ingrate, a juvenile delinquent, an incorrigible rascal, a loser. I'll never forget that.

ELENA: Well, don't go to his office where he has an audience and where he's used to giving orders. Go home, in your house where's he's alone, weak, and vulnerable.

ALFIO: Weak? Vulnerable? You don't know him.

ELENA: You told me he has heart problems.

ALFIO: That's besides the point. With me, he's always behaving like Colleoni.

ELENA: Colleoni?

ALFIO: That monument in front of the hospital. That famous mercenary leader who looks like Mussolini. Hard and nasty. My father has declared war on me.

ELENA: Then go to the battle. Face him. Tell him off. Claim you have rights. Fight back.

ALFIO: What rights? He says I have none.

ELENA: The only son of a millionaire widower? You have all the rights in the world!

ALFIO: Who told you that?

ELENA: I've discussed it with Daddy. He said we could take legal action. That he would represent our case. A couple legally married against his arrogance.

ALFIO: Oh!

ELENA: As a couple, sure, we have rights.

ALFIO: My father has hundreds of lawyers who can prove I am wrong. He'll never forgive me. His lawyers know all the tricks. That's how he became rich.

ELENA: I don't understand. What could you ever do to him to make him this mad!

ALFIO: You know...

ELENA: No, I don't know.

ALFIO: I told you. First, the problem of school. He wanted me to get a degree in business administration at the Cà Foscari University. Can you imagine how boring that is? Who needs a degree if your father's a millionaire?

ELENA: To help you find a job if your father doesn't come around and disowns you. What else did you do to him?

ALFIO: *(Hesitating.)* Then there was the old story of...the maid...

ELENA: Knocked up at sixteen. You pig! Your father is right to call you irresponsible for that one. But he paid her off, no disgrace in the end. How much did he pay her?

ALFIO: Enough to buy an apartment.

ELENA: One-thousandth of your father's fortune. Why does he hate you so much? Why can't he forgive you? Look at us. She has an apartment and we live here! *(Indicates the surroundings.)*

ALFIO: Then the drugs...It's inconceivable to him. You should see how furious he gets. His eyes start popping out of their sockets if you even mention drugs. It's inconceivable to him that a young man would "destroy his being, his brain" that's what he says. "Destroying." If I made a hundred women pregnant—

ELENA: *(Interrupting.)* Just try it and I'll cut your dick off. The way that American woman did. But I'll throw it to the dogs! No chances to stitch it back.

ALFIO: *(Continuing.)* Or if I killed a couple of people by mistake—more or less—it would be less serious, according to him. He would fight for me. Proving—

ELENA: *(Ironical.)* With his hundreds of lawyers.

ALFIO: ...That I am innocent. He would have me plead self-defense.

ELENA: Of course! Anyone with a lot of money can get away with murder. We know that well. Just read the papers.

ALFIO: But drugs...He'll never forgive drugs.

ELENA: But you gave them up! We have been clean for months.

ALFIO: He doesn't believe me. He doesn't trust me. If he saw me... *(Hesitates.)*

ELENA: If he saw you?

ALFIO: *(Hesitant.)* ...On drugs again...

ELENA: Well? What are you trying to say?

ALFIO: He'd have a heart attack.

ELENA: *(Suddenly having an idea.)* That's what you want, isn't it? What we need. Pretend you're high. You've always been a good actor.

ALFIO: "Acting," me?

ELENA: Sure, you act with me all the time.

ALFIO: Bullshit.

ELENA: *(Ignoring.)* Just pretend to be high. You go to his office and pull out a needle. He has a heart attack. You inherit everything.

(The telephone rings. They are surprised and shaken. ELENA is on the verge of answering. ALFIO stops her. One ring, two, three, four.)

ALFIO: No...Not yet. You haven't perfected it yet. You are not convincing enough.

ELENA: I'll never be.

(Three more rings. A silence. ELENA is disappointed.)

ELENA: I should have answered.

ALFIO: Not yet, not yet...You must have the right intonation to convince him. This way... *(He imitates a sweet, maternal, feminine voice with some ability.)* Yes, darling...it's me...how are you? I'm always thinking about you. Yes, I'm close to you...I'm protecting your sleep...I am your guardian angel.

ELENA: Not bad. You answer. *(With some irony.)* You're the one who sounds really "feminine and maternal." You know her voice well.

ALFIO: Very funny. He would catch on! We need a sweet, feminine voice, like yours...

ELENA: *(Impatient.)* When? When? I'm tired of this life of your empty promises!

ALFIO: Soon, it will happen soon, cross my heart.

ELENA: I'm answering it next time! You've been promising for months. It's high time to decide, to try. The die is cast. I am answering, that's it.

ALFIO: I think it would be better if... *(He hesitates.)*

ELENA: What? Do you have second thoughts? Losing your nerve? You said it yourself that he will never forgive you! You told me that this *(Indicating the telephone.)* is the only way.

ALFIO: Not the only way...

ELENA: This one! You said he needs an incredible shock—one big enough to give him a heart attack. It's either me on the phone or drugs again.

ALFIO: Drugs again? No, we promised each other...

ELENA: I said pretend, you jerk! Just pretend to be high, in his office.

ALFIO: And if...

ELENA: If what...

ALFIO: We must consider all contingencies...

ELENA: What are you trying to say? That it's not true that his heart is so weak?

ALFIO: Oh no...The doctors told him... he overworks, he's excitable, he has a very high blood pressure...he must take pills for his heart, when he remembers...He must.

ELENA: "When he remembers"...Is he absentminded?

ALFIO: He's a busy man. At times, he even forgets to eat and then screams at his secretaries for trying to take care of him.

ELENA: Do you think he's a bit off his rocker?

ALFIO: No. He is just arrogant like all dictators.

ELENA: He's got to be a little crazy. I mean—to install a phone on his wife's coffin...

ALFIO: He loved her very much. It was a great romantic love...

ELENA: Yes, but putting a telephone in a mausoleum...I've never heard of that one before. He's lost his marbles. He's not all there.

ALFIO: He was inconsolable when she died. I had never seen him cry. He even hugged me and confided in me. He said: "I want to stay with her, to be near her, to die with her, for her..." Then he had the idea about the telephone.

ELENA: I guess the phone on the coffin is a better solution for him.

ALFIO: I would say so. It's more romantic. He was convinced that when he called home and she wasn't there: he saw the room, he saw the telephone vibrating on the table, he saw her...It's true in a way.

ELENA: That's crazy!

ALFIO: Have you ever tried? It's true. I know it happened to me. I saw my room when no one was answering. I used to call my— *(He stops; he should not have started this subject.)*

ELENA: To call "my"...? who?

ALFIO: *(Hesitating.)* My first girlfriend, many years ago...

ELENA: Who was she?

ALFIO: I didn't mention it because it was only an innocent platonic infatuation. We were both very young. Only a few caresses...

ELENA: *(Jealous.)* "Platonic"?

ALFIO: I swear it! Anyway, when I called her, I "saw" her bedroom even if she didn't answer.

ELENA: And her little bed, I'm sure!

ALFIO: It's true. I even saw her bed. The telephone was there on the night table.

ELENA: And how come you had been in her bedroom?

ALFIO: She was a friend of the family. We'd visit each other all the time, playing childish games. She was twelve...

ELENA: *(Ironical.)* You poor innocent child! Even at twelve!

ALFIO: *(Ignoring.)* That's why I understand my father and his desire to have a telephone here. Once he told me "She hears me, I know. She feels I'm close to her and I make her happy. One day, maybe, she'll answer."

ELENA: And that's when you had this crazy idea.

ALFIO: Yes.

ELENA: And if I answer with your mother's voice...

ALFIO: Maybe...

ELENA: Maybe?

ALFIO: Almost certain...

ELENA: Almost certain?

ALFIO: It shall happen.

ELENA: What shall happen?

ALFIO: You know.

ELENA: Say it.

ALFIO: Don't be cruel...After all, he's my father.

ELENA: He is the cruel one. You don't disinherit a son when you are that rich! You give, you help your son when he's in trouble, when he's in love and wants to get married. *(She indicates herself.)* He's cruel, holding onto his money like that when we're starving.

(A silence.)

ALFIO: You are right, you are right. We would never do this to our child.

ELENA: Is that a promise?

ALFIO: It's a promise. Cross my heart.

ELENA: Parents who are so selfish not to help their children deserve the worst.

ALFIO: The worst.

ELENA: You're doing the right thing.

ALFIO: We're doing the right thing.

ELENA: Yes. I decided to do this with you because I love you, because I am your accomplice in everything. Love, struggle for survival, desire to help those in need. Our children and their friends. If they deserve it.

ALFIO: If they deserve it.

ELENA: Of course! One doesn't throw one's money away!

ALFIO: And who decides if they deserve it?

ELENA: We do.

ALFIO: The new Colleoni, the new dictators, the new rich—

(The telephone rings. They stiffen. They still have some doubts. ELENA stares at ALFIO, who nods vaguely, imperceptibly. ELENA decides to answer.)

ELENA: *(On the phone, with a maternal warm voice.)* Yes, darling...it's me. How are you, my love?

(ALFIO is startled by that new word which he did not suggest.)

ELENA: I'm thinking about you, I am close to you...always...especially at night.

I am protecting your sleep... I am your guardian angel...

(She hears a noise, the falling of a body. She hands the receiver to ALFIO, who listens carefully.)

ELENA: *(Whispering.)* I heard a thump... he fell, I think...

(ALFIO signals her not to talk. Voices from the receiver, confusion, screams. ALFIO tries to hand the receiver to ELENA. ELENA refuses it.)

ALFIO: *(After hesitating, in the receiver.)* Hello, hello, what happened?...

(Voices. Garbled and confused.)

ALFIO: How is he? How is he?

(GUIDO comes back downstage, curious, attracted by the noise.)

ALFIO: It's Alfio, his son... I was talking to him... How is he? What happened?... Oh my God! Call the ambulance! Hello, hello! Try artificial respiration! I'm coming, I'll be there right away! *(He puts the receiver down. He stares at ELENA in silence.)*

ALFIO: *(Exploding with joy.)* It's done! He dropped dead!

GUIDO: Who died?

ALFIO: My father!

(He hugs ELENA with passion, then takes her by the hand, ready to leave.)

ALFIO: Let's go! Let's run home! And to you, Guido, the gift I promised! The chapel is yours! With everything in it: decorations, telephone... and my mother! Do with it whatever you want! It's yours, yours, yours forever!

(ALFIO and ELENA exit, running. They are happy. GUIDO looks at them, astonished. Then he looks at the chapel with satisfaction; it now belongs to him.)

GUIDO: Finally!

(Downstage, GUIDO is playing his [saxophone]. When he has finished playing, he speaks to the audience.)

GUIDO: ...And so, that's how I inherited the chapel... I fixed it up a little... I've used it on different occasions... for a girlfriend... for a family of gypsies... for a tourist, once... for one of the workers who is fixing the cemetery and lives too far away... for some homeless friends. No charge, of course, for the homeless... And now... *(Indicating upstage.)* I'm going to tell you about a few poignant cases of nostalgia... First I want to tell you that my life keeps on being very interesting... I give tours of the most famous graves and I get tips... generous tips, at times. The most generous are the Japanese... I charge special fees if I'm taking pictures or shooting videos for the visitors. They are often bizarre avant-garde scenes. On Stravinsky's grave, people like to take photos with musical instruments. I also rent this *(He shows his [saxophone].)* ... On Diaghilev's tomb... I shoot dancers in different positions... once one of them wanted to be naked! Just imagine, stark naked in a cemetery where everyone is wearing his Sunday best! That time, I got a hundred-dollar tip. I also took photos of a lot of Germans and Austrians who always like to put flowers on Ezra Pound's tomb... Then, one day, I noticed something unusual. A beautiful redhead—like the one who took me to New York—well, I caught her spitting on Ezra Pound. It was the first time I'd ever seen someone spitting on a grave. I told her it was absolutely forbidden, and I threatened to call the police... You guessed. She offered and gave me a generous tip if I allowed her to come back and spit on that grave again, every day for the whole week... I gave her permission of course. And from that moment on, I carefully watched people approaching the grave of our dear Ezra. I caught at least twenty more people who spat on his tomb. Poor man! After all, he was a good poet even though he was a Nazi sympathizer. No one is perfect. In America, I met all sorts of Nazis, racists, bigots, people with a superiority complex. It's just a question of taste, isn't it? Well, thanks to Ezra Pound, I struck gold. I cashed in on a small fortune. Poetry pays, that's for sure! I learned that here, in this romantic cemetery. Now, now...let's go back to my chapel that I sometimes rent and sometimes give for free to friends...There is now an incredibly touching case...please don't tell anyone. There is... *(He hesitates.)* No, not yet...Let's talk first about the political situation in Italy...It's all tied in with a certain Di Pietro, a tough honest judge. He has discovered that in the last fifty years, the Italian ruling party—the White Party of the Christian Democrats was robbing Italy blind. I stand corrected. They were taking bribes, accepting...contributions...it's more elegant to say that...How did it work? Very simple. When the government allocates, for instance, ten billion for a highway, or to repair a palazzo—there are so many here in Venice—they want a gift...a contribution of twenty percent. It's like a commission—a fixed rate they always require, the notorious bustarella, a little envelope containing a large amount of cash. We should call it, in this case, big envelope, a suitcase...It was a way of living and thriving, accepted in high places for decades. Well, they were finally caught—most of them. Some went to prison, others are on the run...Well, most likely you guessed it. My honorable friend, the Senator, as he was risking arrest, he hid here with me! He was number two in the Pink Party, the ally of the "unchristians"—as they are now called. But in my opinion, what happened to him is unfair. He's an honest man...rather honest, relatively honest...let's say, more honest than the others...He explained it to me, and he convinced me...that, though both parties, the whites and the pinks, demanded, accepted these bribes, there is a logic to it. My dear friend the Senator said...

(THE SENATOR appears and speaks to the audience.)

SENATOR: Where on earth is a great amount of money, a huge amount of money in the hands of a few, a negative fact? Let me explain the world of politics. Some people still don't understand us, don't trust us. Let's take it step by step. If I had, for instance, five hundred million lire a month, what would I do with the money?...I would buy a hundred, a thousand, useful things for my family, for my friends. And when you buy a great deal, you deplete supplies and create a need for production. You create jobs for workers. It's logical, isn't it? As easy as pie...or as we Italians prefer to say "As easy as Columbus's egg," the great adventurer who didn't want gold for himself; *only* to benefit the citizens of Genoa...We politicians, we are honest, I can assure you. Everything we do is for the public good. The billions of..."contributions" our party leaders received from...various sources created thousands and thousands of jobs. He who has billions, what can he do with them? Does he keep them in the bank? No. He buys houses, cars, yachts, jewels for wives and daughters of the important elite: judges, lawyers, industrialists. He invites friends to the best restaurants. He buys chic, expensive lingerie for his sweethearts...Jobs, jobs, jobs...and let's not forget the practice of giving generous tips. I feel it's my duty.

I like to give a tip of thirty percent to waiters—more than double an ordinary person would give. All economists agree on the fact that "money that circulates creates wealth for everybody." It's the same with taxes—the well-known Reagan theory that many Italian executives have espoused with enthusiasm. Here it's called the C&B theory, our two great leaders, our financial geniuses. If the rich pay less taxes, the millions they don't pay to the government are invested and distributed directly by them, in purchases that benefit the workers. He who buys more cars, more buildings, more jewels, is obviously creating work for those who produce such articles. It's a theory that works especially well in the south. Don't get me wrong. No offense. I don't want to offend anyone. Some of my best friends are southerners. We politicians in Rome were forced, in a way, to give billions to "entrepreneurs" who were connected with criminal organizations. Well, those gangsters have billions in cash to put on the market. They are therefore very generous to everyone. They dress like dandies and spend generously on their wardrobes. An ordinary man like me spends less, much less. *(Shows his jacket; he exits.)*

GUIDO: In conclusion, in a society where bribery is the norm, there is a thriving economy. Rampant bribery is a sign of wealth for everyone. This is what my Senator convinced me of. Here's an example: Do you remember the boom in Italy a few years ago? It's all because of those bribes that some call...*corruption*. No. My honorable friend never uses this word. He defines it as...a necessary compromise. You want to build highways and create jobs for many workers? Pay bribes, and these bribes—we promise—will come back in circulation as new jobs. This is a necessary and advantageous compromise...Well, after the so-called scandal, we're in trouble...everything's been cleaned up, bribery is on the decline. And you can see the consequences. Depression! And, of course, we have a higher rate of unemployment. My honorable friend has received many subpoenas. A strange word, isn't it? What does it mean? Well, I think it means the authorities are looking for you...Well, well, they couldn't find him...You wanna know why? He was my guest here for a month! *(He indicates upstage behind the curtain.)* ...Now, from time to time, he has a nostalgia for this chapel where he was very happy—we took good care of him. He has this nostalgia of the unusual erotic experiences of the past...

(Spotlight on the chapel. The coffin has been covered with a rich, burnished velvet. A comfortable couch allows the SENATOR to recline like a Roman emperor. He's on the phone while a young woman manicures his nails.)

SENATOR: *(On the phone.)* Tell them to be patient. It's just a question of a few days...Of course they are entitled to a salary, whoever denied that?...It's only a question of time, coincidences, misunderstandings...We have the money, the money is definitely there...It's coming back, I assure you, from Switzerland, from America, from Hong Kong. I told you before...It's just a question of a few days, maybe just a few hours...You have my word of honor as an elected official..."Once a Senator always a Senator" as the Americans say...No, no, no...I don't like those jokes...it's bad taste. I'll call you...that's it. Nobody gets my phone number... *(He slams down the receiver; he's angry and nervous. To GUIDO and THE MANICURIST.)* You see? You are a bit late and they lose respect...Don't they read newspapers? There are problems and it's not easy to pay salaries on time…But you heard me, didn't you? We acknowledge our duty to pay…with interest, if necessary.

GUIDO: If you allow me, Senator… *(He indicates THE MANICURIST.)* …you shouldn't have mentioned…

SENATOR: Mentioned what?

GUIDO: Switzerland, America, Hong Kong…

SENATOR: Everyone knows that some money is stashed away for emergencies. All the political parties do it! *All of them!* It's an accepted, well-known fact…

MANICURIST: *(Naïvely.)* What parties?

SENATOR: All of them! All of them!

MANICURIST: You said before that you are *still*…an elected official, a senator—

SENATOR: I didn't say that, silly girl. It's an American expression. Once a priest always a priest. Once a senator always a senator.

MANICURIST: There's also an old Italian proverb. Once a thief or a liar, always… *(She hesitates, she knows she shouldn't have said that.)* Those things, those qualities…may be…positive in politics. They may be necessary—as you always said.

SENATOR: *(Bored.)* Watch it! You're hurting me! *(Withdraws his hand.)* You women, you don't understand politics…most people still call me "Your Honor the Senator." They remember how efficient I was and I was there for a long time.

GUIDO: According to you, Your Honor, is there hope that…?

SENATOR: Hope for what?

GUIDO: That things may be fixed. Will the good old days be back?

SENATOR: They will, they will. My boss is abroad, but his sidekick, Mr. B, is still here, very powerful. I'm sure he will succeed in bringing back Reagonomics, lower taxes for the rich— *(He catches himself.)* For those who know how to invest and create profits. Generous tips for waiters, drivers, butlers, nurses, and service sector workers. *(Indicates THE MANICURIST.)* Higher wages for blue-collar workers. More money for everyone.

GUIDO: According to them, the ruling parties have been definitely compromised and discredited—

SENATOR: *(Shrugs.)* For instance, they made fun of me because I am…on the plump side.

MANICURIST: Oh no, you are—

SENATOR: *(Ignoring her.)* The new foreign minister is fatter, much heavier than I am. No one mentions it, no one dares make fun of him. Do you see what hatred, personal hatred there is against me!

GUIDO: I would vote for you again, always, but…

SENATOR: *(Staring at him.)* But?

GUIDO: Now they say that your party is all washed up…

(THE SENATOR stares at him in silence.)

MANICURIST: Once a minister, always a minister. I'm sure of that…

SENATOR: Brava! In Italy it's always a question of rank and money. Agnelli is smart. He'll never lose his power. Berlusca is a genius. He has billions and four television stations—thanks to my boss—. He can become president, prime minister, a great leader. Andreotti was very clever. They even found his photo with a Mafia boss he denied he knew. He got away with it. He has been on top. Guiding Italy, for fifty years—

GUIDO: But now he's out.

SENATOR: I proved I was an excellent foreign minister. I had great success, and everyone respected Italy because of me.

GUIDO: Then maybe...

SENATOR: I know everybody and everybody respects me. I'm sure they are going to need me again.

GUIDO: *(Approving.)* Very well, as my priest always said, "Be an optimist if you want to go to heaven."

SENATOR: *(Ignoring him.)* There are many examples of important political figures who have been called back to serve their countries. Churchill, Teddy Roosevelt, Charles de Gaulle...Many many examples. Especially in Italy, the land of... "political musical chairs." Today it's mine, tomorrow may belong to you, the day after tomorrow, it's mine again. And look at America! They still respect and consult Kissinger. Even Nixon managed a comeback.

GUIDO: Kissinger is just a consultant. That's all.

SENATOR: They will definitely be needing me. My diplomatic skills, my experience. I've been very useful. I contributed in demolishing the Soviet Union. I have helped the Croats in their struggle to free themselves from Red Yugoslavia. I told the Americans—bluntly—that we are no longer a colony. They can't give us orders any longer! Do you know what they called our Italian leaders in New York? "Yes men,"—ever-obedient men, always saying "yes" to every command! On the contrary, things changed with my boss and me... *(Reflecting.)* Maybe that's why they trapped me with that tricky TV interview...Millions saw it.

GUIDO: I saw it, when I was in New York.

SENATOR: How did I look? Plump? Jovial? Intelligent?

GUIDO: Intelligent, yes, but...you shouldn't have mentioned your lovers on TV...maybe that was a mistake.

SENATOR: We all make mistakes now and then...*Errare humanum est*...But then I started a hundred useful missions all over the world. Now I am writing a revolutionary book...and they will be forced to call me back, to apologize, and to offer me a prestigious position. The way they did with Churchill and Nixon.

MANICURIST: *(Who has just finished her work.)* You're done.

SENATOR: *(Suspicious.)* What do you mean " done"?

MANICURIST: My work, your hands.

SENATOR: *(Examining his nails.)* Good, good...give the bill to Guido.

(THE MANICURIST hands the bill to GUIDO, who is ready to pay.)

SENATOR: And add twenty percent.

GUIDO: Twenty?

SENATOR: Thirty, you're right. It's better to stick to our generous traditions.

(GUIDO pays her.)

MANICURIST: *(Bowing.)* Thank you, Your Honor, thank you, Your Excellency the Minister.

SENATOR: *(Flattered, with a great dismissing gesture.)* Go, go my loyal friend!

(She exits.)

SENATOR: *(To GUIDO.)* A silly little girl who doesn't read the papers, obviously. But she's cute.

GUIDO: She doesn't read, fortunately.

SENATOR: *(Laughing.)* You are right. She wouldn't understand what she reads. What's the *Gazzettino* writing today?

GUIDO: They don't mention you today. I've the impression it's their way of protecting you, of trying to make people forget.

SENATOR: They'll never understand, never! Are you a card-carrying member of our party?

GUIDO: *(Uncertain.)* No...I had no time to...And then, you know, I was away, I spent those years in New York...

SENATOR: Oh yes, New York! What orgies! What women!

GUIDO: I remember them well. You were very generous in handing some of those women to me. Remember Nancy?

SENATOR: Nancy?

GUIDO: The little one, skinny, dark hair...

SENATOR: Oh yes, I remember! She was all bones. She almost died under me.

(They laugh.)

GUIDO: *(Cautiously.)* I read an interesting article...

SENATOR: Where?

GUIDO: In *Repubblica*.

SENATOR: *(With contempt.)* Ah! Those bastards!

GUIDO: *(Continuing.)* They say that it was the number one in Rome, the leader of the White Party.

SENATOR: Which one?

GUIDO: The big boss. The one who has been ruling forever.

SENATOR: What about him?

GUIDO: It seems that he's the one who unleashed Di Pietro, the honest judge, against you, the Pink Party. He was jealous of your power in the north and he went after you.

SENATOR: That's impossible! He's the one who invited us to join the government and explained the "rules," the "habits," as he called them! He's the one who taught us about bribes!

GUIDO: He was also jealous of your— *(He hesitates.)*

SENATOR: Of my "what"?

GUIDO: Joie de vivre...

SENATOR: *(Flattered.)* That's very possible! He goes to church every morning and there are no women in his life.

GUIDO: He was jealous of that too. Of your freedom and boldness. The title of the article is "Women, Parties, and Jealousies."

SENATOR: *(Reflecting.)* Who stopped him? He was free to screw anyone he wanted!

GUIDO: *(Amused.)* With that sad face of an ex-Jesuit! He can only talk to his little nuns!

(They both laugh.)

GUIDO: What's your opinion, Your Honor? Are the women to blame for all this?

SENATOR: *(Jokingly.)* They are too delicious. *(Consulting his watch.)* At what time is she coming?

GUIDO: *(Consulting his watch.)* With the next taxi boat. What do you think about the article?

SENATOR: I should read it first.

GUIDO: I'll get you a copy. Do you feel you should blame the women for your problems?

SENATOR: Oh no! All great men love women! Mussolini liked to screw, so did Jack Kennedy and his brother. Roosevelt, Eisenhower, Clinton, Bush father, they all had lovers. It's no longer a secret! If you have energy, if you're man enough to lead a nation, you're man enough to attract women and enjoy them.

GUIDO: Maybe you spent too much money? You were so generous. *(Timidly.)* Just out of curiosity, a friendly curiosity…you know I am your admirer, your humble servant…Who was paying the expenses in those hotels for all those parties?

SENATOR: When you are on an official mission, it's the government that pays everything. And we have to give parties to fraternize. It is the duty of every diplomat to give a good impression of his country! *(Getting excited, walking downstage and speaking to the audience.)* What I have done, I have done for my country and for my party!…Let's talk about this honestly. Man to man. If you belong to a club, a church, a community, a party, they all ask for a contribution. Don't they? Often. And we have a tendency to help. We are social animals. A community of brothers. We all need friends, comrades who would do anything for you. If your country calls, you are prepared to go and die for her. If the party calls, it's the same. Ready to die, if necessary… *(Looking around.)* Not in this case, not in this place. *(With his index and pinky extended, he makes the sign of the "evil eye.")* You must always be ready to collaborate…The party is like your family. It's sacred. You always sacrifice for your family. You must make sacrifices for the party. Out of love for your family, you're even ready to steal— *(He corrects himself.)* I shouldn't have used that verb. No one has stolen anything here.

GUIDO: Scrawled on the walls in Milano, I used to see the name of your…boss—the Tunisian one, and by his name, the word "Thief."

SENATOR: Only a perception, a prejudice fed by a partisan media. *(Explaining, as a good teacher would.)* I'll tell you how it went. Rome called us and told us. "We love our White Party; you love your party, the Pinks. All right. A noble and loyal attitude. Every party needs many clerks, many expenses. We have a good track record. Things have been running smoothly these last forty years. We do it out of love for our party, same as you do. You too, love your party, we are sure of it. And of course, you have many expenses, and we assure you our method is honest and fundamentally moral. It has a moral purpose. *(Continuing to explain with patience and clarity.)* The entrepreneurs—they are the ones who suggested it initially—are very happy to give back a certain amount the government gives them to build, structure, design new projects. It's a kickback that goes to the parties, only to the parties…" My boss and I looked at each other, surprised. We thought, if we denounce this method—and we don't have any evidence—we could never be part of their government. They are very religious, good Christians, and they claim that the method is fundamentally moral—that it was the entrepreneurs who suggested it. What's wrong with all that? The money goes to the party. The party is as sacred as a family and needs money like any family. Therefore, we have to go along and accept it. Honestly, I don't see evil in this, absolutely no evil… *(To the audience.)* I swear, we have accepted those kickbacks for the party, and only for the party.

(We hear steps on the cemetery gravel.)

GUIDO: Here she is. She's arriving.

SENATOR: *(Going back into the chapel.)* Let her come in. Close the gate. Thank you, Guido. And remember, I always keep my promises. You will have everything I promised you!

(ROSETTA comes in. She's the same actress as THE MANICURIST with a different wig.)

ROSETTA: *(To GUIDO.)* Ciao!

GUIDO: Ciao!

ROSETTA: *(To THE SENATOR.)* Where do you want to do it today?

SENATOR: Inside.

ROSETTA: Good. I don't like doing it outdoors.

(She enters the chapel. GUIDO closes the gate.)

GUIDO: *(To the audience.)* At times they make love on top of a seductive grave nearby, under the stars. Tonight on a beautiful marble slab that represents Venice, the romantic, irresistible, divine Venice.

―

(GUIDO is playing his [saxophone] for us. We see the same chapel behind him. It's now a small apartment used as an office. The coffin is still there, covered. DORA, GUIDO's wife, is on the phone.)

GUIDO: *(After he has finished playing, to the audience.)* Things are going well...better and better...His Honor has been acquitted and he has been promised a new important position...Our good friend Berlusca is getting more and more powerful. His speeches have a Mussolinian vigor—he's almost as good as my boss. He controls most of Italy. My wife and I—

(He indicates DORA, who is still talking on the phone.)

GUIDO: —Have decided to live here for free...for many reasons...the first one is romantic. She loves me deeply, she is jealous, she wants to stay always with me. Around the clock. We are compatible partners in everything. It works very well. Especially if you organize a small little house *(Indicates the chapel.)* as an office... *(Shrugs.)* Besides it's free. We work very well together... *(He smiles at his wife with love and blows a kiss in her direction.)* Our rent in town was very high. Just look at how much we are saving. We will be able to buy a nice apartment in Venice soon. Perhaps to live there. Perhaps to rent it out to tourists who love Venice, who love the idea of renting a small romantic hideaway for a couple of months...

(He indicates again his wife who is making another phone call.)

GUIDO: Look at my dear wife, how busy she is...all day long. A busy wife is a blessing. Well, thanks to His Honor, we have discovered...kinky sex—that's how they call it in America—it can make you a lot of money. Human beings are looking for new experiences, new sensations, they want what's original, new, stimulating...I'm sure you remember that His Honor had taken refuge here for alleged financial crimes, and then he was acquitted for lack of evidence. Well, even though things are back to normal in his life, His Honor keeps bringing his girlfriends here. First it was inside the chapel, then on the delicate marble slab "Mosaic Map of Venice," then in some more romantic nooks. One day, I discovered a couple making love in the very ornate rich chapel of the noble family Di—The name is not important. I reproached them, and I made them pay a fine. They paid with pleasure, in Swiss francs...They are the ones who first gave me the idea...In the world today, everyone is in a desperate search for something different, the profane laced with the sacred, or both of them together. Just a month ago, they caught a German couple making love behind the sarcophagus of Santa Lucia in the center of the city, near the railroad station...

(Two GHOSTS wearing white sheets cross the stage and wave at DORA. GUIDO does not see them. His wife sees them but ignores them, as if they were part of the landscape; the two GHOSTS are the actors playing ALFIO and ELENA, with different shoes.)

GUIDO: That was a dangerous adventure, but too obvious a place. The police arrested them...The idea was growing more and more in me. I thought...what about renting out special corners of San Michele's, this beautiful quiet cemetery, for...kinky lovers. Right? They do all kinds of crazy things in New York; they make love in the weirdest places. I've learned from them, and now I have a great *network*—American style. We have photos of all the most romantic corners, different prices, for sacrilegious, exciting dates—as some people like to call them. People love the forbidden. Our public relations manager is a native of Chicago. He's excellent...Among our guests, our visitors, our clients, there are some friends of His Honor. He himself often returns to relive the emotions of his exciting exile...We also have a special number of the chosen ones—very refined roués. And prices change according to nationality. My wife suggested that and follows these details meticulously. Germans and Japanese get charged more because they are the ones who received more American money when everybody feared the Red danger. They were good allies and helped us against the Reds. Next come the Jews, who—maybe for psychological reasons, gravitate toward Ezra Pound's grave. The French prefer Stravinsky's flowerbed. The Russians—we only had two couples until now—like the serenity of Diaghilev's grave...We didn't charge the first couple, and we charged the second very little. Poor people, they are now ruined by the "new" economy. I feel sorry for them. The Russians these days are tragically lost—gangsters and prostitutes everywhere. It's a bloody mess.

(The two GHOSTS approach GUIDO.)

GUIDO: I almost forgot...we hired some assistants in white sheets...Authentic, nice Venetian ghosts who work as guards, lookouts during the...romantic encounters. They chase away voyeurs and unwanted visitors *(To the GHOSTS.)* What do you need?

(They gesture with fingers indicating money.)

GUIDO: Oh, it's payday. OK. I have to pay them now.

(The GHOSTS exit with GUIDO. We now hear the voce of DORA, who is still on the phone.)

DORA: All right...I repeat...Your place is the one you see in photo number seven...Your time is Tuesday from six to seven p.m....Don't worry, the next appointment for the next couple is only at eight p.m. Come to the usual place, here, at the central office...I know, I know, it's a maze in here among all these graves...we will meet your gondola at the entrance, avoiding confusion. So we don't waste time...Don't worry, we'll take care of that...I have the map of the cemetery, and I'll give you a copy for next time...See you later.

(She puts down the receiver. Then she writes a few words in a large book. THE SENATOR enters.)

SENATOR: Hi, Dora. Is Guido in?

DORA: *(Slightly surprised.)* Welcome, Your Honor...Guido just left with the guards.

SENATOR: *(Ironical.)* The ghosts?

DORA: They look nice, don't they? It was my idea.

SENATOR: Brava, you're great. When will Guido be back?

DORA: In a little while, I guess. But don't worry. Your preferred slab is reserved... *(Checks in her book.)* for five p.m. It's yours for one hour. Or more, if you like...

SENATOR: No, no. One hour is more than enough when you are under the stars. Has Rosetta arrived?

DORA: Not yet. But she's always punctual...Please sit down.

(She invites him to sit down. His Honor chooses the best chair. He sits down. A silence.)

DORA: Forgive me for my curiosity... but...

SENATOR: Tell me.

DORA: May I ask you something?

SENATOR: The answer is well known. I've been acquitted for lack of evidence. Charges have been dropped. I'm completely exonerated. I'm still interested in politics. There is hope that they'll give me back my job, one of these days.

DORA: No, no. I'm not interested in politics...As a woman, I'm curious to know...

SENATOR: Tell me, tell me, ask me whatever you want to know.

DORA: You said before..."One hour is more than enough when you are under the stars..." How come women are never satisfied when they make love outdoors?

SENATOR: *(Alarmed.)* Who told you? Rosetta?

DORA: Oh no!

SENATOR: Was she talking about me? What did she say?

DORA: No, no. Don't worry. Rosetta is totally loyal. She's not a gossip. She didn't say a word about you.

SENATOR: Nothing? Not even a compliment?

DORA: She smiles. Always smiles. That's a positive sign. It means she's satisfied. I'm sure you satisfy her.

SENATOR: But then, how come you asked that question, mentioning the fact that women aren't satisfied?

DORA: Firsthand personal experience...

(A silence.)

SENATOR: *(Staring at her.)* Guido doesn't...?

DORA: We tried twice on your marble slab, the Venetian mosaic. A disaster...

SENATOR: *(Curious.)* In what sense?

DORA: Just three minutes. And then he runs away. As if the devil were running after him.

SENATOR: That happens. To me too, the first time. Think for a moment. In the open air, when there is still daylight...helicopters and planes flying over the island now and then...with the fear that tourists may see you—

DORA: That's why we hired the ghosts.

SENATOR: *(Continuing.)* It's human for the man...to be quick. According to some biological studies, the instinct of man would be to...procreate in three minutes—

DORA: How selfish!

SENATOR: Guido, does he... *(He's searching for the right words.)* does he give you enough? Does he wait? Does he...postpone?

DORA: At home, everything was perfect. Here in the chapel, it's so so...In the open air, it's disaster.

SENATOR: It's understandable. But give it time. We all improve. Now, I can stay on that romantic slab for forty minutes. From three minutes to forty is a great improvement, isn't it?

DORA: I'm telling you the truth, I don't understand this "konky sex..."

SENATOR: *(Correcting her.)* Kinky sex.

DORA: That type of sex. My best... *(She hesitates.)*

SENATOR: Orgasms.

DORA: I always blush when I hear that word...my best... *(She hesitates; looks for a good word.)*

SENATOR: Copulations.

DORA: That's the word you intellectuals use.

SENATOR: Call it what you want. Your best ones have been...where?

DORA: At home, in our bed. And sometimes in some little hotel...

SENATOR: *(Ironical.)* A forbidden place, a sinful nest. Sin excites everyone. Forbidden things attract everybody. Young people today, from Paris to Moscow, are searching the forbidden: drugs, sexual deviance, new emotions, new experience, fast money at any cost!

DORA: Even in Moscow? Have you been there lately?

SENATOR: It's even worse there. They think capitalism means "kill the old lady today, inherit her apartment, start a new business, and become a millionaire tomorrow." They are too much in a hurry.

DORA: When I was young, I didn't think like that.

SENATOR: They are all rebels today. They love what's forbidden. They are excited and exalted by that.

DORA: *(Studying him.)* Only the young ones?

SENATOR: *(Feeling observed.)* Well, I may have been born fifty years ago, but I still feel young. *(Consults his watch.)* Where's Rosetta?

DORA: She'll be here, don't worry. Your other girl, Gloria, always used to arrive ten minutes ahead of time. This one, the new one, just a few minutes later. Women...

SENATOR: Women...What would we do without you?

DORA: *(Smiling.)* You would be lost.

(A silence. DORA studies him, hesitates. She would like to ask something else.)

DORA: Forgive me if...

SENATOR: Ask, ask anything...

DORA: You...you have a tendency to...

SENATOR: To what?

DORA: ...Variety. You like different women...

SENATOR: All men— *(Correcting himself.)* all except Guido, who is the perfect husband—

DORA: *(Ironical.)* A perfect husband!

SENATOR: I know him well—

DORA: Me too. Don't defend him. He told me about your..."orgies" in New York.

SENATOR: No orgies. He was playing for us. His music could charm snakes. We, some of us that is, those who have a romantic soul and love music, well, some of us got excited, and—

DORA: Spare me the details. Why do you prefer the many...silly whores to one woman, your own woman who loves you and is faithful?

SENATOR: They are not whores. They are loyal, loving, and faithful too.

DORA: How do you know if they are faithful?

SENATOR: *(Uneasy.)* Faithful to me, I know.

DORA: *(Ironical.)* You're very sure of yourself.

SENATOR: As long as we keep them with us, as long as we give them our love and attention.

DORA: And then, one fine day, changing of the guard, changing of the sheets. Why?

SENATOR: My dear lady, what are you making me say? We're always looking for perfection, for a perfect companion...Your husband has been lucky. He found a magnificent woman in you...

DORA: *(Flattered.)* Compliments, compliments... *(Flirting.)* Are you flirting with me?

SENATOR: *(Alarmed.)* Oh no! Oh no! One doesn't lust after the wife of a friend, a loyal friend.

DORA: What do you mean when you say "perfect woman"?

SENATOR: It's difficult to define...

DORA: Try.

SENATOR: *(Reflecting, searching.)* All right. She should be...intelligent, sensitive, sensual...

DORA: All your women seem to be intelligent and sensual.

SENATOR: That's true. I know how to choose well, carefully...

DORA: What's missing then?

SENATOR: Sometimes something is missing...sometimes, it's too much.

DORA: What do you mean? Tell me more.

SENATOR: What's missing is sometimes patience, tolerance, acceptance...

DORA: Acceptance of what?

SENATOR: ...Of the needs of my personality.

DORA: You mean?

SENATOR: We are all different, aren't we? I want...this. Maybe she doesn't...And vice versa.

DORA: And sometimes it's too much, you said. What's too much?

SENATOR: *(Vague.)* ...They want too much...they are impatient, intolerant, and capricious—

(ROSETTA enters. She smiles openly. GUIDO follows her in silence.)

ROSETTA: *(Who has heard the last words.)* Who is intolerant and capricious?

SENATOR: *(To ROSETTA and GUIDO.)* Hi!

GUIDO: Hi!

SENATOR: *(To ROSETTA.)* Dora was asking me about wives. I was telling her I prefer you because you are sweet and...sensitive.

ROSETTA: Sensitive to what?

SENATOR: To everything. A man needs joy and serenity. Who can survive with an impatient, capricious woman? Certainly not me! Let's go.

ROSETTA: *(To DORA.)* The blanket, please. That damned mosaic hurts my ass. It's sheer torture!

DORA: Here.

(DORA hands a heavy blanket to her. ROSETTA gives it to THE SENATOR, who smiles. The happy couple exits.)

GUIDO: *(Admiring them.)* What a lovely couple!

DORA: Your... "loyal" friend paid me a lot of compliments.

GUIDO: He always says good things about you. He admires you.

DORA: These were different. Does he always say I'm hot and "sensual"? How does he know? What did you tell him? Our intimate life?

GUIDO: Oh no. Gentlemen never discuss wives... *(Thinking it over.)* It's strange that before he mentioned something about—

DORA: He wasn't talking about his wife. He was talking about Rosetta, I think. *(Insisting.)* How does he know that I am... "sensual"?

GUIDO: It's obvious. Every real man picks up on it. *(He looks at her with love and admiration.)*

DORA: He also added "intelligent and hot"... how does he know?

GUIDO: With all the work you are doing? Who could ever think of an organization like this? Who would know better than you how to suggest kinky situations?

DORA: Do you trust him?

GUIDO: Sure!

DORA: *(Defiant.)* He let me know that he likes me and...

GUIDO: And...?

DORA: He would like to... you know what I mean.

GUIDO: *(Unbelieving, smiling.)* Come on!

DORA: *(Offended.)* What do you mean? That sounds like an insult! Is that so impossible? Well, I am telling you that it is possible, very possible.

GUIDO: *(Patient and paternal.)* My love, my sweet love. Of course it would be possible. I see how men look at you when we are walking in St. Mark's Square. Nine out of ten dream about you and would like to take you to bed.

DORA: *(Flattered, amused.)* Only nine?

GUIDO: Let's say, ninety-nine out of one hundred but him... not him.

DORA: How can you be so sure?

GUIDO: I'm absolutely sure. It's wiser not to go into details. Trust me.

DORA: *(Determined.)* Tell me.

GUIDO: It's in the past. It's history. It's buried now.

DORA: What is it? Unbury it. This is the ideal place for grave diggers. Unbury the past.

GUIDO: You'll get angry.

DORA: I promise I will not get angry.

GUIDO: Swear.

DORA: I swear.

GUIDO: *(Uncertain, hesitating.)* I remember I told you... Once I was in New York with him—

DORA: Twice, two orgies.

GUIDO: Well... the first time... we were close... in the same room.

DORA: *(Surprised.)* In the same bedroom?

GUIDO: Yes. In the same bed.

DORA: Pigs!

GUIDO: He was with... *(Vague gesture.)* And I was with... another one.

DORA: Two women. That news is at least comforting. And the two whores were close to each other. Were they caressing their tits?

GUIDO: No, no. They didn't touch each other, but...a couple could see what the other couple was doing...

DORA: Like in a real brothel! What's your point?

GUIDO: His Honor saw that I am much better, more endowed than he is. He wouldn't dare to take you to bed. Men hate, fear comparisons.

DORA: *(Struck by this unusual detail.)* That's good news after all... *(Looking at him.)* So I am a lucky girl, am I not?

GUIDO: Yes you are.

(A GHOST motions to GUIDO who exits; the GHOST is now ROSETTA. ALFIO and ELENA enter. They are elegant but depressed. They appear to be tired and discouraged. They approach DORA with curiosity. Who is she? What is she doing there? They observe her with curiosity.)

DORA: Do you have an appointment?

ALFIO: No...

DORA: Well, let's see...let me check... *(Checks in her appointment book.)* Yes... it is possible...I have a nice sexy nest... Just around the corner...Is it the first time for you?

ALFIO: No...

ELENA: No...

DORA: I didn't mean—first time together...I meant first time in our very special paradise, here?

ALFIO: No.

ELENA: No.

DORA: *(Studying them; she has never met them.)* I don't remember...Names? Just first names...

ALFIO: Alfio.

ELENA: Elena.

DORA: *(Looks in her book and does not find their names.)* I don't find you here among our habitual clients—no, I stand corrected—I meant "Guests." You are all welcome guests...You don't mind if I ask a few questions...I'm writing a book about the depth of new sexual experiences...I will not use your names. Just your story, the reasons why...How long have you been married?

(ELENA looks at ALFIO with reproach; they are not married yet.)

DORA: It's all right, it's all right. How long have you been together?

ELENA: Three years. Three long years.

DORA: "Long"...That gives me some hints, already...Is sexual desire fading away?

ALFIO: No... *(Emphatically.)* No.

(ELENA looks at him with a faint smile.)

DORA: It's usual the woman—you... *(Checks the name.)* Elena—who answers that question... *(To ELENA, directly.)* Is it...less?

(ELENA does not answer.)

DORA: I'm sure *(Checks the name.)* your beloved Alfio will allow you, give you the freedom to answer... *(Looks at ALFIO.)*

ALFIO: Naturally. Tell her, Elena. Am I...different?

ELENA: *(Ignoring him.)* It happens to every couple, they say.

ALFIO: Happens what?

DORA: What?

ELENA: Less. Even if they are *not* married.

ALFIO: You have headaches, sometimes. And you...turn me off.

DORA: "Even if they are *not* married." A good, interesting point. After years of marriage people usually feel less—

ELENA: *(Interrupting her.)* Don't tell him. I don't really believe that story of feeling "less"! I would give more. I'd be more grateful, more passionate.

ALFIO: "Grateful"? You never mentioned that.

ELENA: You should have known.

DORA: "Grateful." That's a deep concept. No one, before, ever—

ELENA: *(Aggressive, to DORA.)* What are you trying to say? That I'm lying? That it is not true? I would be! I would be *better!* A perfect, loyal wife!

DORA: "Loyal," it's true. A married woman feels more secure, more grateful. They betray less.

ELENA: Never! I'd never betray him if...if he finally decided to marry me. *(To DORA.)* Thank you!

DORA: I believe you, I believe you...So, sex is not the problem...

ALFIO: It is not.

DORA: Have you ever tried it in different places?

ELENA: What do you mean?

DORA: A movie house, a church, a library?

ALFIO: None of your business!

DORA: *(Hurt.)* Well, well...I'm trying my best, I'm giving you a lovely corner, an exciting nest, and you—

(GUIDO enters. He is very surprised and very cordial.)

GUIDO: Elena! Alfio!

(Hugs them; DORA is surprised.)

DORA: Oh. You know them.

GUIDO: Of course! Didn't I tell you? My good friends, the ones who...gave us the chance to start this...

DORA: *(Timidly.)* Thank you...

(She is puzzled; she has not understood yet; GUIDO ignores her.)

GUIDO: *(To ELENA and ALFIO, very cordial.)* This is wonderful! How are you? Mommy and Daddy are very well, I mean...they rest in peace. I mean...Daddy we put downstairs, but we visit him every day, we visit both of them...We bring flowers, the same type of flowers to both of them...Do you want to visit them?

ALFIO: No.

GUIDO: *(Uneasy.)* This is my wife Dora.

DORA: Glad to meet you. You should have told me that—

ELENA: *(Cutting.)* Yes. We should have.

GUIDO: Do you want us to leave for a little while?

ELENA: No.

GUIDO: *(To ALFIO.)* Maybe you are feeling nostalgic...we can leave and you can... *(Invitation to make love.)*

ALFIO: No.

GUIDO: For old times' sake...Go ahead. Now there is everything you need...

(DORA shows some pillows. ALFIO and ELENA are not interested.)

GUIDO: Or would you prefer a more romantic corner far away from your parents? Dora can show you, take you there.

DORA: I told them—

ELENA: No.

ALFIO: No.

GUIDO: I see you're depressed. What's wrong? What happened?... *(To ELENA, indicating ALFIO.)* Doesn't he feel well?

ELENA: We have lost everything.

GUIDO and DORA: *(Together, alarmed.)* Everything?

GUIDO: How is that possible?

ELENA: Too many trips, bad luck in gambling...

ALFIO: ...And those one hundred lawyers who worked for my father. Jackals. They ate up everything.

GUIDO and DORA: *(Together.)* And now?

ALFIO: It's obvious, isn't it? We're moving back to...our first home, with Mother and Dad.

GUIDO: *(Alarmed, worried.)* ...But you promised! *(He indicates the chapel.)*

ALFIO: Do you know what the lawyers told us?

ELENA: Those swindlers!

ALFIO: *(Continuing.)* They told us that the chapel is still ours because we didn't sign any papers. *(To GUIDO and DORA.)* Do you have anything in black and white from us?

GUIDO: *(Timidly.)* No, but...

ALFIO: Where is the contract? *Scripta manent, verba volant.* As my priest used to say.

(GUIDO and DORA stare at him.)

ALFIO: I shouldn't say my priest. He was just a guy who taught Latin. That was when my father wanted *me* to become a priest. I'm sorry but...

(DORA has a sudden idea. She puts the ghost sheet on ELENA's arm. She signals GUIDO to do the same with ALFIO.)

GUIDO: *(Who has understood immediately, putting the sheet on ALFIO's arm.)* Don't be depressed. I have a wonderful job for you. Dora, show him the books.

(DORA shows them, diligently.)

DORA: *(Indicating with a finger.)* And this is what we took in during the last two weeks.

GUIDO: It's a gold mine, I assure you. We'll go fifty-fifty, as they say in New York.

ELENA: *(Pleasantly surprised.)* Half of...this? *(Indicates a figure in the book.)* Every week?

DORA: Every week.

ELENA: *(To ALFIO.)* Our chance to get married, finally!

ALFIO: *(With a smile.)* Promise! Cross my heart!

(They hug.)

GUIDO: Business is increasing by five percent a month, at least.

(ELENA and ALFIO smile. They see that this is a wonderful solution.)

ALFIO: Black on white?

GUIDO: *My promise* as a friendly...musician! *(Shakes hands with ALFIO.)*

DORA: *(Shaking hands with ELENA.)* My promise as a...a loyal wife!

(They smile. Blackout on the two couples shaking hands. Freeze.)

(CURTAIN. THE END.)

The Academy

The Characters:

THE PROFESSOR
CORSO*
THE SIGNORA
DONATO*
AFRO*
ELIO*
BENITO*
FORTUNATO

Time:

The present

Place:

Venice

---

*During Benito Mussolini's Fascist regime (1922–45), it was common practice to give children born during that period names that glorified Mussolini and his dreams of conquest: thus, Afro (Africa); Benito; Corso (Corsica); Donato (Gift of Providence); and Elio (Place in the Sun).

Italian pop music before curtain. The last song could be "Come Prima, Più di prima t'amerò…" Scene: A large, striking poster with the words: "The Academy." A dusty classroom; stage left, a dais with two chairs, a blackboard, a map of the United States, the Italian and the American flags; stage right, some school benches. AFRO and FORTUNATO enter from left; they are two modestly dressed, virile young men; short hair, sweaters; the relaxed, easygoing attitudes of the Americans one sees in the movies.

AFRO: *(With a gesture, pointing to the room.)* This is the classroom. You'll be glad you came. I've already begun to work. Because I'm just a beginner, not too experienced. You know English better than I do, so he'll let you take care of more important clients. *(Pointing to the two chairs on the dais.)* "She" sits here. Still young, an attractive woman. Everything's up to his wife, remember. So give it your best, a little finesse, you understand. If she flunks you, you're finished here. You can't try again.

(BENITO enters, a young man very much like the other two.)

AFRO: Ask him. He brought his brother. He flunked.

BENITO: *(Languidly.)* Ciao. A new one?

(He shakes FORTUNATO's hand.)

FORTUNATO: Yes, new.

AFRO: *(To BENITO, insistently.)* Tell him about your brother.

BENITO: *(Reluctantly.)* Who knows what was going on in her head? My brother is just like me. Better, perhaps. Sometimes—who knows?—it's a question of incompatibility.

(CORSO and DONATO enter; two more students. CORSO is very tall and robust.)

CORSO: Hi.

DONATO: Hi.

(CORSO and DONATO sit down on the benches and begin talking in the background.)

AFRO: Give her a big smile as soon as she comes in. Everything hinges on the first impression. He doesn't count at all. An ex-Fascist, they say. A sucker for American culture, now.—"If you can't beat them, join them."—Americans are the greatest, the best, tops in everything. They'll save us from the Reds, et cetera. A regular asslicker, a beaten dog who likes to butter up his master. Unemployed, just like us. He's satisfied with his ten percent. He did a good job of organizing here, and that's good for us. I'll loan you the fifty dollars for the registration fee.

(AFRO hands him the money: THE SIGNORA enters; she has a sad air.)

CORSO and DONATO: *(Who, being the first to notice her enter, get on their feet respectfully.)* Buon giorno, Signora.

SIGNORA: Buon giorno.

AFRO: *(Apologizing for not having noticed her immediately.)* I didn't see you come in, Signora. Buon giorno. May I introduce a new applicant, Fortunato.

FORTUNATO: *(Trying to hide the money he's holding and stretching out his hand embarrassedly.)* Enchanted.

SIGNORA: *(With detachment.)* Pleased to meet you.

(FORTUNATO stares at her admiringly.)

SIGNORA: Where is Elio? There's mail for him. *(Holds up a letter.)*

CORSO: He hasn't come yet. I'll give it to him.

(He takes the letter from her.)

SIGNORA: *(To FORTUNATO, making a gesture for him to follow her.)* Come.

(They go out together, to stage right.)

CORSO: *(Looking at the envelope against the light.)* There's fifty dollars in this. A fortune! Not a week goes by…

AFRO: *(Looking enviously at the door through which his friend and THE SIGNORA have gone.)* There's the fortunate one. He was christened Fortunato, and right now he's proving it. This audition is his most beautiful moment here…

(ELIO enters, the same age as the others, but more elegant.)

ELIO: *(Catching the last sentence on the fly and motioning with his head toward the door at stage right.)* A new one?

AFRO: A new one.

ELIO: *(Ironically.)* Still in love with our Signora?

AFRO: Frustrated, perhaps. Only once, it whets the appetite. A woman sticks right here… *(Pointing to his throat.)* if you don't have her completely.

CORSO: Mail.

ELIO: *(Takes letter.)* Oh, my granny!

DONATO: The usual fifty bucks.

ELIO: *(Kissing letter.)* Mia divina! If her venerable age allowed her to come back to Italy, I would treat her better. *(Ironically.)* Tell me, Afro, how would you treat our Signora if she gave you another session?

AFRO: With kid gloves. So would you if given the chance. None of us have really had her.

ELIO: Could be... *(Reads letter that came with the fifty dollars.)* She's dreaming about me, desires me...hopes to come back...Let's hope to God she won't be able to move...Her pains are soothed...She's hungry for tenderness... "Hunger," they say. It's really incredible, the stamina of these American grandmas...

(THE PROFESSOR enters from stage left; he is about fifty-five, lean, severe. They all rise to their feet. ELIO hides the letter with the money.)

ALL: Buon giorno, Professor.

PROFESSOR: *(Formally.)* Please sit down.

(A moment of silence.)

PROFESSOR: *(To ELIO, taking him by surprise with his unexpected question.)* How much did she send you?

ELIO: *(Surprised.)* Fifty...fifty dollars.

PROFESSOR: Turn over the percentage.

(ELIO reluctantly goes to the dais and hands over the money.)

ELIO: *(As he goes back to the seat, nastily; getting revenge for having to pay.)* There's a new applicant in the next room, with your wife.

PROFESSOR: *(Unconcerned, not giving it any importance.)* Let's review a few things from the preceding lesson. Donato, you. What is the capital of Maryland? *(He points with pointer to the state on the map which does not have the names of the cities.)*

DONATO: Annapolis.

PROFESSOR: Of Alabama?

DONATO: Montgomery.

PROFESSOR: Of Kentucky?

DONATO: Frankfort.

PROFESSOR: You, Benito. Which are the thirteen states that first joined the republic?

BENITO: *(Slowly, counting on his fingers.)* Connecticut, Delaware, Georgia, Maryland, Massachusetts, New Hampshire, New Jersey, New York...Pennsylvania... South Carolina, North Carolina...Virginia... *(He can't think of the last one.)*

PROFESSOR: You're one short.

ELIO: Rhode Island.

PROFESSOR: Right. *(To ELIO.)* When was Washington born?

ELIO: February 22, 1732.

PROFESSOR: Lincoln?

CORSO: February 12, 1809.

PROFESSOR: *(To ELIO.)* How many calories does a glass of carrot juice contain?

CORSO: Fifty.

PROFESSOR: A hamburger?

CORSO: Two hundred.

PROFESSOR: A yogurt?

CORSO: One hundred and sixty-five.

PROFESSOR: *(To AFRO.)* An example of high-calorie food?

AFRO: Caviar, anchovies, spaghetti...

PROFESSOR: Low calorie?

AFRO: Celery, jello...

PROFESSOR: *(To ELIO.)* How many calories should a tall, rawboned American woman ingest per day?

ELIO: Minimum, 1,845. Maximum, 2,580.

PROFESSOR: *(Turns to CORSO.)* Vitamin A is good for...

CORSO: Eyesight and glandular functions.

PROFESSOR: *(To DONATO.)* Vitamin C?

DONATO: Bones, teeth, gums, skin.

PROFESSOR: Good, you have not wasted your time or your money. Thanks to our Academy, you are always ready to perform with éclat for our guests from across the sea. For the glory of our nation. Now...

(The SIGNORA enters, followed by FORTUNATO: all eyes are on the woman, who hands a test paper to the PROFESSOR. FORTUNATO sits down next to AFRO, who questions him in a whisper. FORTUNATO continues to look at the SIGNORA, who sits down on the dais; he answers AFRO's questions by nodding his head in a distracted manner.)

PROFESSOR: *(After a short consultation with THE SIGNORA.)* My wife's report: favorable. You passed. *(To FORTUNATO.)* Can you speak English?

FORTUNATO: Yes.

PROFESSOR: This is a bad start. When I say "Can you" you must answer "I can." If I say "Do you" you must answer "I do."

FORTUNATO: I'm sorry. You are right.

PROFESSOR: Now translate: "Le piace l'Italia?"

FORTUNATO: Do you like Italy?

PROFESSOR: Passeggiare.

FORTUNATO: To walk.

PROFESSOR: Amare.

FORTUNATO: To love.

PROFESSOR: Dormire.

FORTUNATO: To sleep.

PROFESSOR: Labbra.

FORTUNATO: Lips.

PROFESSOR: Carezza.

FORTUNATO: Caress.

PROFESSOR: Capezzolo.

FORTUNATO: Nipple.

PROFESSOR: Pelle liscia.

FORTUNATO: Baby skin.

PROFESSOR: Sangue ardente.

FORTUNATO: Hot blood.

PROFESSOR: Luna di miele.

FORTUNATO: Honeymoon.

PROFESSOR: Tenerezza.

FORTUNATO: Tenderness.

PROFESSOR: Desiderio.

FORTUNATO: Desire.

PROFESSOR: Sogno.

FORTUNATO: Dream.

(A pause. The PROFESSOR looks for other questions, reads the name on the test paper.)

PROFESSOR: Translate: "Mi chiamo Fortunato. Lo sono veramente, oggi. Ho incontrato lei."

FORTUNATO: *(Very sure of himself, with a good accent.)* My name is Fortunato. I am really fortunate today. I met you.

PROFESSOR: *(Pleased.)* Good. Did you freelance?

FORTUNATO: Yes, whenever I hit on one of them.

PROFESSOR: Do you receive money?

FORTUNATO: No.

PROFESSOR: You see, what you lacked is organization. The seed was there, your good will; it did not, however, bear fruit. *(He points to ELIO.)* Today he received fifty dollars. All of them receive dollars, every now and then. One of them... *(Making a vague gesture.)* one whom none of you remembers... once received a pair of ruby cuff links, as a present. He resold them for two thousand five hundred dollars. A fortune.

AFRO: *(Whispering to FORTUNATO.)* It's not true. He read it in a novel by Tennessee Williams.

PROFESSOR: *(Taking note of the whispering.)* What's that he's telling you? Don't listen to him. He reads too much. And his imagination runs away with him. All right, Fortunato.

(THE PROFESSOR looks at THE SIGNORA, who nods in agreement.)

PROFESSOR: You're accepted. Let's have the registration fee: fifty. *(To THE SIGNORA.)* Collect the homework.

(As FORTUNATO takes the money to the dais and signs a paper, THE SIGNORA, with the students staring at her morbidly, collects the homework. After signing, FORTUNATO receives a list which he takes back to the bench and reads.)

(THE PROFESSOR waits for silence.)

PROFESSOR: *(In a professorial tone, savoring his words.)* You see, my dear Fortunato—you are indeed fortunate to be with us—I use the word "organization" not by chance. *(Scanning his words.)* This is in fact a first-class organization, just ask. *(A vague gesture to the other students.)* Our Academy was conceived with love, vision, imagination. To attain—even though we suffered and lost the war—a lofty aim. We will fortify—thanks to our pure Latin blood—the other races. *(He takes a deep breath.)* Today, which is the race to whom the destiny of the world is entrusted? The American race. They are the receptacle of all culture, the refined masters of every art, the original worshipers of *real* democracy. No civilization can be compared to *their* civilization. No society has ever reached such a standard of affluence. They're the most perfect embodiment of real accomplishment, the quintessence of progress, the synthesis of the best achievements. Their culture is on the highest level in every field. *They'll* save Europe from the Reds. We must therefore strengthen their race, improve it; we must contribute somehow to the noble task of defending civilization. *(Speaking in a less rhetorical tone.)* Therefore I am here in a school founded with inspired insight to give you an American culture, to put you in the position to exploit to the full your—our—best qualities. In fact the Academy develops the intensive and rational application of our masculine, virile patrimony. The Germans possess a splendid steel industry; the Americans have a first-class missile industry; we...we have created a new industry: the American woman, the American tourist... *(Going into details, in a less heroic tone.)* On the sheet I have just handed to you are listed our branches in other cities, the stores that give us discounts: florists, photographers, bookstores, et cetera. Memorize it. Now let's get to the essentials. Where do you live?

FORTUNATO: Via Garibaldi.

PROFESSOR: A working-class neighborhood, not suitable. You must move around here, to this section. *(To ELIO.)* Is the room near the square available?

ELIO: Yes.

PROFESSOR: You'll introduce him to Madame Lucia later. *(To FORTUNATO.)* A pleasant, well-furnished room. A double bed, liquor, music, telephone, a good and convenient address in this section. She won't take you to her hotel. She'd be ashamed. She won't go to a place far away. Distrust. The premises have to be very nearby. And already *paid for.* In fact, during the first few hours the whole subject of money must be handled with kid gloves, with tact. *(Pointing at him, imperiously.)* Certainly you're asking yourself, so where's the profit? Don't jump to conclusions. We get a daily report from the hotels. They only give us the names of the ladies who stay at least *four days.* *(Stressing.)* Four at least. *(To DONATO.)* Why, Donato? Explain it to him.

DONATO: *(Standing up, repeating a lesson by heart.)* The first day we pay for everything. The second day we allow a very small expenditure. The third day, we tell our little story.

PROFESSOR: What little story? Explain it to him.

DONATO: *(To FORTUNATO.)* The third day we will appear putting on a gloomy face, very, very sad…"What's the matter, darling?"—the old girl, by now head over heels in love, will ask us. "My father has gone bankrupt." A disastrous crash. We've lost everything. Money, home, and honor. She will pay for lunch, then for dinner; she will reimburse us for everything we paid out before this. A one-hundred-dollar banknote leads to another.

PROFESSOR: Please sit down. *(To FORTUNATO.)* It always works. The first day you must make sure to take her address in the States and give her yours. Desperate letters after she has left…I'll write or correct them for you; your English is not perfect…Ingenious, isn't it? If it seems advisable, you will also follow them to the nearby cities. After the announcement of bankruptcy, they will foot all bills. For you it is an agreeable vacation. *(To CORSO.)* Telephone number in Milan?

CORSO: 482559.

PROFESSOR: In Florence?

CORSO: 53771.

PROFESSOR: In Rome?

CORSO: 815683.

PROFESSOR: *(To FORTUNATO.)* Memorize these. The address of headquarters will, however, always be the most important. They will all write to you here.

AFRO: Not all of them, unfortunately.

PROFESSOR: It's your fault. *(To FORTUNATO.)* He's referring to the fact that some don't answer. That will be entirely your fault. It will mean that you haven't done your work with enough tact, sensitivity, intelligence. To conquer a human being is not easy. *(Continuing with lesson, which he knows by heart.)* Our raw material, the American Woman, can be of two types: the woman who *knows* and pays, and the woman who does *not* know and pays anyway. The first is the astute type, usually the wife of some big industrialist accustomed to buying everything. She buys the merchandise on the spot, pays, does *not* want to pay at a distance for something she no longer has in hand. Contrary to what one might think, she is actually the most difficult client. It's a matter of convincing her that she can get more and better of the same merchandise. On the last day, the demanding fiancée whom you were forced to see at brief moments, which were denied to her, will be introduced. You'll bring up the subject with regret, irritation. At that moment, she will understand that you're capable of more and better services. You will also stress your revulsion at having to live here, your yearning to go to America, to accept from her *any sort* of position. Even the position of personal attendant. Only if you have been endearing, persuasive, will you get mail. An invisible thread will bind her to you, compel her to pay. *(Pointing to BENITO.)* Benito, who is so quiet, so apparently reserved, inspires a feeling of confidence and security. He is very successful with this type. We have then the type that doesn't know, the romantic type. These are the ones who produce the best results, even if, quite obviously, the initial overtures are more delicate and difficult. Donato, will you describe these initial overtures?

DONATO: *(Standing up.)* We get the report from the hotel, the snapshot from the photographer. Depending on how tall she is, either Corso or I will go. Waiting around the hotel, shadowing, choice of the most propitious moment for the first act of politeness. Rescue from a wolf—whom we, of course, pay; intervention as an interpreter when she cannot understand why she must pay that particular amount of money in a store, and so on. In desperate cases, when, for instance, we have seen one or two freelancers firmly repulsed, we make friends with an American male, get him to approach her in some way, and to introduce us...We pay for a drink, then for another, and then for the dinner. Detachment, elegance, display of at least a bit of American culture, interest in and admiration for their world. Finally, we ask her to come for a ride in a gondola. I'll point out to you the gondoliers who work with us; the real siege begins. "The gondolier is blind and deaf."—This must be said jokingly, to reassure her. An arm around her shoulders, a caress. After so many courtesies and such behavior, she won't dare to object.

PROFESSOR: A patronizing attitude.

DONATO: A protective, tender, still discreet attitude. Then, slowly...

PROFESSOR: *(Breaking in.)* We must trust our personal instincts, our physical appeal, the aggressiveness which is peculiar to us, us Latins. If you succeeded in the gondola, all the better. Everything will become much, much easier. She will never again recover from the shock—the swift transition from thinly veiled detachment to feverish assault. She'll accept everything, your room, the night, your problems, and then your desperation when your father goes bankrupt... Ask my wife. *(Turning to THE SIGNORA.)* Isn't it true that afterward it is too late? That no woman has the courage to turn back, to refuse?

SIGNORA: It's true.

AFRO: *(Jumping at the chance.)* You, Signora, are the living example of just the contrary. You never gave us a second chance. Why do you refuse?

PROFESSOR: *(Firmly.)* We are talking about American women, another race, another mentality. *(Changing the subject.)* Donato has mentioned culture before. This is why besides English and sex psychology, *(Pointing to THE SIGNORA, as the teacher of this subject.)* we teach history, geography, religion, hygiene, diet, politics, sociology, *et similia*. To make sure that you're up to your job, well prepared, and more interesting. Benito, tell our new student the names of the two presidents whom it is not advisable to praise.

BENITO: *(Standing up.)* Lincoln, because from the Southerner's point of view, he wronged the South, and Roosevelt, because he inflicted heavy taxes.

PROFESSOR: Elio, what question must never be put to a client from Washington, D.C.?

ELIO: *(Without standing up.)* Whether it is true that in Washington they don't vote because the majority of the population is Negro.

PROFESSOR: Who are the most famous Italians every client knows?

AFRO: The Fontana sisters, Sophia Loren... Renata Tebaldi.

PROFESSOR: And who are the men?

AFRO: Pucci, Marcello Mastroianni, Volare—I mean Modugno—Moravia.

PROFESSOR: And Tomasi di Lampedusa: author of *The Leopard*. It was a best seller. *(To CORSO.)* People best to ignore?

CORSO: Charlie Chaplin and Howard Fast.

AFRO: *(Correcting him.)* Howard Fast is now in the clear. He denounced the Reds—years ago.

PROFESSOR: It would still be best to ignore him. He does have a past. *(To DONATO.)* What poet should never be quoted to Jewish clients because of his collaboration with the German Reich?

DONATO: *(Diligently.)* Ezra Pound. Born in 1885. A good friend of Italy.

PROFESSOR: *(To FORTUNATO.)* To appear informed on the subject of poetry, *The Pocket Book of Modern Verse* will do. It contains all the poetry of the last hundred years. The least boring. If you go to our bookstore, *(Points to the list.)* they'll charge you only five dollars. Learn by heart a poem by Frost and one by Sandburg. You'll astound them. Among the authors to be read and quoted: Thomas Wolfe, 1900–1938; William Faulkner, 1897–1962; Ernest Hemingway, 1898–1961; Truman Capote, 1924–1984. Then there are the touchy subjects. Afro, you list them.

AFRO: Segregation, Missiles, Politics, Religion.

PROFESSOR: Ignore segregation and the South. Missiles are not so touchy now. It is again possible to speak about them. They've regained some ground. Two years ago, it would have been an unforgivable faux pas.

AFRO: Politics and religion.

PROFESSOR: What's your line in politics?

AFRO: If I absolutely must talk about it—when all other subjects have been exhausted—to fill up the gaps between one session and the next—

(All laugh.)

AFRO: I tell her that I had a slight interest in Socialism, which I am now losing.

PROFESSOR: *(To FORTUNATO.)* Understand? You never miss. They have some vague notion what it is. If they respect it, they'll try to bring you back to the "democratic variety." Otherwise, they'll be happy to help you get away from the devil. *(To AFRO.)* Please sit down. Religion is another big headache. What with Baptists, Jews, Protestants, Evangelists, Catholics, Presbyterians, Episcopalians, Methodists, and Mormons, it's impossible to make head or tail of the whole thing. What is the wisest behavior, Benito?

BENITO: *(Standing up, recites.)* "I am a Catholic; I'm somewhat discouraged by certain political interferences on the part of the Vatican; nevertheless I still go to church..."

PROFESSOR: *(To FORTUNATO.)* Do you understand? If the client isn't a Catholic, she will like your veiled reproach; if she is Catholic she will not feel too insulted, because she knows that in Italy the relationship between Church and State is completely different from theirs.

(Telephone on the dais rings. THE PROFESSOR answers, takes notes.)

PROFESSOR: Yes...Yes...Good...Age? *(He writes.)* Height? *(He writes.)* Yes...A widow... *(He writes.)* Good...Did you develop it?...I'll send someone to get them...Yes...Thank you... *(Puts down receiver. Turning again to students.)* Bleached blonde, medium height, widowed eight months ago. Has inherited a number of meat-processing plants. Has taken a luxurious suite. Age sixty-seven. Who wants to go?

DONATO: I'll go.

PROFESSOR: *(To THE SIGNORA.)* Three hundred. Get them from my wife.

(THE SIGNORA hands over money and makes DONATO sign receipt.)

PROFESSOR: Now don't forget. First you get the photograph—which you will carefully conceal in your wallet—then you order the flowers. Don't let her spend any money. In the gondola—detachment, melancholy, flashes of culture. And during the last half hour, helped by the moon, the lagoon, the starry night...

DONATO: I will. *(He has collected the money, goes stage left; turning to fellow students.)* Ciao. So long.

FELLOW STUDENTS and PROFESSOR: Good luck.

(DONATO exits.)

PROFESSOR: *(Moved, looking after him affectionately.)* One of my creations goes forth. A part of myself. As all of you are. And each of your conquests is mine. I love through you, with you. Any questions, Fortunato?

FORTUNATO: *(Slowly.)* If we succeed the first evening, in the gondola, why should we continue to pay the second day, too?

PROFESSOR: We know from experience that they are more generous if they are absolutely untouched by doubt. Paying for a few drinks even after having possessed and conquered is proof of impeccable morality. Anything else?

FORTUNATO: The flowers, who pays for the flowers?

PROFESSOR: I have arranged for a discount. It's up to you to pay. Don't forget that I receive only ten percent on all earnings.

(FORTUNATO sits down again, whispers to AFRO.)

PROFESSOR: Any more questions?

(No answer.)

PROFESSOR: Now I must make the rounds of the hotels. To get a list of arrivals. I'll leave you with my wife. For the psychosexual questions. *(To BENITO.)* You have learned enough. Come with me. We'll be back soon.

BENITO: *(To fellow students.)* Bye-bye.

(PROFESSOR and BENITO exit stage left. The four remaining students stare at THE SIGNORA. A silence.)

AFRO: *(Aggressively, ruthless.)* You said before that after a session with each of us, you can't forget. It is difficult for a woman. Is it true, even now that your husband isn't here to prompt you?

SIGNORA: It's true.

AFRO: That a man *can never be forgotten?*

SIGNORA: It's true.

AFRO: That no woman has the courage to say no?

SIGNORA: *(A bit unsure.)* It's true.

AFRO: So where do you get the courage to reject us and to prefer that old man?

CORSO: Does our profession disgust you?

AFRO: What about the first time? You realized even then that we did it just professionally, didn't you? If we come here it's because we've accepted the organization and its rules.

CORSO: Are we any worse than your husband? After all, he is the organizer! If we were able to get jobs...

FORTUNATO: And if one could survive on what they pay...

SIGNORA: He has taught you everything. You owe him everything.

AFRO: And what about you? What do you owe him?

(A pause; THE SIGNORA looks at him sternly, trying to understand the real meaning of his questions.)

SIGNORA: *(Coldly.)* I owe him what every wife owes her husband. Any other questions?

(A short pause.)

ELIO: I'm sick and tired of old women. I want something young. Do I have any hope, ever, with you? Or must I look for a sweet little fiancée?

(THE SIGNORA throws him a very stern look.)

ELIO: *(Intimidated.)* Forget I said it.

(Another embarrassing pause.)

FORTUNATO: What's your personal opinion of guys like us? That we're whores?

SIGNORA: I don't have opinions. It is a profession like any other. If each of you were given the chance to do something more respectable, you would behave better. These are the consequences of our defeat.

ELIO: That's what your husband says. *(To the others.)* She's repeating, just like a parrot. She's in love with him.

CORSO: Incredible.

FORTUNATO: What does a woman expect from a man?

SIGNORA: *(Changing the subject, which is too personal.)* What does an American woman expect? Perhaps a Latin adventure. Perhaps escape. Perhaps a little companionship.

FORTUNATO: And what if the one I hit on does not belong to these categories? What if she's a good girl, like you?

SIGNORA: Don't talk recklessly. You don't know anything about me. And you won't know anything about that client.

FORTUNATO: How can one get to know a woman well?

SIGNORA: One lets her talk, and waits.

FORTUNATO: If she is the serious, clean sort—there are some—she won't feel like talking. She'll wait in silence, studying me. How should I behave?

SIGNORA: It will be up to you then to talk about yourself. At length. So she'll get to know you. And you must be patient if she is silent or sarcastic.

FORTUNATO: What do I talk about?

SIGNORA: He'll teach you. *(Points to the door through which THE PROFESSOR left.)* Hundreds of topics, as the time goes by. For the present, with your first clients rely on inspiration. Various subjects, your life...

FORTUNATO: *(Interrupting.)* My troubles...

SIGNORA: You have no troubles. Don't forget you're a rich boy, with a father who can afford to go bankrupt.

(Brief pause.)

FORTUNATO: Is it advisable to make advances...the first evening?

SIGNORA: Why not? Delicately, tenderly. Women like men who are proper, tender, and at the same time skillful. The man who is sure of himself, who seems detached, unconcerned about the conquest for its own sake, the sexual act in itself. You can. With discretion. Pretending to be uninterested, at the beginning. As a result, taking her by surprise.

FORTUNATO: But at a certain point, she can't help but realize that that's our aim...that all the talk merely hides that goal.

SIGNORA: Don't give her time to think, to react. She'll immediately adapt herself, adjust to the new situation.

(A short pause.)

FORTUNATO: Is a woman able to sense hate, irritation, revulsion? One can't like all of them. And these feelings come to the surface.

SIGNORA: Disguise them with a scene of jealousy, a fit of rage, even a promise of marriage. A lonely, tired woman responds very easily to this sort of thing. She will never forget a spontaneous proposal, a burst of tears, an avowal of love in the Latin manner...Even later, months later, when she'll be about to mail you the money, she'll remember that spontaneity, that violence, the flowers with which you filled her room, "afterward." She will go back to the hotel, dazed, surprised; the flowers will move her more than anything else. He knows it. *(She alludes to THE PROFESSOR.)* And phone her often, with desire in your voice. And remember, you must give her your address, your telephone number, at the beginning, when you're still a "rich" man. It will burn a hole in her bag. She will *have* to call you sooner or later. Or write to you. She's lonely, don't forget. *(Caught up in what she's saying.)* To be a lonely woman is a devastating thing. You will never understand this, you men.

(A short pause.)

FORTUNATO: You're talking with great feeling. You're taking their side.

SIGNORA: *(Smiling sadly.)* Female solidarity.

AFRO: It's your fault if I have failed in some of my jobs. I was so haunted by memory of you that I let someone else steal a client right from under my nose. What's your advice on how to win back a woman?

SIGNORA: You must be a good sport, a good loser. *(Staring at him.)* No woman forgets the man who can love, wait, accept her life, her *choice.* To know how to lose enhances us in everyone's eyes. Even in the eyes of your clients: of those women.

(THE PROFESSOR enters. BENITO isn't with him. He shows some slips of paper.)

PROFESSOR: Benito has found his ideal. They're already at the aperitif. *(Pointing to slips.)* It isn't too bad, today. *(He hands CORSO descriptive note and photograph.)*

PROFESSOR: Well suited for you. Look at her front window. Some knockers! And just read what her bank account is. *(Handing slip to AFRO.)* This one is slim, hieratic. Just right for you. You have an Oedipus complex; white hair doesn't upset you. *(Handing slip to ELIO.)* Take this...the most difficult one. We know how good you are. She is distrustful, prejudiced. She drove one of our men in Rome crazy. If you can't do it...Gentlemen, good luck. *(He dismisses them.)*

STUDENTS: *(Ad lib.)* Thank you, Professor. So long, Professor. Goodbye, Signora. Until tomorrow.

(The three students exit stage left.)

PROFESSOR: *(Paternally, to FORTUNATO, the last to leave.)* You take this, Fortunato. The best one...a thirty-year-old Calvinist from Illinois...This is your first. You don't yet have the stomach for the wrecks. *(Shows him photograph.)* Still young. Look what sad, beautiful eyes...intelligent, sensitive, majored in fine arts...You will combine business with pleasure...She is divorced. *(He pats him on the shoulder.)* Ciao.

(THE PROFESSOR looks after him with fondness as he starts to leave. FORTUNATO goes out slowly, looking at THE SIGNORA without daring to say goodbye to her.)

PROFESSOR: Say goodbye to my wife, come on. *(Points to her.)*

FORTUNATO: *(Timidly.)* Goodbye, Signora.

SIGNORA: Goodbye.

(FORTUNATO exits stage left.)

PROFESSOR: You can see, they are all happy! Give an Italian a taste of erotic adventure and you make him feel triumphant. Italians are children. They like forbidden fruit. It's a religious complex they can never free themselves of. They are intrigued by frustrated wives, rejected wives, divorcées. As long as she belongs to someone else. To an Italian a divorcée is still somehow considered married. An ex-wife. He feels like a hero if he can invade someone else's territory.

(A pause. THE PROFESSOR goes to window, lifts curtain, turning his back to THE SIGNORA, who gazes at him intensely.)

PROFESSOR: *(Without turning.)* How do you like the new one, little wife?

(A silence.)

PROFESSOR: Why don't you answer, little wife?

SIGNORA: After so many...They are all alike.

PROFESSOR: I have the feeling that *this* one will do brilliantly and he'll bring in a good percentage. *(A pause; he studies her reaction.)* He makes a good impression. *(A slight pause.)* Even on you, little wife. I noticed it.

SIGNORA: *(Always sad, impenetrable.)* You're losing your intuition.

(Another brief pause; he studies her.)

PROFESSOR: *(From his window, he can still see FORTUNATO walking away.)* He's built like an athlete. Strong, broad-shouldered... *(Brief pause.)* Do you like athletes, little wife?

SIGNORA: *(After a brief pause; in a burst of desperation.)* "Wife, wife"...why do you insist on claiming for yourself a woman like me...a...a whore? I'm NOT your wife. *(Sorrowfully.)* Why do you continue to humiliate yourself?...You've already done too much for me by taking me off the streets...

PROFESSOR: *(Without turning around.)* I am indebted to you.

(He turns around slowly to her as she stares at him with curiosity.)

PROFESSOR: The whole world is one big screwing. *(He stares at her, explains.)* They wouldn't part with the money for the registration if I didn't give them something in return, something which is mine by law..."my wife"! *(Pointing to where FORTUNATO is headed.)* His gait is confident, you see. He's happy. He's had his boss's wife. Now with some luck he'll get another. He has found a pleasant, steady profession. He goes to meet the great adventure... *(Ironic, loftily.)* Will he fill the great void in the life of a desperate woman? Will he change someone's fate? *(Shrugging.)* For us, what's important is the money today and the percentage of tomorrow. For him, the new industry: The American Woman...

(THE CURTAIN FALLS.)

Note:

There is also a longer version of this play with a second act.

Friends

The Characters:

FOUR INTERESTING LOVERS: two women and two men.

Two apartments. Stage right, the apartment of the man. Stage left, the apartment of the woman. The woman is much more elegant and orderly. It reveals refinement and good taste. Lights stage right, where HE is talking with his best FRIEND.

SCENE I

FRIEND: Where did you meet her?

HE: At this most boring conference. I arrived late, as usual. I sit down. I look to the left. A fantastic profile.

FRIEND: Beautiful? Who does she look like? Which actress? Give me an idea.

HE: To no one. She's unique. I stare at her for a long time, She feels my stare and turns around. She looks at me for a long time, without showing her feelings,

FRIEND: *(Ironically.)* What feelings? She had never seen you in her life!

HE: *(Continuing.)* Then she turns again, slowly, and continues to listen to the speaker.

FRIEND: *(Ironically.)* Evidently more interesting than you. A real love at first sight!

HE: I keep staring at her, she feels the warmth of my look but doesn't turn around. A strong woman.

FRIEND: Very strong! How could she resist you?

HE: She answers the guy next to her in monosyllables.

FRIEND: Her husband?

HE: No, a priest.

FRIEND: Worse. You don't like church-goers. Is she religious?

HE: *(Ignoring, continuing.)* I keep staring at her. She's tense, motionless. She knows I'm staring at her. She feels the warmth of my admiration.

FRIEND: Love at first sight, I told you! And the priest, did he turn around?

HE: No. He wasn't aware of anything.

FRIEND: Strange. They're hypersensitive. They see everything. Especially if they have a "tender" interest. Was he her boyfriend?

HE: *(Ignoring him.)* At the end of the meeting she got up and with a regal bearing, she came toward me.

FRIEND: Finally! She stopped and offered herself to you.

HE: She only stared, passing near me, very close.

FRIEND: Two more seconds. She's really fast. And the priest?

HE: I noticed that he seemed perplexed. She had sprung up and, without even greeting him, she made a beeline toward me, ignoring him.

FRIEND: A tough one. Aren't you afraid of a woman who is so sure of herself? One who abandons the little priest as soon as she feels desired by someone else?

HE: No. I felt admiration right away for the way she acted, for her manner. Nose up in the air, serious, secure.

FRIEND: Ready to leave behind the ones she does not need anymore. Poor little priest, he must have suffered! Did he follow her?

HE: For a little while, like a lamb. Then he gave up, defeated.

FRIEND: Christian humility or fear of a lioness?

HE: Strange, you understood right away that she made me think of a lioness.

FRIEND: And that does not bother you? Didn't you realize right away that it would have been a difficult conquest, a dangerous one?

HE: She attracted me precisely for that...

FRIEND: ...Because, when the conquest is difficult, victory is more gratifying, a real triumph.

HE: I didn't think of it as a "victory," as a physical conquest—

FRIEND: Great! You understood right away the danger!

HE: I only wanted to get to know her, to talk to her. Nothing more.

FRIEND: *(Ironically.)* I know you! I don't believe you!

HE: It's absolutely true! Some women you undress with your eyes; you feel like... *(Gesture.)*

FRIEND: *(Ironically.)* With her, no desire to do it!

HE: Only the desire to look at her, to know her...

FRIEND: And then? What did you do? You made believe you were religious, you went to the priest and got yourself introduced?

HE: No. I followed her. I attracted her, in a way, toward me.

FRIEND: The old tactic of hypnotism.

HE: She stumbled toward me; she almost fell into my arms.

FRIEND: Hypnotism and a bit of luck. It has always been your method, scoundrel!

HE: No. She really stumbled. If I hadn't been there, to hold her...

(Blackout stage right. Lights stage left, where SHE is talking to her GIRLFRIEND.)

SHE: A third-rate hotel. I don't know why they choose such hotels for an international conference. Old rugs, torn and worn out. I stumbled. Luckily there was this interesting man who caught me.

GIRLFRIEND: A madman or a maniac. Did you notice him before?

SHE: No. Never seen him. And that was the third day of the conference. Three days of deadly boredom.

GIRLFRIEND: Up until that moment. What did you do after he caught you falling? Did he take you to his bed or to yours?

SHE: He was very correct. We introduced ourselves. We went to dinner.

GIRLFRIEND: Does he know how to pick wines?

SHE: Third-rate hotel. Everything included. Even the wines.

GIRLFRIEND: That's why he took you to dinner, the spendthrift! If he were a real gentleman he would have invited you out, far away from that cheap tablecloth. Was it made of paper?

SHE: No. Horrible red and white checkerboard squares. He was so nice. I felt at ease right away.

GIRLFRIEND: What did he want from you? After all, you only met by chance, the buckled carpet. You didn't choose each other because there was a physical attraction.

SHE: Such a warm hand. A caressing protecting hand.

GIRLFRIEND: How old is he?

SHE: Forty, fifty. What's the difference?

GIRLFRIEND: At least fifty. It makes a difference. You know when they're at the height of their sexual power? At eighteen!

SHE: That's all you think about.

GIRLFRIEND: And you don't!

SHE: No, I swear it. We laughed a lot. A dry sense of humor, comforting.

GIRLFRIEND: Like your husband's.

SHE: Oh no! My husband only knows how to tell jokes. He rehearses them diligently, to impress our guests. And I have to listen to them month after month.

GIRLFRIEND: Whereas Mr. "Penetrating Eyes"?

SHE: What can I tell you? There were some Germans and some Swiss at our table. He was nice to everyone. He listened patiently. He loves lo listen.

GIRLFRIEND: A cunning fellow. He learned his lesson. At twenty he didn't listen. He jumped on his victims. At fifty he knows better how to be cool and quiet and listen with "patience." To conquer types like you. After dinner, where did he take you? To visit his stamp collection?

SHE: To the beach. We walked barefoot.

GIRLFRIEND: How romantic! And then? He took you there, on the tricky sand that gets into every fold of your body?

SHE: No. We talked about a million things, hand in hand.

GIRLFRIEND: Warmest hand, that I know. And then? At your age there's no time for acting coy. You come to the point. A real man comes to the point.

SHE: By the way, at dinner he introduced me as his wife to the Swiss.

GIRLFRIEND: What a great effort! Those live in the Cantons. Did he introduce you as his wife to the Italians, to those who matter and like to gossip?

SHE: Yes. There were also some Italians. He's very sure of himself. When he said that I was his "consort" I almost had a heart attack.

GIRLFRIEND: Heart. You had hope in your heart. I know you. You stared at each other and thought, both of you, about the thousands of times when you would make love and how. Honeymoon and then…the knowing, delicious calm after the storm. Well then, when did your honeymoon begin?

SHE: Not yet.

GIRLFRIEND: Incredible! We're at the threshold of the year 2000 and these two put it off, wait, stare at each other. Well, when did you finally kiss? At least that! On the beach? On the doorstep of your room? While he was carrying you in his muscular arms, you—a trembling prey?

SHE: No. A kiss on the forehead, at midnight.

GIRLFRIEND: My poor Cinderella! Do you have his picture? I'd just like to see what kind of a man he is!

(SHE hands over the photo. The GIRLFRIEND studies it carefully.)

SHE: A familiar face…Perhaps twenty years ago he was one of my lovers…

(Blackout stage left. Lights stage right where HE is showing a photo to his FRIEND.)

FRIEND: I've seen her, somewhere…

HE: Maybe on TV.

FRIEND: Who's she? An actress?

HE: No. She is married to a big shot. They often attend official ceremonies.

FRIEND: *(Surprised.)* Ah. She's even married?

HE: They're separated. She found him with a secretary in their own bed. She hates him.

FRIEND: *(Admonishing.)* She even knows how to hate. Careful!

HE: She's real, alive, vibrant! I adore her.

FRIEND: Maybe she wants you only out of revenge. She's using you as a sexual object. An instrument of revenge. Well, when did you make love the first time? On the beach?

HE: No.

FRIEND: What? You're taking a walk in your bathing suits, half naked, on the burning sand—

HE: *(Interrupting him.)* After dinner. Dressed.

FRIEND: *(Continuing.)* …Under a romantic moon and you didn't get the urge to…?

HE: I told you. I only wanted to be with her, to talk to her.

FRIEND: About what?

HE: About everything and nothing. It's miraculously easy to talk about everything when you're with a person you love.

FRIEND: What did she tell you? That she was unhappy with her husband?

HE: No, she's very loyal…She didn't say anything too bad about him.

FRIEND: *(Ironically.)* Not "too" bad. It's obvious she said something negative. Did she say he's impotent?

HE: No…She avoided that subject…I have the impression that he's all right in that department.

FRIEND: It's something that should worry you…Or do you consider it a "challenge"? Did you show her that you're a true "master," unbeatable and tireless, the "best"?

HE: And how do you know?

FRIEND: All the stories you told me.

HE: Tales friends tell each other. I'm normal. I'm like you and everyone else.

FRIEND: Don't forget I inherited your little blonde last year. She told me everything. I almost had a heart attack when I tried to compete with the image she had created of you.

HE: They do it on purpose. They tell you "X" did it ten times to goad you into making love twenty times.

FRIEND: Enough! Don't give me numbers or I'll get a complex! When did you decide to make love? After how many hours? How many days?

HE: It's unusual but I didn't have this sexual urge to…It seemed like a sacrilege.

FRIEND: *(Stunned.)* "Sacrilege"? What's happened to you? A premature attack of senility?

HE: I like to be with her…It's as though I've known her for centuries…She said the same thing.

FRIEND: OK. The first time you made love three hundred years ago. When did you take it up again…After how many dates?

HE: I feel she's…a twin, alike.

FRIEND: Now I understand. You don't have sisters. You missed an incestuous experience. Tell me about this incest.

HE: She said a phrase that struck me… She said; "I have millions, set aside. Are you a good administrator?"

FRIEND: No incest, I was wrong! She wants to buy you! Does she know that I am the administrator of *your* millions? And that I make them increase every year?

HE: No. I avoided the subject of money. She knows nothing about me. Nothing about my finances.

(Blackout stage right. Lights in the apartment stage left.)

GIRLFRIEND: What do you know about him?

SHE: He told me everything. He's most sincere.

GIRLFRIEND: Is he rich?

SHE: I don't know the details. I don't like to ask. I love him and that's enough.

GIRLFRIEND: You are in trouble. Did he know you're rich?

SHE: "Know"? We met by chance!

GIRLFRIEND: Guys like that find out first.

SHE: Where? How?

GIRLFRIEND: It was an international conference. Your name is there, with your credentials. A few phone calls and he finds out everything! Your family name is well known.

SHE: Absolutely not. He's a treasure. He's not interested in money. Not at all. I have even… *(She stops; hesitates.)*

GIRLFRIEND: What other faux pas? What did you tell him?

SHE: *(Uncertain.)* I hinted, only hinted that I have money…I asked if he wanted to invest it, for me…

GIRLFRIEND: You're raving mad! You're dangerous! You just barely know a man; you offer him your money. What's the matter with you? Did you lose your mind? What's so special about this man? *(Ironical.)* His "penetrating eyes"?

SHE: I don't know…I feel so much at ease with him…I am sure that we were a happy couple five hundred years ago.

GIRLFRIEND: *(Alarmed.)* Go see someone. You need doctors and special cures, little girl. *(Correcting herself.)* What am I saying? We're both over thirty! You should take care of yourself, my naïve friend! Tell me everything now. You are in mortal danger. What else did you tell him? That you will put your houses, land, factories, and the bank in his name? That you trust him blindly?

SHE: *(Uncertain.)* No…

GIRLFRIEND: What does he do? How much does he earn?

SHE: He's a writer…

GIRLFRIEND: Ninety-nine percent starve. What did he tell you? That he's the exception?

SHE: No. He's extremely honest. He told me he earns enough, to live—

GIRLFRIEND: —Modestly! In some hovel.

SHE: He invited me. I'll see it... *(Suddenly with conviction.)* But even if it were a hovel, it doesn't matter! I love him!

GIRLFRIEND: Let's get back to the point. You told him the truth. Who you are, how much you have, what you're worth.

SHE: I don't believe he heard me...

GIRLFRIEND: He heard you, he heard you! And he'll never give you up! Where can he find a golden goose like you? Be careful, my dear!

SHE: He was strangely puzzled after I had told him about me, about my family. He said: "My mother always reminded me that it is better to marry a poor woman than a rich one."

GIRLFRIEND: Idiotic or wise, that mother. What did he tell you about his family?

SHE: His father was a union man; his mother is strict and determined. A strong woman. The same sign as mine: Taurus.

GIRLFRIEND: He's looking for another mother in you. A rich mother this time. Does he have sisters?

SHE: Two brothers.

GIRLFRIEND: What does he write about?

SHE: Articles, essays, poetry.

GIRLFRIEND: That's a gold mine! He doesn't have a dime. Be careful! Is he interested in politics?

SHE: I think he's not very interested...

GIRLFRIEND: "Think." If he were so sincere he would have told you everything in plain English. Therefore you shouldn't have any doubts.

SHE: No, I don't have any doubts. I love him with all of me.

GIRLFRIEND: Like that sixteen-year-old who told everything to a rascal and found herself pregnant and robbed.

SHE: I'm no longer sixteen and I know what I'm doing.

GIRLFRIEND: She who loves blindly doesn't know what she's doing. What else did he tell you?

SHE: ...He talked about... "class conscience."

GIRLFRIEND: What class? His? Careful! Careful my dear friend! He wants to take you as a hostage, from our world, and take his revenge! He only wants your money!

(Blackout stage left. Lights stage right.)

FRIEND: Isn't it better that she's rich? Until now women have cost you a fortune! You always pay for everything, Italian style!

HE: It's the only negative element from my point of view. I would have preferred her not to be rich. Money ruins relationships and poisons people.

FRIEND: But you continue to accumulate it.

HE: It's an unjust accusation. I was lucky with that book. I trusted you with my money. It's in your hands now.

FRIEND: And I invest it for you. Anyway, water always flows toward the sea. The rich always marry the rich.

HE: She doesn't know what I have. I won't tell her.

FRIEND: Good. You want to be loved for yourself, only for yourself. And now tell your best friend the joy of the first time, the contact, the meeting...in other words, the first fuck. How did it go?

HE: *(Romantic, dreaming.)* It was like a dream...I remember very little, vaguely...

FRIEND: She drugged you and seduced you. And when you awoke?

HE: I felt I was in heaven...

FRIEND: Seriously, how did it go? I always tell you everything!

HE: The conference lasted six days. We were always together. Sometimes I touched her hand...I was almost afraid to touch her...

FRIEND: Afraid?

HE: I didn't want to ruin everything with one wrong move.

FRIEND: What "wrong move"? Women love a man who desires them ardently and...does something about it!

HE: I didn't have that strong desire that compels you sometimes to hug, penetrate. Nothing, for her. I didn't feel that impelling desire to...

FRIEND: And you call that love?

HE: Yes! True love is the desire to be together.

FRIEND: *Be* together, I agree.

HE: The rest comes later, if it comes...

FRIEND: All right. With you, did it come or not?

HE: *(Timidly.)* Yes and no...

FRIEND: Meaning? It works or it doesn't work. With you, did it work?

HE: It was late, the last night...Maybe three o'clock...I accompanied her to her room.

FRIEND: Finally!

HE: I sat in a corner, timidly...She went to shower.

FRIEND: Mamma mia! That is the right sign! She was preparing herself! She wanted you! And you?

HE: I...I was looking for a pen and paper...

FRIEND: Pen and paper?

HE: I wrote two poems.

FRIEND: Poems? Where are they? Let me read them.

HE: The first time, in my life, that I wrote poetry instead of...

FRIEND: I don't believe it! Instead of taking her, you wrote poetry! You are really getting senile!

HE: She liked them. She invited me to lie down beside her.

FRIEND: *(Anticipating, excited.)* Nude, wet, and inviting.

HE: *(Dreaming, moved by the remembrance.)* Maternal...stupendous...

FRIEND: Then? Did it happen or not?

HE: It was all...so sweet...so confused...

FRIEND: *(Exasperated.)* Yes or no?

HE: Yes and no...It was late...We were tired...

FRIEND: *You* were tired. And then?

HE: ...A real disaster...like a young boy...

FRIEND: You, at your age? With your experience?

HE: They are the hazards of true love...I let her down...

(Blackout stage right. Lights stage left.)

GIRLFRIEND: Well then?

SHE: *(After a pause, dreaming.)* It was wonderful.

GIRLFRIEND: Vigorous, tireless, devastating?

SHE: The sweetest...

GIRLFRIEND: The most vigorous?

SHE: The most tender!...

GIRLFRIEND: For hours?

SHE: Stupendous.

GIRLFRIEND: Most powerful?

SHE: Divine.

GIRLFRIEND: Most manly?

SHE: Moving.

GIRLFRIEND: Virile?

SHE: The kindest.

GIRLFRIEND: Mighty?

SHE: The most loving.

GIRLFRIEND: Passionate?

SHE: Delicious.

GIRLFRIEND: Energetic?

SHE: Moving.

GIRLFRIEND: Robust?

SHE: The most sensitive.

GIRLFRIEND: Resistant?

SHE: Solicitous.

GIRLFRIEND: Tenacious?

SHE: Caressingly.

GIRLFRIEND: A real man?

SHE: A real man.

GIRLFRIEND: He made you feel what you had never felt before?

SHE: What I have never felt before.

GIRLFRIEND: He made you cry?

SHE: He made me cry.

GIRLFRIEND: Incredible?

SHE: Incredible.

GIRLFRIEND: Unforgettable?

SHE: Unforgettable... And I wrote it to him.

GIRLFRIEND: *(After a pause, reflecting.)* Will you introduce him to me? *(She smiles; she is probably joking.)*

(Blackout stage left. Lights stage right.)

HE: I was really afraid of having lost her forever...

FRIEND: Very possible! A man like you, at your age, who can't get it up...It's shameful!

HE: I was so preoccupied...I even cried.

FRIEND: *(Preoccupied.)* You need a shrink. What happened to you? You've never cried in your entire life!

HE: *You* have never seen me cry?

FRIEND: Ah, you admit it now! When?

HE: When Pope John XXIII died. A true Christian. A Saint.

FRIEND: Now you have even become religious? That lady has bewitched you! *(Short pause.)* How did you...get back on track? Did you write her a letter explaining?...

HE: No... *(Staring at him.)* She wrote me a letter.

FRIEND: *(Curious and interested.)* Ah yes? And what did she say? She forgave you...the failure?

HE: The moment I received it, I started shaking...really shaking...

FRIEND: It's serious, very serious...I'm beginning to worry...What did she say in the letter?

HE: *(Ignoring.)* I hesitated a long time before reading it...for hours...

FRIEND: And when did you read it? What did she write? The usual story? "We women understand. It happens to all men"? And how do they know it happens to all of us? With how many do they sleep?

HE: A letter that was...overwhelming.

FRIEND: Meaning? Let me read it.

HE: A beautiful letter that I'm still carrying here next to my heart.

FRIEND: Together with the two poems. Let me read them.

HE: Love poems are not to be read by friends. They're gushing from the heart. Very personal.

FRIEND: The letter then. Sprung from *her* heart.

HE: Too intimate. It's only *ours*.

FRIEND: Is it about sex? I love confessions by women. What did she invent to justify your failure?

HE: She didn't consider it a failure at all...According to her...everything had been wonderful.

FRIEND: *(Reflecting.)* Generous and... clever. The letter, come on. We're friends.

HE: No. It would be a violation of an intimate secret.

FRIEND: Tell me at least...Is it sensual?

HE: Illuminating.

FRIEND: Passionate?

HE: Radiant.

FRIEND: Ardent?

HE: Glorious.

FRIEND: Impassioned?

HE: The sweetest.

FRIEND: Burning?

HE: The tenderest.

FRIEND: Obscene?

HE: Divine.

FRIEND: The kind of letter that makes you feel young?

HE: Very young. It brought me back the joy of living!

FRIEND: *(Vaguely jealous.)* I...I have never received such letter...so...rich!

(They both laugh.)

HE: Talking about richness, let's remove the Modiglianis.

(They get up and go to take down three Modiglianis from the walls. Lights stage left. While the two friends remove the paintings, the two women friends continue to talk.)

GIRLFRIEND: *(Surprised.)* Did you write him those things so...openly? The way you told me?

SHE: What I felt, what I feel.

GIRLFRIEND: You don't realize that you are now vulnerable, most vulnerable...

SHE: It's beautiful to be open and vulnerable in love. We have sworn absolute sincerity to each other. You can't imagine what we tell each other. Like two innocent children.

GIRLFRIEND: Innocent, yes. How many letters have you written him?

SHE: At least two hundred.

GIRLFRIEND: *(Alarmed.)* Two hundred?... And in all of them, you confess your thoughts and tell everything?

SHE: Everything. A thousand variations of my love, of my desires.

GIRLFRIEND: Do you realize that...he could blackmail you?

SHE: You're ridiculous and obscene. Bitter and embittered. How can you be so mean as to even think of blackmail? Ours is true love, the deepest.

GIRLFRIEND: Blind and mad infatuation. Haven't you ever read those stories of people who pretend to be in love and then offer proof to the husbands? For a price, during divorce proceedings?

SHE: He would never do it! He adores me!

GIRLFRIEND: *You* say he adores you, you have the impression that he adores you—

SHE: *(Interrupting.)* The first impression is always the most important. Remember what I said when you asked me the first time seeing me happy? I answered: "I met the man with whom I would like to spend the rest of my life."

GIRLFRIEND: *(Continuing.)* —You are too trusting of everybody! When you met your husband, you said the same thing. That he was a fantastic man, in every way. You trusted him. You gave him complete freedom. You come home one day and find him in *your* bed with that bitch.

SHE: The worst of insults. He added insult to injury. I'll never forgive him.

GIRLFRIEND: Your husband has power, political power. He can unleash the police or secret agents on you. Or, think for a moment of this other possibility.

SHE: Which one?

GIRLFRIEND: That he has hired your idol in his service.

SHE: Ridiculous!

GIRLFRIEND: Not so ridiculous! Writers are always in search of ideas, adventures.—And money. He uses him against you during the divorce proceedings. And you're done for! You become the guilty party! And you lose millions!

SHE: *(Defiantly.)* Would you like to know something else?

GIRLFRIEND: *(Curiously.)* Tell me. What other madness have you done?

SHE: I made a cassette tape, when I was alone, in bed, and I was thinking of him. A tape full of love, passion, promises. My voice. Sexy and passionate. *(Ironically.)* Do you think he will use even that against me?

GIRLFRIEND: My dear friend, you're ruined. You're in his hands. Chained, hands and feet. He can do what he wants with you.

SHE: *(Defiantly.)* Let him do it! I'm all his! I don't care about anything anymore! I've met the love of my life. I won't let him go. I'm the one who won't give him up!

(Lights stage right. HE signals to his FRIEND to leave with the paintings. The FRIEND leaves stage right with the paintings. SHE enters from stage left. They stare at each other with love.)

SHE: Ciao.

HE: Ciao.

(Passionate embrace. They adore each other. SHE begins to unbutton his shirt. HE reacts timidly, reluctant. He defends himself, delicately. Backs off.)

SHE: *(Timidly.)* Forgive me, my love…It's been so long since we've seen each other…We've promised absolute sincerity to each other…I'm following my instinct, my desire…

HE: It has been so long since we've seen each other…I want first…to admire you.

(HE walks two steps away. Admires her. They stare at each other with love.)

SHE: Hold me tight, really tight, once more, and then let's talk…

(Another passionate embrace, moving. They adore each other.)

SHE: *(Looking around herself.)* And now let me admire your nest...

(SHE begins to look over the room. SHE notices the empty spaces where the paintings were.)

SHE: There were paintings, here...

HE: They're being reframed. I want all three to have the same type of frame.

SHE: *(Cautiously.)* What kind of paintings? Modern or...?

HE: Or?

SHE: Nineteenth century...I have a few. Mancini, Fattori, Domenico Induno.

HE: No. They're only touristic posters. The cities we like most.

HE and SHE: *(Together, amused.)* Ve-nice...Flo-rence...Man-tua!

(They smile at each other. She takes a Chinese vase and studies it.)

SHE: Ming Dynasty. A very rare piece. Beautiful.

HE: A present from my mother. It's yours, if you want it.

SHE: *(Ignoring the offer.)* Your mother has good taste.

HE: Like you. You always choose the best.

SHE: *(Smiling.)* I...I chose you. She didn't. She had to accept you the way you were. A gift from nature... *(Pointing to the empty spaces.)* If you want, we can put there some of my paintings...I have two or three that are very dear to me... Presents from my father.

HE: If you want.

SHE: *(Noticing dust.)* Do you have anyone who does your housekeeping?

HE: A woman comes once a week. Tomorrow.

SHE: Does she cook, too?

HE: No. I often eat at the restaurant downstairs.

SHE: I love to cook. I'll fix delicious things for you. With joy.

HE: Thank you, my love. *(A short pause.)* Sit here, now, please. I want to talk to you.

(Makes her sit down. HE sits too, at a certain distance.)

SHE: Me too. I love to listen to you. Your voice is a caress...

HE: *(Parrying.)* I beg of you...

SHE: It's wonderful. Speak.

HE: *(Uncertain.)* You were saying last time that it was impossible to quarrel with me and you wanted to find differences, the reasons for...contrasts, conflicts.

SHE: *(Amused.)* It's true. Let's try, let's try to fight. I want to see you also in that aspect. I want to know everything about you.

HE: I've made a list of my defects...They are here. Nine.

SHE: *(Remembering, suddenly.)* By the way, I know that nine is your preferred number.—Ours, now. I have prepared a list of the twenty-seven reasons for which I love you. Three times nine.

(They exchange papers. They smile, amused.)

SHE: *(Reading.)* This is a quality...another quality...another...there's a way to solve this...quality...quality... *(Reflecting.)* Number nine...I am that too, a little bit. See? We have so much in common. What do you say about my list?

HE: *(Smiling.)* It's incredible...How do you manage to see in me...to find so many...positive things?

SHE: I am sure that I could find at least a hundred qualities in you. You're wonderful. You are my man.

HE: At least half of these compliments, I certainly don't deserve.

SHE: Then accept the others. Great! We meet halfway. Always ready to agree. We'll be the happiest couple in the world!

HE: *(Uncertain, moved by her enthusiasm.)* My nine defects...are horrendous. Jealousy, for example.

SHE: It's a quality. I am jealous too. We'll be the most faithful couple in the world. *(Impetuous, sincere, overwhelming.)* I really mean it. I hope so! Promise it! Don't change! It's the only thing that I want with all my heart, with all of myself! I forgive you everything: jealousy, melancholy, occasional depression, too much dedication to work...Everything! Betrayal, no! It hurts too much! It wounds too much! It kills! I would die if you betrayed me!

HE: I swear, my dearest! From the moment I met you, I think of nothing but our love. I see only you, always you. I dream only of you. Only you.

SHE: Thank you, love. Then, you accept thirteen and a half compliments. I accept your nine..."defects-qualities." We are a perfect couple.

(SHE opens her arms. Offers herself, ready to make love to him.)

HE: *(Still uncertain and wavering.)* That last defect of mine...being fundamentally stingy...

SHE: I told you. I am too. Do you know what my father used to call me? The accountant. I take note of everything, even the smallest expenses. Before buying, I look in a thousand stores for the best prices. I haggle for hours...You will have perfect budgets and accounts with me.

HE: I'm only stingy with myself...I don't ever buy elegant or expensive things. That sofa bed, for example, is very old. I could afford another. No...I always put it off.

SHE: How does it work?...

(They stare at each other with love.)

SHE: Let me see.

(A silence. HE slowly shows how it works. HE opens it. SHE holds it open with her knee.)

HE: This way...

SHE: *(While SHE begins to prepare the bed.)* Easy...Comfortable...Soft...A nice bed...

HE: With you I shall never be stingy. Everything that you desire...

(A silence. SHE stares at him. SHE would like to ask him: "Can you afford it?" SHE prefers to postpone the question to another time.)

SHE: If you allow me, I'll change a few things, in this nest of ours...

HE: Of course. I trust you. You can change whatever you want.

(A short silence. SHE stares at him. She would like to ask him: "And who pays the expenses?" Holds herself back.)

SHE: The only thing that I don't want ever to change, never, never, is my love for you. I adore you! *(SHE opens her arms. SHE offers herself.)*

HE: *(Kissing her with transport.)* I adore you!

(Blackout. Brief musical bridge.)

SCENE II

Lights stage right. SHE is still on the sofa-bed. Half nude. HE is preparing tea and pastries.

HE: *(While HE's preparing.)* Remember that first letter of yours, the one where you defined yourself in love. An overwhelming love?

SHE: Of course. It was my *first* love letter. How could I forget it?

HE: Why did you add in a corner "When you answer me, don't talk about bed"?

SHE: *(Uneasy.)* Because it's too intimate a subject...I prefer not to talk about it. Love is love. It's feeling good together. With you everything is marvelous.

(HE hands her tea and pastries. SHE smiles at him, caressing his hand.)

SHE: Thanks.

HE: *(With caution. Calm.)* I am sure that...even with your husband everything was marvelous.

SHE: Don't act the jealous child. The past is past. Only with you it's very special, divine. I love only you. I have never loved anyone like this.

HE: No one?

SHE: *(Half-serious.)* Ah. I forgot our promise of absolute sincerity. To tell you the truth... *(Temporizing, to make him jealous.)* I fell madly in love with someone my age...at thirteen...I didn't eat anymore. I didn't sleep anymore. One day...I dared to kiss him on his cheek. I blushed and blushed, from shame. I went to confession! I never saw him again.

HE: *(Cautiously.)* You were married young, at nineteen...You must have had an unforgettable honeymoon.

SHE: *(Vaguely impatient.)* Love, love, my love. There is only you in my life. Only you exist.

HE: *(Cautiously.)* You told me one day that we needed a little "running in," you and I, before...reaching a perfect understanding...I understood right away that the "running in" is perfect between you and your husband...Habit, ability...He must be great in that department.

SHE: That's enough, my love. I beg you, let's not talk about these silly details. You are wonderful, the best in the world. Let's talk about us, about our dreams.

HE: *(Obeying, jokingly.)* At your orders, Mrs. "Shortcut." Tell me then, my love. If we build a nest all our own, which city would you like it in?

SHE: ...A little house in Venice.

HE: Let it be then. In Venice.

SHE: Very well. In whose name?

(They stare at each other in silence.)

HE: In yours, of course.

SHE: *(Jokingly.)* You know my mother always said: "Blessed are those whose names are at the top of a document." He who owns, dominates!

(A silence. They stare at each other. SHE realizes SHE has said something wrong.)

SHE: *(Seeking to amend.)* It isn't that I want...to dominate. Never...You are my man, you are stupendous. We will always get along.

HE: Always.

SHE: *(Seeking to justify her words.)* I said: "In whose name?" instinctively...

HE: I know.

SHE: Only because I am insecure. I have never had a profession and...

HE: I understand perfectly.

SHE: I am obsessed by the thought of the future.

HE: Happens to many.

SHE: I have never known poverty. I could never face it, I wouldn't know how...

HE: It's the survival instinct! He who owns, protects his money. *(Vaguely ironic.)* Only because one is insecure in this society.

SHE: Forgive me, my love, if I say strange things...from time to time. Forgive me...It isn't my fault if I'm a daughter of merchants...

HE: It isn't your fault.

SHE: But now that I have met you, I'll change...You are great, you are my man. I have nothing to fear with a man who knows how to love like you, with a perfect man like you.

HE: *(Ready to change the subject.)* Me, perfect? I've just written down nine defects because I hold dear the number nine. I have at least another ten.

SHE: Which? I don't see them! But I want to discover them one at a time. And if you have them, I will uncover them. And we will fight a little bit. They say an outburst from time to time is good for the nervous system. Also because we will then make up and we will make love with more passion.

HE: My worst defect is not knowing how to choose gifts. It's a trauma for me, the thought of having to...decide.

SHE: But if you've just offered me the most precious vase of your life, that Ming that's worth a fortune and is a gift from your mother!

HE: Because it's here. Everything I have is yours. What you see, is all yours. I was speaking of gifts for birthdays, anniversaries, the beginning of the year. Looking for them, choosing, having doubts. A search that makes me nervous, makes me crazy. I hate it!

SHE: We'll choose them together. I'll give you hints, making you realize what I like.

HE: Clearly, please. I love clarity.

SHE: I'll put my little finger on it, like this. You will have no doubts and you will make me very happy.

HE: *(Happy.)* Very well! It's a method I've been dreaming of for a long time, forever. Relatives and friends should make a very clear list of what they want. Everything would be easier.

SHE: *(Studying him.)* Strange that you said...relatives and friends...You didn't buy gifts for your lovers?

HE: *(Making believe HE is severe, imitating her.)* I prefer not to speak of those silly details. There's only you in my life.

SHE: Wonderful! And I'll be your angel. The most precious person in your life. I'll help you in everything. I'll choose little gifts...symbolic ones. Things that cost little, so as not to create problems for you.

HE: *(Spontaneous.)* Oh no! You can choose whatever you want! At any price! I hate money!

(A silence. They stare at each other. SHE studies him. HE realizes HE has said too much.)

SHE: I saw a movie with Greta Garbo, years ago. One of her lovers wanted to make her happy by buying expensive gifts. He made many debts and went to prison.

HE: That is a movie. In life one spends what one can afford.

SHE: I'll help you…I'll work if necessary.

HE: *(Wanting to put her to the proof.)* For example…We love to travel…According to me it would be right if we paid the same amount. Fifty percent from me. The rest from you.

SHE: *(Enthusiastic like a child, clapping hands.)* Very good! And what is left then, we can divide half and half.

(SHE feels uneasy. A silence.)

HE: You can keep the whole thing.

(A brief silence, they stare at each other. An uneasy silence. SHE is sorry about what SHE has said.)

SHE: Forgive me, love. My instinct as an accountant has reappeared. Forgive me. It's not my fault.

HE: I know.

SHE: I have never worked in my whole life. I mean, I have never had a salary. I'm insecure…My money could one day terminate. And then?

HE: And then?

SHE: But we could use the interest…It's true that the devaluation has to be calculated but it doesn't matter! We'll use the interest!

(HE continues to stare at her, studying her in silence.)

SHE: *(Suddenly.)* We're talking about horrible things! Here, you see, we'll fight, sometimes, on this subject. It isn't my fault if I come from a family of financiers where money is…important, almost sacred.

HE: *(Vaguely ironic.)* "Sacred."

SHE: I'll learn, I swear! I'm ready to learn everything from you!

(A silence.)

SHE: Say something, my love.

HE: *(Calm.)* I hate waste, pomp, bad taste…Perhaps if you wanted to buy a dress or a fur coat that costs the monthly budget of an entire family…

SHE: *(Interrupting.)* Oh no! I'll do everything possible to make you save!

(They stare at each other. They study each other. SHE is uncertain. Maybe SHE has said something wrong again. SHE feels uneasy, confused.)

SHE: *(Timidly.)* It is natural that a man wants to pay for the purchases, the expenses of his woman…I am sure that you…But I swear, I'll make you save! I'll be very modest… *(Opens her arms, offers herself again with love.)* And very happy! You are my man! I adore you! And I beg of you, forgive me for all the nonsense I'm saying!

HE: *(Embracing with love. Smiling at her.)* You can say all the silly things you want, my love. They are precious. Everything you say is precious. You're fantastic. You are for me mother, wife, daughter. You are my whole world.

SHE: *(Adoring.)* Do you know how I described you when I spoke to my best friend about you? "Heart-warmer." You are my superb "Heart-warmer."

(They embrace with love. Blackout. Lights stage left. The GIRLFRIEND enters, half nude, coming from the bedroom. She sits on the sofa. Places a book in full view on the small tea table.)

GIRLFRIEND: *(Talking to someone who is probably dressing in the bedroom.)* Do you need anything? Another towel? They're in the wardrobe on the left.

(No one answers.)

GIRLFRIEND: *(Lights a cigarette. Leafs the book.)* Come here, close to me...I like to talk, after...

(Another silence.)

GIRLFRIEND: I want to tell you that you were fabulous...You are the only one to have found my "G" spot, the first time...the first man in my life... *(Repenting, attenuating.)* Not that there have been so many men, in my life...I had only two lovers...None of the two had the slightest idea of where it was...They didn't even know what it was...You, where did you read about it? In some American book?

(Enters the FRIEND, who has just taken a shower.)

FRIEND: You were saying?

GIRLFRIEND: ...That I've been waiting for you...sit here, near me...

FRIEND: You were also saying something else...I heard, it seems to me, the word "lovers."...Have you had many?

GIRLFRIEND: Two or three...

FRIEND: Two or three?

GIRLFRIEND: Three. And you are the best. You are wonderful. Where did you learn...all those subtleties?

FRIEND: One learns...by living, loving...

GIRLFRIEND: Have you loved much? Many women, I mean...

FRIEND: There have been some lucky encounters, *(Pointing to her.)* from time to time... *(Notices suddenly the book that she had placed under his eyes. He is very surprised.)* This book, how come you're reading it?

GIRLFRIEND: It's by an author I adore. Have you ever read it?

FRIEND: Of course. I've read all his books!

GIRLFRIEND: Do you know him?

FRIEND: He's my best friend...This is a strange coincidence. *(Suspicious.)* Did you know we are friends?

GIRLFRIEND: No. How could I have? It's not written here, in his biography. *(Shows the cover. After a short pause.)* What kind of person is he?

FRIEND: Sensitive, poetic, absentminded...

GIRLFRIEND: Is it true that he is a great...Don Juan?

FRIEND: He is a lucky man.

GIRLFRIEND: Lucky and...capable, I imagine.

FRIEND: Both.

GIRLFRIEND: How is it that you know? Does he tell you everything?

FRIEND: Everything. *(With an accomplice's smile.)* And he is also generous.

GIRLFRIEND: Generous...how? with whom?

FRIEND: Sometimes he introduces me to his women...When he wants to get rid of them...

GIRLFRIEND: A real friend.

FRIEND: *(Suspicious, staring at her.)* Don't tell me it's the same old story! He took you to bed and now you come to me to talk about him.

GIRLFRIEND: Oh no! I don't know him at all!

FRIEND: Swear!

GIRLFRIEND: *(Serious, letting go irony.)* I swear!...But if...

FRIEND: But if?

GIRLFRIEND: ...If you want to introduce me to him, this could be your revenge...

FRIEND: *(Confused.)* Meaning?

GIRLFRIEND: *(Coquettish.)* The turnaround this time. First you...then him.

(They laugh.)

FRIEND: I see, I see! You are ready for him now. You read four pages and imagine who knows what...

GIRLFRIEND: Seriously...Is he the type of Don Juan that must change women every week, to prove to the world—and to himself—that he is still attractive and desirable?

FRIEND: Yes and no...

GIRLFRIEND: More yes than no.

FRIEND: He doesn't look for them, actively...They happen...I told you he is a lucky man.

GIRLFRIEND: *(Indicating the book.)* That chapter on the huge American lady who appeared to him in the raw and said: "Can you handle this?," is it true?

FRIEND: Very true.

GIRLFRIEND: And he, how did he react?

FRIEND: Exactly the way he described it there. *(Indicating the book.)* He said to her "I'll do my best." And he did his best, modestly. He's a modest man, deep down.

GIRLFRIEND: Are there many women in his life?

FRIEND: Many.

GIRLFRIEND: *(With curiosity.)* Did he ever fall in love?

FRIEND: Never... *(He stares at her. Studies her. He is growing suspicious of so many questions.)*

GIRLFRIEND: Strange...A real man falls in love, at least once...You told me, in that bed, that you love me...

FRIEND: It's true...I have fallen in love quite a few times...I'm in love, now, with you...He... *(Hesitates.)*

GIRLFRIEND: He, never! And probably he brags about it.

FRIEND: I had a great satisfaction a few months ago...

GIRLFRIEND: What satisfaction?

FRIEND: He always makes fun of me, when I fall in love...He says I'm a weakling, it's not true love, true love doesn't exist.

GIRLFRIEND: A cynic.

FRIEND: Listen to this. Lately... *(Staring at her; he is still uncertain and suspicious; hesitates.)*

GIRLFRIEND: Lately?

FRIEND: It seems he's fallen in love madly like a little boy. It serves him right.

GIRLFRIEND: With whom?

FRIEND: *(Avoiding.)* He talks of her night and day. He's done for like never before. Smitten. I would have never imagined that he could...

GIRLFRIEND: Who is she? How did he meet her?

FRIEND: *(Who wants to confide but not too much.)* He calls her divine, stupendous, marvelous...You name it. At least a hundred adjectives, all on the superlative side. It's been a great satisfaction for me. He is finally human, like me and like you.

GIRLFRIEND: Has he left his other women?

FRIEND: It hasn't been easy. He still has a couple of them, I believe. Trying to get rid of them.

GIRLFRIEND: You men! You swear eternal love and then!

FRIEND: I have never sworn it. I'm prudent and wise, like you. You haven't promised me anything, in that bedroom.

GIRLFRIEND: I *gave* love. Isn't it better than promises?

FRIEND: If you want a promise of "relative" eternity, all right. *(Jokingly.)* I promise!

GIRLFRIEND: Fine! I accept your "relative eternity." But tell me about your friend. If it's true that he is madly in love, how can he still go with other women?

FRIEND: He tells me he is trying, that he'd like to break all ties and forget the past, but it hasn't been easy.

GIRLFRIEND: It should be very easy if he's truly in love.

FRIEND: There's one particular one, an Armenian doctor who is very attached to him.

GIRLFRIEND: If he's a real man he should say: "No, it's enough; I'm in love with another woman."

FRIEND: He is a real man. He promised he'll tell her.

GIRLFRIEND: *(Cautiously.)* When one has many women one spends a lot. Where does he find so much money?

FRIEND: See that book? He sold two million copies. It's a gold mine.

GIRLFRIEND: *(Seeking to hold back her surprise.)* He's rich then?

FRIEND: Very rich. If you compare him with me at least. Much richer than me.

GIRLFRIEND: *(Reflecting.)* Strange...

FRIEND: What's so strange? He published many books. One out of ten reaches sometimes the bestseller list. He was lucky with "Friends." An intriguing title. It sold like hotcakes. *(Indicates the book again.)*

(They stare at each other, they study each other.)

GIRLFRIEND: This is not my apartment.

FRIEND: *(Calm, not surprised; with a sense of humor.)* It's not the first time that a beautiful lady like you meets by chance a handsome man like me and asks to borrow an apartment...From her best friend, perhaps. *(While beginning to get dressed.)* Whose is it?

GIRLFRIEND: A very rich lady.

FRIEND: Lucky her!

GIRLFRIEND: As rich as your friend, maybe. Or maybe more...

FRIEND: Lucky both of them. But I don't see the connection.

(They stare at each other. Again he is suspicious.)

FRIEND: You want to tell me that is the bedroom *(Pointing to it.)* of...?

GIRLFRIEND: Of my best friend. The woman that your best friend loves, maybe.

FRIEND: *(Hurt.)* This...was then a trap?

GIRLFRIEND: Golden trap. Did I let you down in bed?

FRIEND: *(Reflecting.)* Oh no, no! I've been very happy. But knowing that I've been selected by you only because I am his friend...it's upsetting, in a way...

GIRLFRIEND: Not only for that. It is a lucky coincidence that you are a handsome man...Sexy and charming. This way the two best women can go with the two best men...A good quartet.

FRIEND: *(Not too convinced.)* Yes...a happy coincidence. Even if it is a little... contrived.

GIRLFRIEND: Many coincidences are bizarre. As my girlfriend says: "Ask the souls for help. They will give it to you."

FRIEND: What souls?

GIRLFRIEND: My friend is very religious. She believes that the souls of the dead help "coincidences." Souls that weigh twenty-seven grams, according to what she has read in a Vatican paper. She thinks that these very light souls are the ones who made her meet her great love, your friend.

FRIEND: She admitted to you that she is in love?

GIRLFRIEND: She admitted it. She loves him blindly. At least that's what she says.

FRIEND: The fact that she's religious doesn't help the relationship...He is an atheist.

GIRLFRIEND: And a liar.

FRIEND: *(Surprised.)* Why a liar?

GIRLFRIEND: He told her he's poor. Why?

FRIEND: That's a complicated story...

GIRLFRIEND: I love complicated stories. Tell me.

FRIEND: *(Continuing dressing.)* He is still a revolutionary. What he was at twenty. He has always hated money, "cause of all ills"—as he says. Then, unexpectedly, he got this windfall. *(Indicating the book.)* A bestseller. He doesn't want to know anything about money. He gave it all to an administrator. He doesn't have the slightest idea of how it is invested. He doesn't want to know.

GIRLFRIEND: Let's hope that the administrator knows his job and doesn't cheat him.

FRIEND: He knows his job and the capital increases.

GIRLFRIEND: *(Reflecting.)* Then he is rich too...

FRIEND: He is.

GIRLFRIEND: *(Directly to the FRIEND.)* If he really loves her, why didn't he tell her the truth?

FRIEND: Because he is very very much in love. He wants to be sure she is in love with him, not because of his money. He even said he would prefer her to be poor. Sheer madness!

GIRLFRIEND: *(Reflecting.)* You are strange, you men. Instead of being happy that a woman has, besides her feminine qualities, wealth.

FRIEND: My friend is...a poet. Absent-minded, intense, a rebel. It won't be easy for a woman to live with him.

GIRLFRIEND: She is difficult, too.

FRIEND: In what way?

GIRLFRIEND: She is also intense, hard, exacting. A perfectionist.

FRIEND: He is not...He is very flexible. I've never seen him angry.

GIRLFRIEND: She's ferocious sometimes. She could even freeze a volcano.

FRIEND: Strange expression. Where did you find it? Are you a poet?

GIRLFRIEND: She said that once, when she was furious with her husband. Do you know what she did to him?

FRIEND: *(With curiosity.)* What did she do?

(She continues to talk softly while the lights go out and he finishes dressing. Lights stage right. The FRIEND is talking to him.)

FRIEND: Do you trust me?

HE: *(Not too convinced, nervous.)* I do, I do. Then, out with it! What do you have to tell me?

FRIEND: A delicate subject…

HE: How did you find out? I bet you paid someone. Everything can be bought with gold, everything can be ruined.

FRIEND: Please, trust me. I'm your best friend. He who cares can always find a way to—

HE: —Swindle his fellow man.

FRIEND: —To help somebody one loves and respects. You! I love and respect you.

HE: *(Impatient.)* Talk.

FRIEND: I don't know how to begin…

HE: Like that. Step by step. Calmly and clearly.

FRIEND: A difficult subject…I hope you don't misunderstand me.

HE: We've lost all the money. So much the better. I'm free and relieved. And I can eliminate this great pretense in my life. My last lie.

FRIEND: No no. The money is increasing. Financially you're OK for the rest of your life. What bothers me is your health.

HE: *(Surprised.)* Health? I can beat you in any sport. Would you like to run a hundred yards right away? Let's go to the park.

FRIEND: Your spiritual health, your soul.

HE: Don't worry. My soul has been taken by her, the woman I love.

FRIEND: Precisely…

HE: You are jealous, admit it, you are jealous because we are madly in love, a perfect couple!

FRIEND: One can't ever be jealous of such madness, such blindness.

HE: *(Impatient.)* Then what have you "found out"? How? Who asked you to? I didn't!

FRIEND: Out of friendship, I did it out of friendship.

HE: *(Rhetorically.)* "How many crimes have been committed in your name, "friendship"!

FRIEND: I care about you, about your future.

HE: I know. I promise you that you shall remain my administrator. *(Lifts his hand, ironically.)* I swear it! *(Seriously.)* Now talk.

FRIEND: Well…I took her best friend to bed. She told me everything.

HE: Ah.

(A brief silence.)

FRIEND: It's true she's rich, it's true she loves you.

HE: Thanks, I knew it.

FRIEND: She loves you intensely, she says.

HE: I know.

FRIEND: She also loved her husband intensely.

HE: I know.

FRIEND: That poor guy had an escapade. She destroyed him!

HE: *(Ironical.)* Ah yes, she castrated him? I didn't know that.

FRIEND: I didn't want to use that word. But it's practically true.

HE: Meaning?

FRIEND: The irony is that you've had hundreds of adventures. Therefore you are vulnerable.

HE: Meaning?

FRIEND: You could fall for it again.

HE: Make yourself clear.

FRIEND: After her, another woman. You have so many opportunities!

HE: Never again. The book is closed. She is my letter "Z." I'll never love anyone else.

FRIEND: You don't even know what love is. *(Correcting himself.)* I mean, until now.

HE: It's a good thing you corrected yourself.

FRIEND: Don't forget what Machiavelli said.

HE: What did he say?

FRIEND: "Who offends a woman, justly or no, in vain can hope by prayer or pleading her mercy to gain." She doesn't know how to forgive. She will destroy you if you look at another woman.

HE: She would be entitled to.

FRIEND: She's going to castrate you.

HE: She'd be entitled to.

(A short pause. The FRIEND is disconcerted by so much firmness and stares at him. He studies him.)

FRIEND: Do you know what she did to him?

HE: No. Tell me about it. Make up your mind.

FRIEND: First thing...she put a detective on his trail.

HE: She had a right to do that.

FRIEND: Then she went to the bank and withdrew all *their money.*

(A short silence. HE is impassible.)

FRIEND: All of it. All his money.

(A short silence. HE is impassible.)

FRIEND: They had a joint account.

HE: You know I don't like to talk about money.

FRIEND: Precisely. She is a terror. If you make a mistake, she cleans you out.

HE: This is what you're afraid of. To be cut out. You'll continue to administer my money, I repeat. It's a clear-cut promise. You know me.

FRIEND: I do not worry about that, I swear.

HE: *(Curious.)* What is it then?

FRIEND: Another thing...delicate, very personal...

HE: You started. Now finish.

FRIEND: You know she's very religious...

HE: I know. She can be what she wants. That's her business! Personal!

FRIEND: She even believes that souls exist and weigh twenty-seven grams.

HE: That's her business.

FRIEND: Listen to what she's arrived at...A very strange thing...

HE: Tell me.

FRIEND: Being religious...

HE: She kneels in church? So what?

FRIEND: She kneels! She kneels!

(HE stares at him with hostility. Now HE's very interested.)

FRIEND: I beg you...I'm telling you only because I'm your friend...to warn and prepare you...

HE: Prepare me.

FRIEND: *(Reluctant, cautious.)* Being very religious... *(Delay.)* she has a strange concept of obedience......out of respect for contracts...

HE: All right. Go on.

FRIEND: I don't know how to tell you... Her friend told me... *(Seeking for a lighter subject.)* But how come you haven't asked me how she is in bed?

HE: It doesn't interest me.

FRIEND: *(Falsely happy.)* She's magnificent! Really...

(No reaction; short pause.)

FRIEND: Well...your lady...has admitted to mine...that...she sleeps with her husband.

(They stare at each other.)

HE: "Sleeps"?

FRIEND: She admitted, candidly...Her friend asked her: "How do you do it? If you really love him, how can you do it in bed with someone else?"...Do you know what she answered? Listen to this; it's incredible. She said to her—verbatim—"I made a contract, in church. It wouldn't be right to take away from him what is due him. Until the final divorce decree, I 'lend' him my body, when he wants it; only my body. My soul belongs to the man I love."

(A silence. HE is petrified by this revelation. HE believes in what his FRIEND has told him. Blackout. Lights stage left. The two girlfriends. The GIRLFRIEND addresses her friend, who is reluctant and nervous; SHE wouldn't like to listen to her GIRLFRIEND; SHE would prefer to ignore her.)

GIRLFRIEND: ...There is something else...

SHE: *(Extremely nervous.)* What else? What you've been telling me until now, I knew. He told me himself. All of it.

GIRLFRIEND: *(With caution.)* Something new...very important...

SHE: *(Ironic, bitter.)* How much did it cost you the...detective?

GIRLFRIEND: A night of love.

SHE: Was it worthwhile?

GIRLFRIEND: For your good, only for your own good.

SHE: *(Ironical.)* How generous of you!

(A silence. They stare at each other.)

SHE: Go on.

GIRLFRIEND: It's something that will hurt you.

SHE: I'm used to being hurt.

GIRLFRIEND: Something that will really wound you.

SHE: I'm used to being wounded. By my husband.

GIRLFRIEND: Something you'd never imagine.

SHE: *(With irony; with fear.)* He's bisexual?

GIRLFRIEND: Oh no. He loves women. Too much.

SHE: I know.

GIRLFRIEND: He confessed to his best friend that he needs variety to excite him.

SHE: I will give him "variety."

GIRLFRIEND: Many women, other women.

SHE: He has promised that he has closed the book. I'm the last one. The letter "Z" of his life. "Z." He said it just like that.

GIRLFRIEND: Men promise and then...

SHE: He's different. Our love is different. He has sworn that he will keep this sacred promise. He said just like this: "sacred."

GIRLFRIEND: "Sacred"? He is not religious at all.

SHE: So what?

GIRLFRIEND: He's an atheist.

SHE: So what?

GIRLFRIEND: Sworn promises don't count for him. He never goes to church.

SHE: That's his business.

GIRLFRIEND: Never!

SHE: We've talked about it. There will be absolute respect for what he does; for what I do.

GIRLFRIEND: He's a liar.

SHE: He *was* a liar.

GIRLFRIEND: He still is.

(A silence. Tension.)

SHE: How do you know?

GIRLFRIEND: His friend told me.

SHE: He's jealous. Jealous of our great love.

GIRLFRIEND: *(Insisting.)* He's a liar.

(A silence. Tension. SHE is disturbed. SHE's afraid of details that could destroy her love.)

SHE: *(Seeking to justify.)* White lies, maybe...We all tell them.

GIRLFRIEND: A very big lie.

SHE: Is he married?

GIRLFRIEND: No.

SHE: Is he a thief?

GIRLFRIEND: No.

SHE: Is he an assassin?

GIRLFRIEND: No.

SHE: *(With irritation.)* Well then? I don't care about other things. I love him and that's all! He's mine! I adore him!

GIRLFRIEND: *(Insisting.)* He's a liar. He told you a very big lie.

(A pause. They stare at each other.)

GIRLFRIEND: To give you an example...He said white; but instead it's black.

(SHE, furious, slams the door and goes out. SHE doesn't want to know anything more. Blackout. Lights stage right. HE and SHE.)

HE: Ciao.

SHE: Ciao.

(They stare at each other. A silence. Tension. HE advances. They embrace. It's obvious, though, that they are both uncertain and upset.)

HE: What's the matter?...You look a bit sad...

SHE: *(Vaguely.)* No...

HE: Did you quarrel with your husband?

SHE: It's not something new. We quarrel all the time. Let's talk about your day.

HE: The usual. I answered a few letters. I wrote a couple of pages.

SHE: Let me read them.

HE: Later. Tell me. Why do you quarrel? About what subject?

SHE: About everything. Let me read your new pages. What are you writing about?

HE: Later. I promise we'll read them together. Tell me how you start a quarrel. Do you start it or does he?

SHE: Any excuse is good. You said that "We'll read them together." Did you write about us?

HE: About us. Give me an example of a quarrel. He comes home late and you...

SHE: He's always punctual. He is always around.

HE: He comes in and insults you.

SHE: No. He's very nice, lately. *(Avoiding.)* You've made me curious. Did you write about us as...lovers?

HE: About us. According to you, why is he so nice?

SHE: Maybe because he feels guilty. Tell me about us. Let's talk about us.

HE: First about him. He's trying to conquer you again.

SHE: Perhaps. He tries. He has repented.

HE: And you...You feel sorry for him...and you're ready to forgive him.

SHE: Never. *(She stares at him.)* I told you once before. A Taurus woman never forgives.

HE: It makes me happy to hear it... *(Studying her.)* Never forgives...Then you wouldn't allow him to kiss you...

SHE: No...For months my lips have kissed only you.

HE: But...since you still live together...

SHE: *(Interrupting.)* I'm waiting for the divorce decree in order to leave.

HE: *(Continuing.)* ...since you still live together...the contract is still valid...

SHE: What contract?

HE: The one that was signed in church.

(A silence. They stare at each other.)

SHE: We have decided that religious problems, our attitude with regard to religion, will never be an obstacle between us. We are free, both of us.

HE: Free to do what?

SHE: To go or not to go. To pray or not to pray.

HE: To kneel or not to kneel...

(A silence. They stare at each other.)

SHE: We had agreed. I go to church if I feel like it.

HE: We're not talking about religion. We're talking about contracts.

(A silence. They stare at each other.)

SHE: *(Slowly, cautiously.)* As a principle, I agree that contracts should be respected... *(Indicating him.)* Promise of love, is a contract.

HE: Signing in church is even more important and binding.

SHE: *(Vaguely.)* It is if...

HE: How do you behave if...your husband asks you to respect the contract?

SHE: I thought that it was understood that...we wouldn't talk about this.

HE: Why?

SHE: One doesn't talk about things that hurt.

HE: "Hurt" whom?

SHE: Me and you.

HE: I prefer to talk about it. What do you tell him when he asks you to respect the contract?

SHE: Strange...You are not religious. You behave like...a fanatic...This is an inquisition.

HE: So be it! Sometimes it's useful.

SHE: For what? To whom? To make us both suffer?

HE: Don't change the subject. What do you say to him? What do you do?

SHE: *(Avoiding a direct answer.)* Did you write this in those pages?

HE: That too.

SHE: Let me read them and then I'll answer.

(He gives her the two pages. She reads them carefully. Lifts her eyes and stares at him.)

HE: Well then?

SHE: *(Slowly.)* I always tell the truth. If you had asked me this question months ago, I would have answered.

HE: Answer now.

SHE: *(Slowly, with reluctance.)* For about one month after having known and loved you...it's true... *(Pointing to the pages.)* you've guessed...I respected that contract...only physically. I have...lent him my body, passively...It didn't seem right to take away from him what he had a right to...

HE: *(Furious.)* Right? What rights are you talking about? Only love has rights!

SHE: *(Shyly, trying to save the situation.)* Our love, today—

HE: *(Interrupting.)* Only the first month? Only the first thirty nights you let him f... *(He holds himself back; he doesn't dare to use that verb. Imperious, furious.)* Answer!

SHE: *(Perturbed, firm.)* I don't like the tone of your voice. I don't like your inquisition.

HE: I want to know.

SHE: Absolute sincerity then. Have you ever lied to me?

HE: *(Calming himself, uncertain.)* ...Trifles...small things...to your advantage...

SHE: For example?

HE: I ate two ice creams and I confessed only one...Or I bragged about having worked the whole day...Instead I also saw a movie—or two. Such things. Trivial sins.

SHE: Did you ever tell me a big basic, important lie?

HE: *(Vague, uncertain.)* Nothing that... would hurt you...nothing against you, to your disadvantage...

SHE: *(SHE has now understood that HE had lied to her and is hiding something basic; ready to go out.)* Tell me only this...Did you ever say—let's make a comparison—exactly the contrary of the truth? White instead of black?

HE: *(Shaken, uncertain.)* In a certain way...

SHE: *(Resolute.)* Yes or no?

HE: Will you allow me to explain?

SHE: *(Intransigent; she's ready to renounce their great love because he lied.)* Yes or no?

HE: Well...yes, but allow me to—

(SHE goes out, hurt, raging; slams the door.)

HE: *(Going toward the door now closed.)* It was for us, only for us, to seal our love... *(Almost to himself, defeated.)* To create a world of real happiness...clean, unspoiled by money...

(Blackout. Musical interlude to indicate the passing of time.)

SCENE III

Lights stage right. One spotlight that shines on him only. With bent head, HE is crying. Light enlarges to include also the GIRLFRIEND who is near him, with a sweet consoling expression.

GIRLFRIEND: *(Very sweetly.)* I have loved only once, in my life...Years ago...He took everything...I am poor now...But I have in my heart infinite richness to give to one man only, a poet who knows how to feel, how to suffer...

(HE lifts up his face and stares at her with a slight gleam of hope. Blackout. Musical interlude.)

SCENE IV

One spotlight that shines on her. Head bent, SHE is crying. The light enlarges to include also the FRIEND, who is standing beside her with a sweet consoling expression.

FRIEND: *(With sweetness, paternal.)* I am a good administrator...in twenty months I can triple any sum...

(SHE does not react.)

FRIEND: And I am loyal, very loyal...I have never told a lie in my entire life... NEVER!

(SHE lifts up her face and stares at him with a slight glimmer of hope. Maybe it is the beginning of two new love stories.)

(BLACKOUT. MUSICAL COMMENT. CURTAIN.)

Terrorist

The Characters:

ADRIANA: a mysterious woman; in her early thirties
RAUL: a South American writer in his early forties
THE MAN

A beautiful living room with bookshelves; a sofa; a table; two armchairs; two chairs. The front door is stage left. There are two windows stage right. A staircase goes up to the bedroom. ADRIANA enters through the window. She knows where the lights are and turns them on; she looks around; she checks different objects looking for possible microphones. She opens a drawer and takes out a gun; unloads it and puts the bullets in her bag. She puts the gun back in the drawer; dims the lights and turns on the radio. Soft music plays in the background. She waits. She hears the key in the lock. She turns off the radio. RAUL enters. He is a handsome man in his forties. He is surprised that the lights are on, but does not worry. He assumes he forgot to turn them off. He goes to the table and puts on it two books with some sheets of paper in them. He finally sees ADRIANA who nods to him warmly, smiling.

RAUL: Now I understand why the light's on...

ADRIANA: You have been forgetting to turn it off...So, I didn't turn it off...We can look at each other better this way...Don't worry...I am a friendly guest.

RAUL: Guest? How did you get in?

(She indicates the window.)

RAUL: My memory is fading...Leaving the lights on, the window wide open... *(He studies her.)* Anyhow, if you came in alone with no bodyguard... *(He looks around.)* I'm not afraid of a beautiful woman...But I am curious of course...Who are you? How come you are here? Have you been here before?

ADRIANA: A guest, a friend, an admirer...Is this the first time you find an admirer in your house?

RAUL: No...Once I found someone upstairs in my bedroom...

ADRIANA: Twice.

RAUL: How did you know? *(He studies her.)* You too? Were you part of the threesome that—?

ADRIANA: No. I wasn't part of that threesome.

RAUL: That was a night with two generous lovers...One looked a little bit like you. Are you sure you were not here before?

ADRIANA: Very sure.

RAUL: So, how do you know them?

ADRIANA: You writers, you tell everything. It was in your short story that the *New Yorker* published last January. Were their names really Betty and Louisa?

RAUL: No. I made those names up. To protect two daring women.

ADRIANA: But was it a true story?

RAUL: Almost. I only embellished some details.

ADRIANA: Which ones?

RAUL: The fact that it was a plot, a bet. That in reality two young women had bet that I wouldn't turn them down.

ADRIANA: It's well known that you like women, that you know how to make love.

RAUL: You don't really believe everything you read. Men often exaggerate.

ADRIANA: Not you. I've read all your books, your short stories, poetry, your very personal, intimate monologues. I know you don't lie and don't exaggerate.

RAUL: Sometimes I omit...In the case of that first woman—Betty, the little blonde...I didn't really want to make love to her. I threatened her with a gun...

(A silence.)

RAUL: I have a gun.

ADRIANA: I know.

RAUL: And I have used it.

ADRIANA: I'm not a blonde. *(Shows her beautiful black hair.)* You wouldn't use that weapon against me.

RAUL: Are you challenging me?

ADRIANA: Maybe...

RAUL: *(Slowly opens the drawer and takes the gun out.)* See? You could be the inspiration for a new novel...I shot a beautiful woman because...

ADRIANA: Because?

RAUL: ...Because I am a suspicious type...Who are you? Why are you here?

ADRIANA: Can I call you Raul?

RAUL: Why not? You are in my house.

ADRIANA: Raul...I'm here for a very simple reason. I saw you with beautiful women, I have read everything you have written...I am in love...It is a thrill to be here with a man like you. To talk, to discover—

RAUL: Discover what?

ADRIANA: In every conversation there are new answers...Maybe, maybe you'll tell me what you have never told anyone. New truths...

RAUL: Truths?

ADRIANA: Is it true that your family was very poor, that your father had to steal to feed your three sisters, that your mother committed suicide?

(A silence.)

RAUL: I never told anyone, I never wrote that I have three sisters. For personal reasons I have written only about two of them.

ADRIANA: I know why. The third one was not your father's child.

(A silence.)

RAUL: Where did you read that?

ADRIANA: Extensive research. With computers one can find out anything.

RAUL: *(Suspicious.)* Why did you do such in-depth research?

ADRIANA: An admirer doesn't limit herself to just reading someone's books. She wants to know the man behind the page. She wants to know, to tell herself if what she has intuited is accurate.

RAUL: What did you "intuit," as you put it?

ADRIANA: That behind your serene exterior you are tormented.

RAUL: *(Studying her.)* What do you want from me? Who sent you? *(Plays with the gun, pointing at her now and then.)*

ADRIANA: No one. Just curious. I just wanted to talk to you, to know a famous writer a little better.

RAUL: Famous? I've only had three books published here in the USA.

ADRIANA: And fourteen short stories.

RAUL: Do you have all of them? I've found only the ones I remember—twelve.

ADRIANA: I have all of them.

RAUL: Good. You're growing on me. Do you really have all of them?

ADRIANA: All of them.

RAUL: If I asked you, would you be ready to—?

ADRIANA: I am. I'm ready for anything.

RAUL: An attractive offer…You could be useful.

ADRIANA: That's not a nice adjective. I don't want to be "useful." I want to be respected and loved for who I am, not for what I can tell you, give you…

RAUL: *(Studying her.)* Maybe, just maybe there is already a woman in my life and I am a faithful lover…

ADRIANA: Faithful?

RAUL: Now I am, maybe…

ADRIANA: Maybe?

RAUL: One woman at a time. I'm intimate with a new woman, only one.

ADRIANA: You were with Elena this evening. You didn't bring her back here.

RAUL: *(Surprised.)* She chose to go to her house, her bed.

ADRIANA: That is not true. You haven't slept with her for three weeks. You talk to her in the restaurant, you caress her hand, but you don't want her. You are tired of her.

RAUL: *(Very surprised.)* Three weeks, the hand I caressed in the restaurant…You know too much. How is that possible? Are you stalking me? Are you a spy? Sent by whom? There was a time, long ago… *(He hesitates.)*

ADRIANA: Long ago?

RAUL: I used to be involved in politics. They threatened me…Who is paying you to spy on me now?

ADRIANA: No one. You said you were involved in politics. On the right, or on the left?

RAUL: If you have read my books, you should know…

ADRIANA: It's true. Most of your characters are…progressive.

RAUL: I was a member of the Communist Party, in Chile. I never denied that.

ADRIANA: You left them in 1989.

(A silence.)

RAUL: You know too much. Show me what's in your handbag or…I'll shoot you. *(Jiggles the gun.)*

ADRIANA: So shoot me. It will be a new emotion. I love new emotions.

RAUL: Give me your handbag.

ADRIANA: No.

RAUL: Look now…I can shoot you legally…I have a gun permit…you broke in. It would be self-defense. Give me your bag.

ADRIANA: No.

RAUL: I'll count up to three and then...*one...two...three...*

(He shoots away from her face; he just wants to scare her; the gun misfires; RAUL is surprised.)

ADRIANA: You see? You gave me a new emotion. A brute who is ready to kill to get what he wants. Here is my bag.

(Hands it to him.)

RAUL: *(Checking the contents.)* Money...driver's license... *(Looks at her.)* it's you. You are less beautiful in this photo. You look older.

ADRIANA: Thanks for the compliment.

RAUL: *(Very surprised.)* Bullets? Are they mine? Are they from my gun?

ADRIANA: Just like in your TV movie: "Terrorist." You see? I copy, too. I stole your idea.

RAUL: That's why you were not afraid! Your "new emotions" were just a story.

ADRIANA: I imitate your style, copying the best.

RAUL: Are you accusing me of plagiarism? Me? I'm one hundred percent original.

ADRIANA: I know. That's why I'm here. You are a great writer. Beautiful descriptions, always. There is love in you.

RAUL: *(Finds a notebook in her bag.)* Stationery from the university? You stole this too?

ADRIANA: Stole?

RAUL: Bullets, a notebook, packets of sugar...they usually come from restaurants...

ADRIANA: No. I brought those from home.

RAUL: Why?

ADRIANA: Because I know you never use sugar. So...

RAUL: So?

ADRIANA: I use sugar, if you decide to make me some tea...I come prepared...Four packets; two per cup. I use two packets.

RAUL: Two? There are four here.

ADRIANA: One before, one after. I love tea.

RAUL: *(While reloading his gun with the bullets he found in her bag.)* So, you're not a thief.

ADRIANA: I'm not.

RAUL: But you came in through the window...

ADRIANA: Out of love.

RAUL: Like in my short story... *(Invites her to say the title.)*

ADRIANA: Too easy. "Windows"

RAUL: And what's the name of my protagonist where a lawyer—I'm not a lawyer—says she's afraid of getting diabetes?

ADRIANA: That was Sara, in "The Snake."

RAUL: Do you feel like a snake, here, today?

ADRIANA: Whatever you want. For you I can be a serpent, a panther, a gazelle, a loving mother.

RAUL: "Mother"?

ADRIANA: You wrote that too. "Every lover is also a mother and a sister."

RAUL: I wrote that in...?

ADRIANA: Three different stories.

RAUL: Are you suggesting I repeat myself?

ADRIANA: With style. You repeat yourself, sometimes, to reinforce your idea.

RAUL: But it's still a repetition. You noticed it.

ADRIANA: Only because I have read every word you've ever written.

(A brief pause.)

RAUL: The notebook from the university. Why is it here in your bag?

ADRIANA: I teach there.

RAUL: What do you teach?

ADRIANA: Spanish.

RAUL: Mi primer idioma.

ADRIANA: Yes. Your beautiful language.

RAUL: That's why you read my first writings...

ADRIANA: In Spanish.

RAUL: Where did you find them?

ADRIANA: In "Hispanamerica" magazine.

RAUL: Do you have a copy?

ADRIANA: I have all of them. The ones with your stories.

RAUL: That's good news. Great! You're going to be amazingly useful. I'm trying to organize all my papers and... *(Suddenly suspicious.)* Why didn't you call ahead? Or knock at my door? Why didn't you contact me like a normal person?

ADRIANA: I wanted...an adventure, a new experience, new emotions.

RAUL: Like the one with my gun? You could have gotten yourself killed.

ADRIANA: You didn't fire at me. Like in "Gloria."

RAUL: Published in...?

ADRIANA: "Hoy." The Spanish magazine.

RAUL: Do you want to be a victim, like Gloria?

ADRIANA: I know very well how that story ends. After a great deal of fear, the abductions, handcuffs, *(She offers her wrists.)* everything ends in passion and abandon.

(RAUL ignores the offer of her wrists.)

ADRIANA: Do you have handcuffs in your bedroom?

RAUL: Maybe...So you came here to become a..."protagonist"?

ADRIANA: I am, in real life. I wanted to be one with you.

RAUL: A part of one of my stories?

ADRIANA: With joy...I want to know more, live more intensely...To become eternal, in your writing.

RAUL: One night of love and then...?

ADRIANA: One always hopes...

RAUL: For what?

ADRIANA: An invitation to come back. *(She indicates the door.)*

RAUL: You took a big risk, not using the door.

ADRIANA: All your women take risks. They never have regrets. It's worth it. There is a book I have read fifty times.

RAUL: *(Curious.)* Which one?

ADRIANA: *Love in the Time of Cholera.* In Spanish and in English.

RAUL: Gabriel Garcia Marquez...We all tried to imitate him. He is unequaled, incomparable.

ADRIANA: Thanks to him, I discovered Latin American literature—with all its passions, hopes, revolutions. That's how I discovered you, too.

RAUL: He's a giant. I'm nothing in comparison.

ADRIANA: You are simply much younger; you have a brilliant future.

RAUL: He's the one who deserves love and admiration.

ADRIANA: He was born in 1928. A long time ago. Old ideas, old traditions. You, you are young. You'll be thirty-seven tomorrow morning.

RAUL: Tomorrow... You know that too.

ADRIANA: I was afraid you'd come back home with Elena...

(RAUL studies her.)

ADRIANA: In "La Petite Morte" you write that you must, you have to make love to someone on your birthday. To feel young.

RAUL: *(Perplexed.)* I don't...I still don't understand how...It seems impossible to me that...a beautiful woman who has read Marquez, who knows so much about me—

ADRIANA: Everything.

RAUL: Nobody knows everything.

ADRIANA: I know your fears, your doctors...

RAUL: What doctors?

ADRIANA: Three. Even the last one.

RAUL: What last one?

ADRIANA: Gottfried. Why do you need a psychoanalyst? You are so anchored in your stories. You know what you want in life. You give wise advice. In your film "Terrorist" you encourage Raul—you used your name for the protagonist; you make him strong; he resists and defies the torturers.

RAUL: It's easy writing, describing, but one always has doubts...

ADRIANA: Like what?

RAUL: The future...

ADRIANA: You explained to Raul, clearly, that after you die, there is only a memory of you, your life, of how you behaved. One only lives in the memory of those who respect and admire you. Or in the memory of those who tortured you to death.

RAUL: *(Who is trying to understand the real reason why Adriana knows so many details.)* Who is my closest friend?

ADRIANA: You have many.

RAUL: What about my first one, when I was a boy?

ADRIANA: Pedro.

RAUL: My dog's name?

ADRIANA: You called him "Fidel."

RAUL: My first girlfriend?

ADRIANA: That's an easy one. You describe her in your first novel. "Lucia."

RAUL: My favorite city?

ADRIANA: Aracataca. You spent three months there, in Marquez's village to discover his secrets.

RAUL: Do I take any pills? I've never mentioned that in my work.

ADRIANA: Tenormin, Lipitor, Cardura.

RAUL: How do you know that?

ADRIANA: I happen to use the same drugstore. The pharmacist there is another admirer of yours.

RAUL: And he told you what I take? I'll report him.

ADRIANA: No, please. I promised him I wouldn't tell you about this...he was very reluctant. I flirted with him. A woman knows how to give hope, a bit of hope. And the man does what she wants him to do.

RAUL: *(Ironical.)* Ah yes—that's what you think!

ADRIANA: I was talking about the pharmacist, only about him.

RAUL: *(After a brief pause.)* Who was I seeing before Elena?

ADRIANA: Angela for three months. You left her because she would wake you up early, caressing you and asking for…more. I wouldn't do that. I'll let you sleep.

RAUL: How can you know these details? Do you know Angela? She told you this? Did she send you here?

ADRIANA: I don't know Angela. No one sent me.

RAUL: But how can you know such intimate details?

ADRIANA: I have a confession to make…

RAUL: Finally!

ADRIANA: What's that proverb? When you love someone, you love everything about him…you want to know everything…Well…

RAUL: Well?

ADRIANA: I have a cousin. I'll introduce him to you. He's a computer wiz. He knows everything about cameras, binoculars, all modern gadgets. He helps me.

RAUL: Why?

ADRIANA: He knows I'm completely in love with you, and he wants to help me.

RAUL: To go to bed with a stranger?

ADRIANA: You're not a stranger. He too admires you. He's a big fan.

RAUL: Has he read my books?

ADRIANA: *(Hesitating.)* I must tell you the truth…I don't think he has read everything you wrote, but we watched your TV film "Terrorist" together.

RAUL: Everyone must have seen it. What's ironic is that I am lucky if I sell five thousand copies of my book. A made-for-TV movie is seen by ten million people.

ADRIANA: They showed it three times. Raul is a wonderful character. It is you, isn't it? Do you identify with him?

RAUL: There's always a little bit of ourselves in our characters.

ADRIANA: He too is a member of a political party…He too wants to change the world…He too talks about justice…He too condemns the rich for their greed…He too quotes Che Guevara…Could you endure the torture he went through? What they did to him?

RAUL: No.

ADRIANA: Are you sure?

RAUL: Not today, not anymore. He was twenty-two when they killed him…maybe at that age I could have had his courage…not anymore today.

ADRIANA: Because you are now rich and successful?

RAUL: Not for that reason.

ADRIANA: Because you changed your political ideas?

RAUL: No…Because I'm physically a coward. At my age, you tell all, you buckle under that kind of torture…

(A silence; ADRIANA studies him.)

RAUL: You've made me confess everything; even that I am a coward. I never told anyone.

ADRIANA: Not even your psychoanalyst?

RAUL: Not even him. That guy is only interested in sex. How, when, where? He says he can understand me better if he knows how I love, how I prefer to make love. All about my sex life, that's what he wants to know. *(A brief pause.)* How did you know about the woman who awoke me in the morning?

ADRIANA: Like I said, my cousin is a genius with the Internet, web, cameras, microphones. He was practically in the house. He sees everything you do.

RAUL: I'll call the police.

ADRIANA: It's all legal. A woman in love can do anything to conquer her love. No judge would convict me. *(A brief pause.)* It's almost midnight. Let's celebrate your birthday. I'll call him tomorrow morning. He'll come here and apologize. We'll become friends. He promised me he'll never do it again. No more microphones. Out of respect for me.

RAUL: For you?

ADRIANA: Respect for us, our...privacy. He wants me to be happy, I'm sure of that...

(They look at each other; they study each other; she shows admiration and desire.)

RAUL: After reading Gabriel Garcia Marquez fifty times, how can you be in love with me?

ADRIANA: I know you...I breathe the same air you do, I am close to you in restaurants, theatres, at a concert.

RAUL: And I never noticed you!

ADRIANA: Unfortunately not, but I love your voice, the warmth with which you speak, the way you say: "Not today, maybe tomorrow…"

RAUL: You have to be human and gentle, that's what I try to be.

ADRIANA: I know. You don't know how to hurt people. You respect women. Your descriptions of them are different...you show respect...

RAUL: So does Marquez.

ADRIANA: No. Here is an example. He describes the widow Nazareth as a "wild mare" choking on her own feverish desire. He uses her and then he shows his contempt when she talks in bed, in her sleep, and reveals she had many lovers.

RAUL: What about his touching love for Fermina?

ADRIANA: He says he loves her while he's fucking other women. He makes a list in his diary. Six hundred twenty-two entries of long-term liaisons plus a few quickies. He calls them "fleeting adventures."

RAUL: He describes his women as beautiful and powerful.

ADRIANA: Yes, they are all fat, with "huge bosoms." And they must always wait for him "stark naked."

RAUL: He loves female beauty.

ADRIANA: He never describes how he caresses the body of a woman. He only says... *(Tries to remember the exact words.)* "she looked like she could be as ferocious as an alligator; that she could eat you alive." What kind of respect is that? It's an indictment. Basic contempt for a woman's desire.

RAUL: What about Ausencia? He loves her for seven long years.

ADRIANA: Love? He fucks her only when he feels like it. He goes to her house only when he needs her, and he wants her to be passive and ready. She must wait for him. Stark naked. He wants his women nude. Like in a parade of prostitutes.

RAUL: He describes Leona Cassiani beautifully. And he didn't sleep with her. I got excited just reading his description of her florid, dark-skinned body.

ADRIANA: He doesn't sleep with her because he was afraid his uncle would fire him. And when he writes that he prefers to screw young women pressing on their bodies until their bones crack? That's contempt, hatred, desire to exploit and torture.

RAUL: You said you read that book fifty times. Why?

ADRIANA: To learn. To understand better how men see us. Florentino swears eternal love for Fermina and uses, exploits, rapes dozens of women. It is a fascinating book that teaches a great deal. He writes on Olympia's pubes: "This pussy is mine." And does not feel remorse when her husband finds that writing and cuts her throat. He is cruel and insensitive.

RAUL: You are exaggerating. Sara, the poetess, tells him: "Love is everything we do naked; looking into each other's eyes, reading poems."

ADRIANA: And then he says she has to suck an infant's pacifier when they make love. Just like a retarded little girl. Do you call that respect?

RAUL: It is a touching detail. A very sexy description. And he shows love when he describes her perfume, her immense colossal breasts, a soprano's bosom. There is love and admiration in that description.

ADRIANA: And then he ignores her when she ends up in a loony bin. There is no remorse in Marquez. He seems to feel relieved when the husband kills his wife, when he gets rid of a crazy woman. He feels free to go to another woman, another lover. You, on the contrary...

RAUL: Me?

ADRIANA: In "Nights of Moon" there are six pages in which you admire Gala's body. You don't rush. You admire, adore, caress...A sensitive experienced lover. I read and reread those pages...

RAUL: Fifty times?

ADRIANA: Maybe...Often...When... *(She hesitates.)*

RAUL: When?

ADRIANA: When I felt desire, desire of you...

RAUL: And after reading them?

ADRIANA: You can guess. You describe it in "A Woman Alone." She's alone, first timidly, then frenetically, until she has her explosive orgasm.

RAUL: Alone...

ADRIANA: I'm ready to relive and let you relive that experience...

RAUL: That one too?

ADRIANA: With you there, yes. Alone, open, excited, waiting for a real man... You, the man I adore...

(A silence; Raul studies her with interest.)

RAUL: Do you remember what Linda did in "Holidays"?

ADRIANA: Of course!

(She gets up and starts a sexy striptease; she lets shoes, stockings, skirt, most of her clothes drop while she walks upstairs, to the bedroom; RAUL follows her with admiration,

excited. Before he goes upstairs, we see a MAN's face at the window. When RAUL disappears upstairs, THE MAN enters through the window; he looks around; he unscrews the heel of ADRIANA's right shoe and takes out a very small microphone; then he takes the pages that RAUL had in the books he put on the table at the beginning of the scene and pockets them. He places a small gun in ADRIANA's bag; looks around, again, to check if everything is in order. He unplugs the phone and turns off the light. He exits through the door.)

———

(The following morning. RAUL comes downstairs and gathers ADRIANA's clothes. He puts them on a chair; he picks up her shoes. The heel of the right shoe is loose and comes off. He is surprised and examines the shoe. He tries to unscrew the heel of the left shoe. He cannot. He notices that the inside of the heel in his hand is empty. He sniffs it. He becomes suspicious; goes toward the table where his books are. He looks for the pages that were in his books. He cannot find them. He is more and more suspicious. ADRIANA, sleepy, tired, and happy, comes down the stairs slowly; she is sensual and feline. She is still wearing the handcuffs of the preceding night.)

ADRIANA: Happy Birthday, love...Did you sleep well? (She sits down.)

RAUL: I did.

ADRIANA: Me too...Thanks, my love... You are wonderful... (Shows the handcuffs.) Do you still want me like this? Am I still your prisoner?

RAUL: They suit you.

ADRIANA: I'll stay like this, then...I like feeling tied up...Being a victim, your victim...I didn't wake you up at five o'clock. Maybe, maybe, you want to show me your gratitude...

(Stares at his crotch, opens her mouth; he accepts the invitation. Standing up, unseen to the audience, he penetrates her mouth. There is violence and anger in him. Oral sex. He is very suspicious and wants to punish her.)

ADRIANA (Speaking with difficulty.) Honey, honey, my love...I almost couldn't breathe...take off these handcuffs, please...

RAUL: No.

ADRIANA: Please...You can put them back on, later...

RAUL: No. I want some explanation... (Shows the heel of the shoe.) It is empty...Only this one...why?

ADRIANA: How should I know? Maybe the shoe is defective...

RAUL: Maybe, in the past, you have used them to spy on someone...There is room in here for a microphone.

ADRIANA: You have imagination.

RAUL: You too. Explain all this.

ADRIANA: Explain what? Please take off the handcuffs.

RAUL: Later... (He studies her.) Have you ever worked for the government?

ADRIANA: No.

RAUL: For a political party, maybe...?

ADRIANA: No.

RAUL: The CIA or FBI?

ADRIANA: No.

RAUL: I had three sheets of paper here... (Indicates the books.) Where are they?

ADRIANA: How should I know? Maybe you lost them...

RAUL: You being here, your visit, begins to feel more and more suspicious...

ADRIANA: You call this a visit? It's an offer of love. I love you, I adore you! And I proved it to you.

RAUL: Do you remember the torture in "Terrorist"? My descriptions are so good because I write from experience...

ADRIANA: So, what are you trying to say?

RAUL: I am familiar with those methods. I was a victim of them...I could apply that torture...I want the truth.

ADRIANA: What truth?

RAUL: Who you are, why you are here, who sent you...

ADRIANA: I told you. I love you, I've read all your books, I admire you...Love and admiration and I proved to you how much I love you...

RAUL: Thank you! But a good spy, at the service of the powerful, dedicated to her job, knows how to pretend that she is in love.

ADRIANA: Did it seem to you I was faking it?

RAUL: To get something, some information or—

ADRIANA: *(Interrupting.)* No, absolutely not. It is only love and desire. Why don't you believe me?

RAUL: Tell me the truth and I'll help you. I'll cooperate with whomever is paying you. Everything I know is for sale, at your disposal!

(A silence.)

ADRIANA: My admiration, my love, my passion are true, real, deeply felt.

RAUL: I don't believe you. By now it's clear, very clear, that you're working for someone. Who?

ADRIANA: No one.

RAUL: Right or left?

ADRIANA: What do you mean? Those are expressions that have lost all their significance.

RAUL: You are wrong. They are still very valid and real today. You either work for the right—Washington—or for the left—Cuba.

ADRIANA: Cuba? Little Cuba? They have no power at all.

RAUL: You are wrong. There is always the possibility of blackmailing me for my history with the Communists.

ADRIANA: That's all in the past. If it's really in the past, they cannot use it. They don't need you.

(A brief silence.)

RAUL: They tried, a long time ago.

ADRIANA: What did they try?

RAUL: A beautiful Cuban woman wanted to invite me to that island. To use my name, my past as a comrade committed to the Socialist dream...You could be the second one. You speak Spanish.

ADRIANA: I assure you. I'm not Cuban. I was never in Cuba. I don't share their opinions, their tactics, their dreams.

RAUL: What about Washington? What do they want from me?

ADRIANA: I don't know. I'm only a woman who admires you and is in love with you. Please take the handcuffs off.

RAUL: No.

ADRIANA: I feel like a prisoner.

RAUL: Good. You are my prisoner. You liked it before. You asked for those handcuffs.

ADRIANA: Yes, as a love game. Now you seem like an enemy. My enemy...You are changing, you are suspicious and hostile...

RAUL: Yes, I am suspicious. I keep you here—handcuffed—my prisoner, until you confess...Maybe, maybe you just feel it's your duty to be a good soldier.

ADRIANA: Soldier? Me?

RAUL: Maybe you are just a good, obedient employee...They told you: "Go to his house, make the sacrifice of fucking him, and—"

ADRIANA: A sacrifice? Oh no, my love!

RAUL: One pretends well when one has a mission. Maybe you just feel this is your mission.

ADRIANA: A mission of love. I didn't pretend, you felt my passion, you know it. True love, true desire.

RAUL: Maybe you are just a zealous patriot, serving your country, your flag, Washington. What do they want from me? Why did they send you here?

(A silence.)

ADRIANA: If you take them off... *(She hesitates.)*

RAUL: If I take them off...?

ADRIANA: I'll tell you...

RAUL: What?

ADRIANA: What you asked me. *(She offers her hands to be freed.)*

RAUL: No. You must tell me first. You must confess.

ADRIANA: I swear, I'm in love with you. I was sincere, I am sincere. You made me feel like a real woman. You made me happy.

RAUL: *(Ironical.)* Good, very good, I believe you. Let's end this farce. Who sent you?

ADRIANA: No one. I... *(Hesitates.)*

RAUL: I'm sure someone did. What do they want to know? Ask me. I'll tell you openly, clearly. I have nothing to hide...Unlike you. Confess!

ADRIANA: What do I have to confess? Love? Admiration? My desire for you?

RAUL: The purpose of your visit. Why you came here. The sacrifice you made to come to my bed. You are a wonderful actress. Where did you study acting?

ADRIANA: Bank Street, near your favorite restaurant.

RAUL: You know that too. You have followed me, spied on me. Who is paying you?

ADRIANA: The university, only the university. That's my only salary.

RAUL: *(With irony.)* And they underpay you, you poor thing, I know. But you have the money for expensive clothes, shoes with special heels so that you can broadcast messages...To whom? Have they followed our whole conversation? Did they also hear your false moans of love?

ADRIANA: True, true! You gave me pleasure, orgasms. You are wonderful!

RAUL: That's enough with the compliments. Who pays you?

ADRIANA: No one, no one...

RAUL: *(Lights a cigarette and approaches her menacingly.)* Do you remember "Terrorist"? How they tortured me with cigarettes?

ADRIANA: Tortured? You?

RAUL: Raul.

ADRIANA: So you are Raul.

RAUL: I identify with him. All writers identify with their characters...If you don't talk I'll burn your nipples...

(He opens her blouse; her breasts are now exposed; he admires them; she studies him trying to hide her fear.)

RAUL: It is such a shame to burn them, to disfigure them...They are too beautiful...But all is fair in war...this is a war, isn't it?

ADRIANA: No, I beg you...Please! Kiss them, suck them like before, last night. They are so sensitive. They excite me. I'm all wet down there where you enjoyed our "tropical paradise"...

(RAUL keeps admiring her body.)

ADRIANA: Kiss me, kiss me, I love you!

RAUL: No. This is war. Washington against...me, an innocent, quiet writer who made the mistake of writing a TV drama..."Terrorist." They all saw it. Maybe they thought the author and the protagonist are the same person. Could he resist if we put him among the Guantanamo prisoners? He would. Torture doesn't work with him. A beautiful pussy will...Raul loves beautiful women and would like to adore them, to fuck them all...You, on the contrary, force me to burn you. First here, and then in the "rosy tunnel of your soul"...

(A brief pause.)

ADRIANA: What's happened? I see a monster in you...

RAUL: We all have a devil in us.

ADRIANA: You, you are revealing it...

(He comes closer to the nipples with his cigarette.)

ADRIANA: No, no, no! I'll tell you.

RAUL: *(Stopping.)* Tell me.

(A silence.)

ADRIANA: It is true that your TV film aroused curiosity...

RAUL: In whom?

ADRIANA: Everyone in my office...We shared comments.

RAUL: "We"? Who is "we"?

ADRIANA: There are also two Cuban professors in my university...

RAUL: So what?

ADRIANA: Anti-Communists, of course... They made a bet.

RAUL: A bet?

ADRIANA: A challenge...They know I adore your novels...

RAUL: So?

ADRIANA: They challenged me...

RAUL: To do what?

ADRIANA: To seduce you...But I swear it is a challenge I accepted with joy...Love is what drives me to you, into your arms; not the challenge; not the money...

RAUL: Money? They offered you money for this? They are treating you like a whore...What's your price? What are you worth to them?

ADRIANA: Ten thousand...

RAUL: You're worth more, I assure you. That's not a compliment. You are great, wonderful. Unforgettable...As a lover and as a...victim that I am forced to torture...How can I forget you? Indelible in my memory...Those two friends of the dictator Batista...Do you really believe they offered you ten thousand dollars? Are you kidding?

ADRIANA: Ten thousand, yes.

RAUL: Their own money? On professors' salaries? You believe that? Did you think it over?

(She thinks; she's confused and fearful.)

RAUL: That money, if it's true it was offered, it comes from Washington... *(Stares at her, studying her.)* Ten thousand...just to seduce me?

ADRIANA: No...I win...I get the money only if I can get you to admit that you are still a Communist and that you work for Castro.

RAUL: I'll be happy to say this on TV. In front of everyone. For free. I am not a Communist, I do not work, spy for Castro, as one of his friends...Satisfied? Did you tape that? Do you have extra microphones on you? Where? In your adorable, tender ass?

ADRIANA: No, I swear...

RAUL: You are an intelligent woman. Do you really believe that two underpaid Cuban professors hand over their own money to you, for a political confession that is futile, absolutely useless?

(A silence, looks at her intensely.)

RAUL: There's something else going on...What do you think, you intelligent woman, beautiful and sweet in the art of making love?

ADRIANA: *(Reflecting.)* Maybe...Now that I think about it...Maybe it's true they are paid by someone in Washington...but just think, Raul...The other side of this story...our love.

RAUL: "Love"?

ADRIANA: Yes, yes. Whatever the motivation, whatever started this stupid bet, there is...What's the saying? "Every cloud has a silver lining." The flip side of the coin is that I love you, I adore you.

RAUL: *(Vaguely ironical.)* You can make anything romantic.

ADRIANA: Even this stupid political situation.

RAUL: "Political"? You're admitting it.

ADRIANA: I admit it. Politics ruins everything. But in this exceptional case, it brought me joy, happiness, the joy of being with you, to be caressed and loved by you...Kiss me, kiss my breasts. They are waiting for your kisses, they desire you. You began like this last night. Like all the glutton children who love their memory of the mother's nipples...

RAUL: I'll kiss them with pleasure, again, if you tell me the truth.

ADRIANA: I told you, I told you everything I know. Point by point. Your TV play, the comments at the university, and the idea, the offer of this challenge.

RAUL: There is something else. I'm not naïve like you. You don't just give away ten thousand dollars for the satisfaction of hearing what they already know. What I've already confirmed one hundred times...

(A silence; he stares at her.)

RAUL: They want something else...What do they want, these people who are using the Cubans as an excuse, an alibi?

ADRIANA: It's possible that there is someone who is pushing them, using them...But me, what's my guilt in this? I was asked to love you and—

RAUL: *(Interrupting her.)* —To trap me.

ADRIANA: A golden trap. I'm happy. The happiest, most satisfied woman in the world. If I die today... *(She regrets saying this in her dangerous situation.)*

RAUL: Yes...Today, maybe...You broke into my house, you threatened me...

(*Shows the gun he took from ADRIANA at the beginning.*) I had to defend myself. Self-defense—acquitted!

ADRIANA: They have...they have that tape... (*Indicates her shoe.*) Seduction, compliments, desires...I never threatened you.

RAUL: You are admitting the tape in that shoe...

ADRIANA: I'll admit to anything you want...

RAUL: Good, good...You knew they had been recording all our words, everything we said. You knew you were lying to me...

ADRIANA: No, no! I've been sincere. Every word, every caress!

RAUL: But you didn't ask me that well-known question: "Are you or have you ever been a member of the Communist Party?" You would have won the bet after that question...Why didn't you ask me? What were you waiting for?

ADRIANA: They were not clear with me, they confused me...

RAUL: You, confused?

ADRIANA: They didn't tell me to ask you that question...

RAUL: Wasn't that understood?

ADRIANA: I told them in advance. I told them: "Raul is a writer, a wonderful writer. A man of letters who is not interested in politics."

RAUL: And they insisted with the ten thousand! (*Ironical.*) How generous of them!

ADRIANA: Who understands the Cubans! Those two hate Castro and they'll try anything to get rid of him! Maybe... (*She hesitates.*)

RAUL: Maybe?

ADRIANA: I had a thought...just a passing thought...

RAUL: Which one? Tell me.

ADRIANA: I thought for a moment that they wanted to recruit you...It would be easy for you to approach Castro and...

RAUL: And?

ADRIANA: ...And do something to him.

RAUL: Really? They must think I'm really good...All right. This game is over! Stop all these ridiculous little stories. (*Threatening.*) Now, now it's time to say goodbye to your throbbing clit... (*He threatens her with his lit cigarette very close to her body.*)

ADRIANA: No, no, no! I'll tell you everything.

RAUL: I'm listening.

ADRIANA: (*Feeling still threatened by the cigarette.*) They are looking...looking for a list of your friends...

RAUL: What friends?

ADRIANA: All of them.

RAUL: I don't have many.

ADRIANA: One is an Egyptian...

(*A pause.*)

RAUL: So what? Why do they need that list, that name?

ADRIANA: They suspect that...

RAUL: That...?

ADRIANA: What do I know, poor little me!

RAUL: Open your knees. (*Tries to open them.*)

ADRIANA: (*Desperate.*) No, no!

RAUL: *(Forcing them open; keeps them open.)* The breasts, no, too beautiful. It would be a crime to disfigure them...

ADRIANA: You are a monster!

RAUL: Better down here...adding fire to the fire...Keep these tender thighs open...Show me that pink wound I want to see, to admire, and then destroy...That intimate nest of your passion—

ADRIANA: Our passion, our passion! Please, my love. You are the man for me. Perfect harmony! In me, in that secret me, that intimacy that you described so tenderly! I love you!

RAUL: What do they want from the Egyptian?

ADRIANA: They don't tell me anything. I suppose they want to know where he is.

RAUL: Why?

ADRIANA: They suspect, maybe, that he was part of the 9/11 plot, the Twin Towers. They told me nothing else.

RAUL: But they told you his name, didn't they?

ADRIANA: Yes—a very complicated name. I wrote it somewhere.

RAUL: I have many Egyptian friends. They all dream of democracy and justice.

Which one are they looking for? *(He moves his cigarette toward ADRIANA's pubis.)*

ADRIANA: No, no! You are not a monster! Only a monster could...

RAUL: Only a monster like you could betray a man the way you betrayed me. You are the terrorist, a woman at the service of evil...Monster against monster. You must pay now. You must feel pain where you felt pleasure, without deserving it because you were lying...

(He is about to burn her. There is a sudden noise near the window. RAUL stops. Gets up and puts his cigarette in the ashtray. He goes to the window. ADRIANA takes advantage of his distraction; she takes her small gun from her bag; shoots and kills RAUL. The mystery MAN comes through the window.)

ADRIANA: *(Offering her hands to be freed from the handcuffs.)* Thank you, thank you for putting the gun in my bag! It's him, it's him! He's the terrorist you are looking for! He confessed it, he confessed a plot with his Egyptian friends...

(A short pause.)

ADRIANA: The handcuffs, please...

(THE MAN ignores her. He takes the gun and erases her fingerprints. He shoots her. It's better not to have dangerous witnesses.)

(FREEZE. END OF THE DRAMA.)

Wars
Three Plays

THE RETURN [from a concentration camp]
THE SEVENTY-FIFTH [Vietnam]
IRAQ (BLINDNESS)

The Return

Characters:

SYLVIA: the fiancée; in her thirties—reserved and soft-spoken; she is resigned and gentle

MASO: the friend: in his late thirties—pale, sensitive, he gives the impression he is hiding from something; he has a nervous way of speaking—quickly

THE MOTHER: in her late fifties; thin, frail; her eyes are sad but her smile is that of a child; she moves with grace

THE ESCORT: same age as Maso but he seems at least ten years older; mature, tall, a man of integrity; reserved and dignified

THE SISTER'S VOICE

At rise: A dimly lit room with a lighted hallway at the rear. There is a door stage right, and next to it a window which faces a small but typical town piazza. On the windowsill there are several flowering plants. One can distinguish an old cupboard; a table with freshly cut flowers, toys, and notebooks; two chairs with jackets hanging on the backs. The fiancée, SYLVIA, is seated at stage left, embroidering her wedding dress. After a few moments we see MASO's face outside, nervously looking into the room.

MASO: *(Unable to see clearly.)* Sylvia, are you there?

SYLVIA: Be careful with the flowers.

MASO: What are you doing in the dark?

SYLVIA: I'm embroidering. Be quiet. She's in the next room.

MASO: May I come in?

SYLVIA: You'd better not. You'll ruin the plants.

MASO: Just for a moment. Then we'll go.

SYLVIA: Not today. You know who's returning.

MASO: More reason to get out. There'll be tears, scenes. Let me in.

(SYLVIA does not move.)

MASO: If you don't open the door, I'll come through the window.

(He threatens to ruin the plants. SYLVIA gets up wearily and opens the door: MASO enters the room. He is nervous and throughout the play he will smoke continually.)

MASO: *(Trying to kiss her.)* Please, just one small kiss...

(SHE tries to avoid him.)

MASO: What's wrong with you?

SYLVIA: *(Trying to avoid him.)* Not today. Please don't.

MASO: *(Glancing around the room.)* All these flowers—this darkness...It's depressing. *(Indicating the lighted hallway.)* Is she in there?

(SYLVIA nods.)

MASO: I'll turn the lights on. *(He turns the light on and looks around impatiently. He leafs through the notebooks, touches the toys, but avoids the two jackets with repugnance, unable to conceal his horror.)* She has dragged everything out...It looks like a circus. What are you doing?

SYLVIA: Can't you see?

MASO: Your wedding dress?

SYLVIA: Yes.

MASO: The—the old one?

SYLVIA: I'm fixing it. I couldn't throw it away.

MASO: *(Pacing nervously.)* ...With that madwoman always in our way... *(He stops, looks at her with supplication; pleads.)* We have to get away from here.

SYLVIA: Not today,

MASO: Are you waiting for him here?

SYLVIA: Yes. And you should too. It would please her. *(She nods toward the hallway.)*

MASO: No, not me! Let's go away, I beg you... *(He succeeds in sneaking in a kiss.)*

SYLVIA: Please, Maso...She's in there. You know how she always watches us. Even when she pretends to ignore us.

MASO: *(Nervous.)* I know. That look frightens me too.

SYLVIA: Remember what she's been through, and what she's still going through. Today... She was up at dawn. She arranged everything herself—the flowers, the toys, the clothes. She even dragged out the notebooks from his grammar school—God knows where she found them. Everything is in perfect order—even his suit. And you'll see—she's in her best Sunday dress...It frightens me too...And the questions she asks all the time...

MASO: *(Running his hands through his hair.)* Don't talk to me about her questions. It can drive you crazy...—"Did he brush his teeth?"—"Did he laugh?"—"Did he cry?"—"Did he talk about me?" Every chance she gets! If we don't leave this place she'll destroy us.

SYLVIA: Today she's going to "see him." She'll be convinced. She needs us now. If we left her, it would kill her.

MASO: Does she ask questions about us?

SYLVIA: Never.

MASO: I'm sure she knows.

SYLVIA: I'm not so sure. She deliberately ignores it. There's never a word, never a reproach.

MASO: Doesn't she suspect that we meet?

SYLVIA: She never asks. Once or twice I started to tell her but she refused to listen. She's always so lost in her own thoughts...

MASO: Her look is so severe, so cold... *(With anguish.)* I'd give anything to get away from this nightmare. We must tell her the truth.

SYLVIA: We may have our chance today. After the return.

MASO: Just remember. We're not getting any younger. We can't let her ruin our lives.

(THE MOTHER appears silently from the hallway upstage. She is not wearing black; tragedy has not changed the gentle sweetness of her face.)

MOTHER: *(To MASO.)* Thank you for coming. Who's at the station?

MASO: *(Uneasy.)* Friends, banners...

MOTHER: How many banners?

MASO: *(Embarrassed.)* ...Two.

MOTHER: And how many friends?

MASO: Many more...All wearing political badges...Even the Mayor is there. And the newspaper boy.

(THE MOTHER is proud. Her eyes glitter like those of a happy child.)

MASO: The headline of the return is marked in red. Everybody is buying the paper.

MOTHER: *(With pride and satisfaction.)* They all love him...Everybody will claim him... *(Bitterly.)* They'll fight over him...

MASO: It's true. Even the priest is there. And the lawyer—Lorenzo.

MOTHER: How many—would you say?

MASO: How many what?

MOTHER: Friends?

MASO: *(Embarrassed because there are not many.)* ...About ten.

(THE MOTHER is disappointed.)

MASO: It's the wrong hour. People are at work...

MOTHER: When will they arrive here? *(She gestures toward the window.)*

MASO: *(Looking at his watch.)* Any minute now. Shall I go and meet them?

MOTHER: *(Sharply.)* No! *(More gently.)* Stay here. Did you see all his things? *(She points to them.)* This is his best jacket... *(She caresses it lovingly.)* ...the last one he bought before he went into the Army...his hunting boots... *(She bends and picks them up.)* Did he ever tell you about the hunting he did?

MASO: *(With embarrassment.)* No, he didn't...With all the problems we had...He never mentioned hunting.

MOTHER: This is his first pipe. At eighteen he was already smoking a pipe...He didn't have the courage to show it to me...I found others later on. Did he have one in the camp?

MASO: *(On guard.)* He made one but he couldn't use it. It didn't work. I told you. We gladly traded any gold we might have for a cigarette or a leaf of tobacco. I gave them my watch...I don't remember what he had. I don't think he had any gold on him.

MOTHER: "Smoke and food together"—you said. "To keep warm." *(Pointing to SYLVIA.)* Sylvia asked me about it the other day. She did not understand what you meant. Explain it to her...

MASO: *(Reluctantly.)* We used to take a mouthful of smoke and an ounce of black bread...We kept it in our mouths without chewing—as long as possible—until it dissolved. To keep our stomachs warm.

SYLVIA: Was your bread black like ours?

MASO: Yours was white by comparison.

MOTHER: These are his notebooks... *(She picks them up, turns the pages.)* His first drawings—a ship, a mouse, an apple...Did he notice the children who were at the camp? Did he ever talk to them?

MASO: We didn't see many of them. He spoke very little. To save his strength. He didn't look at them. It was too painful. To avoid suffering, he tried to ignore them.

SYLVIA: *(Looking up from her work.)* How old were those children?

MASO: The youngest one I saw was twenty-six months. Pregnant women were taken to the gas chamber at once.

SYLVIA: Were the children separated from their parents?

MASO: Yes. In our block alone there were four thousand children. They were unable to work. Consequently they were under "special treatment."

(The two women continue to look at him, waiting for details.)

MOTHER: Tell Sylvia about it.

MASO: *(Nervously.)* A nightmare...The parents usually gave their children whatever jewels, rings, or gold they had. When the time of the "special treatment" came...I remember a little girl—she was a skeleton covered with tears and blood—...In their haste to steal her earring—the Nazis ripped her ear open. It was bleeding like... *(He does not find words.)*

MOTHER: *(Moved.)* Did Enrico see that? What did he do?

MASO: He didn't see it. He was in another block...

MOTHER: *(Turning to SYLVIA.)* He must have talked to you about children...

SYLVIA: *(Bent over her work, with tears in her eyes.)* Yes.

MOTHER: What did he say? Did he want to have many children?

SYLVIA: ...At least two or three. He used to tease me...

MOTHER: *(Participating, curious.)* Why?

SYLVIA: My family has only girls.

MOTHER: That's true. I remember now. He always wanted boys. What did he tell you? Did he make plans for their future?

SYLVIA: *(Uneasy.)* Not really...Only about their education. He wanted them to be good students.

MASO: And yet when you were sent to a concentration camp, only a man with a trade had some hope to survive.

(The two women look at him with curiosity.)

MASO: They were able to resist longer. Those with strong backs, accustomed to hard labor: bricklayers, ditch-diggers, peasants with strong hands. Or those who had a particular trade—like mechanics or tailors. I want my son to be a tailor. They were all able to survive...almost all of them.

MOTHER: *(Severe, with authority.)* There will be no more wars! No concentration camps!

MASO: *(Apologetic.)* I didn't mean that. *(Timidly.)* Me and Sylvia... *(He points to SYLVIA with the intention of bringing in their future.)* Even Sylvia wants her son to study. We'll teach him a trade just in case...

(There is a pause. THE MOTHER turns to face the window, and does not listen to him. MASO continues.)

MASO: Sylvia wants our son to...

MOTHER: Sshhh! *(She points toward the window.)* He's coming.

(They listen. There is no sound from outside.)

MASO: I'll go to meet them.

MOTHER: *(Sharply.)* No! We'll wait in the house, *all of us.* *(She includes him in her gesture.)*

MASO: *(Timidly.)* I doubt if they'll stop here... *(He points toward the window.)* They'll just pass by on their way to the church...

(Footsteps are heard approaching from the piazza—stage left. The tolling of the death knell. SYLVIA joins MASO and reaches for his hand. They stand behind THE MOTHER, looking beyond the window, solemn and moved.)

MOTHER: *(With anguish.)* How small—that box! My child! My poor child! *(She leaves stage right, to meet "the return" of her son: a small box containing his ashes.)*

SYLVIA: *(After a silence, as she clings to MASO.)* Why is it so small?

MASO: It's only ashes...They are not even his.

SYLVIA: Not even...How do you know?

MASO: Thousands...all together...

SYLVIA: It's hard to believe...So young, so full of life...It's terrible, Maso...

MASO: *(Almost to himself.)* The small box gave her the real shock! I was afraid her reaction would be worse...She keeps talking about him as if he were still alive. She even refused his pension.

SYLVIA: But she didn't refuse the medal and the money they give with it.

MASO: *(With irony.)* How generous! A few thousand lire a year!

SYLVIA: Even heroes who survived get the same amount. The value of a medal is symbolic... *(She sizes up the room with greed.)* She *has* some money...She owns this house and spends nothing on herself... *(Looking at MASO.)* She said it would be mine someday. "Ours," I mean.

MASO: *(With anger.)* Oh no! We must get out of here! We must go!

SYLVIA: She won't let us.

MASO: *(In an outburst of defiance.)* And who is she? Who does she think she is?

SYLVIA: *(Slowly.)* The mother of the man who was my...

MASO: Fiancé! That's an old story, that's the past! She is not *your* mother. She can't force you to wait, to die here!

SYLVIA: *(Staring at him.)* You're afraid of her too...

(She notices the irony in MASO's expression.)

SYLVIA: ...Perhaps it's pity. You never contradicted her when she pretended to believe he would return...

MASO: *(With determination.)* But now I will. I'll talk openly. He's really dead now. *(Pointing to the clothes.)* I've had enough of this masquerade. I'm going to tell her right away... *(Weakening.)* ...very soon. So we can leave this place forever!

SYLVIA: I'm going to her now. She's waiting for me.

(THE ESCORT enters silently, without warning. His face cannot be seen clearly. He could be mistaken for the dead son. His mysterious appearance is frightening. After a moment, the stranger steps forward, where we can see him. SYLVIA and MASO realize he is not Enrico.)

ESCORT: *(To win SYLVIA's confidence.)* You must be Sylvia...I suppose... *(He offers his hand.)*

SYLVIA: *(Offering her hand uncertainly.)* Yes, I'm Sylvia. And you?

ESCORT: *(Evading, the question.)* Who is the gentleman? *(He nods toward MASO. He is trying to find out how much he can say, how freely he can speak.)*

SYLVIA: My fiancé.

(After a moment of surprise, the two men shake hands.)

ESCORT: How do you do?

MASO: How do you do.

ESCORT: *(Hesitating.)* I don't know if l can speak freely... *(Deciding to go ahead.)* You see...I'm here on *his* behalf.

MASO: *(Astonished, frightened.)* On *whose* behalf?

ESCORT: *His.* I escorted him in the train.

(A tense pause.)

SYLVIA: You mean—you knew him?

(THE ESCORT is silent. He feels that MASO's presence prevents him from speaking openly.)

SYLVIA: *(Noticing his reticence.)* You can speak. They were friends. Maso knows everything.

ESCORT: *(More at ease.)* May I sit down?

SYLVIA: Of course!

(The stranger sits down.)

SYLVIA: You say you knew him?

ESCORT: We were in the same camp.

(SYLVIA looks at MASO; she wants some confirmation. MASO indicates with a gesture to let the stranger continue.)

SYLVIA: What year was that?

ESCORT: *(Smiling at her understandable skepticism and suspicion.)* He arrived in February 1944.

(SYLVIA looks at MASO again. The date is correct. She wants MASO to tell the stranger that he was in the same camp. But MASO refuses. He wants to study the situation first.)

SYLVIA: *(To encourage THE ESCORT to speak.)* Why did you say:—"On *his* behalf"?

ESCORT: In a way. I knew him well. I even helped him.

(SYLVIA and MASO stiffen, fearing some absurd blackmail.)

ESCORT: *(Noticing their distrust.)* He couldn't have written about me because we never met... *(He feels he has made things worse.)*

MASO: *(Impatient, suspicious.)* Go on.

ESCORT: *(With frankness.)* I belonged to a special Committee. I was a *Lagerschreiber*. A kind of clerk. It was our job to save as many prisoners as possible, especially political ones... The so-called "red triangles." *(To SYLVIA.)* Your... *(He pauses.)*

MASO: *(Volunteering.)* Fiancé.

ESCORT: *(Grateful for the help, more relieved.)* Thank you. *(To SYLVIA.)* He belonged to a political party.

SYLVIA: Yes I know.

ESCORT: Antifascist of course. They were the most persecuted. Selected for special experiments: insemination of disease, immersion in freezing water, intravenous injections of benzine... They were marked with two "N's"—*Nacht und Nebel*—"Night and Fog." Which meant annihilation in three months. We helped them all we could.

SYLVIA: Who is "we"?

ESCORT: We worked in the *Schreibstube*—the office that kept records of the deceased. There were those among us who knew foreign languages. Engineers, jurists, musicians. We were the first to organize a nucleus of Resistance, and we decided to save those who were most in danger: men in politics—dedicated men who would be needed at the right moment...

SYLVIA: And what about Enrico?

ESCORT: He was singled out the first time by Dr. Mengele—one of the most ferocious Nazis. That was in April 1944. We saved him. Then again in June; we hid him in the infirmary. Unfortunately he didn't live to see the Liberation.

SYLVIA: How did he die?

ESCORT: *Sonder Behandlung*—"Special Treatment." The gas chamber... Together with four thousand gypsies and invalids... in August.

SYLVIA: *(With horror.)* Is it true that... those ashes aren't his?

ESCORT: *(Without looking at her.)* It's possible. Who can tell?

SYLVIA: *(Accusing.)* Then what *did* you do for him? What did any of you do? *(She turns to MASO as well, including him in her accusation.)*

ESCORT: *(Apologetic, confused.)* Very little I admit. You don't know what kind of hell, you can't possibly imagine. When we could, we saved the weakest from hard labor. A permit for *Schonung*—enforced rest—meant salvation for many...

SYLVIA: *(With bitter accusation.)* But you, why were you privileged to stay in that office and come out of it alive?

ESCORT: *(Humbly.)* I was fortunate, I know. I was an interpreter. I knew some German, some French...I translated Molière for an officer who loved the theatre, I even organized a gypsy orchestra for him. I'm a musician. *(Wringing his hands.)* It wasn't easy for us either... *(Reliving the past with anguish.)* At six in the morning we were at the gate ordered to play lively music for the prisoners on their way to work...They had to march with heads up. A grotesque procession. They had to walk for miles...We were in the "office"—counting the shoes piled up in the carrion deposit, taking inventory of eyeglasses and wedding rings. The Germans are famous for their scrupulous exactitude...We also made tattoos. We saved Enrico twice by giving him a different number. We weren't supposed to go beyond two hundred thousand. When a political prisoner was on the condemned list we waited for someone to die in the infirmary so we could send that corpse instead.

SYLVIA: *(With humility, regretting her unjust accusation.)* Thank you...

ESCORT: Enrico had only one thing against him, poor boy...

(The two wait anxiously; there is a silence.)

ESCORT: It wasn't his fault, though... *(Looking at SYLVIA.)* He had three gold teeth.

SYLVIA: Yes, it's true. *(With curiosity.)* But what difference could that make?

ESCORT: No one with gold teeth could be saved. By November 1944, seventeen tons of gold had already been collected.

SYLVIA: *(With horror.)* How monstrous!

ESCORT: It was an inferno. Three and a half million men were killed there.

MASO: Two and a half million.

ESCORT: *(Surprised at this correction; slowly.)* That was what the Nazi Commander said in self-defense—"*Only* two and a half million..." The exact number will never be known...I saw them die—by the flocks. It was endless. In the beginning of 1943 I was forced to help build the Bunker Twins: Crematories Two and Three. They were inaugurated by burning eight thousand Jews from Poland. Forty-six ovens could liquidate twenty-five thousand people a day.

MASO: *(Correcting THE ESCORT again.)* Twelve thousand people a day—in that block.

ESCORT: *(Looks at him suspiciously, wondering how he could know so many details.)* How do you...?

SYLVIA: *(Intervening at last.)* He was there.

ESCORT: At Auschwitz-Birkenau?

MASO: Yes, I was at Auschwitz-Birkenau. The man who organized that gypsy orchestra was Captain Broad.

ESCORT: Broad, yes... *(With a mixture of diffidence and suspicion.)* Why didn't you say so before?

MASO: I like to listen. I was reliving that nightmare...

ESCORT: Where did they capture you?

MASO: *(Evasively.)* I worked for some time in D.A.W. Siemens, then at Buna for I.G. Farben. One day I spilled some paint by mistake. They made the usual accusation: sabotage!

ESCORT: What was your job at the camp?

MASO: *Sonderkommando* of the crematories. Under orders of the top murderer: Mohl.

ESCORT: *(With disgust.)* The "Blood-Thirsty Baby." I never saw him, but his very name brought terror to everyone. You're probably one of the few who saw him and can give an account of his crimes.

MASO: *(To SYLVIA.)* He was blond, handsome. He had a baby face. The two things he loved most were his family and flowers.

ESCORT: What unit were you in?

MASO: The barbers. We sent the hair to the mills for weaving.

ESCORT: *(Trying to remember.)* With Supervisor Klein. I can still see him. *(He taps his forehead.)* He used to bring large cans of Zyklon B and went back with carloads of hair.

MASO: He was Pierre's protector. Did you know him?

ESCORT: I knew him.

MASO: *(To SYLVIA.)* This Supervisor Klein saved Pierre, a French boy, only because he had an obscene tattoo on his back.

ESCORT: Our lives hung by a thread. If they liked the color of your eyes, if you knew a foreign language...

MASO: As in your case.

SYLVIA: *(Horrified.)* I'm going to church now. They're waiting for me. *(SYLVIA leaves with relief.)*

(There is a pause. The two men stare at each other in silence.)

ESCORT: You were fortunate. There were nine hundred of you in the *Sonderkommando*. Two hundred were sent to the gas chamber on the seventh of September. Five hundred were shot on the seventh of October. The rest left November 27 for an unknown destination.

MASO: You really know every detail—even the dates. I was among them. I managed to escape.

ESCORT: *(Slowly.)* Those dates are unforgettable. Especially in the last months...

(They look at each other with caution and suspicion.)

MASO: What about you? How did you get away?

ESCORT: I helped them burn the records, the photographs. Then I went to the K.B., the Hospital. They gave precedence to the Crematories—wanting to destroy every last trace. There was no time left to assassinate us.

MASO: They were nightmarish hours. I had almost forgotten... *(Confidentially, looking around.)* Even though the torture hasn't ended for me in this house.

ESCORT: *(Looking at him with surprise and curiosity.)* What do you mean?

MASO: I knew Enrico since we were children. His mother gives me no peace. Questions, questions...She persecutes us both, me and Sylvia, with endless questions. Not out of jealousy, no! *(Trying to explain.)* We became engaged only recently, living a hell with those questions from his mother...

ESCORT: *(Trying to justify her.)* She's a mother...

MASO: She'll do the same with you; you'll see. She'll ask you a thousand different questions.

ESCORT: But I didn't know him personally.

MASO: She'll ask you all the same...Why are you here? *(He looks questioningly, with renewed distrust.)*

ESCORT: I kept putting it off. When it was all over and I returned I couldn't believe I had friends again, a bed, all the bread I wanted, all the cigarettes...

MASO: Some traded their last potato for a cigarette—only to die a little later of starvation. It was terrible. No one can believe it. *(He lights another cigarette from the butt of the one he has been smoking. He is very nervous.)*

ESCORT: I don't quite dare return to normality. When I wake up in the morning—even now—I kiss the pillow, the clean sheet...And I think of those we left there...Poor Enrico—I can still see him—those sad eyes...His was a very tragic case. Almost unique...

MASO: Why?

ESCORT: If only he hadn't had those gold teeth...

MASO: There were many who had gold teeth.

ESCORT: Yes, but...

MASO: *(With curiosity.)* What?

ESCORT: *(Slowly.)* Not everybody knew who had them. There were some who pulled out their own...And no one had confidants or close friends who might inform...

MASO: That's true.

ESCORT: No one trusted anybody. Even the existence of our Committee was known only to a very few. Perhaps not even you...

MASO: *(Confirming this.)* I was told about it later.

ESCORT: When some fortunate individual was taken off the death list, he thought it was Providence, or some miracle.

MASO: No one could guess that some of you had the courage to organize...No one shared secrets, exchanged opinions. We hardly spoke to one another. We watched every word, we saved every sigh...

ESCORT: And we're alive, now. What's your name?

MASO: Maso Cimmi. I was born in 1923.

ESCORT: And I in 1922. I look much older.

MASO: With all we went through...

(A woman's voice is heard calling from outside. With insistence.)

SISTER'S VOICE: Tommi!...Tommi!...Tommi!...

(THE ESCORT leaps to his feet. His face takes on a menacing, terrible expression. Surprise and hatred transform the lines of his face. MASO, who was about to answer the call, is terrified by this sudden transformation and is almost speechless.)

MASO: *(Disturbed, in a low voice.)* It's my sister.

(THE ESCORT seizes him by the neck.)

ESCORT: That's who you are! *You're* "Tommi the Jackal!"

SISTER'S VOICE: *(Nearer the window.)* Tommi! They're all waiting in the church! Come, Tommi!

ESCORT: Tell her you're going. *(Commanding.)* Answer her!

MASO: *(To his sister, in a half-suffocated voice.)* I'm coming...right away.

(THE SISTER leaves. THE ESCORT forces MASO to his knees and holds him there, by the neck.)

ESCORT: Maso, Tommaso, Tommi...I hadn't thought of that. *You* are "Tommi the Jackal!" *(With slow emphasis.) I came for you!* We knew he had been betrayed by someone from his town... *(Unable to convince himself.)* You the "Jackal"... *(With fury, he realizes.)* And you visit his mother...You kiss his fiancée...

MASO: *(Almost choking.)* No...No...I—I assure you that...

ESCORT: "Tommi." That was all we knew. I could have believed anything but that you would be living in his house. Doesn't it haunt you? *It was YOU who killed him!*

MASO: *(Struggling.)* It's not true, no...You know it isn't true...You—you're the only one who can understand. You know what it was like! It was hell!

ESCORT: Dirty traitors like you made it even worse.

MASO: Let me explain, I beg you...

(THE ESCORT releases his grip, but forces MASO to remain on his knees.)

MASO: You know, you saw what they gave him the last day: fifteen blows with the whip. He was in the *Himmelfahrt* Block—which meant sure death. There was *no* hope! They would have sent him to the gas chamber in any case. His body—you must have seen it—it was an open wound...

ESCORT: It *was you* who knew about his gold teeth; it was you who informed! A friend of the family, from the same town...

MASO: It wasn't only me! I wasn't the only one who knew...

ESCORT: But you didn't hesitate to *go first*. And you sold him for three cigarettes.

MASO: *(With difficulty.)* You're right. I did go first...You know how a cigarette can help when you're bleeding, exhausted...It was like a transfusion of energy, of strength for our bodies...

ESCORT: For three R.6 cigarettes.

MASO: You know the brand too. You know everything. I remember—the Commander letting them fall out of his cigarette case...It was the end for Enrico. He couldn't have survived. I shortened his agony.

ESCORT: And as a reward you're taking his fiancée.

MASO: *(Ignoring.)* ...In my case—it could have been that cigarette which saved me... *(With desperation, as he relives the past.)* Somebody else would have spoken, if I hadn't...Why should someone else get those cigarettes? A stranger—someone who meant nothing to him?

(THE ESCORT slaps his face.)

MASO: I—I swear to you...You're the only one who can understand...Only you! I always did the best I could—for all of them...You know what fear and terror held us—you know how they degraded us, dehumanized us...Yet I tried...I really *did*... *(MASO regains some courage, determined to defend himself at all cost.)* For instance—when the Jews hid their babies under their clothes—the clothes that were seized as they entered the gas chambers, I consoled them and helped them! Yes, me! I even went *inside* to reassure them—at my own risk! They could have locked me in there, forgetting me...

(THE ESCORT pulls MASO to his feet and looks straight at him with contempt and disgust.)

ESCORT: You must leave this house forever.

MASO: *(Relieved, with sincerity.)* I promise! Yes, forever!

ESCORT: Your presence here is an insult. You must leave at once, disappear!

MASO: *(With relief, not daring to believe his ears.)* You're right! Of course!

(THE MOTHER enters quietly, unnoticed. They see her. They freeze immediately. There is a silence. THE ESCORT is embarrassed and tries to find a way to explain the dispute, the position in which she found them.)

ESCORT: I am...

MOTHER: *(Cordially.)* Sylvia told me. You're most welcome here.

(A silence.)

ESCORT: *(Confused and embarrassed, alluding to MASO.)* We were having a—an argument. He made a remark in defense of the Nazis. Imagine, we were in the same concentration camp...

MOTHER: *(To MASO.)* I want you to go to church now. They're waiting for you.

(MASO sneaks out of the room quickly, relieved to get away. THE MOTHER'S face is now relaxed, softer.)

MOTHER: Sylvia knows nothing.

(The ESCORT looks at her, not understanding. He is waiting for an explanation.)

MOTHER: I was outside...I overheard... *(She looks at him maternally, serenely; then she says—clearly and slowly—)* I always knew.

ESCORT: *(Stunned.)* You always *knew*? Knew *what*?

MOTHER: *(Without hatred, resigned.)* Everything... That it was he who betrayed Enrico.

(THE ESCORT is speechless. His face shows both shock and remorse for having disturbed the tragic equilibrium of this family.)

MOTHER: *(Speaks very gently, slowly.)* But I need him anyway. He and Sylvia are the only ones who shared with Enrico hours and days that weren't mine. They are the only ones who can tell me about him...I see him in their eyes when they talk about him...I see him living...I feel he's alive...Those moments are the most beautiful in my life...I might even give Sylvia to him...perhaps... *(With a tired gesture.)* And this house of mine...later...

(CURTAIN.)

Note:

All the remarks concerning the camp of Auschwitz-Birkenau are taken from testimonies that correspond to absolute fact.

The Seventy-Fifth

The Persons:

THE SERGEANT (A human stump with one eye, the left arm, and two legs missing)
THE COLONEL
THE PRISONER (He does not speak)

A hospital in Vietnam. THE COLONEL listens patiently, with interest.

SERGEANT: Look at me, Colonel. I gave everything to my Country! Twenty-seven years in the Army. An eye, an arm, and both legs. All my blood! A life of devotion and dedication to my flag. And what do I want in return? Just one favor!

COLONEL: But it's against all regulations and—

SERGEANT: *(Interrupting.)* All? Would it be the first time?

COLONEL: It's not the first time but... we're not in a combat zone.

SERGEANT: This country is nothing but a combat zone.

COLONEL: You'll get your twelfth medal, I promise! We'll send you home first class, with a generous pension.

SERGEANT: You don't understand. Mine is a spiritual need! My mind is organized and precise. You've got to realize that, Colonel. I enlisted at seventeen. Respect for authority, absolute obedience, perfect organization. Everything must be thoroughly calibrated in my mind. And in my life. If not, it breaks my heart.

COLONEL: Easy, easy now! Do you want me to call the nurse to give you an injection?

SERGEANT: No. She comes precisely at noon. I'm ready, psychologically and physically, for that time. Reveille at six. Breakfast at seven. Everything in order, precise like a stopwatch. That's why I picked the Army. So I could love my country in a regulated manner, with unalterable rhythm, with total order and discipline. That's why I need that favor. And I'm not asking for something impossible, I know. You do it every day. Everywhere.

COLONEL: Not in a hospital.

SERGEANT: The hospital is an ideal place for that! Absolutely perfect! Strange that you hadn't thought of it before! Everyone should end up here! They have what it takes: stretchers, linens, refrigerators. I beg you! Please...

COLONEL: Hospitals take care of people. They're taking care of you. Restoring your health and equilibrium.

SERGEANT: Equilibrium? Are you by any chance implying that I've lost my mind?

COLONEL: Oh no! Only that—

SERGEANT: My mind is as precise as a computer. An incredible mechanism. It even surprises me at times. In Japan, I remember, I had decided to kill twenty-five Japs in as many days. One, two, three, twenty-four. Everything was going splendidly. There was a half hour left to midnight on the twenty-fifth day. I had a fever in my blood. I had to keep the promise I had made to myself. And to my country. To eliminate those bastards from the face of the earth. I went out desperate, nervous as hell, feverish. My trigger finger was ready with anticipation. I laid in ambush at the outskirts of the prisoners' camp. Hoping. Five minutes before midnight, one of the prisoners approached the wired fence. An obvious attempt to escape. I shot him in his tracks. Twenty-five in twenty-five days. I had kept my promise. I felt reborn. From that day—and this is interesting because it shows how my brain works—I've had other chances to kill them. I controlled myself because killing the twenty-sixth meant the beginning of a new series. The fever of the fiftieth.

COLONEL: But in your dossier—

SERGEANT: There's the fiftieth, I know. Korean War. I decided to do my duty eliminating another twenty-five gooks in honor of my country at arms. Fifty gooks in fifty days. Note the detail. And the care in organizing my work. I didn't want to suffer the pains of hell—what I went through with my twenty-fifth Jap. Everything came out perfectly. By the fiftieth day another twenty-five bastards went to Hell, where they had come from. War in Vietnam. You know the story, July second—my birthday. Finally: the seventy-second, third, fourth... and then that damned mine that tore me apart. If you don't give me the seventy-fifth, Colonel, I'll die of a broken heart. I don't sleep at night, I'm a wreck. Upset, unfulfilled, defeated. Please, Colonel...

COLONEL: In a battle...everything is allowed. But under these conditions—

SERGEANT: I've been in this profession for twenty-seven years, two months, and fourteen days. I know all about it. We've killed hundreds under "these conditions."

COLONEL: *(Ignoring.)* I promise you, I'll kill one the next opportunity I have. The seventy-fifth, for you. Dedicated to you.

SERGEANT: It doesn't count, Colonel. It has to *be* mine, all mine. *(A brief pause.)* I don't have anything else, Colonel. I always liked women. You want to see what's left, here? *(Raises the sheet, uncovering himself.)* My Country doesn't need me anymore. What good am I now? A stump in a wheelchair. What kind of life is this? At least let me balance the scales. My platinum anniversary with death. Let me keep my vow, I beg you. Twenty-fifth. Silver anniversary in Japan. Fiftieth. Golden anniversary in Korea. Seventy-fifth. Platinum anniversary in Vietnam. Give me a gun for the seventy-fifth and I'll be a happy man. I will have done my duty. Everything in order, precise, splendidly exact. A perfect life. I'll be able to die in peace.

COLONEL: It's not in my power—

SERGEANT: *(Interrupting.)* Everything is in your power. You're the judge of life and death here, we know that.

COLONEL: Not exactly—

SERGEANT: We were in the same helicopter. You pushed out the first one, the second one, the seventh. Number eight talked.

COLONEL: Combat zone. We needed information.

SERGEANT: And those Sunday afternoons. "Gook hunts." Just between me and you, those old folks and ten-year-olds in their

Sunday clothes, they certainly weren't communists.

COLONEL: *(After a final hesitation.)* All right. He's a criminal—caught red-handed. Guilty of innumerable crimes against our troops. We would have executed him tomorrow morning. You're just going to shorten his agony.

(He claps his hands; a Viet Cong with his hands tied is pushed into the room; silence; THE SERGEANT and THE PRISONER stare at each other. THE COLONEL forces THE PRISONER to kneel near the bed; he releases the safety catch of his gun and gives it to THE SERGEANT. THE SERGEANT grips the gun with joy; he is ecstatic.)

SERGEANT: The power of a gun, the power to choose your victim...

SERGEANT: *(To THE COLONEL, after studying him for a few seconds.)* You too. Kneel down next to him.

(THE COLONEL, terrified, obeys.)

SERGEANT: A couple of angels, very good. Heads down!

(THE COLONEL lowers his head; a silence; he waits for THE SERGEANT to make his decision. THE SERGEANT crosses himself with the gun. He decides that it is fair that the seventy-fifth should be himself. He shoots himself through the heart.)

(IMMOBILITY. DARKNESS. CURTAIN.)

Iraq (Blindness)

Characters:

BRIAN, a handsome young man in his early twenties; blind
CATHY, his girlfriend
DAN, brother of Jim, the dead soldier; twenty
ANDERSON, Dan's father; sixty

Time:

2005

A modest living room in Ohio, during the war in Iraq. Chairs, a sofa, a table, four photos at the four corners of the room. BRIAN enters. He is blind; he is guided and helped by CATHY, his girlfriend. DAN, his friend, looks at him with sadness. He gets up and moves toward him.

DAN: Welcome, Brian.

BRIAN: Dan, I recognize your voice. Where are you? I want to shake your hand.

DAN: Here I am.

(DAN goes to him; shakes his hand; they embrace.)

DAN: Hi, Cathy, it has been so long…

CATHY: It has.

BRIAN: I recognized your voice right away. Identical to your brother's. Where is your family?

DAN: Upstairs, I think.

BRIAN: All three?

DAN: Mom and Sis are in the bedroom. They seldom come downstairs. For you, maybe…

BRIAN: How are they feeling?

DAN: They cry all day. Nothing stops their tears. How about your mom?

BRIAN: Ask Cathy.

CATHY: She cries a lot too.

BRIAN: Where is your father?

DAN: Getting us all a beer, I think.

BRIAN: How is he doing? How did he take it?

DAN: Badly but…basically I think he's proud. He still feels like a soldier. One hundred percent American. Proud of war and war heroes.

BRIAN: Your brother was a real hero, I can assure you. That's part of the reason I have come. To tell you about details you are not aware of. We were together for nine months. Inseparable.

DAN: First tell me about you. How are you?

BRIAN: You see me, don't you? Shrapnel cut my optical nerve. I'll never see my beloved Cathy's beautiful face again. *(To CATHY.)* Come here, give me your hand.

(CATHY goes to him; kisses his forehead; he kisses her hand.)

BRIAN: You see? She still loves me. And her face is always here, in my dead pupils. I am *only* happy with people I know. Faces that are always present in my memory. Their smiles, their features, the eyes of my relatives and of my friends. I have the impression of still seeing them. And just think, they will always be young in my memory. There's an advantage even to blindness. Nobody gets old. A silver lining in every cloud—as our Colonel used to say. I'm happy to be here with your family. I remember all of you very well. Where are they? What are they waiting for?

DAN: Dad will be here any moment. Mom and Claudia later, maybe...

BRIAN: Why do you say "Maybe"? Don't they want to see me?

DAN: They don't want to see anybody.

BRIAN: Not even me, your brother's best friend?

DAN: Maybe, let's hope...They promised.

BRIAN: What are they afraid of? Am I so disfigured?

DAN: Oh no, you look just fine. Women, you know. Who understands them? Maybe...

BRIAN: Maybe what?

DAN: It's just my opinion...Wrong, probably... *(He hesitates.)*

BRIAN: Tell me.

DAN: You're alive, here with us...My brother isn't...They are happy for you but...they're human. They would like to have Jim here. Wounded, yes, but alive. With us.

BRIAN: I understand. After all, I just lost my eyesight... *(With irony.)* "Just"...Are they still passionate pacifists, like you?

DAN: Even more so, today.

BRIAN: Your father, on the contrary... Jim's death has not changed his opinion...

DAN: No. He is still the ardent patriot, the warrior who believes in sacrifices—

BRIAN: *(Interrupting.)* —Even his own son's?

DAN: Yes, even his own son's sacrifice.

(A pause.)

DAN: Tell us, tell us what happened, how it happened.

BRIAN: Let's wait for your father. I want to tell him how Jim and I lived in those places for weeks. Always together.

(ANDERSON, the father, enters with glasses of beer.)

ANDERSON: Welcome back, Brian. Welcome to our house, to Jim's house. You, valiant hero. You and Jim, two wonderful heroes fighting for a noble cause.

(Shakes his hand; they do not embrace.)

ANDERSON: I got the beer you like. Here you go. Drink this. *(Hands him a glass of beer; to CATHY.)* What about you, Cathy? Do you want a beer?

CATHY: No, thanks. Your wife and daughter, how are they?

ANDERSON: Why don't you go upstairs and see them? Go to them. They don't understand yet, they haven't accepted.

(CATHY exits to see the two women; the three men raise their glasses.)

ANDERSON: Let's toast to the heroes' return!

(They drink; DAN looks at his father with uneasiness; his brother has not come back.)

ANDERSON: You, you're back, here with us. I can touch you *(Touches him; gives him a pat on the back.)* But Jim is with us, too. Look at the photos. *(Indicates photos of Jim everywhere in the room. Realizing BRIAN is blind.)* Oh, I'm sorry. That was stupid of me. There are photos of Jim in every corner of the room. In uniform. He looks great in uniform. If only... *(He hesitates.)*

BRIAN: If only what?

ANDERSON: Maybe, if you had been together that day, the same day, maybe one could have helped the other, saved the other.

BRIAN: It happened to me in July.

ANDERSON: Yes, we heard about it in July. A call from Jim. He was sure you would make it. He said it was minor. Just a slight wound...

BRIAN: *(Touching his eyes, with irony.)* "Slight"...

DAN: Then, at the end of August, what happened? What did they tell you?

BRIAN: When I was in the hospital, they came and told me that Jim had been invited into some house. A trap. Whatever happened, I'm sure he behaved like a hero.

ANDERSON: Me too.

DAN: *(To BRIAN.)* How do you know? You were not with him.

BRIAN: I've seen him in dozens of situations. Courageous, daring, precise. One of our best snipers. They mentioned his accurate shooting in many papers. In one day he killed eleven of them.

ANDERSON: I have the clippings. I wish he could have seen them.

BRIAN: He would have been happy you were proud.

ANDERSON: How did he feel after that? Proud, happy?

BRIAN: It's not so easy. There are times when we destroy a house by mistake, an entire family, and—

ANDERSON: But those eleven were rebels, armed insurgents, weren't they?

BRIAN: They were.

ANDERSON: So Jim must have felt proud, useful.

DAN: *(Ironical.)* "Useful"?

ANDERSON: *(To DAN, angry.)* You will never understand. You peaceniks have never understood the necessity to eliminate the enemy, the ones who threaten our liberty, our democracy.

DAN: *(Who does not want to continue on that subject; to BRIAN.)* You, how did you find out about Jim?

BRIAN: Our Colonel, who knew we were friends, told me. He mentioned that ambush.

ANDERSON: Was it actually an ambush? Did they confirm it?

BRIAN: *(Vague.)* That's what they told me. Lots of them against three of us.

ANDERSON: I'm sure he wasn't afraid, not even for an instant.

BRIAN: Never. He was never afraid. Not even during the most dangerous missions.

DAN: They were very vague in the telegram we received. What details did they give you?

BRIAN: Not much... I immediately thought of you, felt for you... Even my family, they were all upset by the news...

DAN: But a bit relieved, I imagine, at the thought that you were coming home. Did they tell them about... *(He hesitates, looking for the right words.)* ...your eyes?

BRIAN: No. Only that I was wounded but in good shape.

DAN: They're all happy, aren't they?

BRIAN: Yes, obviously... They can see me, touch me, love me.

ANDERSON: Tell me about Jim, his good times. You know, when he was at his best.

BRIAN: Sure. I have lots to tell you. We were together for such a long time. We were first in Kuwait which was an easy, boring life. Then in Saudi Arabia. A lot of whiskey, on the sly. They're Puritans, they pretend to hate alcohol.

ANDERSON: Women? Did you have women? In Vietnam, we had whores everywhere. Jim was like me. He wanted it all the time, he needed it *(Gesture.)*

BRIAN: It's not easy to find women in those places. You know—the women are veiled and untouchable. Men are jealous and kill the women who betray, who dare to go to bed with someone. I can't even imagine what they would do if they went with an American...

ANDERSON: So, no women? How did you manage? I remember that Jim—

DAN: *(Interrupting him.)* Let him talk, Dad.

BRIAN: In Riyadh we had a couple of nurses.

ANDERSON: Arabs?

BRIAN: American. Generous women who now and then...

ANDERSON: What's the name of Jim's lady?

BRIAN: Shirley. He spent a lot of time with her. I saw her cry when we left.

ANDERSON: *(To DAN.)* You see? You see? A real heartbreaker. Women everywhere. *(To BRIAN.)* What about in Iraq?

BRIAN: Nothing the first three months. It was hell. We destroyed everything. The famous "Republican guards" Saddam was boasting about, we massacred them, we pulverized them.

ANDERSON: And in Baghdad? I've seen photos. A modern city with well-dressed women, Western style. Driving cars, riding motorbikes.

BRIAN: That was before we arrived. They're afraid now.

ANDERSON: Of you?

BRIAN: Of us and of their men. Religious morality is prevailing now. We were surprised to find out that it was a secular society. Now religious fanaticism rules. Women are in trouble.

DAN: What do you mean?

BRIAN: The Iraqis are worse off now. They'll murder each other for twenty years. Poor people, especially the women.

ANDERSON: So, no Iraqi women in your beds? Not even one?

BRIAN: Not even one.

ANDERSON: How can they resist when they see you strutting around, handsome and bold? Armed like war gods! Real, tough males, irresistible!

BRIAN: I'm sure some would like to. There are thousands of widows who are maybe dreaming about us but they are afraid. If they dared they would be stoned to death.

ANDERSON: So, our poor Jim had to live without for months?

DAN: *(Reproaching his father.)* Dad...

ANDERSON: *(To DAN.)* You shut up. You never understood our biological needs and women's desires. They love us, they need us. *(To BRIAN.)* So, in Baghdad, no chance to... *(Gesture.)*

BRIAN: *(Hesitant.)* In Baghdad...This is a delicate story. We have...there was one... *(He hesitates.)*

ANDERSON: Go on, tell us. What's the name of my son's last lover?

BRIAN: It's off limits, it's forbidden to pursue, to sleep with our colleagues. But Jim, with his eternal radiant smile...

ANDERSON: *(To DAN.)* You see? You see? A handsome son, a fascinating God! He always got what he wanted. *(To BRIAN.)* So, he scored, didn't he? What's the name of that big Amazon in uniform?

BRIAN: I cannot, we cannot mention names. It's absolutely forbidden. Military code.

ANDERSON: Military discipline, I understand. Tell us about your raids, your incursions. Every day?

BRIAN: Almost every night. We used to prefer nights. We could see them with our night-vision goggles. They couldn't see us. They were easy targets.

ANDERSON: During the day, where would you meet the Iraqis? Coffee houses, restaurants? How did you circulate among them? Do they applaud you, smile at you?

BRIAN: Some kids smile at us and say: "—please, chocolate, thank you." The only words they know. The adults, all men—they keep women at home—they look at us with hatred and suspicion. They make obscene gestures, they spit and stamp on it, symbolically. Then they look at us straight in the eye. There is no law and order anymore. We are the hated enemy.

ANDERSON: What did Jim say when he felt that hatred? He was always cordial and friendly. Did you try to talk to them? Did you try to make friends?

BRIAN: Oh no! It was absolutely forbidden to go toward them, among them.

ANDERSON: No attempts at real communication, friendship? Chocolate, food, flags, dollars?

BRIAN: No. Jim was upset by that. Like all of us. It's not pleasant to see destruction and death. That day when he had those eleven precise, lucky hits... *(He hesitates.)*

DAN: That day?

BRIAN: We went to that village, later, to find out who those men were, if they had accomplices, family...We saw a little girl crying desperately over a corpse...Jim wanted to talk to her, to comfort her. We had to stop him, hold him back. They would have killed him if he had approached the girl. He left all his rations at the entrance of the village, on a low wall, everything he had on him. Even a flashlight—which is absolutely forbidden. We pretended we didn't notice and took him away. One of us—Gonzalez—was crying like a baby.

ANDERSON: A Puerto Rican?

BRIAN: Yes.

ANDERSON: They are not good soldiers. A real soldier does not cry. Have you ever seen Jim cry?

DAN: *(Intervening.)* I saw Jim cry. When he left Mother and Claudia. Desperate hugs, many tears.

ANDERSON: That's normal when a mother cries. It's human. Jim was such a good son. Have you seen other Puerto Ricans cry?

BRIAN: Puerto Ricans, Blacks, Whites. All races. Especially when we were too quick on the trigger and realized we had hit some civilians.

ANDERSON: It happens in war, unfortunately. Did you speak often about our President?

BRIAN: Almost never. It was taboo.

DAN: But when you did, I'm sure you weren't complimentary. He's responsible for the whole mess.

ANDERSON: *(Angry.)* Don't offend the memory of your brother who sacrificed himself for the President, our country, all of us. He is the best President we ever had. He is proving to the whole world that we are "Number One," the best. We have proven that we can conquer and liberate any country in a few days. Our military power is immense, unlimited.

(CATHY comes back and kisses BRIAN on his forehead; a silence.)

CATHY: *(To BRIAN.)* They would like to see you, give you a hug.

BRIAN: Of course. *(Gets up.)* I'll see them with pleasure. *(Correcting himself.)* I'll *feel* their warmth.

ANDERSON: I'll take him upstairs.

(ANDERSON helps him.)

ANDERSON: *(While he's helping him upstairs.)* Don't say too much. No details. They are too…too sensitive.

(ANDERSON and BRIAN exit. DAN and CATHY are now alone. A silence.)

CATHY: *(To DAN.)* They are inconsolable. Especially your mother…and they do not understand your father's behavior…Losing a son should upset any normal parent.

DAN: He plays the hero, the tough guy, but I'm sure that when we don't see him, he cries too. One day, I walked in on him; he was kissing one of Jim's photos.

CATHY: I'm happy to hear he's human, like all fathers. Did he ever suggest you should volunteer?

DAN: Yeah, six months ago he mentioned it all the time. He insisted it was my duty. He stopped after Jim's death.

(ANDERSON comes back.)

ANDERSON: What a scene! They covered him with kisses. They are smothering him. That fanatic wife of mine pinned a photo of the Pope on his shirt. Fortunately, he didn't notice. *(To CATHY.)* Get rid of it, at the first chance.

CATHY: No. It is a gift, a blessing.

ANDERSON: You too? You women are all religious fanatics. *(To DAN.)* Especially your mother. She keeps mentioning the Polack.

DAN: Mostly last year, when the Pope tried to stop the war in Iraq.

ANDERSON: *(With contempt.)* "Priests." They are always talking peace and then they go to the battlefields to bless the dying. They're only good at preaching and encouraging…

DAN: Encouraging what?

ANDERSON: *(Ironical.)* Not to fear death because Heaven is waiting for them. All religions promise Paradise. *(To CATHY, after a silence.)* Brian is strong and courageous. A real warrior. Are you proud of him?

CATHY: *(Vague.)* I am...

ANDERSON: You are wonderful too. To love him even now that... *(He hesitates.)* You can't look into his eyes and he can't admire you.

CATHY: The sentence that struck me most, when he came back, was: —"It's better like this. It's better to be blind. I'll never see the horrors of war again."

(A silence.)

ANDERSON: I know war is terrible...Me too, I saw horrible things in Vietnam... You have some nightmares at the beginning...Then they fade away. But he's got to know that his sacrifice has brought freedom and democracy to that country...

CATHY: He never talks about it.

ANDERSON: Never of what?

CATHY: Politics, democracy, freedom. They are subjects he avoids.

ANDERSON: What does he say about Bush? About the White House's global vision? Of our desire to bring peace and democracy all over the world?

CATHY: He never mentions him.

ANDERSON: Why, in your opinion? Brian was great here. One hundred percent American, a good patriot, happy about his sacrifice for a noble cause.

CATHY: Out of respect, maybe...No one mentions him at home. It is a delicate subject. Even our friends, the ones against the war, never mention him in our house. Respect, fear, caution...They don't want to rub salt in the wound.

ANDERSON: Hypocrites.

CATHY: He's often depressed...He has nightmares, many nightmares.

ANDERSON: They'll disappear. He should get out more often. Talking about his mission in schools, clubs, town hall meetings.

CATHY: He was invited. He refused to go.

ANDERSON: Too soon, maybe... *(He thinks it over.)* Does he ever say anything negative?

CATHY: No...He avoids it.

ANDERSON: *(Doubtful, to DAN.)* Did he look depressed to you?

DAN: Of course he is. No doubt.

ANDERSON: *(Reflecting, worried.)* I better go upstairs again. I don't want him to depress those two women even more. *(He exits.)*

CATHY: *(After a silence, to DAN.)* A stupid war; blind and cruel.

DAN: Unnecessary. Shameful.

CATHY: *(After a long pause, hesitating.)* I didn't have the courage to tell them the truth...

DAN: *(Surprised.)* What truth?

CATHY: Brian has always known. He only talks about it with me.

DAN: About what? What does he talk about?

CATHY: *(Cautious.)* Maybe I can tell you...Only you...Then you decide if you want to tell your family...Your mother and sister...And, maybe, your father.

DAN: What are you talking about?

CATHY: There was also something about it in the *New York Times*.

DAN: We don't get it here in Ohio. What did they write?

CATHY: *(With caution, hesitating.)* ...The news that twenty-nine soldiers, the most sensitive, the most vulnerable *(She hesitates.)* ...

DAN: So?

CATHY: ...They committed suicide.

(A silence.)

CATHY: Jim was one of them. He shot himself.

(MUSIC. FREEZE. BLACKOUT. CURTAIN.)

Note:

Inspired by three articles in the *New York Times*.

"Che"

The Persons:

RAMON ("CHE")
JULIA, the teacher
BENO and MIGUEL, Bolivian soldiers
THE LIEUTENANT, Bolivian
THE COLONEL, Bolivian
JUAN and ANICETO, Cubans
THE MAN, American

Time & Place:

October 9, 1967—in Bolivia

Music. We hear news bulletins in many languages announcing that "CHE" has been captured. Slides of "CHE" and his guerrilleros.

VOICE: John F. Kennedy said: "U.S. Steel and other leading steel corporations, increasing steel prices, constitute a wholly unjustifiable and irresponsible defiance of the public interest. The American people will find it hard to accept a situation in which a tiny handful of steel executives whose pursuit of private power and profit exceeds their sense of public responsibility can show such utter contempt for the interest of millions." He was murdered.

(A very modest classroom in a two-room schoolhouse in the mountain village of La Higuera. It is rather dark since they must depend on a few small windows for light; there is no electricity in La Higuera. RAMON is lying on a table. He is handcuffed and looks on with some curiosity at the Bolivian soldiers who are showing each other the souvenirs they took from his knapsack.)

RAMON: *(Noticing that they are puzzled about the contents in a small red box; in a calm, kind voice.)* That's adrenalin.

BENO: Adrena—What? Something to eat?

RAMON: No. It's a medicine for my attacks of asthma.

MIGUEL: *(Surprised, studying him.)* Asthma? You have asthma?

RAMON: At times.

BENO: My uncle has asthma. It's an old man's disease. How old are you?

RAMON: Thirty-nine. You're right. I'm old. Only a few revolutionaries reach my age.

MIGUEL: You have asthma, Señor Guevara, and you have chosen...this difficult life?

RAMON: It's a "calling"—they say. If you saw a child in the water, on the verge of drowning, you would jump in—instinctively—to save him. I see millions with water up to their necks, I forget my asthma and plunge into the water.

MIGUEL: Into the fire—I would say.

RAMON: Into the fire—if you like. Some drown. Some burn alive.

MIGUEL: And the asthma doesn't choke you, like his uncle? *(Indicates BENO.)*

BENO: Sometimes my uncle becomes all red. As if he were going to kick the bucket!

RAMON: It happens to me too, now and then. But the duty of a revolutionary is to fight for justice, for you and your families: the poor people—the exploited. How much do you earn in the army?

BENO: What do you mean?

RAMON: How much do they pay you?

MIGUEL: The food is free. It helps my family who couldn't afford to... *(He stops short.)*

RAMON: —To feed you, I know. Don't be ashamed of that. One must never be ashamed of being hungry. It's not your father's or your mother's fault.

BENO: And they promised us money if we kill—

MIGUEL: *(Interrupting and correcting him.)* He means:—"If we capture rebels."

BENO: We get paid now that you're here.

RAMON: The price on my head is many thousands of dollars. Try to get them for yourselves. If that money falls into the hands of your Colonels, you'll get just a few crumbs.

MIGUEL: *(With great interest.)* Thousands of..."dollars"? How many?

RAMON: The last I heard was one hundred thousand. You soldiers should organize a good Union and divide the money among yourselves.

BENO: Unions are forbidden. Too dangerous. But perhaps some kind of religious association.

MIGUEL: Through the Catholic Action. We can ask Father Schiller.

RAMON: He will convince you that the Church is poorer than you. Don't trust him. The money is yours. *You* risked your skin.

MIGUEL: You're right, Señor Guevara. We risked our lives. You were all well armed.

RAMON: And I imagine you are not even volunteers.

MIGUEL: Of course not.

BENO: Of course not.

RAMON: *(To BENO.)* How do you like this life?

BENO: *(Vague.)* We eat well...

RAMON: Better than you eat at home, you mean.

BENO: Yes. And one gets around a lot. Jeeps, trucks, helicopters.

RAMON: Who pilots them? You or the Gringos?

BENO: Not me, not me. I don't know how to do it. The advisers are in charge of—

(MIGUEL signals him to shut up—not to reveal secrets.)

RAMON: "The advisers"...How do they treat you?

(A silence.)

RAMON: I know that your instructors are all from the U.S. I just want to know how they treat you.

(A silence.)

RAMON: All right. I'll tell you what I know. So you don't feel you are revealing any "secrets." Your officers are trained at Fort Gulick—Panama—where they learn English and are paid in dollars. You are trained for nineteen weeks at Camp La Esperanza. You receive orders from the Green Berets of Major Ralph John Shelton—nicknamed "Pappy" Shelton. Green Berets from the English Special Forces in Panama. And many of your instructors are veterans of Vietnam.

(BENO and MIGUEL look at him with astonishment; they never suspected he had such accurate information.)

RAMON: You see? I don't want to know your military secrets. I was just interested to know how they treat you.

MIGUEL: Well.

BENO: Well.

MIGUEL: Very well.

RAMON: I'm happy to hear that. It means they are human. And maybe someday they will realize what they are doing in your country, in many countries. When you say they treat you "well," what do you mean?

BENO: You can ask them for a cigarette. They give it to you. Or for a chocolate, canned food, beer. They have everything.

MIGUEL: Or for medicines. They have doctors who treat patients very well. And if you need a few hours rest they'll let you rest.

BENO: Without insulting you. And without kicking you in the ass.

MIGUEL: The way our officers do.

BENO: The Americans, never! They never kick us!

RAMON: I'm delighted to hear that, really delighted. And tell me—how do they treat your women?

(A brief pause.)

BENO: You know…how these things go…They have money and chocolate and so…

RAMON: And so?

BENO: Those whores go to bed with them!

MIGUEL: Such women can be found anywhere.

BENO: Indians. They're all Indian. And Father Schiller warned us that they're all sick. Venereal diseases.

RAMON: *(With charm and humor.)* It's sabotage! You want to contaminate the Gringos.

MIGUEL: In a way…

RAMON: Bravo! Congratulations! It's the same method used in Vietnam.

BENO: You can never trust women. Especially the Indian ones. I never trusted them. They are dirty.

MIGUEL: The Americans ask them to wash first. And they enjoy watching them shower.

BENO: And then…they use things, rubbers. They have the means to avoid getting infected. They have everything.

MIGUEL: Absolutely everything. Once they allowed me to enter their—

(He stops when he hears footsteps stage right; they raise their weapons, ready to shoot. A soldier enters. He is followed by JULIA, the Maestra, who walks slowly and timidly.)

SOLDIER: Doctor Guevara. I have convinced her! Here is the Maestra!

RAMON: Thank you.

(The Maestra, a beautiful girl in her early twenties, moves carefully; it is obvious that she is uneasy; she is moved at the thought of seeing "CHE.")

RAMON: *(Watching her; with kindness and warmth.)* Come closer please…

(She moves only imperceptibly.)

RAMON: I'm not going to bite you. Look—I am handcuffed…

(She advances timidly.)

RAMON: What's your name?

JULIA: Julia. Why did you send for me?

RAMON: I was told that this is your school. Your kingdom, in a sense. *(Looking around.)* Is this really a classroom?

JULIA: Yes sir.

RAMON: It looks like a stable. No electricity, no chairs, no blackboard. How do you teach?

JULIA: I ask questions, I help them answer. I make them read…

RAMON: This is not a learning environment. In Cuba, we've built thousands of new schools.

JULIA: *(Ignoring.)* Why didn't you send for Father Schiller instead of me?

RAMON: A priest? In a situation such as this?

JULIA: He's a good person.

RAMON: I'm sure he is. But I prefer to see a teacher. If I called a priest, some journalist would write that I repented. Of what? Of caring for my brothers? Of fighting for a new society?

JULIA: New… We didn't hear too much about you, your ideas… Our papers only mentioned that some foreigners were invading our country…

RAMON: "Invading"?

JULIA: You are a foreigner, aren't you?

RAMON: We are all brothers on this continent. We speak the same language, we all suffer and struggle against indifference.

JULIA: Indifference, that's true… The authorities don't listen. We ask for books, pens, paper. They ignore us.

RAMON: Indifference is the cancer of our century.

JULIA: You're right.

RAMON: You're a good teacher.

JULIA: How can you tell? I know so little…

RAMON: I can tell from your words, your reactions. There is thirst for knowledge in you…

JULIA: *(Timidly.)* Yes… I love books… But they say you only believe in guns… They say you came here to kill… Some of you… do that.

RAMON: Ours is a war against the daily violence—the visible one and the invisible one. It's a struggle to eliminate violence against man. Once and for all.

JULIA: Why did you ask for me? Especially for me?

RAMON: I heard you are a good teacher. I always loved teachers. We need them, many of them…

JULIA: Many, yes. It would help…

(A silence.)

JULIA: They told me I can only stay a few minutes… what can I do for you?

RAMON: Come closer, please… I like to look at you… at your eyes.

JULIA: They told me you're dangerous…

RAMON: In a way I am. I believe in changes, improvements. That's dangerous in the eyes of those who prefer the status quo. The few who rule and want things to stay the way they are. Come closer, please.

JULIA: I was told not to...We are being watched.

RAMON: Are you afraid of a man in chains? You've been near them all your life.

JULIA: *(Who doesn't understand.)* Me? Oh no!... *(Suddenly realizing what he meant.)* Ah, you mean...We all are, more or less...

RAMON: *(Constantly studying her.)* Some more, some less.

JULIA: Please, tell me what...what I can do for you...

RAMON: Is there a class today?

JULIA: No, but...I must correct homework.

RAMON: Good girl. I always like diligent teachers. Continue the good work. And teach your pupils the truth.

JULIA: Which truth? There are so many...

RAMON: There is only one valid truth. Our duty to help each other, to help the weak.

JULIA: Yes...that's the truth we should all accept and respect.

RAMON: Make your students aware of the chains. Indicate those who exploit and those who are exploited. Those who lie to maintain their own privileges, and those who are deprived of their rights.

JULIA: We are a poor country, and it's not easy...

RAMON: Your Colonels have villas and servants.

JULIA: A few lucky ones...

RAMON: A few. A cruel oligarchy who revels at the expense of a hungry majority.

JULIA: *(Looking around with fear.)* I don't know, I don't really know. I'm only a teacher.

RAMON: The destiny of the Bolivians who study with you is in your hands. Teach them dignity. Only those who have dignity know how to fight for the freedom of their country.

JULIA: *(Nervous and uneasy.)* May I go now?

RAMON: Here, in my pocket, there is a piece of paper.

(He indicates his shirt pocket and asks her to take it; JULIA is embarrassed and doesn't go near him.)

RAMON: *(To MIGUEL.)* Please, Miguel, you take the paper.

(MIGUEL takes the paper and looks at it; he hesitates; he decides it is not dangerous and gives it to JULIA.)

RAMON: Thank you... *(To Julia.)* It's an article for the *Presencia* in La Paz. It will be easy to get the address.

JULIA: I know it. I read that paper too...All right, I'll mail it. *(She is ready to leave.)*

RAMON: Another thing.

JULIA: Yes...

RAMON: *(Slowly and clearly.)* The CIA has spread the rumor that I have been killed in Cuba. *(Ironically.)* By Fidel "in an outburst of anger." Please tell everybody that you saw me alive...Slightly wounded on the shoulder and the leg. Nothing serious—*definitely not fatal.*

JULIA: *Definitely not fatal.* I understand what you're saying. I will tell everybody. I promise.

(They look at each other with complete understanding; they know they will never meet again. Moved, JULIA now finds the courage to go near RAMON; with gentleness and simplicity, she touches his hand.)

RAMON: *(Grateful, tenderly.)* Thank you, Julia.

JULIA: *(Quietly.)* Goodbye..."Che."

(Music—A brief bridge.)

VOICE: Camillo Torres—a Columbian priest—said: "To be a good Christian means to prevent the exploitation of man by man. It's not enough to give your brother an old pair of shoes or crumbs from your table. You love your brother by giving him agrarian reform, free schools and hospitals, a rational distribution of the wealth, equal opportunities for everybody. One can get all this only by taking political power." He was murdered.

(Brief blackout to indicate the passing of time. THE LIEUTENANT is talking to RAMON. Only MIGUEL is present, in a corner of the room.)

LIEUTENANT: *(To RAMON.)* ...I tell you the truth. The more I think about it, the less I understand...Your family is rich. You left them. You became a physician. Instead of practicing your profession in a city where you're paid, you prefer to take care of these savages—in the jungle. You make a Revolution in Cuba. You win—you become a Ministro. My God, you could live beautifully—with all the privileges of your position: money and women! Instead you come here—to suffer and possibly die. I don't understand you. In Havana they have the best brothels in the world!

RAMON: *(Correcting him.)* They *had.* When the economy was dependent on American tourism.

LIEUTENANT: But Cuba still has beautiful women! With your position and power, you could have hundreds of them! Anything you want!

RAMON: There are men who prefer to fight exploitation and hunger.

LIEUTENANT: But you had won *your* revolution! I can understand winning one! But two, it's absurd! Who has ever won two or more revolutions! No one!

RAMON: As long as there's injustice and hunger, there'll be revolutionaries. And to start a revolution is the first duty of men like me.

LIEUTENANT: Let's reason a little. You're not hungry. Who cares about the "others"? The world is full of hungry people. How can you feed all of them. It's impossible! Look—if I divided my rations and my pay with hundreds of starving Indians, we would all end up hungry!

RAMON: You know very well that we don't want "charity." A few pennies to be shared by many. Society must be reorganized. No more exploitation. No more class distinction.

LIEUTENANT: A society with no class distinction? It's impossible, my friend. You and me—we come from a different environment. Maybe it's some fortunate coincidence—I don't know—but we are a step above—what am I saying?—Many steps above the Indians, the unemployed, the misery around us. I don't mean to boast, Che, but I have a degree! I've studied hard to get it! In a way, I belong to the...ruling class.

RAMON: *(Ironically.)* In a way.

LIEUTENANT: All right. My power is limited. But we—the ones who have studied—we are the ruling class. We are different from the others. We are a class apart.

RAMON: Our duty is to commit suicide as a class so that we can be restored to life as revolutionary workers, totally identified with the deepest aspirations of the people.

LIEUTENANT: It's ridiculous! Some are born white, some are born black. We were born with more intelligence than the others. It's our destiny to rule.

RAMON: While millions starve? While hundreds of thousands are murdered in the streets and in jails?

LIEUTENANT: It takes years, Che. It takes patience.

RAMON: Patience? Oh no! You cannot ask those who are starving to be patient. This is a continent where a hundred and seventy million human beings go to bed hungry! How much longer can they endure suffering in silence?

LIEUTENANT: It's their destiny to live like that. No one is going to save them. Look at the results of the other revolutions. Jesus Christ—who spoke for the humble, the poor, for justice among men. His priests are today fat and self-satisfied and help no one. Look at the Russians. Fat and happy—they don't help anyone. The same with the Cubans! You are the only one who left them. The few on top eat like pigs. The others, starve!

RAMON: Where did you read that?

LIEUTENANT: Somewhere. The world always turns in the same direction. You are the exception, Che. That's why I admire you. You are—how should I say—a romantic. The others abandon the boat when it's sinking. You leave it when it's safely anchored in the harbor.

RAMON: After one step, another must follow.

LIEUTENANT: The Americans would call you a "dropout." No offense, Che, but you are a dropout.

RAMON: It's a compliment. "Dropping out" can be an act of affirmation if you know what you're doing. I did it twice. I dropped out from a comfortable life in Rosario. I dropped out from an easy life in an office in Cuba, after the victory. But I always dropped out from what you call a "safely anchored boat," with a plan in my head. It's the only positive act in a world where violence against the defenseless is still a daily occurrence.

(We hear footsteps coming from stage right. THE COLONEL enters. He is followed by THE MAN and Bolivian soldiers. With them are two prisoners: JUAN and ANICETO. RAMON and the two prisoners exchange smiles. THE COLONEL signals to tie them against the wall, one at the right and the other at the left. The two prisoners are now with their arms stretched out—not unlike the two thieves at either side of the crucified Christ. THE COLONEL hands THE LIEUTENANT some money for the soldiers. THE LIEUTENANT whispers something into THE COLONEL's ear while looking at RAMON. THE COLONEL sits down near RAMON, while THE LIEUTENANT hands some money to the soldiers.)

COLONEL: My dear "Comandante"—as you can see—we have captured your last two men.

RAMON: *(Ironical.)* The last two?

COLONEL: Precisely. Ask my soldiers if you don't believe me. Those two were sleeping like logs. Tired of escaping, no doubt. The last two.

RAMON: *(Ironical.)* If it pleases you, believe it. *(Noticing that each soldier is getting two banknotes; in a deep full voice to the soldiers.)* That's only an advance! Prepare the receipts for the Colonel. *(Caustic.)* I'm sure he will have to justify the many expenses he had.

COLONEL: *(Nervous and irritated.)* Amazing that you still feel like joking!

RAMON: Always. By the way—how much time do I have? What are the orders from Washington?

COLONEL: Washington has nothing to do with this.

RAMON: We all know that you are mercenaries at the service of the imperialists.

COLONEL: In the same way you are the servants of Moscow.

RAMON: If Moscow helped the revolutionaries the way Washington helps the reactionaries, the world would be free in ten years. Or even sooner.

COLONEL: All right. You think whatever you want. I have come with a definite and clear purpose.

(THE COLONEL takes a piece of paper out of his pocket; it's yellow; RAMON recognizes it.)

RAMON: I recognize that. It's the same paper the Admiral asked me to sign.

COLONEL: And you spat in his face before he could show it to you! Are you crazy? He is an *admiral!*

RAMON: He's just another servant of the Pentagon. I don't like servants.

COLONEL: Have you any idea of what this is?

RAMON: It doesn't interest me.

COLONEL: It should. I warn you, Che. It's your only chance—your last hope. *(The COLONEL is sincere; he wants to help him; he wants to convince RAMON.)* You see, Che, I brought your two friends here to prove to you that the revolution in Bolivia has failed. If you admit it—by signing this paper—you'll be free to go back to Cuba.

RAMON: No.

COLONEL: Or to Argentina, if you prefer. To your parents.

RAMON: No.

COLONEL: You certainly know that your battle is over, my friend. If you don't sign, "Che" will disappear forever.

RAMON: Other "Ches" are already fighting against servants like you. And other "Ches" will follow my example in this struggle against indignity and hunger.

COLONEL: You're young, Che. You're only thirty-nine.

RAMON: And who wants to be a hundred—in a cesspool?

COLONEL: If you don't sign, Che, they'll kill you.

RAMON: "They." What an interesting admission!

COLONEL: *(Ignoring.)* You see, Che, I should hate you for what you did to me in Samaipata. But you're a Latino like me—you're an incurable romantic—and I like you...If you don't sign, it's the end, Che, it's death.

RAMON: It will be welcome if such a death will generate new will to continue our struggle.

COLONEL: Just admit a very simple truth, Che. That your revolution in Bolivia has failed. Nothing else. *(Shows him the paper.)*

RAMON: We have not failed. And you know it.

COLONEL: What do you lose by signing? Admit this defeat now. You can have another revolution later, somewhere else, where it's easier!

RAMON: One betrays a Revolution in many ways. Also by saying that it has been defeated. It would be a lie. I will not lie.

(A silence. THE COLONEL looks in RAMON's eyes. He knows he cannot convince him. He gives up. THE COLONEL turns his back to RAMON, and goes to THE MAN, who is waiting for him. They exchange a few words. Meanwhile, ANICETO talks to RAMON.)

ANICETO: When we heard that they had captured you...we couldn't run anymore...We lost our will to live.

RAMON: I understand, Aniceto. But I never thought you would lose your will to live. No one should.

JUAN: It's my fault, Ramon. I couldn't move—I really couldn't. Not even an inch, believe me.

RAMON: You did your best, I'm sure.

(THE COLONEL exits. THE MAN walks to RAMON. RAMON recognizes him and is surprised.)

RAMON: *(Charming, with an ironic smile.)* What a coincidence! From New York to La Higuera! How could I forget you? You smoked all my cigars—while smiling at me with half-closed eyes...Never trust anybody who can't look you straight in the eye.

MAN: You fool! Why did you ever come to Bolivia? You knew that these people can't be saved.

RAMON: Some people look at slaves and say: "Why try? It's hopeless!" I dream of slaves set free and say: "Why not?"

(A silence.)

MAN: I have my orders. I'm sorry...

(THE MAN raises his hand and signals THE LIEUTENANT and soldiers to get into position to shoot. When he lowers his hand, they fire. JUAN and ANICETO die. But the soldiers were unable to carry out the execution of RAMON. They deliberately missed him. THE MAN goes very close to RAMON. They look straight into each other's eyes. THE MAN slowly takes out his revolver and kills RAMON. THE MAN throws his special bag to BENO. BENO goes over to RAMON's body, takes a knife out of the bag, and lifts RAMON's right hand. This time we clearly see that he has done this time and time again. He cuts off the right hand of dead guerrilleros for their fingerprints. He takes the dismembered hand and holds it up, displaying it as if it were a trophy. Spotlight on JULIA.)

JULIA: *(Downstage, to the audience.)* "Che" said: "We love the world so much that we need to plunge into the adventure of changing it." *He was murdered.*

(FREEZE—BLACKOUT. CURTAIN.)

Note:

There is also a two-hour version in English, Italian, and Spanish.

Anniversary
A Thriller

The Characters:

THE FATHER—a handsome man in his early fifties
THE DAUGHTER—no resemblance to her father; in her early twenties
THE SERVANT—a handsome (black) man in his late twenties; formal and efficient

Time and Place:

Today; in New York City.

An elegant dining room with a long table. From a corner downstage, THE FATHER watches, through closed-circuit television, the arrival of THE DAUGHTER. THE SERVANT opens the door, bows: he takes her suitcase and places it in a corner. He helps THE DAUGHTER with her coat. Not a word is exchanged between the two. THE FATHER looks at her with admiration. For a long time.

FATHER: *(With open arms.)* My love!

DAUGHTER: *(After a brief hesitation.)* Daddy!

(A long embrace; they look at each other with curiosity, studying each other. As if it were the first time they met.)

FATHER: Welcome home, honey.

(THE DAUGHTER looks around while THE SERVANT adds some final touches to the decorated table.)

FATHER: Everything's the same. Just as it was last year. *(Pause.)* Every detail, just as you left it the last time.

(THE DAUGHTER looks at the objects with curiosity. She doesn't seem to recognize them.)

FATHER: The same armchair. You sat here; you were tired. *(A silence: he studies her.)* The same mirror. You admired yourself in it. I was behind you, like this...I said—: "We make a great couple, don't we? If we weren't father and daughter... *(Refrains.)* ...We look well together."

(They stare intensely at each other, studying each other, A long silence.)

FATHER: You remember?

DAUGHTER: I remember.

FATHER: Sit here, sweetheart. Peter will serve us right away—You remember Peter?

(THE DAUGHTER and THE SERVANT exchange glances. A faint polite smile.)

DAUGHTER: I remember him.

FATHER: Ever faithful! Without him this anniversary would be incomplete. Impossible.

(THE SERVANT smiles briefly, goes about his duties.)

FATHER: The ritual homecoming...every year at the same time. Punctual and precise, you cross that threshold as I wait with my heart throbbing. Full of love and anticipation.

(He embraces her again, hugs her lovingly.)

FATHER: Thank you.

(They sit silently at the two extreme ends of the table. THE SERVANT brings each one a different aperitif. He knows their taste. Maybe it is true the three know each other.)

FATHER: *(Raising his glass.)* To your beauty!

DAUGHTER: To…my "birthday"!

(They drink, staring at and studying each other.)

FATHER: I missed you. Twelve long months. It feels like an eternity. What were you doing during that eternity?

DAUGHTER: I traveled.

FATHER: Where?

DAUGHTER: *(Vaguely.)* California, Florida.

FATHER: By yourself?

DAUGHTER: By myself.

(Silence. THE FATHER stares at her. THE DAUGHTER avoids his gaze. THE SERVANT begins serving. A silence)

FATHER: Weren't you bored—all alone?

DAUGHTER: No.

FATHER: How did you spend your time?

DAUGHTER: Swimming, walking, reading…

FATHER: What did you read?

DAUGHTER: Simone de Beauvoir, Anaïs Nin, Kate Millett, Germaine Greer.

FATHER: Those women.

DAUGHTER: Those.

FATHER: Did they teach you how to hate men?

DAUGHTER: …To understand them.

FATHER: What did you understand?

DAUGHTER: Many things.

FATHER: Tell me.

(A silence.)

DAUGHTER: Ideally men want to have us there, ready and available, panting with desire, only when they feel like it. *(Vaguely sarcastic.)* When the mood strikes them. Once a week.

FATHER: That's not true.

DAUGHTER: Yes, it is.

FATHER: I desired your mother every night.

DAUGHTER: *(Vaguely ironic.)* You "desired."

FATHER: She was the one who didn't want me.

(A silence. THE DAUGHTER smiles faintly, mysteriously.)

FATHER: Did you know?

DAUGHTER: No.

FATHER: Did she ever tell you why?

DAUGHTER: No.

FATHER: Never?

DAUGHTER: Never.

FATHER: Swear to it.

DAUGHTER: *(Ready and sincere: raising her right hand.)* I swear. We *never* spoke of you.

(A silence. They eat, ignoring THE SERVANT's presence.)

FATHER: Why did you choose to read those books?

(A vague ironic gesture from THE DAUGHTER.)

FATHER: ...Do you need to know *more* about men?

DAUGHTER: Of course. It's a lifelong study.

FATHER: What else did you...find out?

DAUGHTER: Men have a basic fear of women.

FATHER: Not me.

(A silence; they study each other.)

DAUGHTER: That they have more hang-ups than we do.

FATHER: What kind of hang-ups?

DAUGHTER: All sorts...

(THE FATHER is waiting with curiosity; she keeps him in suspense.)

DAUGHTER: Insecure...Vain...Conceited...Selfish.

FATHER: Women too. It is the human condition.

DAUGHTER: They're more unfaithful than women...more—

FATHER: *(Cutting in.)* Those books will poison you!

DAUGHTER: Would you prefer me to say they're angels, faithful and dedicated, better than women?

FATHER: The truth, only the truth.

DAUGHTER: *(Shrugging.)* What's the truth?

FATHER: You're just like us. *(Cautiously, accusing.)* Unfaithful and fickle like us. Human...from "homo hominis"; human like us. You shouldn't deny that—

(A silence; THE DAUGHTER seems to ignore him; she nibbles without looking at him.)

FATHER: *(Suddenly.)* Who are you living with these days?

(A silence.)

FATHER: The same as last year?

DAUGHTER: No.

FATHER: Who is it this year?

DAUGHTER: You don't know him.

(A silence.)

FATHER: The one who sends you off to California or Florida—alone? *(A brief pause.)* Why?

DAUGHTER: He's insecure, confused, selfish.

FATHER: Insecure about what?

DAUGHTER: He's afraid of a female presence.

FATHER: Yours?

DAUGHTER: Mine...Others.

FATHER: Are there other women in his life?

DAUGHTER: I don't think so.

FATHER: Were there others, before you?

DAUGHTER. Possibly. Attempts. Men always try.

FATHER: Women, too.

DAUGHTER: Naturally.

FATHER: "Naturally." Nature can be blamed. It's easier.

(THE FATHER stares at her: THE DAUGHTER tries to ignore.)

DAUGHTER: *(Uneasy.)* It is easier.

FATHER: You didn't need those books to find out he's selfish and full of hang-ups.

DAUGHTER: Those books confirmed my own experiences.

FATHER: "Experiences." *(He studies her in silence.)* Did you have many…friends when you were alone on those beaches?

DAUGHTER: No.

FATHER: *(Vaguely ironic.)* How come?

DAUGHTER: I don't believe in casual friendships.

FATHER: *(Ironic.)* "Friendships"…

DAUGHTER: Love affairs. They give men weapons against women.

FATHER: What weapons?

DAUGHTER: *(Staring at him.)* Good reasons to despise us.

FATHER: "Good" reasons… *(Interested in that theory.)* An interesting thesis. "Don't drink when you've got your badge on. They might think that all Republicans are drunks."

DAUGHTER: Or whores.

(A silence; THE FATHER looks at her with admiration.)

FATHER: I'm proud to see that there are still gung-ho feminists, and that you are one of them. Ardent and dedicated. *(Looks at her with eyes full of love.)* All right, I believe you.

DAUGHTER: *(Vaguely sarcastic.)* Thanks!

FATHER: *(Deliberately, studying her.)* A year in white, then.

DAUGHTER: In white.

FATHER: Almost pure.

DAUGHTER: Pure.

FATHER: Only one man—the one who sends you far away to—

DAUGHTER: Not even him.

FATHER: Not even the first time, when you met him?

DAUGHTER: *(Staring at THE FATHER and studying him.)* No…He was wearing the badge and was drunk.

FATHER: And when he woke up the next morning?

DAUGHTER: He was surprised to see me in his bed. He couldn't remember asking me to stay. I told him he promised *forever*.

FATHER: And later, during the year? Did he…?

DAUGHTER: I waited with anticipation. Perfumed and romantic. Sentimental and naïve. Vibrant and passionate. Vulnerable. The way they want you.

FATHER: What happened?

DAUGHTER: Nothing.

(THE FATHER seems relieved and happy. This is good news for him. He eats with more relish. A silence.)

FATHER: Do you think he might be gay?

DAUGHTER: Not actively. *(Studying him.)* He's afraid to take the big step. He's afraid of everything.

FATHER: What about his friends? Did he have any? Did he introduce you to them?

DAUGHTER: No. He's very jealous. Jealous of everybody. And I mean everybody.

FATHER: Women too?

DAUGHTER: Women too.

FATHER: *(Thinking it over, with concealed joy.)* In twelve months, then, not even a caress, a—

DAUGHTER: *(Confirming.)* Not once.

FATHER: *(Happy.)* My baby! Pure and innocent. As immaculate as last year, when

I kissed your forehead, after our tender, delightful celebration.

DAUGHTER: Just the same, Daddy. *(Studies him; stares at him.)* Just as you've always wanted me to be. Pure and untouched.

FATHER: I'm glad, I can't tell you why but I'm glad. All fathers react the same way—I was told. "Naturally." It's human nature.

DAUGHTER: Men.

FATHER: *(Ignoring.)* Anyhow, before…

DAUGHTER: Before what?

FATHER: Do you remember what you told me last year?

DAUGHTER: No.

FATHER: Your trip to Europe. The Italian lover.

DAUGHTER: *(Vague.)* The past is past.

FATHER: The French one.

DAUGHTER: *(Nervously.)* I can't remember, Daddy. Let's talk about you. What have you been up to these last few months?

FATHER: You know my life. Office, bank, always alone.

DAUGHTER: Always?

FATHER: Almost.

DAUGHTER: You said you "desired" her every night.

FATHER: When I loved her. It's only when you love that you desire ardently, intensely.

(A silence. THE DAUGHTER nibbles. THE FATHER studies her with curiosity.)

FATHER: Don't you agree?

DAUGHTER: We are all different.

FATHER: Could you make love without loving?

DAUGHTER: What do you mean?

FATHER: Sex. Just sex.

DAUGHTER: *(Hesitating.)* I'd prefer not to, but theoretically—

FATHER: Theoretically?

DAUGHTER: You're a handsome man. Daddy. There must have been hundreds of women in your life. Did you love all of them?

FATHER: Less than a hundred. I loved all of them.

DAUGHTER: I congratulate you.

(A silence.)

FATHER: What about you?

DAUGHTER: Daddy…

FATHER: Why don't you want to talk about it?

DAUGHTER: There are things one doesn't discuss with one's father.

FATHER: That's why there is so much misunderstanding in the world. And so much suffering. Because we avoid those subjects…

(A silence.)

FATHER: Maybe you ran away from home because we didn't find the time to talk to each other.

DAUGHTER: "Love." I thought I was in love and I didn't want to talk about it. *(Straight in his eyes.)* I wanted to "feel."

FATHER: Did you "feel" with him?

DAUGHTER: I did.

(A silence.)

FATHER: *(Almost to himself.)* Not a letter, not a postcard, nothing! You could have let me know you were alive…

DAUGHTER: *(Nervously, vague.)* I didn't think you would forgive me. Some fathers don't.

FATHER: I loved you desperately. My only daughter... *(Suddenly.)* Why did you betray me?

(THE DAUGHTER is confused; THE SERVANT is now behind THE FATHER. With signals, he encourages THE DAUGHTER to answer: there is clearly an understanding between them.)

DAUGHTER: I...I didn't want to. You hardly talked to me then. You were a stranger to me and I couldn't...

FATHER: And now?

DAUGHTER: It's easier. You're opening up. You say you love me "desperately." You never told me that before, never.

FATHER: *(Feeling hurt, jumping to his feet.)* Never? *(Going toward her.)* I told you a hundred times a day!

DAUGHTER: *(Confused and intimidated.)* I don't remember.

FATHER: You don't remember? *(Advances toward her.)* Your mother, why did your mother leave me? Do you know why? *(Accusingly.)* Because I was devoting too much of my time to you! That's why!

(A silence. He is aggressive, nervous, perhaps dangerous. THE SERVANT resolves the situation by filling up his glass, moving his chair. He is humbly suggesting that he should sit down. THE FATHER is undecided. He calms down, and goes back to the other end of the table. A silence.)

FATHER: *(Sitting down again.)* Forgive me...But to hear you say I ignored you... *(Loud again.)* It's false, absolutely false!...I took you everywhere, you know that...Everywhere.

DAUGHTER: *(With curiosity.)* Where?

(A silence; they stare at each other.)

FATHER: To the theatre, all the time...And I would hold your hand, remember?...To the park, every Sunday...And I bought you everything you wanted...To the seashore, on my vacation...And I taught you how to swim.

(A silence; they study each other.)

FATHER: Can you swim?

(It is a strange question; THE SERVANT studies her hoping she may find the right answer.)

DAUGHTER: *(After some hesitation.)* Yes...

(A silence.)

FATHER: Diving into the pool, remember?

(THE DAUGHTER, uncertain, nods; they look at each other; someone is lying.)

FATHER: You got to be better at it...better than me, after only a few weeks... Have you learnt any new diving techniques?

DAUGHTER: No.

FATHER: Too bad... *(Looks at her with admiration.)* Any tennis, lately?

DAUGHTER: No.

FATHER: *(Deliberately, studying her.)* You were always so active, enterprising, full of initiative, curiosity...Are you still that way, with your thirst for adventure, come hell or high water?

DAUGHTER: I never was that way.

(A silence: they study each other.)

FATHER: Once you got lost in the woods...You wanted to prove that you had a good sense of direction...We had to organize a search team, with dogs and police, to find you...We did...Do you remember?

DAUGHTER: *(Uncertain and confused.)* No.

FATHER: We found you crying under an oak tree...Your dress muddy and torn...Hungry, thirsty and sorry...

(A silence; he studies her; she avoids his gaze.)

FATHER: You kissed my hand, gently...

(A silence; he continues to stare at her, hoping she will look at him.)

FATHER: Humble and guilty...Like today.

(He hopes for a reaction; THE DAUGHTER finally looks up and stares at him; there is a look of defiance in her eyes.)

FATHER: You were twelve years old...I remember what happened to me, at ten, eleven—

DAUGHTER: I'm different. I always block out unpleasant things.

(A silence.)

FATHER: What about your first man, the one who took you away from me? The others who—

DAUGHTER: *(Interrupting.)* Everything and everybody. That's how I cope with life. It's my only way of surviving. My only hope.

FATHER: Hope...At least I never lost that...The hope you'd come back, maybe for good.

(A silence; they study each other.)

DAUGHTER: Here I am...

(A silence.)

DAUGHTER: Born again...This *is* my birthday...

FATHER: *(With tears in his eyes.)* Mine too, love...Thank you.

(THE SERVANT has brought out a new dish; THE DAUGHTER looks at it; she does not like that kind of food: she refuses it.)

FATHER: *(Surprised.)* It's baby lamb with wild rice, your favorite dish!

DAUGHTER: *(Uneasy, confused.)* I'm—I'm not hungry now...not any longer... *(Smiles at THE FATHER.)*

FATHER: I ordered it for you, especially for you... *(Indicating.)* The same flowers, the same menu...Everything for you...Our special day...It's the one day that renews my hope in life, for the future, for us...

(THE SERVANT again places the dish in front of her. He looks at her disapprovingly. He practically compels her to accept it. THE DAUGHTER nibbles reluctantly.)

FATHER: And then we have veal cutlets, Caesar salad, eggplant parmesan, zucchini.

(THE SERVANT places the dishes at THE DAUGHTER's side, one after the other.)

DAUGHTER: *(Ill at ease.)* Thank you... *(Smiles at him faintly.)*

FATHER: As you can see, I remember your taste perfectly...

DAUGHTER: I'm flattered. *(Vaguely ironic.)* How can you remember so many details?

FATHER: *(Vague.)* "Love"...

DAUGHTER: My memory is not always...

FATHER: *(To THE SERVANT.)* Two lumps of sugar in her coffee...

(THE SERVANT carries out the order.)

FATHER: Just a drop of milk...

(THE SERVANT carries out the order.)

FATHER: Pecan pie...

(THE SERVANT cuts a slice and places it near THE DAUGHTER.) Coffee ice cream. *(To THE SERVANT.)* Later.

DAUGHTER: Thank you. Daddy. You're wonderful.

(A silence.)

FATHER: What do you remember about me?

DAUGHTER: Trying to make me feel guilty?

FATHER: Try to remember.

DAUGHTER: *(Searching.)* ...Affectionate, generous, paternal...

FATHER: You can say that about anyone.

DAUGHTER: You're the exception. You're more generous than anyone.

FATHER: What else?

DAUGHTER: *(Searching.)* ...Terribly busy—but you always found some time for me.

FATHER: Always.

DAUGHTER: ...Elegant...smelling nice—

FATHER: What kind of cologne do I wear?

DAUGHTER: *(Completely lost; she does not know; she mumbles in search of an idea.)* Well...I...

FATHER: You gave me a small green bottle every year—up 'til the year when...Our last time together. *(A brief pause.)* What cologne?

DAUGHTER: *(Trying to remember.)* Wait...I think...It seems to me...

(THE SERVANT succeeds in slipping a note—just scribbled—under THE DAUGHTER's napkin; THE FATHER does not notice it.)

DAUGHTER: *(Reading without being noticed.)* Vetiver.

FATHER: *(Surprised and pleased.)* You're beginning to remember, you see? Congratulations! What else do you remember?

DAUGHTER: Very little. Daddy. I'm sorry. You know I've always been absentminded.

FATHER: "Absentminded"—you say... *(Sad and bitter.)* Did you forget our address, the phone number?

DAUGHTER: I didn't write. Daddy, not to reopen old wounds. That first man in my life never wrote or phoned me. I prefer it that way. It helps me forget. I suffer less. I wanted you to suffer less, not to suffer at all, if possible.

FATHER: Didn't you ever feel a need for me, for a father who would advise and protect you?

DAUGHTER: A thousand times. At least a thousand. I would have wanted a father, I needed one—

(She suddenly refrains; that is an unexpected confession, a mistake; THE FATHER stares at her; she corrects herself.)

DAUGHTER: A father by my side, I mean, when I needed him most. In moments of desperation.

FATHER: I was here.

DAUGHTER: I didn't know I could count on you.

FATHER: And today? Do you know it now?

DAUGHTER: I do.

FATHER: Will you forget again?

DAUGHTER: Never again.

(THE DAUGHTER stares at THE SERVANT, who is again behind THE FATHER, as if she were waiting for him to cue her; THE SERVANT encourages her to continue.)

DAUGHTER: For me...in a way...it's almost as if I didn't have a father...

(A silence.)

FATHER: (Studying her.) What do you mean?

DAUGHTER: (Vague.) I left home too soon—I was only sixteen...That's when you need someone to guide you—a friend, a father...

FATHER: I loved you...I was always with you...Advising, protecting...I answered all your questions. I even gave you a picture of Michelangelo's *David* when you wanted to know how a man looks.

DAUGHTER: (Smiling, surprised; with curiosity.) How old was I?

FATHER: Only six.

DAUGHTER: And I asked you...?

FATHER: To see, yes, to show you, how a man...

DAUGHTER: (Amused, smiling.) And you?

FATHER: I bought you a book on anatomy. And some copies of paintings, sculptures.

DAUGHTER: (Almost to herself.) Six years old...If I could go back in time. Daddy...I'd adore you.

FATHER: Do you want to go back in time?

DAUGHTER: If it were possible...

FATHER: (Sure of himself.) Everything is possible.

DAUGHTER; Really? (With hope.) How?

FATHER: Are you ready?

DAUGHTER: Ready and waiting.

(THE FATHER signals to THE SERVANT to put out the lights. He turns on a film projector. It is a home movie. THE FATHER may resemble THE FATHER. THE DAUGHTER may be completely different.)

FATHER: (Improvising, according to the scenes.) ... Near the pool, you see...you fell in twice. I rescued you, ruining my best suit...That beach ball, I remember it well, it was enormous...—You could never get your arms around it...Look at the tenderness in those spontaneous precious kisses...I never asked for them...You adored me...the garden...You danced very well, look...You wanted to be a ballerina...Your first dive, a good one...grace, joy, happiness...We were happy... (Etc., etc., ad lib.)

(THE FATHER is very close to THE DAUGHTER now. He speaks tenderly in her ear. THE FATHER and THE DAUGHTER are still watching the film. THE SERVANT observes them through the same closed-circuit television that THE FATHER used at the beginning of the play. THE FATHER is now caressing THE DAUGHTER. Intimately. The way a lover would. Her shoulders, hips, breasts. THE DAUGHTER continues watching the film, ignoring THE FATHER's actions. THE SERVANT observes with extreme interest. But he is not surprised. He is calm and self-assured. He controls his reactions very well. The film rolls along. Suddenly, it becomes "bold"—X-rated. A nude couple in bed. THE DAUGHTER, imperturbable, continues to watch all the details. As if it were still an innocent film. THE FATHER is no longer caressing her. Instead of watching the film, which he probably saw many times before, he studies THE DAUGHTER with curiosity and admiration. He likes her; he admires her behavior. The end of the film. The spell is broken. THE SERVANT comes back and turns on the lights. A silence. THE FATHER and THE DAUGHTER are uneasy, now. They try to forget and ignore what has just happened.)

FATHER: (Returning to his seat and signaling THE SERVANT to bring in ice cream *and liqueurs.)* You saw how much love is in my heart...I adored you...For me—for me you were everything. A daughter is everything. It's a reflection of yourself, gentler, more beautiful, more vulnerable...I loved you the way I loved myself—more than myself. I told myself a hundred times: —"I'd go through fire for her. If she were drowning I'd jump in to die with her..."

DAUGHTER: Instinct.

FATHER: There is in me this desire to protect, worship, save...And you... You too, you saw how much you loved me... Sometimes, unexpectedly, you'd hug me tight and you'd kiss me...My heart would melt in those moments...Yours was true love, spontaneous love. You kissed me on the lips—lips strangely moist—instinctively sensual—lover's lips...You squeezed me tight, you held me close...Tenderly. Sweetly. All mine. You loved me, you really did...

(A silence; she tries to avoid his eyes.)

FATHER: *(Suddenly.)* Why did you betray me? *(There is grief in his voice.)*

(A silence; THE DAUGHTER is upset and confused: she does not know what to say.)

DAUGHTER: *(Uneasily.)* Betrayed—in what sense?

FATHER: Running away from home, with another man.

DAUGHTER: I admit I made a mistake. I shouldn't have...

FATHER: *(Interrupting.)* You shouldn't have kissed another man more tenderly than you ever kissed me! *(He is desperate; he tries to control himself.)* He meant more to you, I know...Did he...? *(He is very upset, very jealous; he wrings his hands; it is difficult for him to control himself.)* When I think about it, I want to die...

(A silence; THE DAUGHTER regards him with compassion.)

FATHER: *(Suddenly.)* Were you jealous of your mother?

DAUGHTER: *(Very surprised.)* Me?

FATHER: Some daughters, many daughters are jealous of their mothers.

DAUGHTER: I wasn't.

FATHER: Daughters know...They spy... They're curious. You came into our room many times, early in the morning, to spy on us...To spy on what we were doing, on our awakening...Once you saw me naked—still asleep—you whispered it in my ear, blushing. Remember?

DAUGHTER: I remember.

FATHER: Was it true?

DAUGHTER: It was true.

FATHER: What did you think? What kind of impression?

DAUGHTER: What do you mean?

FATHER: How did you react? A naked man is not handsome when he is asleep. What was your first impression? Fear? Surprise? Repulsion?

DAUGHTER: *(Improvising.)* Surprise. Michelangelo's *David* looks different.

FATHER: Great works of Art do. Did you run away from home because I wasn't as good-looking as *David*?

DAUGHTER: *(Maternal, reproaching him.)* Daddy...

FATHER: Yes or no?

DAUGHTER: No.

FATHER: Why then? Why do you reappear only on your birthday? Where do you live? How?

DAUGHTER: *(After a hesitation.)* I left home because I was in love with that man. *(A brief pause; taking courage.)* I'm here only on my birthday because that's the only time you invite me.

(A silence; it is the truth; THE FATHER is uneasy.)

FATHER: Your mother, do you see her often?

DAUGHTER: No...

FATHER: How many times a year?

DAUGHTER: Hardly ever.

FATHER: How many?

DAUGHTER: *(Intimidated.)* Two, three times.

FATHER: Your mother was insanely jealous of you.

(THE DAUGHTER feels she is being studied. She does not know what to say.)

FATHER: Constantly. When we argued, do you know why?

DAUGHTER: No.

FATHER: Because of you. She accused me of neglecting her, since you were born. It was true, in a sense. When one becomes a mother, she is no longer a lover.

(THE DAUGHTER looks at him with curiosity.)

FATHER: No longer...Mistresses? Do you think I took on mistresses when I began ignoring your mother? No, never...Before you were born, yes, I did. Afterwards, never...

(THE DAUGHTER smiles at him gratefully. This is a compliment.)

FATHER: You changed my life...Your skin, as soft as petals...your tiny hands...I was delirious with joy. Many fathers prefer having a son—to leave him their scepter, their power, their money. Not me, I wanted a daughter...Who would grow up in a unique, special way. Beautiful, intelligent, regal, pure...I wanted my daughter to be pure. *(Stares at her. Suddenly.)* How many lovers did you have, after...after your..."seducer"?

DAUGHTER: *(Surprised, confused.)* Two, only two...

FATHER: Two mistakes, other mistakes, many more, I know...The perfect man doesn't exist.

DAUGHTER: *(Resigned.)* He does not, I know.

FATHER: *(With hope.)* Do you realize it now?

DAUGHTER: Yes...

(They study each other; THE DAUGHTER lowers her eyes: she is uneasy; the questions are getting difficult.)

FATHER: Your mother, did she know you were running away with him?

DAUGHTER: No.

FATHER: How did she find you? How did she get your address?

(THE DAUGHTER is confused: she looks at THE SERVANT for advice and help. THE SERVANT encourages her to continue.)

DAUGHTER: I don't know...I found her one day at my door—

FATHER: *(With morbid jealousy.)* Were you in bed? In bed with him?

DAUGHTER: No. He had gone out.

FATHER: What did she say?

DAUGHTER: She asked me to come home.

FATHER: Did she talk about me? About my suffering?

DAUGHTER: Yes. She said I should go home because of you too. For your sake. You were...very worried.

FATHER: "Worried"? Is that all she said, that bitch?

DAUGHTER: More or less...

FATHER: What else did she say?

DAUGHTER: *(Uncertain, improvising.)* That I was too young, that I was making a big mistake—

FATHER: About me—what else did she say about me?

DAUGHTER: That...you were waiting for me...That you were depressed, hurt.

(THE FATHER stares at her again. In a different way, now, for a long time. There is some tenderness in his eyes. THE DAUGHTER does not know what to do and lowers her eyes.)

FATHER: Did you confide in your mother?

DAUGHTER: At times...

FATHER: And she?

DAUGHTER: She too. At times...

FATHER: How many lovers did she have?

DAUGHTER: Oh no! She never spoke about that.

FATHER: But you knew!

DAUGHTER: I knew what?

FATHER: That she had lovers.

DAUGHTER: No.

FATHER: Did you suspect it?

DAUGHTER: No, I didn't.

FATHER: Not even the slightest suspicion?

DAUGHTER: *(Confused.)* Perhaps...There is always that possibility—

FATHER: Did you ever see him?

DAUGHTER: Who?

FATHER: Her lover. The last one.

DAUGHTER: No.

FATHER: Did she come to your..."nest" alone?

DAUGHTER: Alone.

FATHER: Swear!

DAUGHTER: *(Intimidated.)* I do—honestly...

FATHER: *(Calms down; he seems satisfied. Staring at her.)* I believe you...You're an honest girl...sincere...I know you don't know how to lie...That you'd prefer not to lie. *(He looks at her with admiration and kindness; she is passing the examination with flying colors.)* Is it true you prefer not to lie?

DAUGHTER: It is true, Daddy... *(Lowers her eyes.)*

FATHER: ...That you feel better when you tell the truth, the whole truth, and nothing but the truth?

DAUGHTER: *(Timidly.)* Yes.

FATHER: Well, then...

(He studies her; she looks at him.)

FATHER: Tell me about *your* mother.

DAUGHTER: *(Surprised, diffident.)* You mean...

FATHER: Your *own* mother.

DAUGHTER: *(Unbelieving.)* My own mother?

FATHER: Yours.

(She is surprised. It is a huge turnaround. A new relationship. We discover she is not his daughter. She looks at THE SERVANT. He nods. THE DAUGHTER can finally talk about her real mother.)

DAUGHTER: *(Relieved.)* All right...The truth, the whole truth?

FATHER: Everything.

DAUGHTER: My mother...Irish father and Italian mother. Catholic. Very religious. Honest to the point of naïveté. Honesty personified. At fifteen, she wanted to become a nun. She wanted to dedicate all her energies to alleviating the sufferings in the world. Through the intensity of prayer. My father told her to pray less and study more. He convinced her that the wounds of the world could be eliminated in other ways.

FATHER: *(With curiosity.)* How?

(A silence; THE FATHER is very curious about this answer; THE DAUGHTER realizes she must be careful.)

DAUGHTER: By becoming a good wife, a good mother, a dedicated teacher.

(THE FATHER smiles. He likes this type of answer.)

DAUGHTER: She taught for twenty-one years in a Catholic school...I was one of her pupils...She was very strict with me...Because she loved me. She died last year, of a broken heart.

FATHER: *(With interest.)* Why?

DAUGHTER: My father's disappearance...No one knows where he is.

FATHER: Dead?

DAUGHTER: I don't think so... *(A brief pause.)* Maybe he was just tired of living in this hell of a city...Maybe he started a new life in some quiet unknown corner of this world...

FATHER: Tell me more about him.

DAUGHTER: *(Uncertain.)* Him...My real father?

FATHER: Him.

(THE DAUGHTER looks at THE SERVANT. He nods. She can talk about her father too.)

DAUGHTER: He was very active, politically...He had no time for me...He wasn't capable of loving the way *you* love...Your daughter is lucky.

(THE FATHER reacts nervously. THE SERVANT drops a plate. Maybe it is a warning. She shouldn't have mentioned the real daughter.)

FATHER: *(Ignoring THE SERVANT and composing himself.)* Do you have brothers and sisters?

DAUGHTER: No.

FATHER: Do you live alone?

DAUGHTER: Alone.

(A silence; THE FATHER is reflecting.)

FATHER: *(With admiration.)* Alone... Young, gentle, beautiful. You have all the qualities of my— *(He holds back; he avoids mentioning his lost daughter; he cannot.)* What's your name?

(THE DAUGHTER looks at THE SERVANT again to ask him if she may answer this question; THE SERVANT's face is impenetrable this time; she must decide by herself, alone.)

DAUGHTER: Mary Therese Keenan.

FATHER: *(Pleased, enchanted.)* Mary...a pure innocent name...symbol of a Virgin...Your mother chose an ideal name for you. When were you born?

DAUGHTER: *(Still unable to catch THE SERVANT's eye.)* October 18.

FATHER: Libra...Romantic, sensual, undecided... *(He gets up and goes to open the safe; he leaves it open; he places a little box of jewels on the table. To THE DAUGHTER.)* Open it.

(THE DAUGHTER timidly opens the box; she takes out some magnificent jewels; she admires them, one after the other.)

FATHER: They were intended for her, my angel...a gift from her grandmother... *(Indicates the house and everything in it.)* Everything here, for my daughter...I worked and built for her...for her happiness. Did Peter tell you?

DAUGHTER: No.

FATHER: *(Swallows hard; there is a lump in his throat; he can hardly talk; he is too emotional. With tears in his eyes.)* She started taking drugs...She fell in love... left home one night...disappeared...No trace, ever... *(Savoring the name.)* Mary...Mary...I...I live alone, you see...I would like... *(He is uneasy; he is about to make an important decision.)* I like you, Mary...I would like to...I could adopt you legally...The document is right here, ready...All you have to do is sign your name...Mary Therese Keenan... *(He writes her name on the document.)* ...my signature... *(Signs the document.)* ...and yours...

(He pushes the document toward THE DAUGHTER who is surprised, uncertain, immobile.)

FATHER: Please...

(THE SERVANT drops another plate; THE FATHER is annoyed by it and looks askance at him; THE DAUGHTER ignores THE SERVANT this time; she wants to make up her own mind.)

FATHER: I...I would be happy, happy again if you came to live with me here...I...I need a woman who can be everything to me...mother, sister, daughter...a loving creature near me...

(They stare intensely at each other; it is a daring proposal, with many implications; THE DAUGHTER is trying to decide; maybe THE FATHER is the perfect man for her. THE SERVANT intervenes by putting the small suitcase down next to THE DAUGHTER.)

FATHER: *(To THE SERVANT.)* What's wrong with you?

SERVANT: *(Humbly.)* The other ones, the other years—

FATHER: This year is different! Mary is different!

(A silence; THE DAUGHTER does not dare look at THE SERVANT; THE SERVANT keeps away but leaves her suitcase next to her.)

FATHER: *(Kneeling down beside THE DAUGHTER, with love.)* A woman who will be everything in my life...Everything...Mary, make me happy. *(Humbly.)* I've only a few more years...

(THE DAUGHTER is tense, undecided.)

FATHER: Make me happy by giving me back a daughter who knows how to love...Erasing from my life all these phony, hypocritical "birthdays"—full of lies—nothing more than a sick staging of unfulfilled dreams... *(With a pleading voice.)* Please, sign that paper and we'll be together, forever...Father and daughter...Maybe lovers...Maybe...Only if you want to. You must make that decision... *(With hope.)* Maybe tomorrow...A month from now...A year from now...Whenever you want.

(THE DAUGHTER is uncertain; the offer is tempting; it is THE SERVANT who is clearly against this agreement.)

DAUGHTER: Why me?

FATHER: Because it's you.

DAUGHTER: *(Uncertain.)* Did you offer the same thing to your other...birthday guests?

FATHER: *(Offended.)* Never! Ask Peter.

(They both look at him; THE SERVANT's answer is ambiguous: a vague smile that could mean yes or no.)

FATHER: Speak up, Peter! Tell Mary the truth. Did I ever offer my life to anyone before?

SERVANT: *(Hypocritically.)* The truth? *(Hesitates.)* If you want it, if you really do…

FATHER: *(Impatient.)* The truth, yes! Did I ever ask them to stay for good?

SERVANT: *(Hypocritically.)* Well…to stay, yes—

FATHER: *(Furious.)* For the night! Little tramps supplied by your pimping! Paid for the night! Did I ever offer my life, my house, my future to any of them?

SERVANT: *(Vague.)* No…

(THE SERVANT, using his foot, pushes the small suitcase toward THE DAUGHTER; closer to her, within reach; THE DAUGHTER ignores the action.)

FATHER: *(To THE DAUGHTER.)* Did you hear that? Never, never! This is a special day in my life! *You* are born into my life today! You, you, Mary! Today we start a new life. Together—

(He places the document in front of THE DAUGHTER; it is obvious that the temptation is too strong; she is about to give in. THE SERVANT picks up the suitcase, puts it on the table, and opens it.)

FATHER: *(Furious.)* What are you doing? What do you want here? Put that thing away!

SERVANT: *(Calm, imperturbable; he shows a hundred dollar bill.)* I'm going to pay her, as usual— *(He is about to put the bill in the suitcase.)*

FATHER: How dare you, idiot! Get out! I don't need you any longer! Get out!

(THE SERVANT ignores him; he slowly searches into the suitcase; he takes out a revolver. THE DAUGHTER does not show any surprise; THE FATHER is shocked, frightened; he backs away.)

SERVANT: *(Deliberately, pointing the gun.)* I've been your servant for years…Your slave and…"pimp." We've decided—the two of us— *(Indicates THE DAUGHTER.)* to do something about it…Today.

(THE FATHER is speechless; he never suspected THE DAUGHTER might be THE SERVANT's accomplice.)

SERVANT: *(To THE DAUGHTER, slowly.)* Do you want to shoot him—to give me another proof of your love?

(A silence; THE DAUGHTER does not react; she is "absent"; evidently, she does not want to shoot; THE FATHER is speechless, terrorized; THE SERVANT decides it is up to him to shoot.)

SERVANT: *(To THE FATHER.)* Sorry…I have to do it…Women are too gentle for this sort of thing…They can't stand blood… *(Ironical.)* Goodbye, Master…With money and jewels, your "pimp" will become a free man…

(He steps forward, fires one shot to his heart, at close range. THE FATHER collapses. SERVANT checks his heartbeat. THE FATHER is dead. THE SERVANT, who is still wearing his white gloves—thus leaving no fingerprints—carefully places the revolver in THE FATHER's right hand. His finger on the trigger. To make it look like suicide. THE DAUGHTER is still immobile, "absent." As if she hadn't seen a thing.)

SERVANT: *(With admiration, complimenting her.)* Great, Mary! You were magnificent! *(Takes out several stacks of bills from the safe and puts them into the suitcase. Then he takes the box of jewels and places it next to the money.)* Are you ready? *(A brief pause; he studies her.)* We can go now.

(THE DAUGHTER slowly goes to see THE FATHER. She stares at him. She kneels down to the body.)

SERVANT: The sooner we go, the better. What are you doing?

DAUGHTER: His finger is not on the trigger. It slipped off.

(She leans to place the finger back on the trigger. She picks up the dead man's hand, and shoots in the direction of THE SERVANT. One, two, three times. She kills him.)

(Slowly, she eases back the hand of the "murderer." So, it will appear that THE FATHER killed THE SERVANT. She takes the document to be signed and goes to sit in THE FATHER'S "throne." Sitting at the head of the table, she signs the document. Now she is in charge. She is the mistress of the house. She is born again. This is her "birthday.")

(CURTAIN. THE END.)

Note:

Winner, first prize, Arta Terme Theatre Award.

Missionaries

The Persons:

MOTHER CATERINA: in her early sixties
FATHER EDWARD: in his early thirties

Place:

A modest apartment in Africa

Two doors. The one upstage leads into the bedroom. The one stage right leads outside. FATHER EDWARD is pacing nervously. MOTHER CATERINA enters.

FATHER EDWARD: Mother... *(He calms dawn; controls himself.)*

MOTHER CATERINA: Where is Sister Mary? She didn't come home last night.

FATHER EDWARD: *(Signaling that she should lower her voice, indicating the bedroom door.)* She's asleep. She's resting.

(MOTHER CATERINA approaches the door, but he stops her.)

FATHER EDWARD: She's tired...

(A silence, they stare at each other.)

FATHER EDWARD: Please sit down.

(She hesitates.)

FATHER EDWARD: I was hoping to have a chance to talk with you...Now, please... You know, you're like a mother to me. Sweet and wise.

(She is flattered by the word "mother.")

FATHER EDWARD: Please...

(He indicates a chair. She sits, ready to listen.)

FATHER EDWARD: Would you like a cup of coffee?

MOTHER CATERINA: No.

FATHER EDWARD: Tea?

MOTHER CATERINA: No.

(A silence.)

FATHER EDWARD: Mother, I am plagued with doubts.

MOTHER CATERINA: Everyone has doubts.

FATHER EDWARD: Here in Africa... *(He hesitates.)*

MOTHER CATERINA: Tell me.

FATHER EDWARD: Are we really useful here?

MOTHER CATERINA: Of course we are. How many years have you been here?

FATHER EDWARD: Four.

MOTHER CATERINA: I have been here ten years. I feel useful.

FATHER EDWARD: Since I've been here seventy percent of my parishioners have died. Terrible, agonizing deaths.

MOTHER CATERINA: It's God's will.

FATHER EDWARD: Mother...you know very well that if we had more medicines, more food, more money, they wouldn't die.

MOTHER CATERINA: Providence sends us what it can. It is in the divine design.

FATHER EDWARD: It's not enough and you know that. Why doesn't the Holy Father send us more mon—?

MOTHER CATERINA: *(Interrupting.)* His goodness is infinite. His wisdom is infinite. He does what he can. He has the whole world to protect and help. Wherever there is poverty, war, hunger.

FATHER EDWARD: Why doesn't he admonish the billionaires, the selfish ones who navigate in gold and don't help?

MOTHER CATERINA: He's doing that constantly. He preaches love and charity.

FATHER EDWARD: Obviously they're not listening to him. We don't have medicine, tools, money.

MOTHER CATERINA: There is so much need in every corner of the world. They distribute part of the charity they receive according to the slice that has been assigned to Africa...to the many African countries where people are suffering.

FATHER EDWARD: We read that there are individuals who earn two, three million dollars a day. It's incredible! Billions are wasted while we, here...

MOTHER CATERINA: We must have faith. And we must take the initiative with our own direct contacts. I know, personally, a nice gentleman in Los Angeles. I write him directly twice a year. He always sends me two hundred dollars. You should do the same. Why don't you write directly to your rich friends?

FATHER EDWARD: Rich friends, me? I don't have any.

MOTHER CATERINA: Write to associations, to the mayor of your city, to your professors. Do you remember them?

FATHER EDWARD: I remember a teacher. She was an angel. Tender, human, serene. You remind me of her...You're angelic, like her...I often thought of my teacher when I saw you speaking and scolding the young sisters.

(A silence.)

FATHER EDWARD: Thank you for listening. Your words are so soothing to me. Like a caress...It's the first time in many months...

(A silence. They stare at each other.)

FATHER EDWARD: I have been hoping to talk to you for a long time... *(He hesitates.)* You avoid me...in church, at the mess, everywhere...Why?

MOTHER CATERINA: We sisters, we don't notice anyone. We are immersed in prayer.

FATHER EDWARD: We priests pray too; but we also look around and smile.

MOTHER CATERINA: We never let our eyes meet the eyes of a man. It's our way. Part of our duties.

FATHER EDWARD: We are your brothers in Christ.

MOTHER CATERINA: Men.

(A short silence.)

FATHER EDWARD: I've seen you with Father James. You talk to *him*. So why not with me?

MOTHER CATERINA: I avoid you because... *(Hesitates.)*

FATHER EDWARD: Why?

MOTHER CATERINA: You know why.

FATHER EDWARD: Why?

MOTHER CATERINA: I found you with that…black woman.

FATHER EDWARD: You need tolerance. Mother. They offer themselves. They need comfort.

MOTHER CATERINA: Comfort?

FATHER EDWARD: Kind words…They have lost fathers and brothers. They're desperate.

MOTHER CATERINA: Catechism. You must teach them how to love Jesus. He alone can comfort them. Only our Lord heals and saves.

FATHER EDWARD: They listen. They pray. And then they offer themselves. They need—

MOTHER CATERINA: Money. They're prostitutes.

FATHER EDWARD: Yes. They are. And it's true that they're a bigger danger today with all the diseases. Therefore…

MOTHER CATERINA: Therefore?

FATHER EDWARD: I don't involve myself with them anymore.

(A silence.)

FATHER EDWARD: I've been looking for true love.

MOTHER CATERINA: You found that, the day you dedicated your life to Jesus.

(A silence.)

FATHER EDWARD: Even Father James has been with…black women. You still talk to him. I think there's another reason why you haven't spoken to me… *(He points to the bedroom door.)*

MOTHER CATERINA: You're right. That is the reason. This is a very serious sin, a deadly sin.

FATHER EDWARD: Mary told me that—

MOTHER CATERINA: *(Interrupting.)* Sister Mary.

FATHER EDWARD: That you reproach her, that you persecute her.

MOTHER CATERINA: It's my duty to reproach her. But I never persecute anyone.

FATHER EDWARD: She feels humiliated.

MOTHER CATERINA: She should. It's my responsibility to admonish her and advise her. I consider her to be my daughter. One of my daughters.

FATHER EDWARD: Mother, ours is a great love.

MOTHER CATERINA: Our great love must be for Jesus, only for Jesus and his church.

FATHER EDWARD: We are human.

MOTHER CATERINA: With a mission. We must serve with humility and faith. "Peace and Obedience" is our motto. Obedience to Church law and to our vows. We have promised our lives to our Lord.

FATHER EDWARD: Mary— *(Correcting himself.)* Sister Mary is young. She has feelings, desires.

MOTHER CATERINA: She is the Lord's bride. She promised her purity to Him. Our religious commitment imposes that rule on us.

FATHER EDWARD: We are still religious. Mary and I. Very religious.

MOTHER CATERINA: How? How can you pray? How can you confess yourselves? How can you be serene knowing what you are doing—carrying that guilt around with you?

FATHER EDWARD: When we meet we first kneel down and pray together. Our Lord sees that our love is sincere and I'm sure He forgives us.

MOTHER CATERINA: Jesus sees everything from Heaven and He suffers. You are making Him suffer.

FATHER EDWARD: We feel His benevolent look. We kiss His image. He forgives us.

MOTHER CATERINA: Well, I don't! The Church doesn't! The Holy Father in Rome would not forgive you if...he knew.

FATHER EDWARD: He will never know. It's our secret. A pure love...

MOTHER CATERINA: Pure?

FATHER EDWARD: Yes... *(Points to the bedroom again.)* When two people are truly committed to each other—

MOTHER CATERINA: *(Getting up.)* I don't want to talk about this anymore. Wake her up. I'm taking her with me.

FATHER EDWARD: *(Begging her to sit again.)* Just another minute...I have something else to tell you...I need your advice.

MOTHER CATERINA: Ask Father Mario. He's the oldest among you. He's your spiritual guide.

FATHER EDWARD: He wouldn't understand. You can. I know you can. You are my mother in this moment. My sweet mother who is looking at us from heaven and is blessing us.

(She crosses herself.)

FATHER EDWARD: She is blessing you too. She is blessing you because you have the goodness to listen to me and advise me.

MOTHER CATERINA: Only our Lord is infinite goodness. Stop this madness of yours. This insidious sin. Only then will you be forgiven.

FATHER EDWARD: I wanted to tell you... I have come to a turning point.

MOTHER CATERINA: *(Alarmed.)* What kind of turning point? Are you thinking of leaving the Church? That's an even worse sin. It's a betrayal.

FATHER EDWARD: No...no...I've decided...Never again...never again...that sin...the sin of the flesh.

MOTHER CATERINA: Very well my son. You have my blessing. And Sister Mary agrees with you?

FATHER EDWARD: She does. She has forgiven me.

MOTHER CATERINA: Well, well...And I will forgive her if she promises... *(She hesitates, a brief silence.)* Did she promise you clearly? No more sins of the flesh?

FATHER EDWARD: Never again.

MOTHER CATERINA: She has decided then. She's convinced?

FATHER EDWARD: *(Avoiding a direct answer.)* We have a problem...

MOTHER CATERINA: What problem?

FATHER EDWARD: Unfortunately...With natives...I used protection...

MOTHER CATERINA: Using that is another serious sin. Our Holy Father doesn't condone those...devices.

FATHER EDWARD: Doesn't he prefer us alive? He needs us alive.

MOTHER CATERINA: You are in need of him. Of his omniscience. Of his guidance.

FATHER EDWARD: Well, with real love, our Holy Father is right, it's not necessary to use protection.

MOTHER CATERINA: *(Alarmed.)* So, what are you trying to tell me?

FATHER EDWARD: We didn't use anything and...

MOTHER CATERINA: And...?

FATHER EDWARD: Well, she got pregnant.

MOTHER CATERINA: *(Crossing herself.)* Oh my God, oh my God, what a calamity! What a shame! That's why she hasn't been feeling well lately.

FATHER EDWARD: When she found out she wept. We knelt down together and prayed for hours waiting for divine guidance. Hoping that our Lord would help us, that the pregnancy would be a false alarm.

MOTHER CATERINA: Was it?

FATHER EDWARD: No.

MOTHER CATERINA: What a scandal! We must keep this a secret. You promised not to see her again and she has done the same. She has fortunately come to her senses. Swear that you will never look for her again. You'll never see her again.

FATHER EDWARD: I swear.

MOTHER CATERINA: A sacred promise?

FATHER EDWARD: Sacred.

MOTHER CATERINA: Wake her up. I'll take her with me and no one will ever know.

FATHER EDWARD: Thank you, Mother.

(MOTHER CATERINA moves toward the bedroom door.)

FATHER EDWARD: Another minute, please...One last thing...

MOTHER CATERINA: *(Alarmed.)* What?

FATHER EDWARD: *(After a brief hesitation.)* She lost a great deal of blood...

MOTHER CATERINA: Then, what are you waiting for, you fool?

(MOTHER CATERINA bursts into the bedroom. A silence. A scream. He crosses himself.)

MOTHER CATERINA: My God! *(Reenters, showing a towel soaked with blood.)* What have you done, you criminal? What happened?

FATHER EDWARD: *(Slowly with extreme clarity.)* She asked me to help her...We tried to...Then, suddenly, all that blood...

MOTHER CATERINA: Why didn't you call? Why didn't you come get me?

FATHER EDWARD: Sister Mary begged me not to...She didn't want a scandal... She begged me. She asked me to stay with her. Her hand in my hand, praying... *(A brief pause.)* She died like that. Praying like an angel.

MOTHER CATERINA: Like a sinner, you mean; not like an angel!

FATHER EDWARD: I listened to her, I shared her fears. She couldn't accept the idea of the scandal...She wanted to protect me, you, the other sisters, the Church...

MOTHER CATERINA: Swear. Swear on this crucifix *(Hands it to him.)* that no one will ever know.

FATHER EDWARD: I swear.

MOTHER CATERINA: Swear that the devil, your lust, will never enter your heart again.

FATHER EDWARD: I swear.

MOTHER CATERINA: *(She throws him the bloody towel. She hits him on his face. She puts it on his shoulder with horror.)* Make every trace of blood in that room disappear.

FATHER EDWARD: I'll do whatever you say.

MOTHER CATERINA: *(Ready to go out.)* I'll arrange everything...no one must enter here. No one must see.

FATHER EDWARD: Mother, I would like to...

MOTHER CATERINA: What? What would you like, you coward?

FATHER EDWARD: To say mass for Mary at the funeral.

MOTHER CATERINA: *(She thinks for a moment. She is on the verge of exploding but controls herself.)* Funeral, funeral... You're right. Everybody knows you were friends. It would be expected. Preferable. It will avoid suspicions. All right. You will say Mass for Sister Mary. *(She crosses herself.)*

FATHER EDWARD: Thank you. Mother.

(She looks at him with contempt and exits. He kneels down and crosses himself.)

FATHER EDWARD: Forgive me. Lord...It was true love. True and sincere, I swear it. A great love...And if I was wrong, if I sinned... *(He beats his breast.)* Mea culpa, mea culpa, mea maxima culpa.

(BLACKOUT.)

Sincerity

The Persons:

CLAUDIA: a beautiful woman, very sure of herself
BOB: intelligent, sensitive, timid

Time and Place:

Today, in New York. Bob's apartment.

CLAUDIA enters and studies BOB with curiosity, with interest.

CLAUDIA: Glad to meet you.

BOB: Me too. Very glad. Please sit down.

(BOB is uneasy, uncertain. CLAUDIA keeps observing him, studying him.)

BOB: Can I offer you anything?

CLAUDIA: Nothing.

BOB: Tea?

CLAUDIA: No.

BOB: Coffee?

CLAUDIA: No, thank you.

BOB: *(Nervous and uneasy; he does not know what to do.)* Anything else?

CLAUDIA: *(Cordial, but vaguely ironical.)* I said "nothing." It means nothing.

BOB: I'm sorry. It's a habit. My mother taught me to say "no" three times. I could say "yes" and accept on the fourth time. I had forgotten that with you...

CLAUDIA: Karl told me about you.

BOB: What did he say?

CLAUDIA: He described your personality. Habits, wishes, tastes, hobbies. They coincide with mine.

BOB: Good. I am happy to hear this. What else did he tell you?

CLAUDIA: That you are intelligent, sensitive, timid.

BOB: Timid...not always...but with you, particularly...you must admit this is an unusual situation.

CLAUDIA: Why unusual?

BOB: We meet for the first time. Karl must have told you a great deal about me.

CLAUDIA: Not a great deal. Just what he knows.

BOB: We have been friends for years. He knows a lot. What did he tell you?

CLAUDIA: About some of your adventures. A dozen of them.

BOB: *(Alarmed.)* A dozen? No. We went together four or five times...

CLAUDIA: More. You don't have a good memory.

BOB: Did he tell you about us and the two Californian girls?

Sincerity

CLAUDIA: Yes.

BOB: And what happened when one of the two husbands...?

CLAUDIA: That too.

BOB: And about the night when we ended up in jail because...?

CLAUDIA: Yes. Everything. From a man, I want complete sincerity. The whole truth, nothing but the truth.

BOB: One can ask for that only when... one is intimate.

CLAUDIA: I have known Karl for a long time.

BOB: Are you still lovers?

CLAUDIA: No. What did he tell you about me?

BOB: Compliments. Only incredible compliments.

CLAUDIA: Did he tell you how it ended?

BOB: No...he was rather vague on that subject. Mysterious.

CLAUDIA: He lied to me. I hate hypocrisy and lies.

BOB: Me too. That's why I asked Karl...

CLAUDIA: "Asked"?

BOB: More precisely...I was telling him I don't trust...

CLAUDIA: ...Women, I know. He told me.

BOB: I was burned once...

CLAUDIA: I know the story. The woman who told you she was pregnant. You mustn't hate all women because one of them lied to you.

BOB: I don't hate all women. I hate ambiguities, vague shades of truth, false modesty, deceit.

CLAUDIA: It's not only women who are guilty of that long list of sins. Men too. They teach us to lie from the cradle.

BOB: I've tried many times to be sincere. It costs.

CLAUDIA: It costs.

BOB: A high price, at times.

CLAUDIA: So much the better. The rare victories, friendships, relationships, are more precious.

BOB: For instance, if you tell a woman that you love her deeply, passionately...

CLAUDIA: Don't say it. Prove it.

BOB: *(Surprised and fascinated.)* Karl was right. You are special, unique. Have you ever lied?

CLAUDIA: When I was very young, the first years. White lies. Then one day, years ago, I decided never to lie again. I kept my word.

BOB: *(Looks at her with admiration.)* How is that possible?

CLAUDIA: It is possible.

BOB: Do you have many friends?

CLAUDIA: Just a few. It doesn't matter. It's better to have a few loyal friends than many hypocritical ones. What about you?

BOB: Not many...Karl...my first love who unfortunately...

CLAUDIA: ...lied, I know. Karl told me. And he told me about your conversation. You swore all women lie. He told you: "Call this number. Claudia never lies."

BOB: Yeah. Exactly like that. But I am still...a bit uncertain...

CLAUDIA: ...And insecure, mistrusting. Here I am. Ready for anything!

(A brief pause.)

BOB: *(Timidly.)* I have always dreamt of an absolutely sincere woman. No pretense, no masks...

CLAUDIA: Here I am. You found her.

BOB: ...If I told you now...let's go to my bedroom and... *(A vague gesture.)*

CLAUDIA: I would say... *(Studies him; keeps him in suspense.)* ..."No." We don't know each other.

BOB: I'm sorry. Forgive me. You see? I started on the wrong foot.

CLAUDIA: No. You desire me. You announced it with honesty and clarity. It's a good beginning.

BOB: A positive one?

CLAUDIA: Positive.

BOB: *(Encouraged.)* There is therefore hope that we...

CLAUDIA: There is always hope. Start by using my name: Claudia.

BOB: Of course, Claudia...

(A brief pause.)

BOB: Karl, how did you meet him?

CLAUDIA: A friend introduced us.

BOB: For how long have you been...?

CLAUDIA: Lovers? Six weeks. On Wednesdays and Saturdays.

BOB: You are very precise. Did you tell him about...the other men in your life?

CLAUDIA: When he asked.

BOB: Do you prefer a man to ask or not to ask?

CLAUDIA: I want him to be sincere with himself and with others. If he feels like asking, he should. It's a way to know each other. To know *you*.

BOB: *(Surprised.)* To know...me?

CLAUDIA: Of course. The type of questions reveals, betrays, the personality of the inquisitor.

BOB: I am not an inquisitor.

CLAUDIA: Not yet.

BOB: Forgive me if...I just want to know you better.

CLAUDIA: It's the right way. We are beginning to really know each other.

BOB: Your personality is strong, dramatic, very vital...you frighten me a little bit.

CLAUDIA: You told me another truth, what you feel. You are beginning to interest me.

BOB: "Beginning?"

CLAUDIA: It takes time.

BOB: Days, weeks, months?

CLAUDIA: At times.

BOB: And other times?

CLAUDIA: Just a few hours.

BOB: *(Encouraged.)* Am I the type who might...succeed in a few hours?

CLAUDIA: "Succeed"?

BOB: Wrong verb. I'm sorry. It's the type of language we get used to. Brainwashing. They brainwashed us for years. I meant..."succeed" to become a good, intimate friend.

CLAUDIA: Everything is possible.

BOB: Thank you. I am...faintly encouraged...and fascinated, I must tell you the truth.

CLAUDIA: The truth. Good.

BOB: I never met a woman like you.

CLAUDIA: And I never met a man who was not afraid of the truth. You too are afraid of it.

BOB: I must admit that the truth, some truths, may hurt you, wound you. For instance, would you tell a man that he doesn't know how to make love?

CLAUDIA: Using the right words. Humanly, gently, tenderly. When you love, you know how to cement a relationship.

BOB: "Cement"?

CLAUDIA: I didn't mean cement as a binding unity, a marriage. I just meant how to improve a relationship. Speaking openly, exchanging ideas, opinions, feelings. Revealing oneself. In short, telling the truth.

BOB: *(With great admiration.)* You are incredible, adorable. Do you always tell the truth to your mother?

CLAUDIA: I answer all her questions. With absolute sincerity.

BOB: To your father?

CLAUDIA: My father is dead.

BOB: If he were alive, would you tell him everything?...Names of your lovers, how many...

CLAUDIA: If he had that unusual, morbid desire to know details, I would give them to him. I would tell him everything.

BOB: At the cost of hurting him, upsetting him?

CLAUDIA: He who has the need to ask for everything is prepared for those answers. He had guessed them, felt them. He already knew them. He will not be upset.

(A silence.)

BOB: If I asked you...Look, I am not asking. If I asked you how many lovers you had, would you answer?

CLAUDIA: Sure!

BOB: Would you give me their names...addresses?

CLAUDIA: First names, sure. I've forgotten their addresses.

BOB: You mean...really forgotten?

CLAUDIA: Let's say...canceled. If I made an effort, I might remember them. It isn't worth the effort.

BOB: You are extraordinary, Claudia. Anything to drink?

CLAUDIA: Nothing, thank you. *(A brief pause.)* Later, maybe.

BOB: *(Encouraged.)* I read in that "later" a...vague promise. Was that a promise?

CLAUDIA: To go to bed? No. We don't know each other.

BOB: A little bit more by now, you must admit. We are beginning to know more about...

CLAUDIA: I admit it.

BOB: Do you like me...a little bit?

CLAUDIA: You are dropping your mask. I appreciate that.

BOB: *(Nervously, uneasy.)* I am...emotional...the way I was with my first date.

CLAUDIA: This is our first date.

BOB: First one, unusual, unique. I am touched, happy.

CLAUDIA: I can read that in your eyes.

BOB: Do you also read...some fear?

CLAUDIA: I read that too.

BOB: Which virtues, qualities, must a man have to deserve your love?

CLAUDIA: It must be manly.

BOB: You mean...?

CLAUDIA: You don't know the meaning of "manly"?

BOB: *(Timidly.)* A real...male, I guess. Sexually active and aggressive?

CLAUDIA: No. You all fear that. I was speaking about other virtues: sincerity, loyalty, courage, love for his fellow man, for mankind. That is manly.

BOB: *(Happy.)* I think I have those qualities. Sometimes, when women say "manly, a real man," they mean passion, frequency of sexual activity...

CLAUDIA: It's not the number of fucks that counts. It is their quality.

BOB: ..."Quality"...Let's say mine is inferior to...compared to other men... would you tell me?

CLAUDIA: We're all different. One loves in one thousand different ways. If you asked me that question, I would answer.

BOB: Kindly?

CLAUDIA: With human warmth. Those who love, know how to love.

BOB: I like what you say, the way you say it. Then, if I were not the best, it wouldn't be because I don't love you?

CLAUDIA: We might grow together, learn together.

BOB: Claudia, you say wonderful things. Reassuring ones. I see you can be sincere. Always?

CLAUDIA: Always. Do you still doubt it?

BOB: No more. Less and less.

CLAUDIA: Good. We're beginning to understand each other.

BOB: That's a good sign. Anyhow...I must confess I have a hard time to be totally sincere...

CLAUDIA: In what situations?

BOB: In my office, for instance...I would like to be sincere. It's not easy.

CLAUDIA: What are you afraid of?

BOB: Rubbing them the wrong way, their irritation, their hatred...being fired.

CLAUDIA: Only a few are sincere. You would be the exception. They would admire you.

BOB: I have a friend, a priest I have known for years. If I told him the truth, the way I really feel about religion, he would have a heart attack.

CLAUDIA: Try. He esteems you. Maybe you'll save him.

BOB: From what?

CLAUDIA: The illusions he believes in. Faith, lack of faith, ideologies, they are contagious. They may redeem.

BOB: *(Thinking it over.)* "Redeem"...Did you ever frighten anyone?

CLAUDIA: Many. Those who don't have "manly" characteristics.

BOB: Which are...loyalty, courage, love for mankind?

CLAUDIA: Precisely.

BOB: If we should—I hope so—become lovers—

CLAUDIA: *(Interrupting.)* I prefer the expression: "Make love to each other."

BOB: Forgive me. Old habits. Atavic language. The brainwashing I mentioned before. The chains we carry.

CLAUDIA: That was me too. Up to a certain birthday. Then I promised myself to change, to renew myself.

BOB: Which birthday was that?

CLAUDIA: My twenty-first. Until that age, I lied too. Instinctive, at times. Without realizing it. The habit to deceive.

BOB: I fear that now. I could lie to you by...mistake.

CLAUDIA: A faux pas can be forgiven.

BOB: I was trying to say, I would be extremely sincere with you. I would ask for everything.

CLAUDIA: You would have all the answers.

BOB: I was hinting at something else.

CLAUDIA: I understood. You would have all the answers.

BOB: All of them?

CLAUDIA: Everything is allowed, human, acceptable under the wings of love.

BOB: *(Very moved, feeling his heart.)* I'm excited, happy, moved. I am trembling inside.

CLAUDIA: A very human admission. I like it.

BOB: Have you had many lovers?

CLAUDIA: Many.

BOB: How long... Your most important relationship?

CLAUDIA: The most important, twelve days. The longest, eight months.

(A brief pause.)

BOB: Did you love all of them?

CLAUDIA: Only if you love, it's worth loving. Once, one thousand times.

BOB: *(Alarmed.)* One thousand?

CLAUDIA: *(Vaguely ironical.)* Less than one thousand, don't worry.

BOB: I don't worry. It's that...

CLAUDIA: You are just curious. Ask. I never lie.

BOB: Your first time... many years ago?

CLAUDIA: Not many. Seven years ago.

BOB: Was it... pleasant?

CLAUDIA: I didn't have an orgasm, if that's what you want to know.

BOB: First time, generally...

CLAUDIA: Neither the second, the third, the tenth. It takes time.

BOB: *(Studying her.)* It takes time... But things improve, later.

CLAUDIA: Do you want to know if I am frigid? I'm not. No woman is.

BOB: Evidently... You're passionate, ardent, alive...

CLAUDIA: *(Ironical.)* Alive, you can see that.

BOB: Is it easy for you now, to have... happiness?

CLAUDIA: Let's call them orgasms.

BOB: Is it easy for you, now, to have orgasms?

CLAUDIA: Easier.

BOB: But it doesn't happen all the time...

CLAUDIA: It's well known. It doesn't happen all the time.

BOB: The last time you... Did you have it?

CLAUDIA: Three weeks ago. No orgasm.

BOB: And for that reason, you punished him; you cut him out of your life.

CLAUDIA: Don't worry. There were other reasons.

BOB: What reasons?

CLAUDIA: He was false, mean, selfish.

BOB: *(Slowly studying her.)* ..."Selfish"... I must confess that a woman accused me once of being selfish. You see, I'm sincere!

CLAUDIA: I appreciate that.

BOB: Maybe... you could tell me the same thing... Your last lover, was he selfish in... what sense?

CLAUDIA: *(Smiling.)* One can be selfish in one hundred ways.

BOB: I was talking about him, only about him. I am curious about the reasons why...you broke the relationship...You left him, didn't you?

CLAUDIA: I did.

BOB: Why?

CLAUDIA: He seemed intelligent, open. Deserving love. He was not.

BOB: Selfish...in bed?

CLAUDIA: Is that what worries you? He was human. Sometimes selfish, sometimes unselfish.

BOB: Was he selfish that last time?

CLAUDIA: That last time? No. He was mean and false. We had a quarrel. I hate those who lie. I showed him the door.

(A silence; she stares at him.)

CLAUDIA: What are you thinking about?

BOB: About that man, his last time with you...

CLAUDIA: ...You are thinking about his selfishness, that you suppose it was physical. No. He was altruistic, sexually. Selfish, spiritually.

BOB: What does it mean..."altruistic, sexually"?

CLAUDIA: You don't know?

BOB: I know. But I would like to hear your version.

CLAUDIA: He who prefers to love instead of being loved. *(She opens her legs; a charming offer.)*

BOB: *(Thinking it over.)* ...A beautiful definition...I think I belong to that category.

CLAUDIA: You seem worried. What about? Shoot.

BOB: Sure, certainly...I don't want to lie to you...Lately, women, in many books, give extreme importance to female orgasm...you, what do you think? Is it that important?

CLAUDIA: It is important. It is not absolutely necessary.

BOB: Good...so much the better...In a feminist book I read that a woman is entitled to twenty-four orgasms...

CLAUDIA: *(Amused.)* A year?

BOB: Oh no! That would be easy.

CLAUDIA: A month?

BOB: According to that feminist...twenty-four a day.

CLAUDIA: That's ridiculous! Tell me about yourself. Are you afraid of women?

BOB: Me? Oh no! No fear at all!

CLAUDIA: Have you had many negative experiences?

BOB: No.

CLAUDIA: Physical problems?

BOB: No.

CLAUDIA: Psychological problems? Those who doubt their virility, often fail.

BOB: Me, fail? Never!

(A silence; she stares at him; he is uneasy.)

BOB: ...Once, only once...I was very young...a prostitute who was in a hurry...I didn't succeed in...

CLAUDIA: It happens to everybody. Was she cruel to you? Did she make fun of you?

BOB: Oh no! She was very kind. She pretended everything was all right.

CLAUDIA: You see? Women are not monsters after all. And that prostitute had many reasons to hate men.

BOB: What reasons?

CLAUDIA: You know. Many. She had a chance for a revenge against a man—you—and she didn't take it.

BOB: You, do you have reasons to hate men?

CLAUDIA: No. I hate anyone who lies. Men and women. No discrimination.

BOB: *(After a brief silence.)* Forgive me if I take advantage of this unusual situation to ask "before"...to know everything, clearly. I love clarity.

CLAUDIA: Me too. Ask.

BOB: Are you the type of woman who... needs to be loved every day?

CLAUDIA: Loved, yes. Fucked, no.

BOB: *(After a brief hesitation.)* Do you... take the initiative?

CLAUDIA: Only if I feel like it.

BOB: Do you often feel like it?

CLAUDIA: I never counted the waves of my emotions. Do you count yours?

BOB: Don't misunderstand me. Human appetites are different. Since I have this unique, incredible occasion to know before...to know everything...

CLAUDIA: Go on.

BOB: In your opinion, an ideal man, for you, how many times a week should...?

CLAUDIA: Only when he feels like it.

BOB: *(Happy.)* Good, very good, wonderful...let's suppose that one week—let's say, a maximum of ten days—if I were terribly busy with my work, worried, absentminded, and I had no time for...?

CLAUDIA: Among the virtues of the "manly men" there should be also love for his work.

BOB: Oh, I love my work, I love it a great deal! Sometimes I am taken by a creative fever for weeks and weeks... *(He corrects himself, alarmed.)* I don't mean I don't need making love for weeks and weeks. Generally...

CLAUDIA: Generally?

BOB: *(Vague.)* I have never ignored, neglected my woman for more than ten, twelve days, maybe, at times. Seldom. Only in my creative periods.

CLAUDIA: *(Vaguely ironical.)* How many times a week is your...desire to make love?

BOB: *(Uncertain.)* Two, three times.

CLAUDIA: *(Staring at him.)* The truth.

BOB: You told me that you saw Karl Wednesdays and Saturdays. Twice a week is ideal for me, the perfect frequency.

(CLAUDIA studies him; stares at him.)

BOB: One hour, more or less...after the TV news...around midnight...

(CLAUDIA keeps staring at him.)

BOB: You choose the days...Mondays and Thursdays, Tuesdays and Fridays...or Wednesdays and Saturdays. It's the same for me.

CLAUDIA: *(Ironical.)* You are very generous...

BOB: Are you being sarcastic?

CLAUDIA: I'm not.

(A brief pause.)

BOB: *(Looking at her with admiration.)* Claudia, you are the ideal woman...I feel it, I'm convinced of it...I'm falling in love...Your sincerity, your personality...We have in common the whole world, the same vision, the same way of thinking...Maybe we should...Maybe we are born for each other.

CLAUDIA: Maybe.

BOB: I'm asking you honestly, with all sincerity, with all my heart...Do you want to be my friend, my companion, my lov— *(Correcting himself.)* my woman?

CLAUDIA: One condition.

BOB: Which one?

CLAUDIA: Your questions reveal a problem...a complex.

BOB: *(Alarmed.)* What complex?

CLAUDIA: You are uncertain, insecure. You are afraid of women.

BOB: It's not true! I adore them!

CLAUDIA: It's possible. But I need a confirmation, "before."

BOB: *(Alarmed.)* What confirmation?

CLAUDIA: I want to ascertain, to be sure that...

BOB: Sure of what?

(CLAUDIA indicates BOB's groin.)

BOB: Here?

CLAUDIA: Here, now.

BOB: *(Uncertain, upset.)* It's rather unusual...

CLAUDIA: I am unusual. You said so yourself.

BOB: Wouldn't it be better if...? *(Indicates the bedroom.)*

CLAUDIA: No. It's better to be clear and sincere, now. Your words. I want to see if it's worthwhile. *(Indicates his groin again.)*

BOB: You mean here, now, like this?

CLAUDIA: Here, now, like this.

(A brief pause.)

BOB: Please, don't insist. It's embarrassing, humiliating...You are ruining everything.

CLAUDIA: Clarity and sincerity, remember? A hundred percent.

BOB: We have so many things in common...music, traveling, desire to understand and respect...Our love for the truth. We are a perfect couple.

CLAUDIA: Truth must be full and absolute. Now.

BOB: Please, don't insist.

CLAUDIA: Don't disappoint me. Show me you can face reality. We must be realists in life. If it's worthwhile, it's worthwhile. One must know how to accept reality.

BOB: *(Begging her.)* Please, Claudia. You are destroying an ideal, perfect relationship...

CLAUDIA: The truth, the whole truth, nothing but the truth.

(A silence; BOB decides reluctantly to obey her; with his back to the audience, he shows himself to CLAUDIA; she observes him in silence; her face is impenetrable for at least ten seconds; then she smiles.)

CLAUDIA: You wanted a sincere woman, you found her. *(She looks at his groin again.)* It's worthwhile... *(Begins to unbutton her blouse.)*

(A long pause. Keeping the audience in suspense.)

BOB: *(Slowly, clearly, deliberately, with a firm voice.)* Too late, Claudia...I'm afraid of you. A woman like you, sincere like you, is frightening.

(IMMOBILITY. DARKNESS. CURTAIN.)

About the Author

MARIO FRATTI is a drama critic and playwright. He was born in Italy but has been living in New York City since 1963. He is considered one of the most prolific American playwrights. His plays —including *The Cage*, *Suicide*, *The Return*, *Refusal*, *Refrigerators*, *The Academy*, *Seducers*, *Madam Senator*, *Victim*, *Che Guevara*, *Young Wife*, *Birthday*, *Mothers and Daughters*, *Eleonora Duse*, *Mafia*, *Gift*, *Races*, *The Bridge*, *Lovers*, *Friends*, *Encounter*, *A.I.D.S.*, *Porno*, *Two Centuries*, *Dolls No More*, *Family*, *Sister*, *Leningrad*, *Passionate Women*, *Erotic Adventures in Adventure (Promises)*, *Beata, the Pope's Daughter*, *Terrorist*, and *Iraq (Blindness)*—have been performed in more than six hundred theatres in nineteen languages. The musical *Nine* (his adaptation of Fellini's *8½*) won the O'Neill Selection Award, the Richard Rodgers Award, the Outer Critics Award, the Leone di San Marco Literary Award, the Heritage and Culture Award, eight Drama Desk Awards, and seven Tony Awards.

About the Publisher

THE NEW YORK THEATRE EXPERIENCE, INC. (NYTE), is a nonprofit corporation that uses new and traditional media to provide advocacy and support to the New York theatre community. In addition to its publishing program, NYTE operates the free website nytheatre.com and produces the weekly *nytheatrecast* programs. To learn more about NYTE's programs and about how you can support this organization, visit its website at www.nyte.org.

Copyrights

The Friday Bench copyright © 1970–2007 by Mario Fratti.
Suicide Club copyright © 2001–2007 by Mario Fratti.
Alessia copyright © 1996–2007 by Mario Fratti.
The Piggy Bank copyright © 1978–2007 by Mario Fratti.
The Fourth One copyright © 1990–2007 by Mario Fratti.
Dolls No More copyright © 1973–2007 by Mario Fratti.
Porno copyright © 1990–2007 by Mario Fratti.
Dina and Alba copyright © 1996–2007 by Mario Fratti.
The Bridge copyright © 1970–2007 by Mario Fratti.
Confessions copyright © 1986–2007 by Mario Fratti.
The Coffin copyright © 1962–2007 by Mario Fratti.
A.I.D.S. copyright © 1997–2007 by Mario Fratti.
Brothel (The Doorbell) copyright © 1958–2007 by Mario Fratti.
The Letter copyright © 1972–2007 by Mario Fratti.
Mothers and Daughters copyright © 1999–2007 by Mario Fratti.
Beata, the Pope's Daughter copyright © 1994–2007 by Mario Fratti.
The Wish copyright © 1967–2007 by Mario Fratti.
Erotic Adventures in Venice (Promises) copyright © 1996–2007 by Mario Fratti.
The Academy copyright © 1962–2007 by Mario Fratti.
Friends copyright © 1991–2007 by Mario Fratti.
Terrorist copyright © 2003–2007 by Mario Fratti.
Wars copyright © 2006–2007 by Mario Fratti.
The Return copyright © 1945–2007 by Mario Fratti.
The Seventy-Fifth copyright © 1991–2007 by Mario Fratti.
Iraq (Blindness) copyright © 2003–2007 by Mario Fratti.
"Che" copyright © 1967–2007 by Mario Fratti.
Anniversary copyright © 1994–2007 by Mario Fratti.
Missionaries copyright © 2002–2007 by Mario Fratti.
Sincerity copyright © 1999–2007 by Mario Fratti.

PLAYS AND PLAYWRIGHTS 2002
Edited by Martin Denton, Foreword by Bill C. Davis

ISBN 09670234-3-2   Retail $15.00

The Death of King Arthur by Matthew Freeman
Match by Marc Chun
Woman Killer by Chiori Miyagawa
The Wild Ass's Skin by J. Scott Reynolds
Halo by Ken Urban
Shyness Is Nice by Marc Spitz
Reality by Curtiss I' Cook
The Resurrectionist by Kate Chell
Bunny's Last Night In Limbo by Peter S. Petralia
Summerland by Brian Thorstenson

PLAYS AND PLAYWRIGHTS 2003
Edited by Martin Denton, Foreword by Mario Fratti

ISBN 09670234-4-0   Retail $15.00

A Queer Carol by Joe Godfrey
Pumpkins For Smallpox by Catherine Gillet
Looking For The Pony by Andrea Lepcio
Black Thang by Ato Essandoh
The Ninth Circle by Edward Musto
The Doctor of Rome by Nat Colley
Galaxy Video by Marc Morales
The Last Carburetor by Leon Chase
Out To Lunch by Joseph Langham
Ascending Bodily by Maggie Cino
Last Call by Kelly McAllister

PLAYS AND PLAYWRIGHTS 2004
Edited by Martin Denton, Foreword by Kirk Wood Bromley

ISBN 09670234-5-9   Retail $16.00

Sugarbaby by Frank Cwiklik
WTC View by Brian Sloan
United States: Work and Progress by Christy Meyer, Jon Schumacher and Ellen Shanman
The Shady Maids of Haiti by John Jahnke
Cats Can See The Devil by Tom X. Chao
Survivor: Vietnam! by Rob Reese
Feed the Hole by Michael Stock
Auntie Mayhem by David Pumo
The Monster Tales by Mary Jett Parsley
Sun, Stand Thou Still by Steven Gridley

PLAYS AND PLAYWRIGHTS 2005
Edited by Martin Denton, Foreword by Steven Drukman

ISBN 09670234-6-7　　　　　　　　　　　　　　　　　　　　　　Retail $16.00

Vampire Cowboy Trilogy by Qui Nguyen & Robert Ross Parker
second. by Neal Utterback
Bull Spears by Josh Chambers
Animal by Kevin Augustine
Odysseus Died from AIDS by Stephen Svoboda
Maggie May by Tom O'Brien
Elephant by Margie Stokley
Walking to America by Alberto Bonilla
The 29 Questions Project by Katie Bull & Hillary Rollins
Honor by TheDrillingCompaNY
Kalighat by Paul Knox
Platonov! Platonov! Platonov! or the case of a very Angry Duck by Eric Michael Kochmer

PLAYS AND PLAYWRIGHTS 2006
Edited by Martin Denton; Foreword by Trav S.D.

ISBN 09670234-7-5　　　　　　　　　　　　　　　　　　　　　　Retail $17.00

The Top Ten People of the Millennium Sing Their Favorite Schubert Lieder by Alec Duffy
Burning the Old Man by Kelly McAllister
Self at Hand by Jack Hanley
The Expense of Spirit by Josh Fox
Paradise by Glyn O'Malley
Yit, Ngay (One, Two) by Michael Lew
Pulling the Lever by Rising Circle Theater Collective
The Position by Kevin Doyle
The Dirty Talk by Michael Puzzo
The First Time Out of Bounds by P. Seth Bauer
Aurolac Blues by Saviana Stanescu
The Whore of Sheridan Square by Michael Baron

PLAYS AND PLAYWRIGHTS 2007
Edited by Martin Denton, Foreword by John Clancy

ISBN 978-0-9670234-9-6　　　　　　　　　　　　　　　　　　　　Retail $18.00

Lenz by bluemouth, inc.
Office Sonata by Andy Chmelko
Kiss And Cry by Tom Rowan
They're Just Like Us by Boo Killebrew
Convergence by Bryn Manion
Red Tide Blooming by Taylor Mac
The Adventures of Nervous-Boy by James Comtois
Another Brief Encounter by Stan Richardson
Corps Values by Brendon Bates
Diving Normal by Ashlin Halfnight
'nami by Chad Beckim

Also from The New York Theatre Experience, Inc.:

PLAYING WITH CANONS: Explosive New Works from Great
Literature by America's Indie Playwrights
Edited by Martin Denton

ISBN 978-0-9670234-8-9   Retail $26.00

Want's Unwisht Work by Kirk Wood Bromley
La Tempestad by Larry Loebell
Titus X by Shawn Northrip
Genesis by Matthew Freeman
The Eumenides by David Johnston
Principia by Michael Maiello & Andrew Recinos
Uncle Jack by Jeff Cohen
Story of an Unknown Man by Anthony P. Pennino
The Brothers Karamazov Parts I and II by Alexander Harrington
Bel Canto by Reneé Flemings
Salem by Alex Roe
Bartleby the Scrivener by R. L. Lane
Frankenstein by Rob Reese
Northanger Abbey by Lynn Marie Macy
The Man Who Laughs by Kiran Rikhye
Bald Diva!: The Ionesco Parody Your Mother Warned You About by David Koteles
Fatboy by John Clancy
The Persians...a comedy about war with five songs by Waterwell

Additional information about the *Plays and Playwrights* series (ISSN 1546-1319) can be found at www.nyte.org/pep.htm.

Plays and Playwrights books are available in bookstores and online, or from the publisher:

The New York Theatre Experience, Inc.
P.O. Box 1606, Murray Hill Station
New York, NY 10156